The ULTIMATE

FOOD LOVER'S

GUIDE *to*

HOUSTON

a Second edition

Copyright 2011
Lazywood Press

ISBN: 978-0-9665716-0-8

Written, edited, designed and printed in Houston, Texas
Second edition

Copies of this book are available at special discounts when purchased in bulk for premiums and sales promotions as well as for fund-raising or educational use. To buy books in quantity, contact Jane Kremer at (713) 973-0207 or jane.kremer@my-table.com.

EDITOR-IN-CHIEF Teresa Byrne-Dodge
ASSOCIATE EDITOR Nikki Metzgar
DESIGN Jennifer Blanco, spindletopdesign.com
ASSSISTANT EDITOR Rachel Kitchens

www.my-table.com

PHOTOGRAPHY/ILLUSTRATION CREDITS

JENNIFER BLANCO Canino's Produce *p. 14* · Catalina *p. 79* · House of Pies *p. 214* · Irma's *p. 217* · Kraftsmen Bakery *p. 66* · Liberty Station *p. 107* · Shade *p. 288* · Vintners Own *p. 122* Hot dog *p. 212* · Lap top *p. 78*

JOHN EARLES Agora *p. 76* · Amazing Cake Supplies *p. 13* · Araya Artisan Chocolate *p. 55* · B&W Meats *p. 25, 35* · The Breakfast Klub *p. 155, 350* · Chocolat Du Monde *p. 56* · Crave Cupcakes *p. 46-47, 59, 332* · French Riviera Bakery & Cafe *p. 64, 75* · Gelato Blu *p. 49* · Houston Dairymaids *p. 18* · India Grocer *p. 27* · Inversion Coffee House *p. 81* · Mam's House of Ice *p. 51* Moeller's Bakery *p. 68* · Moontower Inn *p. 251* · Phoenicia Specialty Foods *p. 10, 25, 30, 162* Raja Sweets *p. 70, 324* · Relish *p. 20* · T'afia *p. 295, 297, 324* · Té House of Tea *p. 87* · Waldo's Coffee House *p. 83*

WILLIAM HARDIN Al's Quick Stop *p. 128* · Avalon Diner *p. 138* · Anvil *p. 88-91* · Balkan Market *p. 23* · Beaver's Ice House *p. 143* · Bistro Le Cep *p. 146* · Brasil *p. 151* · Brasserie 19 *p. 6, 152* · Broken Spoke Cafe *p. 157* · Buffalo Hardware *p. 43* · Cadillac Bar *p. 160* · Carter & Cooley *p. 171* · Ciao Bello *p. 174* · Cyclone Anaya's *p. 178* · Danton's Gulf Coast Kitchen *p. 181* · Del Frisco's *p. 4, 182* · Down House *p. 93, 186* · Feast *p. 195* · Frenchy's Chicken *p. 200* · Gatlin's Barbecue *p. 201* · Jerusalem Halal Meat Market *p. 37* · Kim Son *p. 227* · Les Givral's *p. 236* · Natachee's Supper N' Punch *p. 253* · Niko Niko's *p. 256* · Ninfa's *p. 230, 257* Olive & Vine *p. 19* · Ouisie's Table *p. 262* · Pete's Fine Meats *p. 38* · Pink's Pizza *p. 272* Plonk *p. 120, 246* · Pronto Cucinino *p. 275* · Queen Vic Pub & Kitchen *p. 276* · Reef *p. 280* Revival Market *p. 21* · Ristorante Cavour *p. 283* · Spec's *p. 116, 350* · Star Snow Ice & Teriyaki *p. 56* · Treebeards *p. 309* · Yum Yum Cha Cafe *p. 319* · Zydeco Louisiana Diner *p. 323*

CLARK LARA Chez Roux *p. 172*

The ULTIMATE

FOOD

LOVER'S

GUIDE *to*

HOUSTON

a Second edition

from the

EDITORS OF **MY TABLE** MAGAZINE

TABLE OF CONTENTS

....

INTRODUCTION

FORKS READY?

HOUSTON HAS BEEN MY HOME FOR NEARLY 30 YEARS. FOR 27 OF THOSE YEARS I'VE BEEN WRITING ABOUT THE city's food scene. Which means I have had one of the best jobs in town.

When I first started writing about restaurants for *The Houston Post*'s Sunday magazine in 1984, wines-by-the-glass came in two flavors: house red and house white. There were no farmers' markets, Hong Kong Food Market, Super H Mart, Central Market, Mi Tienda or Phoenicia Specialty. There was no such thing as wraps. Sushi was still pretty scary. And who could pronounce, much less spell, "chipotle"?

Around the late-1980s, however, the Houston food scene began to catch fire, and I am lucky to have observed the conflagration up close.

The rapid change owes much to the immigrants who have added their influence to the city's stockpot. The foods and cooking styles from Latin America, Asia, the Middle East and Europe have resulted in a local food culture built layer upon delicious layer. That inspired stew makes Houston more than simply a city. Today it's one vast ethnic groaning board.

In 2011, not a day goes by without a new restaurant, craft beer bar, bakery or specialty food shop trumpeting its opening. And the rate of evolution seems to be ever increasing with pop-up restaurants, seasonal markets and food trucks adding to the hurly-burly. It's everything we editors at *My Table* magazine can do to stay abreast of what's cooking and who's pouring in our sprawling metropolis.

The purpose of this book is to lead you to where the sips and bites are best. The last thing we ever want to hear is, "You haven't touched your food." Let this book be your guide to all that's classic, quirky, exotic, unexpected, down-home and downright delicious in one of the most vibrant, food-loving cities in America.

Note: Every effort has been made by the researchers, fact-checkers and editors to make *The Ultimate Food Lover's Guide to Houston* as accurate and useful as possible. However, many things can change after a guidebook is published—establishments close or relocate, phone numbers, hours and prices change, restaurants come under new management, etc. Avoid frustration and call before traveling.

We want to hear from you concerning your experiences with this guidebook. We especially welcome word of noteworthy openings and closings. While we may not be able to respond to all comments and suggestions, we will take them to heart and make certain they are shared among the editors. Please email me at *teresa.byrnedodge@my-table.com*. ★

Cheers,

Teresa Byrne-Dodge, EDITOR/PUBLISHER

KEY to SYMBOLS		
🚗 = WORTH THE DRIVE	✏️ = EDITOR'S PICK	⬤ = MAP QUADRANT

ACKNOWLEDGEMENTS

....

A GUIDEBOOK SUCH AS THIS IS COMPOSED OF COUNT-
LESS DETAILS THAT MUST BE TAMED, ORGANIZED AND
put to work. No one could do it alone. My deepest appreciation goes
to the people whose experience, digging, handholding and enthusiasm
made this project happen.

Among the many, I must single out three, including graphic designer/
cartographer/photographer Jennifer Blanco, whose Spindletop Design
made this such a beautiful book. Bouquets of thanks also to associate
editor Nikki Metzgar, who was still a Rice University intern when she
worked on our first edition but has had three years of (*ahem*) season-
ing in Houston's food-writing world since then. She combed through
every listing and was especially keen on making the selections included
in Chapter 4. And thanks to Rachel Kitchens, this year's intern, who ·
had the brain-numbing job of entering every listing into a database in
order to create the indexes, not to mention visiting several restaurants
a week.

I'm also indebted to the many writers and reviewers who contrib-
uted to the text of this edition of the guidebook. All of these folks
are *My Table* magazine contributors or write for our twice-weekly
e-newsletter, *SideDish*. They include Dennis Abrams, William Albright,
Robin Barr Sussman, Jenny Wang, Renee Bruner, Eric Gerber, Sarah
Bronson, Stephanie Madan, Jodie Eisenhardt and Mai Pham. It's a
pleasure to work with all of you, and I'm grateful for your humor, good
sense and generosity.

On the proofreading side, sisters Jeanne Cooper and Jen Cooper
gave the page proofs their most critical eye. Is Jen Cooper's name
familiar? It's because she is the graphic designer of *My Table* magazine.
For this project, however, she put on her ex-English major's hat. My
gratitude, too, to Paula Murphy, the magazine's director of marketing
and special events. She is always ready to bounce around ideas to make
a project a little shinier and more fun. How does a guidebook get from
the printing plant into your hands? That's the genius of Jane Kremer,
the guidebook's associate publisher for distribution.

Finally, my thanks to Taylor Byrne Ray, who is associate publisher of
My Table magazine as well as my first-born child. To her credit, she is
rarely fazed by the flames shooting out of my ears.

MARKETS

PICK-YOUR-OWN-FRUIT

WHY WOULD WE DRIVE AN HOUR OUTSIDE THE CITY, DELIBERATELY EXPOSE OURselves to the Texas heat and possibly crickets, all to labor for produce that is not even bargain priced? Because it's fun, that's why. Check the websites for current picking conditions.

ATKINSON FARMS
3217 SPRING CYPRESS RD., SPRING
☎ (832) 381-8202
atkinsonfarm.com
Pick your own strawberries in season. There's also pasteurized whole milk and sweet butter every day, as well as a farm stand.

E&B ORCHARDS
28268 CLARK BOTTOM, HEMPSTEAD
☎ (979) 826-6306
eandborchards.com
Homemade peach frozen yogurt calls like a siren, but since you're already out there, you might as well pick some peaches (and nectarines and blackberries) yourself.

KING'S ORCHARD
11282 CR 302, PLANTERSVILLE
☎ (936) 894-2766
kingsorchard.com
Out near Renaissance Festival country, this family operation is open from February to August for blueberry, peach, tomato and flower picking.

MATT FAMILY ORCHARD
21110 BAUER HOCKLEY RD., TOMBALL
☎ (281) 351-7676
mattfamilyorchard.com
These 40 acres grow a wide variety of produce, including blackberries, figs, persimmons and pumpkins. The annual fall Harvest Festival is a fun family event.

CHMIELEWSKI'S BLUEBERRY FARM
23810 BAUER HOCKLEY, HOCKLEY
☎ (281) 304-0554
chmielewski-blueberry.com
Visit during the spring for picking on eight acres of Southern Highbush and Rabbiteye blueberries. Local honey—the bees pollinate the blueberries—is for sale, too.

FROBERG'S FARM
11875 CR 190, ALVIN
☎ (281) 585-3531
frobergsfarm.com
Summer means strawberries, and that's the calling card at this Alvin orchard. Also taking top billing are the homemade strawberry, buttermilk and lemon cream pies.

{ *Specialty Markets* }

AMAZING CAKE SUPPLIES

5611 BELLAIRE BLVD.
west of Chimney Rock
☎ **(713) 665-8899**
amazingcakesupplies.com

D7

THIS LITTLE SPECIALTY SHOP WAS PLANNING to move a few doors north in the strip center about the time we go to press with this book, and it's easy to see why. It is absolutely crammed with stuff needed and beloved by pastry chefs and serious home bakers. But unless you belong to that group of cooks, you might be confounded by some of the things found here: airbrushes, edible "disco dust," oil-based candy colors, rolling pins of various textures, fondant and isomalt sticks. Thousands of items needed to

Tart pans at Amazing Cake Supplies

make and decorate pastries and candies line the shelves or hang from hooks, from the gay newly-wed cake-toppers to jungle cookie cutters to a collection of books and DVDs. The store often hosts classes ("Intro to Gum Paste," anyone?), which might inspire anyone set on appearing in the film sequel to *Kings of Pastry*.

• BELDEN'S

99 BRAESWOOD SQUARE
at Chimney Rock & N. Braeswood
☎ **(713) 723-5670**

30 min **B8**

OF HOUSTON'S FEW RE-MAINING INDEPENDENT supermarkets, this is one beautiful store, with gleaming floors, plenty of space in the aisles and remarkable customer service that almost makes this seem like a small-town grocery store. Even the entrance, where seasonal flowering plants and herbs are often sold, is kept manicured. Inside, you'll find an excellent meat department (including quite a range of organic meats), produce that is fresh and attractively displayed, smoked fish, gourmet goods (check the freezer case for Mamie's Famous Cheese Wafers shipped in from Alabama), an onsite bakery famous for its warm baguettes and a surprisingly large and sophisticated wine collection. The city's Jewish community comes here for the extensive

MARKETS

selection of kosher products, including wine, meat and poultry (there is a full-time *mashgiach* on the premises), cheeses, dry goods and candy.

• CANINO'S PRODUCE
....

2520 AIRLINE *just inside Loop 610*
☎ **(713) 862-4027**
caninoproduce.com

16 min **E5**

CANINO'S IS SET UP LIKE A BIG SEMI-OPEN SHED and filled with produce and seasonal finds. Out front in the fall, nuts are freshly roasted and pecans are shelled on the spot. In the spring, you'll find carts full of tomato and chile plants and buckets of fresh strawberries. Inside, it's just produce—bins and bins of it—along with eggs, dried beans and jarred jams, salsas and honey. There's nothing terribly rare here, but the

Inside Canino's Produce

melons, particularly watermelons, are said to be the best in town, and you'll find an extensive selection of chiles. Plus, the prices can't be beat. Out behind is the Airline Farmers' Market, but you may not take your Canino's shopping cart with you. (Plan your shopping excursion accordingly.) Open daily at 6 am.

• CENTRAL MARKET
....

3815 WESTHEIMER *at Weslayan*
☎ **(713) 386-1700**
centralmarket.com

13 min **D6**

WE'LL JUST SAY IT: WE LOVE THIS STORE. Pyramids of a dozen types of everything line the labyrinthine set-up. Not only is there an overwhelming degree of selection, each item seems to have been carefully chosen for quality. Pricey? Some things, yes. Worth it? Yes. On any given day, there are about 700 items in the sprawling produce section. Bulk-bin items such as fair-trade coffees, sea salts, organic grains, and sweet and savory snacks are yours to scoop into plastic bags, weigh and tag yourself. The meat, cheese, charcuterie and fish counters are models of excellence in selection and helpfulness of the employees. In addition to groceries (and we mean *groceries*—go elsewhere for your laundry detergent, kitty litter, Miss Clairol and such), Central

Market has an outstanding prepared-foods section and a deli sandwich counter good enough to warrant long weekend lines. The store, which celebrated its 10th anniversary in Houston in June 2011, is serious about being a good community partner and sponsors or donates to scores of local causes.

DOÑA TERE TAMALES

....

8331 BEECHNUT *west of Hwy. 59*
☎ **(713) 270-8501**
multiple locations
tamalesdonatere.net

C7

WE GENERALLY FROWN UPON IMPERIALISM unless the empire in question is a tamale empire. The bare bones establishments of the Doña Tere tamale domain sell excellent Mexico City-style versions of the masa pockets. That means they're plumper than the Tex-Mex kind, sometimes wrapped in banana leaf rather than cornhusk and stuffed with fillings like chicken mole or pork. The *Oaxaqueño*, an enormous roll of creamy masa bursting with chicken, is a must-have. Most selections are perfectly complemented by a tangy and spicy green salsa. If you're feeling adventurous, do try the *atole*, the sweetened porridge-like drink made of cornmeal traditional in Mexico and Central America.

FREDLYN NUT COMPANY

....

9350 WESTPARK *near Fondren*
☎ **(713) 781-2710**
fredlyn.com

 C7

SEE THE BIG PINK SQUIRREL ON THE SIGN? PULL over now. Thank goodness for that squirrel, because otherwise Fredlyn Nut Company might be overlooked as just another wholesale storefront on this somewhat bland stretch of Westpark. Come inside and be prepared to sample. Raw, roasted, sweet, salty or dipped in chocolate—the variety of nuts, seeds and dried fruit is mind-boggling. Luckily everything can be tasted until you find the perfect mix. The sweet-and-spicy pecans and cranberry crunch are delicious, as are the savory butter toffee peanuts. The new crop pecans arrive every November, and hard-to-find black walnuts are here, too. Pick up a snacking portion for a pittance at warehouse prices or send in a list of all the names on your holiday list to have gifts custom-packaged and delivered. Fredlyn, which has been in business for 40-plus years, stores all its raw nutmeats at 37 degrees until time to roast, usually twice a week in the off-season.

MARKETS

TEXAS CHEESES

TEXAS IS KNOWN FOR PEACHES, BARBECUE AND, THE WAY THINGS ARE GOING, PERHAPS one day for its cheese. These nearby dairies are among the state's best. Look for their cheeses in Houston stores and at farmers' markets.

BLUE HERON FARM
blueherontexas.com
Husband and wife team Christian and Lisa Seger traded jobs in Houston for 10 acres and a herd of goats. Their chèvre comes in various flavors, and the goat milk caramel is especially good.

CASTRO CHEESE CO.
☎ (713) 460-0329
castrocheese.com
Started in 1971 and using the queso fresco recipe learned on her grandmother's farm in Mexico, Maria Castro's crumbly La Vaquita cheeses are sold throughout Texas.

CHEESY GIRL
☎ (281) 334-4628
cheesygirl.com
Susan Holle's cheekily named cheeses like Satin Doll camembert and Femme Fatale chèvre are made with plant-based rennet.

POLA ARTISAN CHEESES
☎ (281) 414-2509
☎ (713) 774-1214
These Houston cheesemakers procure cow and goat's milk from farms in Bryan, Moulton and Waller for a rotating selection of cheeses such as Beer Bathed Tomme and Grape Leaf Goat.

PURE LUCK FARM & DAIRY
☎ (512) 858-7034
purelucktexas.com
Amelia Sweethardt takes the milk from her herd of Nubian and Alpine goats and turns it into exceptional chèvre, bleu and feta.

SWEDE FARM
swedefarm.com
Tim and LeeAnne Carlson raise goats near Waller and sell their milk, yogurt, kefir and cheese at Urban Harvest farmers' markets.

VELDHUIZEN FAMILY FARM
☎ (254) 968-3098
veldhuizencheese.com
The Veldhuizen family is committed to raw milk cheesemaking. Our favorites include the Saint Arnold beer-bathed Redneck Cheddar.

• GEORGIA'S FARM TO MARKET

....

12171 KATY FWY. *near Kirkwood*
☎ **(281) 940-0990**
georgiasmarket.com

 10 W ✈ **B6**

T URNS OUT, THERE'S A HIPPIE PARADISE IN WEST Houston and it's called Georgia's Farm to Market. The eponymous Georgia is Georgia Bost of Georgia's Texas Grassfed Beef, which is available at 18 local farmers' markets and now at this health food megastore. (Ever cowpooled? You and three carnivorous friends can split a side of local beef.) Organic produce, bulk herbs and spices and every fascinating alternative remedy you can imagine are well stocked in the spacious aisles. The biggest draw, however, is the buffet. Unlimited fresh-squeezed juices, an omelet station during brunch, an epic salad bar and all kinds of vegetarian and meat items abound while live music keep diners entertained. All this and despite the store's size and health food focus, it still manages to feel homey and unpretentious.

HOUSE OF COFFEE BEA

....

2348 BISSONNET *at Morningside*
☎ **(713) 524-0057**
houseofcoffeebeans.com

 E7

B ACK IN 1973—JUST TWO YEARS AFTER THE VERY first Starbucks opened in Seattle —Houston welcomed the House of Coffee Beans. While customers can purchase a fresh cup of joe here, House of Coffee Beans is first and foremost a whole-bean purveyor and always has been. All roasting is done in small, hand-tended batches in a pre-World War II German coffee roaster that was acquired, disassembled and ultimately renamed Madam Hasbean. Blended and unblended coffees, dark and espresso coffee, decaffeinated and flavored are available and all are certified fair trade.

○ HOUSTON DAIRYMAIDS

16 ....

2201 AIRLINE *at Nadine*
☎ **(713) 880-4800**
houstondairymaids.com

E5

I T SOUNDS A BIT ANACH-RONISTIC TO BE A DAIRY-maid or cheesemonger in this day and age, but cheese love cannot be bound by time or space. This small local company operates largely as a

MARKETS

Cheese tasting at Houston Dairymaids

wholesale business, providing artisan dairy products to restaurants across town, but it also gives the public access to fine cheeses at farmers' markets and at its small Heights warehouse. On Fridays and Saturdays, customers are invited into the warehouse to sample cheeses and a variety of other snacks, including Slow Dough Bread Co. baked goods, Texas jams and olive oil. Although owner Lindsey Schecter works closely with 10 Texas cheesemakers in particular, hawking everything from the Veldhuizen Family Farm's Saint Arnold Washed Redneck Cheddar to creamy Pure Luck Dairy Chèvre, well-established cheeses from across the country are available here as well.

⊘HOUSTON PECAN COMPANY
. . . .

7313 ASHCROFT *at Evergreen*
☎ **(713) 772-6216**
houstonpecan.com

22   **D7**

⌐T'S A CULINARY TRU-
 ⌐ISM THAT GOOD FOOD
requires good ingredients, and

since 1942, faithful Houston followers have turned to Houston Pecan Company for the nuts and fruits they include in their baking, as well as snacks like wasabi peas, glazed fruit and Corn Nuts. This small store creates its own trail mixes like Hawaiian and cranberry nut crunch as well as different sizes of gift tins and bags and a small selection of kosher items. You can order online, but the staff is so friendly and helpful it would be a shame to miss that and the toasty sweet smell of warm pecans.

✗HUBBELL & HUDSON
. . . .

24 WATERWAY AVE.
near Lake Robbins Dr.,
The Woodlands
☎ **(281) 203-5600**
hubbellandhudson.com

NORTH OF **D1** 🚕

⌐⌐HIS INDEPENDENT GRO-
 ⌐⌐ CERY STORE, THOUGHT
by many to be on par with Central Market (though much smaller), really had to bring it to distinguish itself. And bring it they did, with 25,000 square feet of food excess. The dry-aged beef is hung in-house and on display at the immaculate butcher shop, and the cheese/charcuterie selection is the largest in this northern part of the Houston metro area. A prepared-food section proffers stellar sandwiches and salads to be eaten on

the patio. And for a finer, sit-down meal try the adjacent bistro, which is under the direction of chef Edelberto Gonçalves. Alaskan halibut in saffron aioli cream and perfectly grilled steaks procured from the market equal entrees at any of the more upscale restaurants in town. But specialty food market and fine dining are not all of it: The third H&H component is the upstairs Viking Cooking School. (Hubbell & Hudson also recently opened Hubbell & Hudson Kitchen, a mini-version of the original, at 4526 Research Forest in The Woodlands.)

LEIBMAN'S WINE & FINE FOODS

. . . .

14529 MEMORIAL
near N. Dairy Ashford
☏ **(281) 493-3663**
leibmans.com

B6

LOCALLY OWNED AND OPERATED BY SOUTH African ex-pats Ralph and Ettienne Leibman for the past 32 years, Leibman's is *the* gourmet food stop in west Houston. There's a commendable array of fine holiday-themed chocolates, hostess gifts and store-brand Leibman's Select jams, salad dressings and dips, but the store is also justly famous for its deli. The Captain's Choice sandwich, made with turkey and cranberry chutney, and the petite reuben are among the favorite lunch options, as is the Chicken Salad Afrique. When perusing the wine aisles, keep an eye out for South African selections, which are the specialty here.

OLIVE & VINE

. . . .

12848 QUEENSBURY LANE
in CityCentre
☏ **(832) 377-1610**
oliveandvineshop.com

B6

THREE GUESSES AS TO WHAT A FUSTI IS. NO? Fustis are the stainless steel dispensers that contain each of the 36 different varieties of olive oil and vinegars at this Euro-style specialty store, and they greatly improve the shopping experience by allowing customers to taste each product before buying. Susan and Wayde Burt, the husband and wife team behind Olive and Vine, have curated a variety of olive oils that will not only improve your home cooking but also give you a swift education. Depending on its country of origin, type of olive and amount of poly-

MARKETS

Olive oil options at Olive & Vine

phenols, each fresh bottled-to-order oil tastes distinctly different on its own. And then there are the infused varieties. Meyer lemon EVOO would be delicious on fish, and roasted garlic is perfect for snacking. Mix and match with the shop's traditional or flavored balsamic vinegars.

PENZEYS SPICES

516 W. 19TH ST.
east of N. Shepherd
☎ **(713) 862-6777**
penzeys.com
E5

LTHOUGH PENZEYS IS A NATIONWIDE ESTablishment, it is a favorite stop for local restaurants when fulfilling spice needs. Penzeys runs much of its business online (you can download the catalog), where spices can be bought in bulk and shipped freshly ground (or whole) from Wisconsin, but the store itself is also an enjoyable experience. The decor favors a *faux* antique look, with never-used wooden crates and spice bags lining the walls. But there is generally little reason to look up given what is on the shelves, from the three types of vanilla to Penzeys spice mixes. Each bottle comes with helpful serving suggestions and recipes and the staff is very amenable to answering questions. Give your nose a workout and sniff-test sample jars to your heart's content.

• RELISH

3951 SAN FELIPE *at Willowick*
☎ **(713) 599-1960**
relishhouston.com
D6

F REVIVAL MARKET IS SOMETHING OF A BOYS' club (we're talking ownership and infatuation with meat), then Addie D'Agostino's new specialty foods market (it opened in June 2011) might be its feminine counterpart. It's washed in white and sunlight, and it feels like something you might find in the Hamptons. In stock: products from local purveyors including the Houston Dairymaids, Greenway Coffee & Tea, The Grateful Bread and Atkinson Farms. The store's true calling card, however, is the selection of prepared foods. Texas peach salad with brandied pecans, prosciutto and crumbled goat cheese or the jalapeño pimento cheese sandwich are the answer to the lunchtime stomach rumble. Party trays and gift baskets can be ordered in advance.

The counter at Relish

• REVIVAL MARKET

. . . .

550 HEIGHTS BLVD. *at W. 6th*
☎ **(713) 880-8463**
revivalmarket.com

16   **E5**

THE DRIVING FORCE BE-HIND THIS ÜBER-LOCAL market, coffeeshop and cafe hybrid is a collective of true food nerds. Owners Morgan Weber of Revival Meats and Ryan Pera, formerly of the Grove, man the counter and curate every jar of Heights honey and orange yolk farm-fresh egg. Rebecca Masson of the Fluff Bake Bar provides the retro mallomars and snickerdoodles, and the cheese comes from the Houston Dairy-maids. What really awes are the assortment of one-of-a-kind house-made jams, vinegars and barrel-aged syrups—and the meat counter, of course. Already grilled and smoked meats might just change your life a little, and the staff is trained to send you home with thorough in-structions on how to cook the raw cuts you purchase. The tiny space is made the most of, with baristas producing the best flat white in the city, and the lunch counter frequent-ly has a line eight people deep waiting to order thick-cut bacon sandwiches and shrimp salad.

RICE EPICUREAN MARKET

. . . .

5016 SAN FELIPE *at S. Post Oak*
☎ **(713) 621-0422**
multiple locations
riceepicurean.com
D6

LONG BEFORE CENTRAL MARKET WAS INVENTED, Rice Epicurean Market was Hous-ton's first upscale food store, and many of its older and well-to-do customers have remained loyal over the years. It is also the oldest family-owned supermarket chain in Houston, which has not changed hands since its founding. The store features all the usual suspects, in-cluding gorgeous produce, gourmet deli section and prepared foods, fine wines and a bakery. The salad bar options are varied and con-stantly fortified with new items, making it a solid lunch spot. REM is also Houston's exclusive purveyor of See's Candies: Choose from some 90 varieties of candies, nuts and chews, available pre-boxed or cus-tom-boxed according to your whim.

Deli counter at Revival Market

MARKETS

WHOLE FOODS

701 WAUGH *at W. Dallas*
☎ **(713) 284-1260**
multiple locations
wholefoodsmarket.com

E7

ESPITE BEING AN IN-VENTION OF WAYWARD free-love Austinites, all types of organic and natural foods appreciators both hippie and yuppie flock to this bright, principled business. You won't find your typical brands of soda or lunchmeat here. Instead, products aimed at satisfying the store's "whole body" commitment, including the chain's 365 brand, line the shelves. If health food isn't your thing, never fear. Dietary supplements may get their own dedicated section in the store but so do warm, cheesy pizzas, cheese and charcuterie counter, olive bar, wine selection, seafood section and excellent butcher. At this location, the newest Whole Foods in Houston, there's even a Bayou Bar where you will find both wines and beers on tap—a perfect way to ease into the week's grocery shopping.

{ *Ethnic Grocery Stores* }

• 99 RANCH MARKET

1005 BLALOCK *at Katy Fwy.*
☎ **(713) 932-8899**
multiple locations
99ranch.com

5

C5

OT A LOT OF TEXANS WILL ADMIT TO CALI-fornia being better than us at anything, but this Asian grocery chain out of Los Angeles is proof that the Golden State is doing something right. The produce and seafood selection are extensive—you'll find everything from kaffir leaves to sushi-grade fish—and the bakery generates fresh bread from different cuisine types every hour. The food court is one of the store's best aspects, and the three-meat Chinese barbecue plate makes for an inexpensive and easy take-out dinner for two. Weekend crowds are intense and the parking lot is undersized, so weekday visits are advised in consideration of your mental health.

ASIA MARKET & CONVENIENCE

1010 W. CAVALCADE
between Airline & N. Main
☎ **(713) 863-7074**

Assorted packed meats at Balkan Market

THIS TINY HEIGHTS MAR-KET KEPT A LOW PROFILE for years, catering to the Cambodian, Laotian and Thai community. The shelves are stocked with canned goods, such as date palm, dried shrimp, chile pastes, coconut jelly and salted black beans, and the refrigerated section has produce (e.g. huge bags of mung bean sprouts), fresh noodles and seafood. Not long ago, the owners renovated the store a little to take advantage of the growing reputation of their prepared-food counter, which serves up excellent Thai food.

BALKAN MARKET

10928 WESTHEIMER
at Lakeside Country Club Dr.
☎ **(713) 532-6588**

ON THE ONE HAND, HOUS-TON IS DIVERSE ENOUGH to have a Bosnian market and on the other, we only have one and there's barely enough *ajvar*, or red-pepper spread, to go around. The second outpost by the family that also owns Cafe Pita+ just across the road, Balkan Market stocks mostly imports from the Eastern European peninsula. One wall has goods for preparing a traditional Balkan meal, including pickles and Shokata sodas; toward the back of the shop, there is a refrigerated section that features dried meats and hard sausages, as well as dairy products (butter, thick creamy cheesy spreads, freshly made brined cheese). Wafer sandwiches with different flavors of nougat are popular, especially the Croatian Jadro brand. For Nutella fans, there is Eurokrem, which is similar and possibly better.

DROUBI'S BAKERY & DELI

7333 HILLCROFT
between Bellaire & Bissonnet
☎ **(713) 988-5897**
multiple locations
C7

THERE IS SUCH A THING AS A DANGEROUS FAL-afel sandwich, and it's not what you think. This type of sandwich is simply so good that it just won't do to wait until arriving safely at home before eating it, causing a person to drive with her knees to leave her hands to her meal. The crunchy, fried-to-order falafel at Droubi's is such a sandwich. The Hillcroft store is admittedly getting on in years, a bit dimly lit inside, and parking is tight. But Droubi's pita bread is sold citywide for a reason. You should also try the *zatar* bread dusted with wild thyme and other herbs with a cup of hot tea. Besides the dry goods, halal meat counter and corner kitchenware shop, there is a small cafe area serving up fresh hummus where some customers choose to sit and enjoy their shawarma in the glow of foreign television programming.

FIESTA MART

· · · · · · · · · · · · · · · ·

8710 BELLAIRE BLVD.
at S. Gessner
☎ **(713) 981-0858**
multiple locations
fiestamart.com

IESTA WAS FOUNDED BACK IN 1972 AND catered to the local Hispanic market with the slogan "lower food prices." In reality, Fiesta carries a selection of international foods that trumps most other grocery stores while still concentrating on staples from Mexico. It's an eclectic operation—some stores are definitely nicer than others—but the chain continues to deliver on its original motto. Inside many of the stores customers will find a sno-cone stand, bakery (with empanadas, pita and bagels), prepared foods section or deli, and a serviceable selection of beer and wine. (The W. Alabama location has an outstanding wine selection, in fact.) In the larger Fiestas you will probably also come across men's pants, religious icon candles, perhaps a travel agent. Produce is equally diverse: sometimes wilted, but sometimes brilliantly fresh and cheap.

• GOLDEN FOODS SUPERMARKET

· · · · · · · · · · · · · · · ·

9896 BELLAIRE BLVD.
just inside Beltway 8
☎ **(713) 772-7882**

14

O STRAIGHT TO THE SOURCE, OR AS CLOSE as you can get in Houston, for traditional Chinese ingredients. This green-domed supermarket is not so huge as Hong Kong Food Market #4 in the Hong Kong City Mall, but it's clean and still manages to stock a wide selection of product. Exotic produce (e.g. dragon fruit and piles of strange-looking melons and squashes), a dozen types of soy sauce and a extensive seafood counter where your fish are cleaned on the spot are givens, but there are also powdered milk tea mixes,

Deli counter at B & W Meats

Slow Dough's pretzel buns

Pies and puffs at Phoenicia

DAREDEVIL DINING

MAC 'N' CHEESE AND DOUBLE SCOOPS OF ICE CREAM ARE COMFORT FOOD ALL RIGHT, but it's time to face the truth: We're getting a bit soft. So put down that bowl of custard and challenge your palate with these "Fear Factor" foods.

THANH PHUONG
3236 E. BROADWAY, PEARLAND
☎ (281) 412-7868

Ease into the world of out-there eats with some game meats, common in traditional Vietnamese cooking. Deep-fried rabbit and venison carpaccio are on the menu here.

FEAST
219 WESTHEIMER
☎ (713) 529-7788

Houston's favorite nose-to-tail dining establishment might make a killer crispy pork belly, but that means you have to eat your tongue and liver, too.

KIKI CAFE
9126 BELLAIRE BLVD.
☎ (713) 772-8883

If innards normally make you squeamish, try the Taiwanese fried pork intestines. They look like airy bacon crisps—and more or less taste that way, too.

HUGO'S
1600 WESTHEIMER
☎ (713) 524-7744

It was a desperate man who first ate a grasshopper. We'd say the man who eats Corn Nuts, which is what these spiced fried bugs taste like, is similarly desperate but we try not to judge (much).

CAFE RABELAIS
2442 TIMES
☎ (713) 520-8841

Do not be fooled by the delicate name of the *andouillettes*. They are in fact steamy, coarse-ground tripe sausages. The smell alone will burn the hair out of your nose.

SAMBA GRILLE
530 TEXAS
☎ (713) 343-1180

The cooks in the back don't even flinch when they drive skewers straight through beef hearts and grill them. Also keep an eye out for the black corn fungus, *huitlacoche*.

Japanese Ramune soda (the kind with the marble seal) and various vegan *faux*-meats. Of special note is Willie Barbecue & Meat, a Chinese barbecue stand that sells freshly roasted ducks, chickens and *char-siu* (barbecued pork) by the pound. It's back in the left-hand corner.

•HONG KONG FOOD MARKET

. . . .

11205 BELLAIRE BLVD.
between Wilcrest & S. Kirkwood
in Hong Kong City Mall
☎ **(281) 575-7886**

l⁴

YOU CAN EASILY SPEND HOURS BROWSING through this ginormous Asian grocery store, which anchors the Hong Kong City Mall. Give yourself plenty of time to peruse the large produce, meat and seafood selections—we counted 31 types of whole fish on one occasion. Pick up useful housewares, including a wok or steamer. Stock up on Sriracha, *sambal* or soy sauce. Working from the right side of the store to the left, the first department is the bakery, which features fresh buns and colorful sticky rice concoctions. Produce is next—watch for great bargains here, especially mushrooms, greens and, in season, mangos—then tofu of every style. There are herbal remedies, a dozen types of ramen, dried herbs and roots and a seafood counter supplied with every-

thing from king crab to geoduck. Organization could be improved, but that would only make it less of an adventure.

INDIA GROCERS

6606 SOUTHWEST FRWY.
at Hillcroft
☎ **(713) 266-7717**
C7

LIKE A LIGHTHOUSE IN A STORM, INDIA GROCERS is the beacon visible from the freeway that let's you know you're entering Houston's Little India (or the Mahatma Gandhi district, as it's also known). This small, clean store, owned by the affable Yatin Patel, makes the most of its space. It's well stocked with South Asian cooking supplies, dried spices, herbs and seasonings difficult to

Assorted grains at India Grocers

find in other parts of town. Smiling down upon the rows of chutney, jarred sauces and British candies are posters of virile-looking cricket players. The produce section deals in the basics, like okra and potatoes, but the refrigerator cases contains myriad frozen meals for when you're too tired to cook despite just accumulating all the best ingredients. (Hey, it happens.)

KHÔ BÒ

11209 BELLAIRE BLVD.
west of Wilcrest
in Hong Kong City Mall
☎ (281) 988-6630
multiple locations
khobohouston.net

EXAS IS WELL ESTAB-LISHED AS A JERKY lover's Shangri-La, but as it turns out Vietnam kicks that delusion in the butt. Luckily, Houston is a melting pot, and the two locations of this store offer us access to an unfathomably broad selection of exotic dried meats. There's regular ol' black pepper teriyaki beef jerky, but there's also shredded curry flavor beef jerky, barbecue squid jerky (heads on) and baked pork liver jerky. The two stores—tidy and attractively laid out—have even more in the way of dried fruits, nuts and confections. Among the more interesting snacks and culinary ingredients are shredded

preserved green mango with chili, mixed fruit chips (jackfruit, banana, pineapple, taro and yam) and Japanese candied ginger.

MI TIENDA

1630 SPENCER HWY.
at S. Perez, Pasadena
☎ (713) 941-7550

I TIENDA IS H-E-B'S LATIN-THEMED MEGA-market, aimed at immigrants from Mexico and Central America. A gringo may well feel like an intruding tourist here, where pesos are accepted and employees approach you with rapid-fire Spanish. The signs, labels and magazines at checkout are all in Spanish, too, but once the staff realizes you can't speak Spanish—and non-Spanish-speakers are in the minority—they'll either switch to English or begin to pantomime indulgently. Groceries are inexpensive, and the focus is on Mexican specialties. A simulated village, decorated festively with _papél picado_ (cut paper) streamers, takes up half the store and serves up hot food that most customers choose to enjoy in store. Choose from ceviche, combo plates, tamales by the dozen and refreshing _aguas frescas_.

NIPPON DAIDO

11146 WESTHEIMER *at Wilcrest*
☎ (713) 785-0815
B7

 UICK-KNIFE BENIHANA-STYLE CHEF ASPIRANT or not, you too can enjoy authentic Japanese food in your own home. How? Shop at Nippon Daido where all your sashimi-grade fish, containers of smelt roe and octopus tentacles dreams can come true. The store is impeccably clean, with no errant fish smells wafting through the air. A small vegetable section is stocked with produce found in traditional Japanese cooking, and packaged goods like noodles, powdered wasabi, nori, miso, dashi and sushi rice are available as well. Daring foodies will take a peek in the freezer section for all the different varities of *natto*, the fermented soybean breakfast food commonly enjoyed in Japan and reviled everywhere else in the world for its smell.

◦NUNDINI FOOD MART

500 N. SHEPHERD
between I-10 & W. 6th
☎ (713) 861-6331
nundini.com
14 **E6**

 RIVING PAST ON SHEPHERD YOU'D LIKELY mistake Nundini's for just another warehouse, which, technically, it is. The quaint, rather mismatched food mart is the retail portion of this Italian food importer, and what it lacks in atmosphere it makes up for by stocking the best. Dry pastas, meats, cheeses, sweets and other Italian goodies at wholesale prices line the shelves and perhaps most importantly, there is a panini bar. Fresh sandwiches like the Genova, a simple combination of quality salami and provolone on ciabatta, are a fantastic lunch option when paired with a scoop of the excellent gelato or even better, the flavor-packed sorbetto. Party trays are also available, and the cannoli has been known to impress. Nundini Chef's Table is the new bistro (circa 2011) located within the market.

PHOENICIA SPECIALTY FOODS

12141 WESTHEIMER
west of Kirkwood
☎ (281) 558-8225
phoeniciafoods.com
 B7

 PON ENTERING THE SPRAWLING WAREHOUSE that is Phoenicia, the scent of spices is overwhelming. And while probably not designed for the purpose of making customers giddy with excitement, it very well does.

MARKETS

Freshly packaged pita and other breads in Phoenicia Specialty Foods

This family-owned market carries products from countries around the world while specializing in Mediterranean and Middle Eastern cuisine. The olive bar is one of the best deals in town, and halal beef and whole lamb are available in the meat section. At the lunch and prepared-foods counters, you can purchase Armenian string cheese or babaganoush, among other things, by the pound. Digestive biscuits are shelved beside Kinder Eggs and jars of mango chutney, and there are entire aisles devoted to canned beans and pickled items. Look for a large selection of dates, fruit leathers and wines from Lebanon, Turkey and Eastern Europe. Need a hookah? Buy it here, along with a supply of flavored tobacco. **Note:** A second Phoenicia is under construction downtown at 1001 Austin due to open Fall 2011.

RUSSIAN GENERAL STORE

....

9629 HILLCROFT
at S. Braeswood
☎ **(713) 665-1177**

THERE ARE SOME INTERESTING TIDBITS TO BE gleaned from perusing the aisles of this specialty store. For example, did you know that in Russia there are carts that sell a mildly alcoholic, soda-like beverage called kvass? It's available at this modest shop in Meyerland alongside all sorts of other traditional Eastern European foodstuffs. The deli section is a particular gold mine, with all manner of inexpensive Russian smoked ham, hunter's sausage and buttery hot smoked mackerel. The house-made pickles come in several varieties, and packaged cookies catering to the foreign palate are always interesting little purchases. Pick up some frozen *pelmeni* dumplings and Georgian wines, and you'll be fully prepared for that Iron Curtain-themed holiday party you saw on Sandra Lee's *Semi-Homemade*.

•SUPER H MART

1302 BLALOCK
between I-10 and Westview
☎ **(713) 468-0606**
hmart.com

4 **C5**

I F YOU'VE NEVER HAD THE OPPORTUNITY TO EAT Korean fried chicken, well, what is it exactly that motivates you to carry on? A lone stand in the food court of this South Korean-owned supermarket chain is poised to up-end your life with its tender, garlicky brand of fried goodness and a side of pickled daikon. Other stands hawk *bibimbap* (the rice-egg-vegetable-and-chile-paste assemblage) and spicy tofu stews to fuel you before hitting the immaculate and well-priced produce aisle. This clean and cheerful grocery really does have a lot to offer. The amazing seafood counter has many types of live fish; simply point to the sign that describes how you want your fish cleaned, and it will be done. Pick up marinated *bulgogi* for Korean barbecue and super-thin-sliced beef for *shabushabu* (Japanese hot pot) in the meat case. Peruse an entire wall lined with kimchee of every

kind. There's even a glit [...] European bakery at the fro [...] store. This chain, which h [...] compared to a Whole Foods for Asian foodstuffs, is well-priced, customer friendly and fun to shop.

VIET HOA INTERNATIONAL FOODS

8300 W. SAM HOUSTON PKWY. *at Beechnut*
☎ **(832) 448-8828**
viethoa.com

B7

W HEN VIET HOA FIRST APPEARED on Houston's Asian grocery scene, it quickly proved itself to be bigger and badder than the competition. Especially large but one of the cleaner and better organized of its peers, the store carries pretty much everything in the wide world of Asian cooking ingredients, and then some. The seafood counter is a wall of live specimens (frogs, check!), and fish is custom-cleaned. So when the line at the Boiling Crab next door is too daunting, you can opt to prepare your own shellfish. The cheap lunch counter offers a little more selection than other similar supermarkets, and, in particular, the barbecued meats are recommended. Beyond the assortment of sauces, produce and an enormous selection of ramen, there are also sections for furniture and even shoes. Hungry? Grab a *banh mi* at the sandwich counter.

{ *Farmers' Markets* }

AIRLINE FARMERS' MARKET

(aka Farmers' Marketing Association)

....

2520 AIRLINE *at Sylvester, behind Canino's Produce*
☎ **(713) 862-8866**

 E5

HIS OPEN-AIR MEXICAN FOOD WONDERLAND IS not your typical locavore-friendly farmers' market. Very little, if anything, here is organic or local: It's a resale market. And instead of escarole and duck eggs, the featured products are more typically mountains of chiles and buckets of hominy. The stalls blend a bit confusingly with Canino's Produce in the front, but take to both and wander through on a Saturday morning as the crush of families hunt for the best prices for mangos and corn. Try to buy only two onions from the tent in back and you'll get a befuddled look on the vendor with the forklift, who according to the cost per pound is only asking for 25 cents in exchange. Stuff your pocket with dollar bills, as most things are $1 or $2, and the vendors accept cash only. After shopping, take advantage of the taco trucks that are parked in back.

CENTRAL CITY CO-OP

....

2515 WAUGH *at Missouri*
☎ **(713)524-9408**
centralcityco-op.com

 E6

HERE ARE TWO WAYS TO ADOPT THE MICHAEL Pollan lifestyle through this modest, local food co-op: Either pay the dollar "entrance fee" at the Wednesday market at Grace Lutheran Church (9 am to 6:30 pm) and shop like you would elsewhere, or become a member and pick up your share of fruits and vegetables every week. Depending on the season, there could be eggplant, red potatoes or Honeycrisp apples. Ordering online is an option, too, although the volunteers on location are very friendly. Note: There is never meat available here, although depending on the week you might find vendors selling eggs or founding member Pat Greer with her pre-made vegan snacks.

MIDTOWN FARMERS' MARKET

....

3701 TRAVIS *behind t'afia one block north of Alabama*
☎ **(713) 524-6922**
tafia.com

 E6

HEF/RESTAURATEUR MONICA POPE'S ECLEC-

FOODIE TOURS

SEE THE CITY AND LEARN SOMETHING ABOUT HOUSTON'S FOOD CULTURE, TOO.

WHERE THE CHEFS EAT
visithoustontexas.com/ culinarytours

Some of Houston's best-known chefs have signed on to conduct the hugely successful *Where the Chefs Eat* tours. Bryan Caswell, Chris Shepherd and Monica Pope are among the chefs who have led the five-hour Sunday afternoon tours to Houston's lesser-known ethnic restaurants and markets. Each tour has a theme—e.g. street food, Latin American, barbecue, Chinatown—and each sells out almost the moment that tickets (typically $180) go on sale. Tour participants, limited to 20, rendezvous at Central Market and travel in a small air-conditioned bus. There's always a cooler of beer and fun goodie bags.

FOODIE FLOATS
☎ (713) 752-0314
buffalobayou.org

Gliding down the Buffalo Bayou on a pontoon boat at twilight is magical enough. Now add a foodie component. The Buffalo Bayou Partnership hosts Foodie Floats, a seasonal series of boat tours on Houston's main waterway. You might sign on for a tour that features a beer and cheese tasting with the Houston Dairymaids and Saint Arnold Brewing Company, or a Spanish tapas and wine tasting co-hosted by Central Market. Tours typically begin at 6 pm and last about 90 minutes. Tickets are $40 to $50.

FARMERS MARKET BIKE RIDES
☎ (713) 524-3567
bayoucityoutdoors.com

Dust off your bike for the Saturday morning All Farmer's Market Tour Rides, sponsored by Bayou City Outdoors. Bring your backpack and meet up with fellow bikers at 8 am—the group can number 50 or more when the weather is nice—at the Onion Creek cafe in The Heights. The group typically rides to three to five markets around the city (eight to 12 miles total) and returns about noon. Participation is free.

tic Saturday morning farmers' market is one of the city's smaller venues, but the vendors are well-chosen. It's half outside under tented stalls and half inside T'afia restaurant—a blessing to both shoppers and perishable foods on sunny days. One of Pope's innovations is that she hosts a free cooking class to teach shoppers how to use the week's seasonal produce. Other pluses: There's always something to breakfast on, and the market is easy to reach via the MetroRail.

RICE UNIVERSITY FARMERS' MARKET

. . . .

2100 UNIVERSITY *at Montclair*
farmersmarket.rice.edu

FOR THOSE WHO LIKE TO AVOID THE MAD-deningly weekend crowd, this popular Tuesday evening (3:30 pm to 7 pm) market is the perfect solution. It's especially magical in the winter when the sun sets early and you shop by lantern and candlelight. Though not as populated as Eastside, more than 30 vendors with everything from organic dog biscuits to sugar-dusted chocolate whammies (God's gift to cookie lovers) set up shop each week. Stop by Blue Heron Farm for some delectable goat milk caramel and Angela's Oven for almost-croissants.

Just be cautious near the animal-adoption booth—those cute mugs can be irresistible.

• URBAN HARVEST FARMERS' MARKETS

. . . .

3000 RICHMOND *at Eastside*
☎ **(713) 880-5540**
multiple locations
urbanharvest.org

19

THE BIGGEST FARMERS' MARKET IN HOUSTON IS Urban Harvest's Saturday morning affair (8 am to noon) on Eastside, not far from Lamar High School. Aside from the city's biggest selection of fresh and prepared foodstuffs, there are always chef demos, live music and knife sharpening. You'll find meat, dairy, seafood, orchids, cut flowers, bakers and produce stands. Vendors to look for include Hatterman Poultry Farm (fresh eggs), Pola Cheese and The Grateful Bread (slab bacon, vanilla extract and more). The best produce and flowers sell out early and parking is messy (street parking, plus some—but not all—nearby lots), so the earlier you arrive the better. At the City Hall Farmers' Market, which takes place on Wednesdays from 11 am to 2 pm and is similarly operated by Urban Harvest, the offerings are more for eating on the spot. Prepared-food stands, including Melange Crêperie and

Nisha's Quick N Ezee Indian Food, keep the lunchtime crowd happy, and we highly recommend a macaron from Maison Burdisso for dessert before returning to the office. Finally, the Highland Village market, on Sundays 10 am to 1 pm, includes brunch offerings, shopping and lots of activities for children.

THE WOODLANDS FARMERS' MARKET

. . . .

7 SWITCHBUD PLACE
in Grogan's Mill Center
grogansmillvillage.com
NORTH OF **D1**

THIS SEASONAL MARKET, WHICH RUNS FROM EARLY April until the end of June, brings vendors commonly spotted in Houston out to The Woodlands. Located inside the Village of Grogan's Mill on Saturday mornings, it features an array of artisan food. Keep an eye out for Wood Duck Farms, Georgia's Grassfed Beef and the Texas Hill Country Olive Oil Company. There's usually live music, and it seems as though the entire community appears en masse to do their weekend shopping.

{ *Butchers* }

B & W MEAT CO.

. . . .

4801 N. SHEPHERD
a couple blocks north of W. 43rd
☎ **(713) 697-2844**
bwmeatcompany.com
E5

MORE THAN 50 YEARS OLD, B&W MEAT CO. looks like a supermarket with a huge meat section...until you realize that the aisles are stocked with cookout-ready sides and supplies. Wide aisles and a roll of numbered tickets portend crowds, though lines move fast here. The reason for its popularity is clear: fresh meat of all kinds at prices to feed a family on. Sausages made inhouse for about a dollar a hefty link are bestsellers, including andouille, boudin and alligator, some smoked or made with spices, garlic or jalapeños. (We enjoyed links of deer, grilled.) The range of selection impressed not only because we could choose between the leg of a lamb or a frog, but also for the

Pork sausage at B & W

thoroughness with which each animal is covered, from hocks to gizzards to tongues, in addition to the familiar steaks and ribs. B&W also does custom processing.

BURT'S MEAT MARKET

....

5910 LYONS AVE.
between Shotwell & Hoffman
☎ **(713) 674-0064**
burtsmeatanddeli.com
 F6

 ANY PEOPLE IN HOU-STON, INCLUDING THE Breakfast Klub owner Marcus Davis, say that the pan sausage from Burt's is the best breakfast sausage in the city. This old Cajun-Creole meat market (circa 1948) is located in the Fifth Ward just north of I-10. Other choice picks: the boudin, andouille, smoked tasso, various combination "family packs" (which might include turkey wings, pork bones and bar-becue links) and soul food take-out dinner items such as ox tails, gumbo, ribs and chicken and dumplings.

GUY'S MEAT MARKET

....

3106 OLD SPANISH TRAIL *at Telge*
☎ **(713) 747-6800**
E7

HOUGH NEITHER IS IN THE NAME, GUY'S TRULY excels at two things: nostalgia and smoked burgers. This meat market and lunch counter is a Houston institution. The original opened on Almeda in 1938, and Guy's son Brad Dickens began smoking burgers in 1988. Each morning the store puts 200 partially cooked burgers in the smoker and all of them sell out before noon. Be sure to arrive in time because other menu items, like the ribs and brisket, get low marks. Aside from the slabs of beef behind the glass case, Guy's also sells frozen chili and Cajun-style stuffed chickens.

HEBERT'S SPECIALTY MEATS

....

4714 RICHMOND
just inside Loop 610
☎ **(713) 621-6328**
multiple locations
hebertsspecialtymeats.com
 D7

HOUSTON OUTPOST OF CAJUN COOKING, Hebert's (pronounced "A-bears") offers marinated and seasoned meats as well as Louisiana favor-ites like boudin, étouffée, crawfish pie and a gumbo stock that sells faster than the store can make it. The shop is a simple tile-floor, wood beam-ceiling affair with friendly staff ready to recommend an item and tell you how to cook it. But what Hebert's is really known for is deboning and stuffing practically anything that walks, flies or swims. The lengthy product list includes everything from an especially good shrimp-stuffed chicken to stuffed rabbit, stuffed bell peppers to stuffed brisket and the zenith of stuffed-ness, the turducken. Everything is prepared at the Dairy Ashford location, and the recipes are "straight from Louisiana," the original store being located in Maurice, La.

JERUSALEM HALAL MEAT MARKET

....

3330 HILLCROFT
south of Richmond
☎ **(713) 784-2525**
C7

UT OF ALL THE AVAILABLE OPTIONS, PERhaps being crushed by a tumbling avalanche of imported food items

Sweet treats at Jerusalem Halal

overloaded onto the highest shelves as they are at this modest meat market wouldn't be the worst way to go. Customers queue up for halal meat, permissible by Islamic law, inside the butcher room, where requests for meat cut to order are made. There are also tons of dry goods—snacks, herbs, dried legumes and cooking mixes plus kettles, cooking pots and tableware. There are 14 brands of pomegranate molasses alone, though things can be a bit grimy from years of inattention. If you care to eat in, you'll find a buffet of kabobs, hummus and a daily rice special served at the tiny counter tucked in the back.

LA BOUCHERIE

....

3323 FM 1960 WEST
near TC Jester
☎ **(281) 583-8177**
cajunmeats.com
C2

URDUCKEN BEING THE BIGGEST CELEBRITY TO come out of Maurice, La., it hogs most of the spotlight when people discuss this Cajun specialty butcher shop. Of course the turducken is a mighty food, but so is the five-chicken sampler, each bird stuffed with jalapeño cornbread, crawfish jambalaya or shrimp and sausage jambalaya. In fact, so many meats are stuffed with various ingredients that we can only assume that Cajuns only consider food

MARKETS

edible once it's been filled with something. Cooking instructions are practically foolproof, thankfully, and the store also sells *maque choux* (kind of a Southern-style succotash), seafood gumbo and tasso, which make holiday meals a snap.

LA MICHOACANA MEAT MARKET

1348 N. SHEPHERD *at W. 13th*
☎ **(713) 862-6129**
multiple locations
lamichoacanameatmarket.com

E5

LA MICHOACANA IS MUCH MORE THAN A meat market today. This modest Mexican grocery chain was founded in 1986 by a Houston family before spreading its wings to other Texas cities. It now has nearly 100 locations throughout Texas and beyond and is the largest independent Hispanic grocery store chain in the country. It's a safe bet for inexpensive cuts of meat from fajita meat to ribs, baked goods, salsas, *queso fresco* and *crema*, and cones of *piloncillo*, the hard dark sugar. In Mexican meat market tradition, a hot food counter frequented by blue collar workers dishes up a respectable taco, as well as *chicharrones*, *barbacoa* and more.

PETE'S FINE MEATS

5509 RICHMOND
east of Chimney Rock
☎ **(713) 782-3470**
petesfinemeats.net

D7

THE OWNER OF THIS 50-YEAR-OLD SHOP (PERUSE some of the framed yellowed news clippings) seemed almost regretful that they might not always have lion. We want to assure Pete's Fine Meats that we are beyond happy that someone has been wrestling actual pythons and ostriches to bring us the rest of the eclectic, high-quality menu. After ogling a deep-red stack of prime sirloin, we opted for a kangaroo shoulder so lean the meat was purple (but tender after a day's marinade). Try the jerky or the tamales, or com-

Prepacked quail at Pete's Fine Meats

plete your meat with smoking woods and original seasonings. With hearty, fully stuffed hoagies and buffalo burgers for just five bucks, plus sides like deviled eggs, the in-store deli is the ideal place to refuel in the middle of the day. Pete's Fine Meats can also process just about any animal you bring in, cook anything you order and cater for just about any group size.

{ *Fishmongers* }

AIRLINE SEAFOOD
·················

1841 RICHMOND
between Hazard & Woodhead
☎ **(713) 526-2351**
E7

HERE'S AN UNSPOKEN UNDERSTANDING ACROSS the city that the humblest-looking shops often have the friendliest staff and best product, and that's definitely true of Airline Seafood. Most of its business is whole-sale to restaurants, but the bare-bones shop is open for retail customers to get their grubby hands on the large international selection of finfish and shellfish (from mahi mahi to enormous sea scallops to shark). Still, owner Steve Berreth has made a specialty of ultra-fresh Gulf Coast seafood: drum, flounder, croaker, sheepshead, grouper, cobia, various snap-

per and much more. Aside from the raw fish selections, Airline also makes its own *campechana* rife with seafood and avocado, as well as smoked salmon, gumbo, stuffed crabs and crab cakes.

CONNIE'S SEAFOOD MARKET
·················

2525 AIRLINE *at Aurora*
☎ **(713) 868-2144**
multiple locations
E5

NE OF MANY STORES IN THE FRESH MARKET corridor down Airline, Connie's does not suffer from the competition. The hordes of customers, reaching peak volume at lunch, seek the relatively inexpensive seafood at this "you buy, we fry" spot. While Connie's functions as a fishmonger, most of the square footage is apportioned for the dining room, where uncomplicated fried and garlicky grilled fish is served. There's a lot of buzz about the cross-cultural fried rice that can be ordered with the seafood, but we've never been particularly enchanted by it. (Still, it's better than the fries.) Buy either raw or cooked seafood by the pound: shrimp, frog legs, mussels, crawfish tails, snapper, trout, etc. The Airline location in particular is friendly to families.

MARKETS

CHARCUTERIE

SURE, "I'M WITH BACON" T-SHIRTS ARE ABSURD, BUT YOU CONSIDERED WEARING ONE FOR A moment, didn't you? Of course, bacon is for peons compared to the meats being cured inhouse at these Houston restaurants and markets.

REVIVAL MARKET
550 HEIGHTS BLVD.
☎ **(713) 880-8463**
This little Heights market is the sacred temple of sustainable, great-tasting meat. House-cured anything shines, and the gleaming meat counter is stocked with everything from freshly butchered duck to beef fajitas.

STELLA SOLA
1001 STUDEWOOD
☎ **(713) 880-1001**
From your table at Bryan Caswell's "Texas Tuscan" eatery, you might be able to spy the rows of sausages aging to edible maturity. Follow the charcuterie starter with roast suckling pig for two.

POSCOL VINOTECA
1609 WESTHEIMER
☎ **(713) 529-2797**
This is a true Italian wine bar, meaning the best way to experience it (and life) is to order a bottle and the board of house-made sausage, salumi and head cheese and linger a while.

BRASSERIE MAX & JULIE
4315 MONTROSE
☎ **(713) 524-0070**
The authentic brasserie atmosphere doesn't inspire romance so much as it does desire for a medley of meats. Indulge in house-made pâté or a crock of pork rillettes.

THE GRATEFUL BREAD
thegratefulbread.com
You can find Al Marcus at several area farmers' markets each week, hawking his excellent slab bacon, andouille and pancetta.

BLOCK 7 WINE COMPANY
720 SHEPHERD
☎ **(713) 572-2565**
Whether arranged atop a crispy flatbread or served alongside the cheese plate, Block 7's house-made sausage is perfect for sipping vino.

J&J SEAFOOD MARKET

3825 WOODVALLEY
north of Loop 610 near Stella Link
☎ **(713) 661-6102**
jandjseafoodmarket.com
D8

WHILE IT SEEMS SMALL, DRAB AND a little on the edge of the busier parts of town, just a lungful of air inside this shop quickly steers the senses to fresh fish and/or a hot dinner. Owned and operated by the Ong family for 30 years and two generations, J & J Seafood Market fillets (and fries, if you wish) any fish on display on the spot, be it catfish, salmon, gar, perch, drum, flounder, bass or red snapper, mostly from the Gulf. Let them know if you want to take home the bones and heads for stock. Also on the ice are fresh crabmeat, oysters and shrimp. The cooked menu is full of tasty sides, including hush-puppies, shrimp fried rice, crabcakes and fried okra, mushrooms and zucchini. Prices are excellent. Their newest offering: boudin.

LOUISIANA FOODS

....

4410 W. 12TH ST.
east of N. Post Oak Rd.
☎ **(713) 957-3476**
louisianafoods.com
D5

IF YOU'VE EATEN SEAFOOD IN HOUSTON, CHANCES are it came from Jim Gossen and Louisiana Foods. Gossen, Billy Landry and Floyd Landry founded this largely wholesale operation back in 1972. The guys, of course, went on to operate a number of Houston restaurants, many of which were sold to Tilman Fertitta. Gossen still runs the seafood facility, where employees work the phone lines sourcing all things gilled from all over the world, and he makes sure the seafood here is stellar, even going so far as to guarantee that the red snapper is, in fact, *Lutjanus campechanus*. A number of Cajun specialties, such as gumbo and fried catfish, are available at the storefront alongside flounder, amberjack, and burlap sacks of oysters. The downside is that the retail shop is open just 25 hours a week, 10 am to 3 pm Monday through Friday. On Saturdays, however, stop in for P.J. Stoops' Total Catch Market (9 am to early afternoon), which makes a fetish of by-catch and so-called "trash" fish. Just because these fish are small and kind of ugly doesn't mean they don't taste great.

MARKETS

{ *Kitchen Outfitters* }

ALLIED KENCO SALES

....

26 LYERLY *at Airline*
☎ **(713) 691-2935**
alliedkenco.com

E4 🖎

BERING'S

....

6102 WESTHEIMER
near Fountain View
☎ **(713) 785-6400**
multiple locations
berings.com

THERE ARE CERTAIN THINGS YOU SHOULD always leave to professionals. But in Texas, meat is not among them. This butcher-supply house specializes in sausage- and jerky-making equipment, meat-smoking and curing products as well as outdoor cooking supplies. Grinders, mandolines, dehydrators and all sorts of brining products are at your disposal. Owner Cody Brown didn't set out to operate a meat-lover's nirvana back in 1982; he originally catered to professional butchers' equipment needs. But serious backyard meat guys kept coming in, and today Brown oversees an enormous retail outlet and even publishes a 160-page catalog. What else will you find here? Tenderizers, sausage casings, various seasonings and cures, bottled spices, turkey-frying kettles, smokers, cutting boards and knives. Lots of knives.

IT'S A MARK OF OUR SOCIETY'S ADVANCEMENT THAT we bring hostess gifts to parties, and the best hostess gifts in Houston are often found at Bering's. European ceramics, coffee contraptions, cloth napkins, high-end glassware and fine coffees are ideal for gifting or your own entertainment splurge. Expect a smart collection of cooking tools at these popular Houston-born hardware stores that pack a surprising amount of great merchandise into their small sites. Cookbooks, aprons, basic to innovative kitchen and baking tools, cutlery, fine cutting boards and small appliances are a few of the staples. The pleasant neighborhood feel and a staff that seldom turns over is a reminder of times back when things moved more slowly. ***Note:*** The Westheimer location recently had a large expansion of its culinary department so there are more lovelies than ever.

BUFFALO HARDWARE

· · · · · · · · · · · · · ·

2614 WESTHEIMER *at Kirby*
☎ **(713) 524-1011**

IN A PINCH, RIVER OAKS DENIZENS RELY ON THIS tiny family-owned corner store for hardware. But they also come here when there's more time to peruse the slightly chaotic selection of quirky gifts and intriguing cookware. From baking sheets, cutlery, beautiful bamboo cutting boards, small appliances and even a current cookbook and food book selection, you can usually find what you need. Especially if what you need is a brioche mold or meatball grilling basket. If you get lost in the dark rows of wondrous kitchen items, ask a helpful salesperson. They know the inventory well; they have been doing this for more than 60 years.

PAYAL

· · · · · · · · · · · · · ·

5615 SAVOY DR. *off Harwin*
☎ **(713) 782-2150**

INDIAN STAINLESS STEEL KITCHENWARE—THALI dishes, teapots, cups, pressure cookers, bowls, pans, woks and tiffins (India's famous stacked food carriers)—lines the walls and is piled high throughout this warehouse/retail shop. It's a great shopping adventure, one of those stores hidden in a warehouse development that you would never find on your own. Curiously, the shop also sells incense and jewelry.

MARKETS

Shelves lined with various baking pans at Buffalo Hardware

PITT'S AND SPITT'S

· · · · · · · · · · · · · · · ·

14221 EASTEX FRWY. *near Lee*
☎ **(281) 987-2474**
pittsandspitts.com

HIS MAKER OF CUS-TOM PITS, GRILLS AND trailers is nationally known but Texas specific in its style of preferred food preparation. They'll advise you to smoke your meat rather than cook it directly over the fire and to use wood rather than charcoal, like any respectable Texan would tell you. The store also stocks spices, sauces, cooking woods, accessories, cookbooks, etc. Want a taste of big-time barbecuing? Pitt's and Spitt's has their own video on YouTube, made with the Houston Texans band at a tailgating party.

TONY'S BAR SUPPLY

· · · · · · · · · · · · · · · ·

5201 S. WAYSIDE DR. *at Long*
☎ **(713) 641-2277**
tonysbarsupply.com

ONY'S BAR SUPPLY FEELS LIKE IT SHOULD be to the trade only, and that's exactly the kind of place you want to do your shopping. Founded in 1963, this restaurant supplier carries everything for a bar except (as

the website notes) the alcohol. You'll find bar appliances such as sinks and refrigerators, chemicals for cleaning draft-beer lines and concession machines. What the home cook and host will be more interested in is the glassware and bartender kits that will make you look like a solemn professional while the cocktail swords and Jell-O shot syringes shout party.

TOSS IT UP

CAN'T DECIDE WHAT TO EAT IN THE SWELTER-ING SUMMER HEAT? HIT THE SALAD BAR BUFFET and let your eyes guide you. It can be an inexpensive, healthful and quick lunch.

JASON'S DELI
2611 S. SHEPHERD
☎ **(713) 520-6728**

All-you-can-eaters flock the salad buffet as an alternative to the popular sandwiches. Standard toppings like jalape-ños, celery, bacon bits, nuts and carrots, plus potato and pasta salads, muffins and garlic toast. Note: We observed buffet untidiness at some locations.

SALATA
1200 MCKINNEY
☎ **(713) 739-9000**

Servers toss your pick from a selection of fresh lettuces and signature Salata dress-ings. Fifty awesome toppings including quality proteins like pesto chicken, baked salmon and crabmeat, plus toasted pumpkin seeds, dried cranberries, favas, snow peas and more.

GEORGIA'S FARM TO MARKET
12171 KATY FWY.
☎ **(281) 870-9999**

Vast ultra-tidy buffet for healthniks. Choose from several sprightly lettuces, raw veggies, delightful fresh herbs, sunflower seeds, sprouts, peppers, cheeses, marinated salads, pineapple salsa and guacamole. Great ginger-lime dressing.

• SWEET TOMATOES
8775 KATY FWY.
5 ☎ **(713) 365-9594**

Huge 55-foot salad buffet with myriad colorful, fresh salad fixings and tasty ranch dressing. Pluses include six hearty soups, warm tossed pasta, bountiful bakery sweets, focaccia and soft-serve ice cream with darling miniature cones.

WHOLE FOODS
2955 KIRBY
☎ **(713) 520-1937**

Super selection of salady stuff: chicken, tofu, baby shrimp, boiled eggs, fresh fruit, homemade croutons, beets, artichokes, edamame, shredded zucchini, premium crumbled cheeses and organic Whole Foods dressings.

BAKERIES & SWEETS SHOPS

{ SIDEBARS }

{ *Frozen Confections* }

AMY'S ICE CREAMS

·················

3816 FARNHAM *at Greenbriar*
☎ **(713) 526-2697**
amysicecreams.com

BERRIPOP

·················

3825 RICHMOND
at Weslayan
☎ **(713) 960-1940**
multiple locations
berripop.com

USTIN'S MOST WELL-LOVED EXPORT (SEC-ond to Austin City Limits) has really cleaned up its act over the past few years. The old wooden tables etched deeply with layers of initials have been replaced by untouchable vinyl ones, but the kids working behind the counter are still tatted up enough to keep up the quirky vibe. The slightly chewy texture of the ice cream is unbeatable, as is the Belgian chocolate flavor (far superior to dark chocolate). Try the Shiner beer and the cinnamon if available. Toppings are the average crushed candy and fruit selections but there are always two flavors of non-dairy ices for the diet restricted. The photo booth has malfunctioned for half of its existence, but that doesn't stop teenagers from piling in on Friday nights while couples and families linger at nearby tables.

HE PALE PEAKS OF SWIRLED FRO-YO AT this houston yogurt chain are almost as cute as the bright bubblegum interior. Neon colors and pop music videos appeal to a tween crowd while the healthful aspect of the designer yogurt, which boasts active live cultures at only 125 calories per four-ounce cup, attracts their chaperones. Not-too-sweet flavors such as watermelon and açai berry ro-tate in and out, although plain, raspberry-pomegranate and blue-berry are constant, and toppings range from healthful diced kiwi to no-excuses cheesecake chunks. Un-like other similar joints, portions are not self-serve, and in addition to churning out portions, servers also make soymilk smoothies and parfaits.

CONNIE'S FROZEN CUSTARD

....

12545 JONES _at McCracken Circle_
☎ **(281) 469-3444**
conniesfrozencustard.com
B2

AILING FROM THE MID-WEST, FROZEN CUSTARD has not yet become a Texas thing. So not only is Connie's offering a quality product—a fresh batch is frozen every hour—it's also so rare locally that people travel from all over the city to satisfy the craving. In typical custard-stand tradition, cones are sold out of a tiny hut with little seating area. There are only two flavors, chocolate and vanilla, but each can be made into glorious concretes, another Midwestern invention. (A concrete is simply a well-blended custard plus ingredients.) The Pretzel Caramel Crunch will make you question your Lone Star loyalty.

FAT CAT CREAMERY

....

☎ **(713) 974-2956**
fatcatcreamery.com

NEWCOMER ON THE ICE CREAM SCENE, Sarah Johnston's Fat Cat Creamery in The Heights makes small batches of ice cream with local ingredients. You can get your pints at Revival Market and Georgia's Farm to Market, and single servings are currently available at Black Hole Coffee House and Antidote. So far there's just the three basic Neapolitan flavors, but tasting unlike any you've probably had before: strawberry buttermilk with Hendrick's Gin, milk chocolate made heady with local stout and a tender Mexican vanilla.

GELATO BLU

....

5710 MEMORIAL _at Birdsall_
☎ **(713) 880-5900**
gelatoblu.com
E6

HOUGH GELATO IS A FREQUENTLY ADULTERATED food in America, this pocket-sized shop gets full marks for authenticity and quality. Owner Chuck Irwin spent a year in Italy immersing himself in the language and culture in order to deeply understand gelato and sorbetto. The Raffaello flavor (apricots stewed in Pinot Grigio with pistachios) is stunning, while the light sweetness of simple _stracciatella_ (vanilla with chocolate shavings) is cut

Various flavors from Gelato Blu

by the darkness of the chocolate. The coffee is also expertly made, which means the gelato *affogato*—a scoop swimming in a shot of espresso—is the dessert equivalent of a power couple. Free WiFi and kid-friendly movies on the television are bonus reasons to drop in. But in case you can't, Gelato Blu provides product to several restaurants around town.

GELATO CUP

. . . .

9889 BELLAIRE BLVD.
at Beltway 8
☎ **(713) 271-1082**
D7

NOT CONTENT WITH ITS SMALL VILLAGE OF bubble tea shops, Chinatown has recently seen an explosion of gelato spots. Of course, they're not perfect replicas of those in Italy, nor are they trying to be. Flavors for the Asian palate from stinky durian (triple dog dare you to try it) to nutty, creamy black sesame complement the more conventional chocolate, pistachio and coffee at this particular store. A number of other desserts—including a delectable sesame ball in ginger soup, shave ice and a kooky-sounding ice cream burrito wrapped in Vietnamese rice paper—are reason to experiment. Like anything in the neighborhood that's worth its salt, Gelato Cup gets very crowded during peak hours so bring your accommodating nature and cash.

HANK'S ICE CREAM

. . . .

9291 S. MAIN *between Murworth & Buffalo Speedway*
☎ **(713) 665-5103**
hanksicecream.com
E8

FOR NEARLY 20 YEARS, HANK'S HAS BEEN A Houston institution. There isn't much to say about its location in a dingy strip center near Reliant Stadium, but the pink walls of the store itself are covered in memorabilia and autographed photos from local celebrities.

Despite all that tradition, owner Hank Wiggins isn't afraid to go nouveau with some of his flavors. Next to classics like chocolate and butter pecan, there are always different experimental flavors like Grape Nuts and creamed corn for the more adventurous. All are served up in either a Styrofoam cup or a crisp waffle cone, as custom dictates.

JUICE BOX

. . . .

9889 BELLAIRE BLVD.
at Beltway 8
☎ **(713) 484-8085**
B7

THIS CHEERY, EVER POPULAR TAIWANESE-STYLE juice bar gets slammed every weekend with teens and families seeking cool refreshment. The menu is organized into fruit "series," in which watermelon, strawberry and avocado, etc., get turned into juice with yogurt or juice with Calpis (a milky Japanese soft drink) and smoothies. The item of note, however, and what you'll spy on pretty much every table, is the milk shaved ice: A large bowl of downy shaved ice topped with fruit—mango, melon, strawberry, kiwi—condensed milk and a quality scoop of ice cream. It's enough to feed up to four people, or just you on a sad day.

LA PALETERA

. . . .

5720 BELLAIRE BLVD.
at Renwick
☎ **(713) 667-8311**
multiple locations
lapaletera.com

D5

LA PALETERA HAS GROWN FROM A TRADITIONAL Mexican popsicle stand to a full-blown franchise with more than a dozen locations across Texas. The colorful interior is plastered with posters advertising the wares: fruit cups served with lime and chili powder dip, sno-cones and *paletas*, or sturdy popsicles both water and cream based. Chunky pecan, creamy mango and rice pudding are perhaps at the pinnacle of human popsicle achievement, and the ice cream, also made at the factory in San Antonio, is

similarly good in a range of flavors from coconut to stunning *leche quemada* (burnt milk fudge). A few savory items like hot dogs and Frito pie complete the nostalgic return to childhood.

MAM'S HOUSE OF ICE

CORNER OF 20TH & RUTLAND
mamshouseofice.com

E5

MAM'S IS A LOT LIKE SANTA CLAUS—IT ONLY shows up a certain time of year to dispense treats, and if you blink an eye you might miss out. The authentic New Orleans-style snoballs—fluffier and creamier than a Texas sno-cone—doled out of an adorable blue trailer draw long lines in the peak summer months, and business hours tend to change depending on weather and truck maintenance. But once the wait

A sno-cone at Mam's

COOKING CLASSES

YOU KNOW WHEN YOU LOOK AT ABSTRACT ART AND SAY TO YOURSELF, "I COULD TOTALLY DO that"? It happens with food at restaurants, too, and in both cases it's probably not true. Until you've got yourself a little education, at least.

CENTRAL MARKET
3815 WESTHEIMER
☎ **(713) 993-9860**
Not only do courses cover a medley of cuisines, CM is able to pull in nationally known cookbook authors and local chefs to instruct. Keep an eye out for classes designated "hands-on."

ANVIL BAR & REFUGE
1424 WESTHEIMER
☎ **(713) 523-1622**
In some circles, a well-made cocktail is dinner, and the best bar in town offers classes covering everything from the versatility of a certain spirit to cocktails of a bygone era.

WELL DONE COOKING CLASSES
1208 E. 29TH
☎ **(832) 782-3518**
Small, laid-back classes invite you to gather your friends, bring wine and get your hands messy preparing three-course meals and specialties such as "food men love."

VIKING COOKING SCHOOL
24 WATERWAY AVE.,
THE WOODLANDS
☎ **(281) 203-5608**
Aspiring cooks on the north side will want to seek out this school inside Hubbell & Hudson. The school is equipped with seductive, high-performance Viking appliances.

SUR LA TABLE
1996 W. GRAY
☎ **(713) 533-0400**
Well known for its practical classes, Sur La Table's intro-level "Knife Skills," for example, moves from slicing vegetables to breaking down chickens and filleting fish.

CREATING CULINARY OPPORTUNITIES
☎ **(713) 622-6936**
Only one local cooking school can claim the hands-on class instruction of acclaimed teacher, chef and cookbook author Giuliano Hazan. Sessions are quick to fill.

is over, a long list of kooky flavors such as Tiger Blood (berry and coconut), King Cake, mojito or plain ol' blueberry stuffed with a scoop of vanilla ice cream await. Opt to get your sno drizzled with condensed milk, whipped cream or marshmallow fluff, and once you've snagged your refreshment, join the other happy customers milling about the empty lot that serves as Mam's home base to finish up before hiking back to the car.

MORELIANA NATURAL ICE CREAM

10181 WESTVIEW
east of Conrad Sauer
☎ (713) 932-6262
C5

TRADITIONAL ICE CREAM VARIATIONS SUCH AS vanilla, chocolate and pecan can be found here, but the real gems are the less-common flavors such as sweet corn and a brightly flavored mango and cheesecake ice cream. Many selections change to reflect what is in season. The popsicles are tempting, covered in a soft frost and with fresh berries bulging out of their angular edges. You might also find homemade tamales and other traditional Mexican items available to go, but there doesn't seem to be a permanent spot on the menu for them. If you're looking for bins of mix-ins and

candy flavors, this little mom and pop parlor (next to a kimchee factory) probably isn't for you. The "natural" flavors lean towards a tart gelato-like spectrum, with the fruit controlling the sweetness versus added sugar.

SWEET LOLA YOGURT BAR

304 GRAY *just west of Bagby*
☎ (713) 521-1333
sweetlolayogurtbar.com
E6

TO STEP INSIDE OF SWEET LOLA IS TO KNOW WHAT the life of a purse pooch must be like—frilly, feminine and a tiny bit claustrophobic. The pink, green and chandelier-strewn frozen yogurt shop doubles as a home accessories store, and the format is self-serve. Whatever is in your cup, be it multiple flavors and however many toppings, costs $9.92 per pound. The yogurt itself is organic and fat-free, and the flavors, from Frosty Frosting to Caramel Macchiato, change regularly. Fan favorites include Blush (an almond cherry), ONilla (orange-vanilla) and lavender. The toppings are the best part and definitely not fat-free: Guittard mint pearls, caramel debris and house-made peanut butter croutons are laid out buffet-style in a clear attempt to ruin any healthful intentions.

SWIRLL

·················

2531 UNIVERSITY *at Kirby*
☎ **(713) 526-7947**
multiple locations
swirlls.com

O F ALL THE SHOPS TO POP UP DURING THE FAT-free frozen yogurt craze, Swirll is king among the local chains. With several locations optimally located near Rice University, River Oaks and Sugar Land Town Square, gaggles of girls glide in for their pick of the eight soft-serve stations. There is, of course, the tart original flavor, but also pomegranate, green tea, raspberry and a few more indulgent-in-name-only offerings such as cheesecake. The layout is weigh-then-pay, and once you've taken as much or as little fro-yo as you want, head to the toppings station for fruits, cereals and *mochi* (Japanese rice cake), then the cash register.

TAMPICO REFRESQUERIA

·················

4520 N. MAIN *at Edsee*
☎ **(713) 880-3040**
multiple locations

O FFERING ICY TREATS LIKE *RASPAS* AND *LICUADOS* (the Latin American version of the sno-cone and smoothie, respec-tively) this shabby blue and yellow shack is like a beacon on a hot day. And yet the best time to visit may be the late evening, thanks to a closing time of 10:30 pm. When the cool breeze sets in and the nuclear summer sun disappears, there's no better way to spend a summer night than sitting at one of the picnic tables with an *elote* (a parfait of corn, mayonnaise, butter, crema and chili powder) and a banana *licuado* rife with cinnamon. There are dozens of high-fructose-heavy sno-cone flavors like strawberry cheesecake and peach, but the natural flavors—especially the *limón*—are the way to go.

{ *Chocolate & Candy* }

ARAYA ARTISAN CHOCOLATE

·················

2013 W. GRAY
just east of S. Shepherd
☎ **(832) 967-7935**
multiple locations
arayachocolate.com

I N A MOVING TALE OF AMER-ICAN COMMERCE, OWNERS Stefano Zullian, wife Carla and her sister Silvana quit their day jobs to spend some time learning the gourmet chocolate trade from friends in Venezuela and relocate to Houston to set up shop. Armed with stocks of Venezuelan El Rey chocolate, considered some of the

A gift box of chocolates at Araya

best in the world, the team dreams up recipes with the Houston palate in mind and whips them up in a Katy kitchen. Tender little packages of orange marzipan and hazelnut praline in ganache rest in orderly rows within the glass case. Among the bestsellers are pink salt, strawberry balsamic and margarita, each complex, decadent and beautiful. High gift-giving potential is increased even more by the limited-edition, artist-designed boxes.

CANDYLICIOUS
. . . .

1837 W. ALABAMA *at Driscoll*
☎ **(713) 529-6500**
multiple locations

E7

CANDYLICIOUS IS MORE THAN A SWEETS SHOP: It's a theme park and a paean to the world of sugar. The owners would do well to charge admission for all the entertainment value that comes with pointing out kitschy or unique items to your companions.

Floor-to-ceiling treats from the retro candy necklaces and wax lips to international licorice and gummies form a rainbow of dazzling color. Seasonal novelties and "cakes" built out of candy would please any recipient, and beyond the sugar are non-edible trinkets like metal lunchboxes and games. Everything in the store is designed to make a kid pass out from excitement. Depending on your tastes, you might get a sugar rush, too.

THE CHOCOLATE BAR
. . . .

1835 W. ALABAMA *at Driscoll*
☎ **(713) 520-8599**
multiple locations
theoriginalchocolatebar.com

 E7

WHAT OWNERS ERIC SHAMBAN AND GILBERT Johnson are really doing is performing a public service. By providing towering layers of cake, dozens of ice cream flavors and house-made truffles all suffused with chocolate, they are truly a force for good in the world. Every night of the week, an eclectic crowd gathers in the purple palace for a treat. Of the ice cream selection, Snowberry and Toffee Coffee Time are excellent, and the White Russian cheesecake is groan-worthy and not just because it's expensive. The novelty chocolates, molded into everything from hammers to diplomas, make for fun gifts, and customers can peer through a window into the candy-making facility in the back. Weekly swing nights and live music make a night out of things but the sweets are occasion enough. Notice the address? The Chocolate Bar is next to Candylicious.

CHOCOLAT DU MONDE

....

5302 MORNINGSIDE
at Rice Blvd.
☎ **(713) 520-5600**
chocolat-du-monde.com

 E7

CHOCOLAT DU MONDE IS FOR SERIOUS CHOCOLATE lovers—there's no shoveling mountains of chocolate-covered raisins here. You enter the shop with composure and peer into the glass case of fine European chocolates thoughtfully and, okay, with some childish giddiness. Belgian choco-

late is a specialty, and Chocolat du Monde is the exclusive seller of posh Neuhaus and Leonidas chocolates in Houston. Dagoba, Scharffenberger and Joseph Schmidt also line the shelves and surprisingly, so do a few vintage and increasingly rare candy bars like Charleston Chew, Clark and Zero. Owner David Heiland can often be found behind the counter and can recommend a truffle flavor or ganache, but it's fun to just wait until your teeth have cracked the chocolate shell to discover what's within for yourself.

CHOCOLATE PIZAZZ

....

9055 GAYLORD
just east of Campbell
☎ **(713) 932-0991**
chocolatepizazz.com

 C6

THE AFFLUENT MEMO-RIAL VILLAGES HAVE indulged in Chocolate Pizazz's creations since 2006, and the buzz has flashed throughout Houston's chocoholic community. Special events and corporate gifts are just two of the spectra this small shop caters to. Chocolate-dipped cookies, pretzels, potato chips and popcorn are made fresh on location and come in endless combinations, complete with candy crumbles and sprinkles. Available in store and online are dark chocolate variations

Chocolat du Monde's display of chocolates

of anything offered on the menu as well as dipped fruit, toffee, peppermint bark, chocolate-covered marshmallows, matzoh, moon pies and more. The owners love for their products to pack a punch and offer many options for bright and playful or chic and streamlined gift wrap and packaging.

KEGG'S CANDIES

8168 WESTPARK *at Braxton*
☎ **(713) 784-3000**
multiple locations
keggscandies.com
D7

 HATEVER YOUR IMMEDIATE IM-pulse might be, very little looting actually goes on during the unguided tours of the Kegg's chocolate factory on Westpark. Despite the lack of supervision, visitors content themselves with a view of the copper pots and chocolate enrobing lines that produce these Houston confections and a post-tour treat. The Kegg family set up its small shop in Meyerland Plaza in 1946, expanded across the city in the following years and has since reduced back down to the factory and one retail store. Shelves are stocked with truffles, chocolate-covered Nutter Butters and fudge, but Kegg's calling card is the pecan crisp, a sweet, brittle-like dessert with less crunch and less sugar than regular versions.

POPARAZZI'S GOURMET POPCORN

8236 KIRBY *at Old Spanish Trail*
☎ **(713) 667-4767**
poparazzispopcorn.com
E8

HE SCIENCE THAT GOES INTO MAKING ONE FOOD taste like a completely different food is complex and precise, but the family that owns this specialty popcorn store excels at it. There are around 100 different flavors of popcorn, from taco to banana nut, and as odd as they may sound, the taste reproduction is pretty spot-on. Sweet versions like blue coconut and cotton candy are tinged pastel colors but standard kettle corn, buttered and white cheddar are also in supply. The servers are more than happy to apportion samples, and the hungry people visiting the nearby Med Center especially love to visit.

{ Bakeries }

THE ACADIAN BAKERS

604 W. ALABAMA *at Audubon*
☎ **(713) 520-1484**
acadianbakers.com
E7

UIRKY THOUGH IT MAY BE, THE MARQUEE ADORNED

with paintings of goofy cartoon pastries and the tagline "Baker to the Stars," this neighborhood fixture since 1979 is justly famous for its liqueur-spiked party cakes. A flipbook and framed photos illustrate the myriad decorating possibilities and flavors, but amaretto buttercream is a wedding bestseller, and the king cake and brownie chocolate mousse are popular for other occasions. Elaborate custom cake decoration is a specialty here and delivery is an option for a fee should you not want to risk damaging your frosted replica of a tequila bottle or football helmet by transporting it yourself. Over at the lunch counter, the hamburgers and box lunches get high marks.

ALPHA BAKERY & DELI

. . . .

11209 BELLAIRE BLVD.
inside the Hong Kong City Mall
☎ **(281) 988-5222**
B7

DIGGING THROUGH THE PILE OF PLASTIC-WRAPPED Vietnamese goodies is a bit like searching for buried treasure. There are sweetened rice cakes, neon-colored jelly formations and waffles, and while many of the items are unidentifiable to the uninitiated, bargain prices make adventurous sampling a low-risk gamble. This tiny store is even better known for its *banh mi* sandwiches, constructed on bread made inhouse, dirt cheap and sold as fast as they can be made to the line of people forming outside the door. Activity inside is definitely frenzied, and there isn't much help from the counter service with limited English skills. Just grab what you want, pay in cash and be brave.

•ANGELA'S OVEN

. . . .

204 AURORA *at Harvard*
☎ **(832) 239-0437**
angelasoven.com
E5

16

HANDMADE LOAVES, SCONES AND CROISsants from Angela's Oven are ubiquitous at Houston farmers' markets, but as of 2010 there is now also a lovely little storefront in The Heights. Come here for your market favorites, as well as pastries too delicate to travel. All of Jerry and Angela Shawn's baked goods are preservative-free. We're especially fond of their baguettes.

CHEZ BEIGNET

. . . .

10623 BELLAIRE BLVD. *at Wilcrest*
☎ **(281) 879-9777**
B7

BACK WHEN IT LIVED INSIDE THE LOOP, THIS beignet shop's Vietnamese following seemed a bit surprising. Now that German owners Joachim and Teda Jantzen have relocated to a strip mall in Chinatown, it's the beignets that look out of place, at least on paper. In reality, locals love to gather under the blue icicle lights at night for an indulgent snack and some youthful romance. Grab a tray and a mug to help yourself to the earthy chicory coffee, then place your order for beignets. Fried to order and blisteringly hot to touch for a few minutes after that, these fluffy donuts heavily festooned with powdered sugar are best not shared. It's not quite the same as sitting at a sidewalk cafe in New Orleans, but the experience is distinctly Houston.

COCO'S CRÊPES & COFFEE

....

216 GRAY *at Valentine*
☎ **(713) 521-0700**
multiple locations
cocoscrepes.com
E6

CRÊPES ARE IN GENERALLY SHORT SUPPLY IN Space City, but you wouldn't think it to see how they've taken hold in Midtown. Surrounded by apartment complexes, cramped Coco's successfully achieves that intangible cafe feel with neighborhood pedestrians dropping in at all times of day for a meal or to take advantage of the WiFi. Choose from the classic sweet and savory crêpe filling combinations like Nutella and strawberries or chicken with roasted vegetables, or mix and match ingredients to invent your own. We recommend the Moroccan sausage, caramelized onions and mozzarella in particular but be warned: Service can be slow and disorganized.

CRAVE CUPCAKES

....

1151-06 UPTOWN PARK
near Post Oak Blvd.
☎ **(713) 622-7283**
multiple locations
cravecupcakes.com

12   **D6**

THE MINIMAL GLASS AND STAINLESS STEEL interior of these designer cupcakes shops are not unlike the high-end stores in The Galleria that make you feel shabbier for stepping into them. But as luck would have it, there are sugary treats to combat feelings of self-doubt. Gourmet, imported ingredients go into beautifully decorated cakes, baked in small batches throughout the day, each topped with a color-coded,

Rows of cupcakes at Crave

flavor-identifying candy button. In addition to red velvet, Nutella and the like, there is also a selection of breakfast cuppies in cake donut, lemon poppyseed and maple walnut. Coffee is extremely well done here, and if you have an amazing metabolism, perhaps you will want to partake in the lattes that are blended with frosting.

CROISSANT BRIOCHE

....

2435 RICE BLVD. *at Morningside*
☎ **(713) 526-9188**
E7

AIRING TWO OF THE MOST POPULAR FRENCH baked goods in the shop's name may seem at first a bit overreaching. The epitome of both croissant and brioche? But in actuality the mini brioche muffins and enormous croissants deserve placement on the storefront marquee. This little Rice Village cafe keeps most of its checkered tablecloths occupied throughout the day, be it with students, couples or the retired chowing down on lunch specials and sipping expertly pulled espresso. The picture-perfect desserts are what draw you in, and while most are spot on, like the éclair, there are a few misses here and there. Still, there's no lovelier way to while away a Saturday morning than at a table with the newspaper and a ham and cheese croissant.

• DACAPO'S PASTRY CAFE

....

1141 E. 11TH *at Studewood*
☎ **(713) 869-9141**
dacapospastrycafe.com
17 **E5**

F YOUR GRANDMOTHER WERE TO OPEN HER OWN bakery, it would probably be something like Dacapo's, where everything is both homemade and homey. Located in a quaint old commercial building with retro black and white tile flooring, Tresa and Lisa Biggerstaff's little spot on the corner has been a comfortable choice for a sweet treat or lunch for 15 years. Well-proportioned chicken salad sandwiches are built on housemade bread, and the banana split cake, fresh pear cake and banana chocolate chip cookies are divine. One interesting specialty of Dacapo's is the cake top: Shaved off whole cakes during the icing process, the domed tops are made into small icing sandwiches.

•DESSERT GALLERY

....

3600 KIRBY *at Richmond*
☎ **(713) 522-9999**
multiple locations
dessertgallery.com
18 **E7**

ONG BEFORE FANCY PANTS CUPCAKERIES started cropping up, Sara Brook was the undisputed queen of stylish sweets in Houston. With two locations done up in whimsical Alice in Wonderland-style purple and red, much of her fame comes from the excellence of the Luscious Lemon cake and Old-Fashioned Diner cake, a moist yellow cake layered with balanced chocolate buttercream. Pretty much any other dessert item you can imagine can be found here—cream-filled cupcakes, chocolate-covered strawberries, pies and even sugar-free and dairy-free options. Dessert Gallery also does a fair business catering box lunches. Screened cookies—the staff can replicate your logo or a photo—and cakes are another specialty, often ordered for birthdays and corporate events.

EL BOLILLO

. . . .

2517 AIRLINE *at Aurora*
☎ **(713) 861-8885**
multiple locations
elbolillo.com

VERY TIME A CHURRO IS FILLED WITH *DULCE de leche* (caramel-like milk-based spread), an angel gets its wings. For that we all owe El Bolillo a debt of gratitude. This Mexican bakery in The Heights is the neighborhood bread source for locals and a destination for foodies city wide. An efficient pay station where cashiers tally purchases quick as

lightning sits at the center of a rotunda of pastry cases. Use the tongs and trays to snatch up whatever your heart desires, be it the aforementioned churros, sugar-dusted *conchas* (shell-shaped buns) or empanadas. Some of the sweet rolls can be dry, but the cream-filled cones will dance in your head while you sleep. *Telera* bread (for making tortas) and the namesake *bolillos* are stellar sandwich material, and fresh tortillas are spat out of the *tortilleria* in front of your very eyes. If that wasn't enough, the custom cake-decorating service will fulfill any design request no matter how ridiculous.

•EPICURE CAFE

. . . .

2005-C W. GRAY *at McDuffie*
☎ **(713) 520-6174**
epicure-cafe.com

HE SMELL OF FRESHLY BAKED CINNAMON ROLLS is widely considered to give life meaning. And it's what first greets you upon entering this River Oaks cafe, often packed to the gills with families during the day and neighborhood intellectuals coming from the adjacent River Oaks movie theater in the evening. Buttercup yellow walls and goofy paintings of obese chefs keep things quirky in that very Houston way. Lunch and dinner entrees with a European flair are solid, espe-

BAKERIES & SWEETS SHOPS

FOOD TRUCKS

SOME THINGS THAT ARE BETTER ON WHEELS: SHOES, SUITCASES, HAMSTERS AND YOUR lunch. Houston has long had a taco-truck culture, but 2011 saw a boom of gourmet gone mobile. Check social media for the most up-to-date location information.

EATSIE BOYS
@EATSIEBOYS ON TWITTER
Three young men and food lovers joined forces to create comfort food with an Asian twist. Favorites include Frank the Pretzel (a juicy chicken sausage on a pretzel bun) and the Pork Snuggies.

TIERRA CALIENTE
WEST ALABAMA ICE HOUSE LOT
This is an old guard taco truck, complete with a cash-only policy and questionably sourced meats. We love it, the *lengua* tacos and *salsa verde* capsaicin high, anyway.

OH MY! POCKET PIES
@OHMYPOCKETPIES ON TWITTER
Hand-pies sweet and savory hit the streets early in the trend, and now the truck's Salisbury steak and s'mores pies have a loyal following.

BERNIE'S BURGER BUS
@BERNIESBURGERS ON TWITTER
Some of the best burgers in the city are being served out of an old school bus. Chef Justin Turner's juicy beef patties are topped with house-made condiments.

ZILLA STREET EATS
@ZILLASTREETEATS ON TWITTER
Three words: fried Nutter Butters. Between those and the chicken and waffles, it's truly amazing what can come out of such a small space.

MELANGE CRÊPERIE
@MELANGECREPERIE ON TWITTER
The best crêpes in town are made at a tiny mobile stand by the hands of Sean Carroll. Wait time for a ham and cheese crêpe is long, but totally worth it.

cially the daily specials and when paired with fresh berry lemonade, but the pastry is where this cafe shines. Gorgeous napoleons, Linzer cookies and princess tortes deliver on flavor, and the chewy chocolate chip cookies are among the most delectable in the city.

FLUFF BAKE BAR

....

☎ (832) 374-8340
fluffbakebar.com

REBECCA MASSON, KNOWN LOCALLY AS "THE SUGAR Fairy," is one of Houston's most exciting pastry chefs, though she does not currently have a retail storefront—Fluff Bake Bar is her virtual bake shop for the time being. Trained in Paris and active on the local foodscape, Masson is seemingly everywhere. In 2010, she won the Houston Chowhounds' mushroom throwdown with a baked sweet sweeping all the guys' savory offerings, and she heads up a dog-rescue fundraiser with guest celebrity chefs twice year. In 2007 she won the Houston Culinary Award for Pastry Chef of the Year. She can bake just about anything, but is especially beloved for her fluffernutters, macarons and baked Alaska. Special events are her calling. Fluff Bake Bar products are available every day at Revival Market, and special orders can be picked up there as well.

•FLYING SAUCER PIE CO.

....

436 W. CROSSTIMBERS
at Garden Oaks
☎ (713) 694-1141
flyingsaucerpieshop.com

18

THE FLYING SAUCER HAS BUILT ITS REPUTATION and perfected its pies for nearly half a century, and the long holiday lines are the stuff of legend. Upon entering this Independence Heights bakery, you'll be confronted with stacks upon stacks of juice-bleeding tins and a wall sporting a mural of astronauts with pies for heads. There's no seating area but on a normal day you can expect to have a 10-inch pie in your hand moments after stepping up to the counter. Most popular are the strawberry cream, rippling with whole strawberries, and a masterful pecan, which has the perfect combination of smooth interior and caramelized shell.

•FOODY'S GOURMET

....

1400 ELDRIDGE
north of Briar Forest
☎ (281) 496-3663

14 W

LOCATED ADJACENT TO LE MISTRAL, THE POPular West Side French restaurant, Foody's Gourmet is run by Le

BAKERIES & SWEETS SHOPS

Mistral's chef David Denis and his brother (and front-of-the-house guy) Sylvain Denis. It's a dual concept: The bakery supplies custom bread and rolls to restaurants all over the city, baking according to specific individual recipes. But it's also a retail bakery, offering croissants, baguettes and other loaves, macarons and quiche to the local housewives and Energy Corridor business neighbors. There's a patio between Foody's and Le Mistral that is perfect for enjoying coffee, a croissant and the newspaper in our milder months.

•FRENCH GOURMET BAKERY & CAFE

. . . .

2250 WESTHEIMER
between S. Shepherd & Kirby
☎ **(713) 524-3744**
multiple locations
fgbakery.com

8 W E6

THERE ARE THE POLY-MATH BAKERIES, AND there are the specialized. French Gourmet is definitely the latter. Skip straight past the savory lunch items, pass go and head to the confections. Thumbprint cookies crowned with a fat dollop of chocolate are perhaps the best available offering, although the ginger stars are the tender stuff of childhood Christmases. French-style cakes like the Moka Rum—thin layers of yellow cake laced with rum

and sandwiched with coffee buttercream—are exquisitely beautiful. The almond croissants have been known to inspire impassioned speech. Pick up a bag of fresh rolls for tonight's dinner before exiting.

•FRENCH RIVIERA BAKERY & CAFE

. . . .

3032 CHIMNEY ROCK
between Westheimer & Richmond
☎ **(713) 783-3264**
15 D7

SUNSHINE-YELLOW WALLS CREATE THE PLEASANT atmosphere in which regulars mingle with brothers Louis and Robert Wu, who have owned this well-regarded French bakery for the past 30 years. The baguettes, boasting a crust that shatters and a light interior, are contenders for best in the city, as are the melt-in-your-mouth croissants whether plain, filled with ham and cheese

Fresh pastries at French Riviera

or almond crème. In fact, everything here is done well, from the café au lait to the salami and pâté sandwiches at lunchtime. The chicken salad has become so popular that it's sold in quart containers. Alas, during the peak lunch hour the rush requires that most orders be take-out.

• FROSTED BETTY BAKESHOP

....

833 STUDEWOOD *at E. 9th St.*
☎ **(713) 862-4500**
multiple locations
frostedbetty.com
E5

OWNER NICOLE MORA AND HER FAMILY BEGAN Frosted Betty as a mobile cupcake truck operation before taking off the training wheels for brick and mortar locations in Katy and The Heights. Known for adult flavor combinations like maple bacon, chocolate cardamom and almond ricotta raspberry, the shop bakes the not-too-sweet cupcakes fresh every morning with full fat butter instead of shortening. Specialties include the mini-cupcakes that make perfect party platters, cake balls and vegan and gluten-free cupcakes. The truck still makes appearances at farmers' markets and events from time to time, and locations are always posted on the shop's social media pages.

GLUTEN FREE HOUSTON

....

1014 WIRT
just north of the Katy Fwy.
☎ **(713) 784-7122**
glutenfreehouston.com
D5

RANDI MARKOWITZ SUFFERED FROM CELIAC disease, triggered by a severe sensitivity to gluten. After being hospitalized and years of searching for a reliable local source for gluten-free foods, she finally decided she needed to do it herself. Years of tossing, revising, experimenting and testing finally gave birth to Gluten Free Houston. Today you can pretty much find it all here: gluten-free hamburger buns, breads, dinner rolls, pies, muffins, lasagne, biscotti, macaroni and cheese, pizza. She even sells take-and-bake chocolate chip cookie dough that is gluten free. Retail store hours are limited: noon to 5 pm on Wednesday through Friday and 8 am to noon on Saturday. Otherwise, Markowitz is busy filling orders for stores and restaurants all over town. She also fills orders via the Internet.

BAKERIES & SWEETS SHOPS

• HOT BAGEL SHOP

....

2009 S. SHEPHERD *near Welch*
☎ **(713) 520-0340**

17　　**E6**

ONG REGARDED BY THE COGNOSCENTI AS THE best bagel source inside the Loop—New York Bagel & Coffee Shop is the best outside-the-Loop bagel bakery—this exceedingly modest spot was recently downsized as the adjacent store took away its eat-in area. That's better than going out of business altogether, which was the rampant rumor until the recession put redevelopment plans for the tiny strip center on ice. Anyway, the Hot Bagel Shop is about half the size it once was. The cooler that held the various cream cheeses is gone, and now you order that at the counter along with everything else. All the bagel varieties are here, including the "everything," as well as salty/oniony bialys and kolache-like "bagel dogs" featuring Oscar Mayer wieners.

HOT BREADS

....

5700-A HILLCROFT *at Harwin*
☎ **(713) 785-1212**
houstonhotbreads.com

C7

HIS LITTLE INDIA BAKERY GOT ITS START ACROSS the pond in Madras, India, back in 1988. U.S locations are limited to three, and Houston is lucky to have one. Though the shop produces a variety of conventional cookies and cakes, it's the Indian-European fusion pastries that are exceptional. Eggless, halal and vegetarian options abound, but everyone should try one of the mini pizzas, really pizza in name only as chicken tikka or paneer replace tomatoes on the buttery crust. Finish off a bargain *channa* (seasoned chickpea) lunch wrap spread with mint chutney by ordering a salty sweet masala shortbread cookie. Wash down a chicken croquette or goat curry croissants with a lassi or chai.

• KRAFTSMEN BAKING

....

4100 MONTROSE *at W. Main*
☎ **(713) 524-3737**
multiple locations
kraftsmenbaking.com

E7

PROJECT OF ICONIC HOUSTON CHEF SCOTT Tycer, who was also behind Gravitas and the now-shuttered Textile, this wholesale bakery-cum-deli is serious about craft. Crusty loaves, often fermented for eight hours before baking, are nestled in restaurant breadbaskets across town. Sandwiches and pastries draw laptop-toters and stately groups of ladies into the retail store-

The BLT at Kraftsmen Baking

fronts, although portions and presentation are often unimpressive. The Green Gobbler, which incorporates apple butter, turkey and a brioche roll, is a nice play on the savory and sweet. Both locations are lovely places to while away an afternoon, the brick exterior of Montrose covered in vines and The Heights dining room awash in soothing neutral tones.

LA VICTORIA BAKERY
. . . .
7138 LAWNDALE *at S. 75th St*
☎ **(713) 921-0861**
lavictoriabakery.net

HIS EAST END TREASURE, RUN BY TWO sisters, produces Mexican-style breads, pastries, a variety of brightly hued sweets and elaborate cakes worthy of their own reality show.

Come here for breakfast tortas or *gorditas* of egg, potato and bacon, grilled Mexican biscuits, crisp flautas and, around Day of the Dead, the crucial sweet breads shaped as skulls—everyone else does. Tamales are a bit more expensive than the competitors but the supple masa is worth it. The dining room, though not much to look at, is utilitarian and clean should you choose to enjoy your purchases inhouse. Parking at this converted service station is a battle, but what is life but struggle followed by *tres leches*?

• MICHAEL'S COOKIE JAR
. . . .
5330 WESLAYAN *at Bissonnet*
☎ **(713) 771-8603**
michaelscookiejar.com
16

HE MICHAEL IN QUESTION IS MICHAEL SAVINO, A CIA-trained pastry chef with the Four Seasons hotels in Houston and Dallas on his resume. He doesn't take the cookie craft lightly, although to experience his handiwork is to become lighthearted. His two collections include the European "Fancy" line of currant shortbread, almond Florentine and the like, while the "Americana" line features classic favorites like chocolate chip with blocks of semisweet and the perfectly textured snickerdoodle and ginger molasses. Each cookie is a work of art, hence their popularity for weddings, but they're also genuinely delicious examples of baked goods reaching their full potential. Aside from the small retail location, these goodies are also available at partnered locations such as Antidote and Carter & Cooley Company.

• MOELLER'S BAKERY

4201 BELLAIRE BLVD.
at Stella Link
☎ **(713) 667-0983**

18   **D7**

ONE OF THE TRAGEDIES OF MODERN EXISTENCE is that no one eats petit fours anymore. But these enchanting squares of light-as-air cake topped with pastel flowers are the specialty at Moeller's, which has been producing treats since 1930. The proof is in its ancient original oven, now on display outside the front

Moeller's delicate petit fours

door. Aside from the wee French cakes, molasses cookies, coconut snowballs and addictive orange rolls line the pastry cases of a seemingly long-lost era. Plus, the staffers are some of the most affable between here and the Rio Grande.

OOH LA LA

23920 WESTHEIMER PKWY.,
Katy, west of the Grand Pkwy.
☎ **(281) 391-2253**
multiple locations
oohlalasweets.com

🚗 **A7**

AMERICA'S CUPCAKE OBSESSION STILL RUNS rampant. As if enthusiasts weren't getting enough of them, this Katy bakery has plumped up the size of its cakes considerably. Softball sized cakes are crowned with swirls of colorful icing and candy adornments befitting their flavor. Owner/pastry chef Vanessa O'Donnell, a veteran of the Houston Country Club pastry kitchen, has cooked up funky yet approachable flavors like Margaritaville and Boston cream pie to complement the usual suspects. The kitschy storefront also offers a great deal more than cupcakes, the pies and cake truffles being the most popular alternatives. Rest assured, there's even a drive-thru for when you're really jonesing for a fix.

• PARISIAN BAKERY

....

**8300 W. SAM HOUSTON PKWY.
(BELTWAY 8)** *at Beechnut*
☎ **(281) 776-0503**
multiple locations

CONSIDERING THE OFFER-
INGS OF PLACES LIKE THIS
French-Vietnamese hybrid mini-
chain of bakeries, it's a wonder
why anyone patronizes fast-food
joints. Here, quick and cheap
meals come with a side of cultural
adventure. There may not be a
drive-thru, but the dining rooms
of each of the three locations are
clean and decorated in kitschy
French red, white and blue and
potted plants. For the main course,
try one of the steamed pork buns
accented with green onion and
boiled egg or savory brioche kol-
aches of sorts topped with chicken
or ham. The *pâté chaud*, a puff
pastry stuffed with pork, is some
of the best in the city and best
washed down with fresh sugar
cane juice. For dessert, try a green-
tinged *pandan* (a Thai leaf) waffle
or the deep-fried banana eggroll.

PÂTISSERIE JUNGLE CAFE

....

9889 BELLAIRE BLVD.
at Beltway 8
☎ **(713) 272-6633**

IN ITS PREVIOUS LIFE A
FEW BLOCKS DOWN BEL-
laire, Jungle Cafe was the bubble
tea spot for teens. After moving
to a spiffy new location, Jungle
Cafe transformed into a sleek,
modern pâtisserie. The vibe is a
little "you break it, you buy it,"
thanks to all the shiny surfaces,
minimalist empty space and all
the rules—including a camera ban.
The beautiful confections made
of airy cake and mousse, coated in
ganache and topped with decorative flourishes cost a pretty penny
and even more if you're not paying
in cash (there's a confusing pricing
scheme). But the French-style treats,
which are light and less sweet than
American desserts, manage to be
worth all the trouble.

PETITE SWEETS

2700 W. ALABAMA
west of Kirby
☎ **(713) 520-7007**
petitesweetsinfo.com

AIRY, LIGHT-FILLED AND
SIMPLY OUTFITTED,
Petite Sweets opened in Sep-
tember 2011. Pastry chef Susan

Molzan (she also owns Ruggles Cafe Bakery and is winner of the 2002 Houston Culinary Award for Outstanding Pastry Chef) is baking onsite daily. Included in her repertoire: artisan macarons, handmade marshmallows, mini cupcakes, cookies and frozen custard. Almost everything (except the whoopee pies) is tiny and adorable, as delicious to look at as to eat. Don't pass up the carrot cake balls.

PIE IN THE SKY

. . . .

632 W. 19TH *at Shepherd*
☎ **(713) 864-3301**
multiple locations
pieintheskypieco.com
E5

OW WITH TWO ESTABLISHED NEIGHBORHOOD joints (the original being in Conroe), owner Marlene Stubler has come a long way from selling pies out of a gas station. The Heights location fits into the 19th Street small-town feel perfectly, and the modest dining room done up in bright green proudly displays the crayon masterpieces of local children. Although pie is the restaurant's namesake, the full array of diner food such as an enormous patty melt on buttery Texas toast and hearty breakfasts deserves as much of your attention. Pies come with almost every filling imaginable from Southern favorites like buttermilk and sweet potato to sour

cream raisin and peach streusel. They might be improved by the absence of drizzled syrup designs but still make compelling arguments to save room for dessert.

RAJA SWEETS

. . . .

5667 HILLCROFT *at Harwin*
☎ **(713) 782-5667**
C7

OU DON'T HAVE TO BE A SUGAR FIEND TO enjoy Raja Sweets—which offers outstanding butter chicken and goat curry alongside some of the best Indian desserts in town— but it certainly doesn't hurt. The family behind all these top-notch recipes opened the doors to their business 25 years ago as of April 2011. Since then, their syrup-soaked *gulab jamun* (doughnut balls) and crunchy *jalebi* (sugary Indian-style pretzels) have gained quite a reputation. A variety of colorful *burfi*, a condensed milk dessert, and sacks of samosas or pakora are also for the taking.

Burfi in Raja Sweets

RAO'S BAKERY

....

6915 CYPRESSWOOD
at Southampton Dr., Spring
☎ **(281) 251-7267**
raosbakery.com

🚗 **C1**

PEN SINCE 1941 IN BEAU-
MONT, RAO'S FINALLY
brought its legendary cakes, gelato
and pastries to the Houston area
via Spring. Widely known for its
seven varieties of king cake around
Mardi Gras time, they also have
a selection of more than two
dozen gourmet cakes available
whole or by the slice. The six-
layered Dobasche—a triple serving of fudge, vanilla and walnuts
—is impossible to resist. Rao's also
has a breakfast, lunch and dinner
menu that is heavily called upon
by the Sunday post-church crowd.
The paninis are worth a try, too,
but it's the cakes, tarts, cream
puffs and other pastries that will
keep you coming back.

RUGGLES CAFE BAKERY

....

2365 RICE BLVD. *at Chaucer*
☎ **(713) 520-6662**
rugglescafebakery.com
E7

HIS COZY OFFSHOOT
OF THE RUGGLES REST-
aurants serves up more casual,
inexpensive fare at the counter.

Basic salads, sandwiches and
pastas are given nice touches like
mango salsa in the veggie wrap
and chipotle mayo on the pork
loin sandwich, even better with
sweet potato fries. The desserts,
which range from *tres leches* to
the Charlotte's Web (a chocolate
cake melded with espresso pudding and Heath bar bits), are usually
the chief reason to visit and could
feed a small family. Of course, some
of the Rice University students who
flock here eat enough individually
that there's no need for sharing.
The patio is a nice place to enjoy
a full meal and improved by the
BYOB wine policy.

RUSTIKA BAKERY

....

3237 SOUTHWEST FWY.
at Buffalo Speedway
☎ **(713) 665-6226**
rustikacafe.com
D7

MONG THE SIMPLEST
OF HOUSTON'S CULI-
nary pleasures is the breakfast
taco. At Rustika, the brainchild of
Mexico City-born Francis Reznick,
her version is more akin to a burrito. This and other Mexican-style
breakfast options jazzed up with
salsa verde merit a weekend visit,
and coffee and a full pastry case
are suitable for meetings or afternoon lounging. There are a number of Argentinean pastries like
empanadas stuffed with chicken

mole and tender *dulce de leche*-filled *alfajore* cookies as well as strudel and *palmiers* (the "elephant ear" puff pastry treat). The clean, homey interior makes for a cheerful environment to toss back a few baseball-sized chocolate-covered macaroons as well.

SIX PING BAKERY

. . . .

9384 BELLAIRE BLVD.
near Ranchester
☎ **(713) 773-0658**

 D7

USUALLY THE INDECISION OF BEING CONFRONTED by several appealing options inside of a bakery is resolved by a combination of guilt and prohibitive cost of buying multiple pastries. But at this closet-sized Chinatown shop where many items cost around one dollar, it's more likely you'll decide to just scoop everything into a bag and worry about calories later. Pick up a tray upon entering and grab whatever looks good—foot-long bacon-sprinkled breadsticks, taro-filled buns and cake rolls. Definitely take home a pack of mini-kolaches made with a slightly sweet egg bread for breakfast the next day, one of the curry pork rolls and the airy chocolate sponge cake. Occasion cakes layered with hazelnut cream or mango and the like are also well done. Cash only.

SLOW DOUGH BREAD CO.

. . . .

1314 ROY
two blocks west of Durham
☎ **(713) 568-5674**
slowdoughbreadco.com

E6

OWNER/BAKER HEATH WENDELL WORKED IN European bakeries before coming to Houston to launch this remarkable bakery in April 2009. Today he and partner Marlo Evans supply custom bread to dozens of Houston's best restaurants (e.g. Branch Water Tavern, Down House, Da Marco, Feast) and the hippest food trucks (e.g. Eatsie Boys, Good Dog Hot Dogs). There is still no storefront where you can purchase bread, but you'll find Slow Dough loaves and rolls at Relish, Georgia's Farm to Market and Revival Market.

SPRINKLES

. . . .

4014 WESTHEIMER *at Drexel*
☎ **(713) 871-9929**
sprinkles.com

D6

THE UPSCALE LOS ANGELES CUPCAKERY THAT started it all has found its ideal Houston home in a tiny storefront in Highland Village where hungry, well-heeled shoppers like to stop in for a treat even if it means waiting in a line outside the door.

Beauty may be on the inside, but these haute cupcakes are dolled up to match the gourmet ingredients, from Belgian chocolate to Madagascar Bourbon vanilla. Playful flavors such as ginger lemon and chai latte rotate in and out while mainstays like dark chocolate and red velvet remain constant—and with vegan and gluten-free iterations. Choose from a variety of graduation, wedding or baby shower decorations when ordering a celebratory dozen.

STONE MILL BAKERS

. . . .

2518 KIRBY *at Westheimer*
☎ **(713) 524-6600**
multiple locations
stonemillbakers.com

TONE MILL IS PROUD OF THE FACT THAT IT GRINDS its own wheat and the breads are made without added fats, oils and preservatives. All that healthful stuff aside though, the fluffy freshness can't be beat. Whole-wheat sourdough, Montana wheat and jalapeño cornbread are the most-purchased loaves. Avoid the cookies, which are fantastically large but lacking in flavor, and order one of the sandwiches instead, specifically the curried chicken salad on cinnamon raisin bread, a mouth-pleasing harmony of sweet and savory. The deli closes at 5:30 pm, and aside from the standards, certain breads are available only on certain days of the week. Avoid disappointment by going online or calling ahead to see what's available.

SUGARBABY'S

. . . .

3310 S. SHEPHERD *at Branard*
☎ **(713) 527-8427**
ilovesugarbabys.com

UPCAKE EXPERTS OR YOUR FIVE-YEAR-OLD will tell you that the crucial feature of any cupcake is the icing-to-cake ratio. The ideal number varies for everyone, but Sugarbaby's caters to the icing lovers. And the icing is good, especially the peanut butter buttercream. Flavors are fun without being overly complicated; other than the basic chocolate, strawberry and red velvet, the menu includes Hummingbird, German chocolate and lemon raspberry, which are baked fresh every morning. Mini tarts, cakes and dainty macarons are available for the icing-averse. The shop itself is basically a life-size rendition of one of Barbie's more rococo dream houses, with black and white tiling and bright pink walls. Parking in the back is tight, but there is ample seating inside.

BAKERIES & SWEETS SHOPS

SWEET

· · · · · · · · · · · · · · · ·

801 TOWN & COUNTRY BLVD.
in CityCentre
☎ **(713) 647-9338**
sweethouston.com

THERE'S REALLY NO SUCH THING AS BEING "TOO pretty to eat," but the treats at Sweet come pretty close. The bustling adult playground that is CityCentre was crying out for a dessert shop, and this one truly delivers. The space is small but beautiful, with an upscale vintage vibe and towers of cupcakes swirled with fluffy frosting. The red velvet wins the title of Most Adorable, with clouds of cream cheese frosting and a heart-shaped garnish, while the tiramisu cupcakes sweeps flavor. Both rest in an environmentally friendly unbleached liner just as coffee is served in corn cups. French macarons are the bakery's other specialty, pistachio being the most popular and also most commonly out of stock as a result.

THREE BROTHERS BAKERY

· · · · · · · · · · · · · · · ·

4036 S. BRAESWOOD
at Stella Link
☎ **(713) 666-2253**
3brothersbakery.com

THE FIFTH GENERATION-BAKERY OWNERS—BOBBY Jucker calls himself an SOB: Son Of a Baker—had been selling superlative challah and bagels to a loyal following since 1949 until 2008's Hurricane Ike hit. For months of closure, it looked like the business wouldn't recover from the damage. When the doors to Three Brothers did reopen with a whole new, modernized look—complete with flashy flatscreens screening pastry pictures—a collective sigh of relief went up in thanks. Along with traditional sourdough French bread, corn rye and German farmer's bread, the bakery produces a wide range of cupcakes, danishes and *parve* (kosher) treats. It's the place in town to go for black and white cookies and *rugelach*, and many a bride has celebrated her union with a custom tiered cake—the bakers specialize in goofy decorative elements.

COFFEEHOUSES & TEA SHOPS

{ SIDEBARS }

{ *Coffeehouses*}
AGORA

1712 WESTHEIMER *at Park*
☎ **(713) 526-7212**
agorahouston.com

☜ **E6**

H OUSTON WENT INTO WIDESPREAD MOURN-ing when Agora burned in the Halloween fire of 2010. Less than a year later, the coffeehouse rose from the ashes largely the same and with a fan base more passionate than ever. On sunny days, groups of older Greek men and scruffy artsy types sprawl on the patio while in the cool, dim interior, individuals type up their novels or latest business plan. The creaky converted house is full of "perfect spots"—one next to an upstairs window with a view of bustling Montrose, another with a backgammon board. Aside from the usual lineup of caffeinated beverages, Agora stocks a generous variety of foreign, craft and obscure beers and wines. Avoid the shots of Chocovine but do partake in the mini-Toblerone.

ANTIDOTE COFFEE

729 STUDEWOOD *at 8th St.*
☎ **(713) 861-7400**
antidotecoffee.com

E5

L OW-SLUNG VINTAGE FUR-NITURE AND CAFFEINE are scientifically proven to encourage creative thought, which explains how Antidote has become a modern day salon for like-minded Heights residents. Students and writers come armed with laptops, and old friends linger over pots of French Lemon Ginger tea. The drip coffee is potent, and the *cajeta latte* swirled with Texas goat milk caramel demands a try. Snacks are well sourced, including cheese plates from the Houston Dairymaids, baked goods from Michael's Cookie Jar and vegan tamales. A side patio strewn with colorful furniture and happy hour during which select beers are $2 and a double espresso is only $1 give good reason to swing by several times a day.

Second floor seating in Agora

BLACK HOLE COFFEE HOUSE

. . . .

4504 GRAUSTARK
at Castle Court
☎ **(713) 528-0653**
E7

IDDEN IN A RESIDENTIAL SECTION OF MONTROSE, the owners of Antidote Coffee have proven their knack for creating pitch-perfect recreational spaces once again. Generous legroom means visitors will rarely have to elbow for a table or seat, and with the baristas making full use of the kitchen, the building is often filled with the smell of something baking, be it pumpkin spice granola or chocolate chip cookies. Sandwiches, quiche and various baked goods from local pastry chef Rebecca Masson line the glass case, and a chalkboard menu spells out the beverage options including the Antidote (coffee with a shot of espresso) and the Dirty Chavez (a latte with low milk content). The beans are from Marfa company Big Bend Roasters, and while the lattes will certainly give you the necessary caffeine fix, folks visit less for gold standard coffee than for the experience as a whole. That, and beer and wine on discount during happy hour.

BLACKSMITH

. . . .

1018 WESTHEIMER
at Yoakum
☎ **(281) 983-5700**
blacksmithhouston.com
E6

ARISTA DAVID BUEHRER IS FINALLY MOVING OUT of the basement at Greenway Plaza. Buehrer and partner Ecky Prabanto announced in August 2011 that they are joining with the partners of Anvil Bar & Refuge, Underbelly and The Hay Merchant to redevelop the building that formerly housed Mary's (Houston's oldest openly gay bar) into a coffeehouse. Plans call for a small but full kitchen, so you will be able to get a bite to eat with your coffee. Minor construction and planning for the shop had begun as we go to press with this book. Blacksmith has a projected opening date of Spring 2012.

CAFE LA TEA

. . . .

9102 BELLAIRE BLVD.
near Ranchester
☎ **(713) 988-3188**
cafelatea.com
C7

HINATOWN'S VERSION OF THE AMERICAN COFFEEshop is superior in several ways. Clean, inviting and outfitted with plenty of comfy seating, Cafe La Tea is a quiet place to use the WiFi

COFFEEHOUSES & TEA SHOPS

LINGER WITH A LAPTOP

FRANKLY, WE DON'T KNOW WHY ANY BUSINESS OWNER WOULD ALLOW US TO SHOW UP, USE the electricity, publicly Skype our girlfriends and hog the bandwidth "writing our novels," but we're grateful they do. How else would we get "me time" away from the cat?

AGORA
1712 WESTHEIMER
☎ **(713) 526-7212**
In the evenings, the lights at this Houston favorite dim and more people order beer than coffee but during the daylight hours, no one will give you a second glance for camping out, be it with a laptop or picture book.

BLACK HOLE COFFEE HOUSE
4504 GRAUSTARK
☎ **(713) 528-0653**
Inside this trendy Montrose coffeehouse, it's a bit of a scene with hip industry folk and local musicians whiling away hours over espresso and granola. Still, it's quiet enough to work, and folks often spend entire afternoons here.

FIOZA CAFE
9002 CHIMNEY ROCK
☎ **(713) 729-8810**
Meyerland got a little cooler when this independent coffee shop opened. Not only do the baristas make beautiful latte art, there are plenty of snack items to fuel your laptop time.

TÉ HOUSE OF TEA
1927 FAIRVIEW
☎ **(713) 522-8868**
This serene teahouse is the perfect spot to find quiet over a pot of Persian peach tea. There's no more zen hangout spot in the city—and vegan vittles to boot.

WALDO'S COFFEE HOUSE
1030 HEIGHTS BLVD.
☎ **(713) 869-0700**
Plenty of space and quiet rooms make this an ideal place to get studious—if you aren't the type to be distracted by pink paint.

or bring a date. But they do one better by offering exceptional coffee both rich and smooth, occasionally decked with foam art, and a lovely, bottomless green tea. Beyond that is an eclectic fusion menu that should definitely be availed of but stick to the Taiwanese items—the house pork chop garnished with pickled mustard greens is top notch and comes with unlimited coffee at lunch. The handsome pastries. such as mango mousse or posh rounds of tender chocolate cake, are excellent, if slightly expensive for the neighborhood, and the frozen yogurt unexpectedly gets rave reviews.

Exterior of Catalina Coffee

CATALINA COFFEE

2201 WASHINGTON
east of Sawyer
☎ **(713) 861-8448**
catalinacoffeeshop.com

 E6

THERE COMES A TIME IN EVERY MAN'S LIFE WHEN he realizes that not all cups of coffee are created equal. Most fall in the middle tier, a few are extraordinarily burnt or weak, and a few —a very rare few—are a revelation. Does that sound like hyperbole? Catalina is the undisputed best coffeehouse in the city, and the baristas are mad scientists with different brew methods and instruments. There are no amateurs here. Owner Max Gonzalez roasts his

own beans as the Amaya Roasting Company, and if you've never had a Cubano (espresso with sugar and half-and-half), *cortado* (espresso cut with milk) or *doppio* (espresso double shot), this is the place to broaden your horizons. The cozy, sun-dappled setting inside a 1928 A&P Trading Post is frequently crammed with people on the weekends, probably due in part to the croissants being so addictive.

DIRK'S COFFEE

4005 MONTROSE *at Branard*
☎ **(713) 526-1319**
E7

YOU KNOW THAT DIRK'S IS "OF MONTROSE" BY the quirky announcements like "Sleep is for the weak" displayed on the shop's marquee. Due to its small space, it's a popular spot to grab and go on the way to work in the morning, but a few neighborhood regulars still camp out with a newspaper (there's no WiFi) at one of the few tables in the sunny interior or out on the front patio with a view of passing traffic. The servers have been known to be surly at times, but at least they know their way around an espresso machine.

FIOZA CAFE

....

9002 CHIMNEY ROCK
at Caversham
☎ **(713) 729-8810**
fioza.com

OSTLY INUNDATED WITH NATIONAL CHAINS, MEYerland residents (and especially its youth) threw up a cheer when this locally owned coffee shop opened in their 'hood. A warm glow, creamy white plush seating and a peaceful level of quiet make this a popular spot for students but also for casual business meetings or light lunch with friends (doors close relatively early in the evening). Working with Houston's own Fontana coffee, the baristas excel at latte art and great espresso but there are also coffee confections such as the s'mores latte and peppermint mocha for those that like a sugar fix. Excellent cake and bubble tea round out the menu. Feel free to add tapioca pearls to any of the drinks. Just go absolutely nuts with it.

GREENWAY COFFEE

....

5 GREENWAY PLAZA
at Richmond
☎ **(832) 377-7773**
greenwaycoffee.com

AVID BUEHRER IS A COFFEE EVANGELIST. HE spreads the good word not only from his business inside the Greenway Plaza food court—not the first place you'd expect to find such beverage excellence—but also around town at various restaurants with fixer-upper coffee programs. Buehrer frequently collaborates with others, namely Anvil Bar & Refuge, for coffee cocktails and events and offers private espresso bar "catering." Back at his home base, expect well-textured lattes complete with foam art and farm fresh milk from Way Back When Dairy. The usual options, from regular drip to iced, are available but you wouldn't be mistaken to order a sugar cane latte. The hours are abbreviated (7 am to 4:30 pm) due to the location inside this office complex, but a visit is worth finding the time.

INVERSION COFFEE HOUSE

....

1953 MONTROSE *at W. Gray*
☎ **(713) 523-4866**
inversioncoffee.com

E6

ATTACHED TO ART LEAGUE OF HOUSTON AND in the former site of the 2005 giant vortex Inversion house installation, this coffee shop definitely has art cred. The 30-foot ceiling and metal tables and chairs lend an industrial loft feel that sometimes gets read as more commercial, but Inversion is definitely an independent. The coffee is among the best in the city, from a simple drip cup to a *cortado* (espresso cut with milk), and the baristas are skilled at latte foam art. A library level of quiet pervades as students lay claim to tables for hours to study and make

Inversion Coffee House

use of the WiFi. Some sugar-heavy but admittedly delicious choices include the Chocolate Cherry Bomb and Butterscotch Brouja and quite a few cold sandwiches and pastries are available as well. Bernie's Burger Bus, a mobile kitchen, sometimes parks outside.

JAVA COFFEE & TEA CO.

....

2727 FONDREN *at Westheimer*
☎ **(713) 974-0443**
javacoffee.com

C7

BECAUSE TRYING TO BUY RESPECTABLE COFFEE while being confronted with all the commercial versions at the grocery store can be all too unsatisfactory, we sometimes need the guidance of an expert. And the owner of this 30-year old business, Bill Lawder, is such an expert. The west Houston storefront is the face of a wholesale business that roasts and blends beans from around the world. It's where the coffee novice can begin to understand what "wet processed" and shade-grown really mean for his morning cup of joe or the aficionado can pick up that rare bag of Tanzanian Peaberry. A variety of teas are also in stock, and a number of sample blends are brewed each day for taste testing.

{ 81 }

KATZ COFFEE
1003 W. 34TH *west of Shepherd*
☎ **(713) 864-3338**
katzcoffee.com
E5

AMESAKE AVI KATZ FOUNDED KATZ COFfee, a small-batch custom roaster in The Heights, in 2003. Though not a coffeehouse as such, the company creates and roasts proprietary blends for many of the city's coffeehouses and restaurants, from Agora to Waldo's Coffeehouse. You can also buy whole-bean Katz Coffee—all of their coffees are Fair Trade Certified—at Whole Foods, Central Market and Midtown Farmers' Market. In addition to coffee, Katz sells teas and Torani Syrups.

MINUTI COFFEE
. . . .
909 TEXAS *at Main*
☎ **(713) 226-7500**
minuticoffee.com
F6

OR THE DOWNTOWN COFFEE DRINKER WHO wants to get away from the corporate chain and closer to the little guy, this sleek Italian-inspired shop will fuel you through your workday. The Molinari brand beans hail from Modena and while some slightly goofy names such as Shakerato and Ice-O don't give much of a clue

as to what those drinks actually are, the standard lattes, macchiatos and teas keep things sane. The indoor seating area, splashed a chic bright red, is very modern but many patrons also retire to the equally lovely front patio area where the bustle of the big city can really be felt. The evenings are especially busy, when people drop by for a glass of wine or a panini, to partake in the occasional wine tasting or live music.

SALENTO
. . . .
2407 RICE BLVD.
at Morningside
☎ **(713) 528-7478**
salentowinecafe.com
E7

UST LIKE A KID ANXIOUS TO GROW UP, SALENTO is trying to shed its coffeehouse roots and mature into a posh wine bar. While the owners may be frustrated by its existence in the in-between, the steady West U crowd doesn't seem to mind. Students with laptops linger over single-origin brew until evening when the lights are dimmed, and an older crowd, often set on romance, turns up for the Argentina-heavy wine list. There aren't as many selections by the glass, but happy hour presents a solid discount on house wines. The typical cafe fare is enlivened by South American touches from breakfast empanadas to Argentinean-style wheat bread. Weekly live music and tango draws a cosmopolitan crowd.

TAFT STREET COFFEE

. . . .

2115 TAFT *at Welch*
☎ **(713) 522-3533**
taftstreetcoffee.org

E6

ECRETED AWAY BEHIND LUSH FOLIAGE, DIM, spacious and industrial Taft is a respite for the weary. Super-friendly baristas greet you as soon as you enter and often offer to top off your mug along the way. The menu includes the usual espresso drinks made with organic beans and a few sandwiches (try the peanut butter, jalapeño and jam) and baked goods. Local art adorns the walls and a few shelves constitute a not-too-shabby bookstore. Altogether, Taft is not just a spot to stare at your computer screen but an active community gathering place. The shop is attached to a church, however, so if you don't enjoy your latte with a side of booming contemporary praise rock coming through the walls, you might want to avoid the place on Sundays.

WALDO'S COFFEEHOUSE

. . . .

1030 HEIGHTS BLVD. *at E. 11th*
☎ **(713) 869-0700**

E6

HE VIEW FROM YOUR WINGBACK CHAIR IN THIS quaint Heights bungalow and coffeehouse could easily be mistaken as one of your grandmother's house, if she was particularly into local art and pink paint. Cozy side rooms crammed with big tables and antique chairs sprout out from the livelier main coffee bar area so the studious and the chatty can each pick their preferred noise level. The coffee is Katz brand, and the friendly baristas, breakfast croissants and plump, moist brownies improve every visit. Bring beer or wine for a $5 corkage fee and snag a seat on the front porch with a view of the scenic Paul Carr jogging trail.

Waldo's porch seating

CATERERS

R USSIAN OLIGARCHS AND PRO ATHLETES THROW THE ABSOLUTE BEST PARTIES, AND YOU KNOW they hire a caterer. Excellent food is a given, of course, but most of these six caterers, which represent every price range, can also help you with hand-addressed invitations, valet parking, flowers, rentals and entertainment.

A FARE EXTRAORDINAIRE
2035 MARSHALL
☎ **(713) 527-8288**

Society caterers Karen Lerner and Rachael Volz have been creating beautiful parties since 1985. They can assist with photography, bartenders, limos, gift bags, you name it.

BAILEY CONNOR CATERING
8741 KATY FWY.
☎ **(713) 932-8335**

This boutique outfit provides a range of services and foods from corporate breakfasts to weddings to afternoon tea.

CATERING BY CULINAIRE
2900 MILAM
☎ **(713) 524-2337**

Chef/owner Barbara McKnight has access to top venues and also owns the late Judge Roy Hofheinz's mansion where she can host seated dinners for up to 70.

CITY KITCHEN CATERING
8101 AIRPORT BLVD.
☎ **(713) 847-8004**

Gary Mercer and Scott Murphy own this high-end catering company specializing in glamorous, mid-size events. It's one of the youngest companies on this list.

JACKSON AND COMPANY
☎ **(713) 523-5780**

Houston's preeminent society caterer for 30 years, Jackson and Company is still the firm for events that must impress. The company also operates the Corinthian, a glamorous downtown venue.

JAMI'S FINE FOODS
6600 S. RICE, BELLAIRE
☎ **(713) 661-5264**

Made with pride by husband-and-wife team Jami and Steve Smith, Jami's Fine Foods provides box lunches and ready-to-eat meals for carry-out as well as custom-catered events.

{ *Tea Shops* }

BOBA ZONE

....

10613 BELLAIRE BLVD.
at Wilcrest
☎ **(281) 983-5700**
bobazonedrinks.com

ONE OF THE YOUNGER GENERATION BUBBLE tea spots located in one of the building-boom-era strip malls, Boba Zone fulfills the typical expectations of its genre. Teens flock for the tapioca tea, light snacks and free WiFi in a suitably comfortable environment. The Royal Milk Tea is hands down the most popular menu item, but flavored iced tea and the honeydew shake are also heavy hitters. The popcorn chicken doesn't have quite as loyal a following, but since Boba Zone is open relatively late at night, the fried rice does have a certain undeniable appeal.

⋅THE PATH OF TEA

....

2340 W. ALABAMA
just east of Kirby
☎ **(713) 252-4473**
thepathoftea.com

THIS TRANQUIL, ALL-ORGANIC HAVEN FOR tea lovers lets the bloodhound in you call the shots. Peruse the bar lined with dozens of tins of Japanese green, herbal tisanes and Sri Lankan black tea and choose by scent—an extremely accurate indicator of the flavor. Portions can be purchased to go, and certified tea master and owner Thia McKann will be happy to aid in your selection. Candle-warmed pots come in two sizes, and a wall of charming, mismatched cups requires further decision-making. There aren't many electrical outlets, so there's a smaller crop of laptops than at most beverage shops, but the warm yellow and blond wood tones make for an inviting place to read the paper or catch up with friends. Feel free to bring in food from Field of Greens next door, and know that the cupcakes here have a secretive but devoted following.

STAR SNOW ICE #1

....

9188 BELLAIRE BLVD.
between S. Gessner & Ranchester
☎ **(713) 988-8028**

(SEE NEXT)

STAR SNOW ICE & TERIYAKI

....

9889 BELLAIRE BLVD.
at Beltway 8

THE CONTESTANTS ON *TOP CHEF* HAVE NOTHING ON

Mango chunks with shaved ice and condensed milk at Star Snow Ice

the man breaking down papayas and pineapples behind the counter at Chinatown's Star Snow Ice when it comes to knife skills and speed. The fruit is for the variety of shakes and shave ice at one of the neighborhood's most senior and well-loved bubble tea spots. Staples like milk tea with tapioca are excellent but for a little adventure try adding the egg pudding. The second location (with "& Teriyaki" in the name) also has a full lunch menu with cheap and delicious Taiwanese dishes including fried silken tofu cubes and a generous fried pork chop with fried egg and bok choy. Lines are often out the door at both locations; cash only.

TAPIOCA HOUSE

· · · · · · · · · · · · · · · · ·

9104 BELLAIRE BLVD.
between S. Gessner & Ranchester
☎ **(713) 272-6468**

E ARE INDEBTED TO THIS CAFE FOR making possible the Earl Grey milk tea with lychee. Tapioca House brims over with not just flavors, but drink types: juice, cold versus hot tea, iced versus hot coffee, endless combinations with sinkers, or even the exploding "flavor balls," a more volatile Fruit Gusher. The mixed teas are more than a sugar craving satisfied, falling towards the milk end of the spectrum. Around us convened chatting youths at snacktime and families at mealtime. Let the smell of dinner entice you to try some fresh Thai chicken nuggets, big spicy knots in a bag with a still-floury twig of basil, eaten with a stick. Bring cash to spend under $5.

• TÉ HOUSE OF TEA

....

1927 FAIRVIEW *at Woodhead*
 ☎ **(713) 522-8868**
tehouseoftea.com

¡٩   **E6**

OUT OF ALL THE BEVERAGE HOUSES IN MONTROSE, Té offers an experience altogether more serene. Instead of hip rock music blasting, a respectful quiet persists for most of the afternoon while students slave over their textbooks in the tidy, sunlit room. Some 130 varieties of tea from a pretty pink hibiscus mint to a smoked Earl Grey are available in different teapot sizes, and once the tea arrives at your table, you'll be instructed to let it steep properly. Té makes the best, most authentic mug of chai in the city and offers a full menu of light and sometimes vegan eats. Weekend breakfast is lively, with couples and friends lined up for crêpes or Asian-influenced salads and rice bowls, and by evening Té is often venue to a popular tango night or movie screening.

Hot tea served at Té House of Tea

THE TEAHOUSE

....

2089 WESTHEIMER
at S. Shepherd
☎ **(713) 526-6123**
multiple locations
teahousebeverage.com
 E6

THERE ARE PLENTY OF BUBBLE TEA SPOTS AROUND Houston but Teahouse is an empire with locations in Chinatown, Northwest Houston, Dallas and this one in River Oaks. It's a favorite spot for teens too young for bars, couples and pretty much anyone acquainted with the addictive nature of chewy, slightly sweet tapioca balls (or boba). The menu includes countless drink options from strawberry green tea to taro coconut cream blend and more sinker options beyond tapioca, like almond pudding and lychee gelatin. A simple black cream tea is a safe bet, but the vivid red cherry ice blend is tempting on hot days and there are more authentically Taiwanese flavors, including longan and red bean. Board games are available if you want to make a night out of it.

WINE & SPIRITS

{ SIDEBARS }

{ *Bars* }

ANVIL BAR & REFUGE

1424 WESTHEIMER *east of Mandell*

☎ **(713) 523-1622**

anvilhouston.com

E6

IT'S SAFE TO SAY THAT ANVIL CHANGED THE FACE of drinking in Houston. There are several things our city had never heard of before Anvil opened. One of them is the bitter, pink aperitif Campari and the other is waiting in a line out the door. The bar and its passionately artisanal cocktails set the standard for excellence that many have since tried to imitate. Cocktails like the Ethel Groves—a combination of gin, lemon, St. Germaine and thyme—feature fresh juices and house-made infusions designed by mad-scientist bartenders. Beer and wine are treated with similar care. Just don't expect to be served too quickly (per-

The bar in Anvil

fection takes time). The menu of featured drinks changes with the seasons, but you can always trust that the selection will be delicious.

BARCADIA

2600 TRAVIS *at McGowen*

☎ **(713) 523-2525**

barcadiabars.com

E6

OUR INTENTIONS SITTING AT THE BAR MAY NOT always be innocent, but the vintage arcade games at this always-busy Midtown bar offer some good clean fun. The beer selection is better than it has to be, with 24 on tap and about 75 more by the bottle. A full range of liquor is also at the ready, and the bartenders are famously friendly. With a Fireman's #4 in hand, challenge a cutie to a game of Mortal Kombat or oversized Connect Four on the patio. Tuesdays are our favorite days to visit because that's when Texas drafts are only $3. The crowd that visits is a broad mix, we assume because of the wide appeal of giant Jenga, though skews younger, probably for the same reason.

THE BIG EASY

5731 KIRBY *at Robinhood*

☎ **(713) 523-9999**

thebigeasyblues.com

E7

THE SHABBY STAND-ALONE PAINTED MARDI

Gras colors look a bit out of place surrounded by the expensive real estate of Rice Village. But the Big Easy is a landmark for keeping the blues and zydeco scene alive and thriving in Houston. It's the kind of place to both drown your sorrows while swigging Lone Star (or something stronger) and discover living legends of their respective musical genres while you're at it. There's rarely a cover charge, although when the weekend rolls around and bigger names take the stage, it's pretty much standing (or dancing) room only. There's also a distinct chance you will be outdanced by a couple twice your age.

BLANCO'S BAR & GRILL

3406 W. ALABAMA
at Buffalo Speedway
☎ **(713) 439-0072**
houstonredneck.com

HY DO FOREIGNERS ALWAYS THINK Texans tote guns and ride horses everywhere? Just because we like to start happy hour at 11 am and two-step in our cowboy boots doesn't mean we're rednecks. Or does it? Blanco's regulars don't mind the appellation, although they don't mind much when they've got a cold Pearl or Lone Star in hand. The dance floor's got ample space for waltzing with your darlin' to the sounds of fine, live Texas bands that saunter in Wednesdays to Fridays. On Saturday nights Blanco's closes for private parties, and on Sundays they pray and sleep.

BOHEME

307 FAIRVIEW *at Taft*
☎ **(713) 529-1099**
barboheme.com

HINGS SEEM TO COME TOGETHER JUST SO AT Boheme. Low light, brick walls and mismatched sofas exude an artsy but unpretentious air. An eclectic mix of local art and perfectly worn edges lends itself towards reading in solitude during daylight hours and romance at night. Bottles of wine line an entire wall but as it's kept at room temperature, we more often opt for a cold beer or a margarita on the rocks. Bartenders are notoriously unresponsive, but it's worth it for the happy hour deals—$5 sangria, $4 house wine and $3 beers—that last all day on Sundays and Mondays. Choose a seat on the back patio on balmy nights and let the breeze sweep past you as a few of Houston's best frozen mojitos get the conversation going.

CONTINENTAL CLUB

3700 MAIN *at Travis*
☎ **(713) 529-9899**
www.continentalclub.com

THE SECOND LOCATION OF AUSTIN'S FAMED LIVE music venue is practically a nightlife amusement park. If the nightly rockabilly, country and blues bands up on the red-velvet-lined stage don't appeal to you (and they should, they're very good), there's a second room in the back with pool tables, shuffleboard and an occasional barbecue stand. The patio, which is shared with Big Top next door and the Pachinko Hut, is decked out with Elvis' name in string lights and a few picnic tables for the smokers. Patrons young and old gladly lay down the occasional $5 cover, and no one is a wallflower. As the Thursday night Beatles cover band will tell you, everyone is happy just to dance with you.

GOODE'S ARMADILLO PALACE

5015 KIRBY *near Westpark*
☎ **(713) 526-9700**
thearmadillopalace.com

YOU CAN'T MISS THIS SPOT, FOR TWO REASONS: (1) there's a 14-foot concrete armadillo out front, and (2) Jim and Levi Goode's museum/saloon/live music show/beer garden is so tasty and so much fun it would be a crying shame to drive on by without going inside. So now you've crossed the threshold, what catches your eye? Maybe the leather Western saddles that take the place of regular bar stools. Maybe all the paraphernalia hanging around that pays tribute to the great Texas traditions. Maybe the fact that the cubed venison chili has never met a bean. Maybe you like the shuffleboard, pool, domino games and cold beer iced down on the patio. Vittles here include Frito pie and armadillo wings, and there are specialty drinks made from good whiskey if beer's not your thing. There's always somebody live fiddling up a storm (see the website for music schedule).

GRAND PRIZE BAR

1010 BANKS *at Montrose*
☎ **(713) 526-4565**

THERE'S AN UNNAMABLE QUALITY TO GRAND PRIZE that draws in good things. Any given night of the week there might be a mac 'n' cheese throwdown between two big-name chefs, and it's a favorite haven for local musicians. There's a full bar on each floor offering super cheap beer as well as a menu of expertly crafted

THE $2 LONE STAR TEST

THERE ARE A FEW QUESTIONS YOU SHOULD ALWAYS ASK YOURSELF WHEN WALKING INTO a bar for the first time. Does the bar have Lone Star? Is it $2? If not, are you sure you're in a bar? If it's less than $2, do you feel safe?

CATBIRDS
1336 WESTHEIMER
☎ (713) 523-8000

Any true Montrose bar stocks $2 Lone Star, and Catbirds is sometimes referred to as the Cheers of the neighborhood. The difference is that no one here is wearing shoulder pads.

POISON GIRL
1641-B WESTHEIMER
☎ (713) 527-9929

At the late end of Saturday night, almost every table at PG is littered with a cluster of empty Lone Star bottles. Honestly, these people deserve some kind of promotional deal.

THE MINK
3718 MAIN
☎ (713) 522-9985

Wind through the bar in front, an alley and a patio to the music venue in back to rub elbows with folks whose main food groups are Lone Star and cigarettes.

BOONDOCKS
1417 WESTHEIMER
☎ (713) 522-8500

This bar is just a massive dance party in disguise. Every weekend, a DJ spins dance tunes on the second floor, which shakes from the movement of the crowd.

JIMMIE'S ICEHOUSE
2803 WHITE OAK
☎ (713) 861-9707

Our favorite longnecks are indeed less than $2 at Jimmie's, and between being able to smoke at the bar and a terrifying bathroom, it's definitely a dive, but a friendly one.

BIG STAR BAR
1005 W. 19TH
☎ (281) 501-9560

Everyone at this hideaway from Grand Prize proprietor Brad Moore is clutching a Lone Star, whether huddled by the firepit in the back or inside selecting New Wave from the jukebox.

cocktails like the Aviation or a Vieux Carre. A red glow masks the shabby nature of the mismatched seating, but by 11 pm on Saturday, it's pretty much standing room only. Our favorite photo booth in town emits two photo strips in record time and offers the choice between color and black and white. Then again, solid drinks, ample seating without loss of intimacy and a jukebox loaded with David Bowie isn't exactly unnamable.

KELVIN ARMS
2424 DUNSTAN *between Kirby and Morningside*
☎ **(713) 528-4730**
E7

OUTED AS HOUSTON'S ONLY SCOTTISH PUB, THE most "Hoot mon" identifier about the place is its regal roll call of fine Scotch whisky. If beer is your poison, 20 varieties are on tap, with Fullers ESB, Belhaven Twisted Thistle IPA and Boddington's among the listed brews. Second most Scottish hook is the shrine to Sean Connery, with photos and junk celebrating Scotland's favorite son. On August 25, they even throw 007 a birthday party. Happy hour 3 to 7 pm draws in crowds who seem to like the Vault Room—a real vault, vintage 1940s, inside the converted bank building. There are darts and game boards, but we noted no music from Scotland on the jukebox.

LEON'S LOUNGE
1006 MCGOWEN *at Fannin*
☎ **(713) 659-5366**
F6

EARLY 60-YEAR-OLD LEON'S WAS ONCE gritty. It was the kind of place where a grizzled regular would approach you and take 10 minutes to describe the pleasures of cold beer and some other weird stuff before asking if you have a boyfriend. Then, in 2010, the bar was purchased by the owners of Under the Volcano, closed for nearly an entire year and reborn a butterfly. The landmark red phone booth is still outside, but inside chandeliers, lush red drapes and pin-tucked furniture lend themselves to a modern Gothic feel you want to snuggle in. And, by God, there's a cocktail menu. Try the Green on Red, a rum drink garnished with showy red pepper. Men in pearl snaps lean against the narrow alley in the back to enjoy a smoke, and weekends are invariably packed.

MARFRELESS
2006 PEDEN *at McDuffie*
☎ **(713) 528-0083**
marfrelesshouston.com
E6

ARFRELESS IS POPULARLY BILLED AS A make-out bar for an older crowd. We're not sure that still holds true, but don't let us stop you from getting to second base. That's your date's job. First you'll have to find the place, though, which has no signage. Look for the blue door under the fire escape behind the River Oaks Theater. Candles flicker everywhere, and the music is classical. Most of the trysting goes on upstairs. Classic cocktails like the Pimm's Cup and Tom Collins plus a few oddballs including the Taste of Honey (Wild Turkey honey liqueur and Sprite) are mostly very well-made and not particularly expensive, though Wednesdays mean half off wine by the bottle.

NOUVEAU ANTIQUE ART BAR

2913 MAIN *at Tuam*
☏ **(713) 526-2220**
art-bar.net

E6

MM. WHAT DO YOU THINK THE OWNERS are trying to tell us with the name of this bar? It's pretty indirect but one has to assume it has something to do with classy art stuff. Once inside, deafening club music confuses the message but the space is breathtaking. Hundreds of Tiffany-style lamps extend a soft glow over every surface. Couples looking for a cocktail sidle up to the bar alongside rowdy boozers looking for a Jaeger shot, and since the space is as big as a football field, no one is too bothered.

The enormous space is divided into enough seating areas to offer some privacy, which is perfect considering the amorous effect the environment seems to have on ladies.

POISON GIRL

1641-B WESTHEIMER
at Dunlavy
☏ **(713) 527-9929**

E6

OISON GIRL IS THE QUINTESSENTIAL NEU-montrose bar. Inside the pink building, you'll spot local musicians in statement eyeglasses and the guy from your donation yoga class. Out on the patio, nestled between a life-size Kool-Aid man and one-legged Cabbage Patch doll, everyone is smoking. Whiskey and Lone Star are the drinks of choice, and you'll probably leave without having spent more than $10. Test your pinball wizardry on the Family Guy machine (it's the best one), or play something on the all-Texas jukebox. On the third Thursday of the month, the bar hosts Poison Pen, when three local authors read short samples of their work. Usually rowdy, booze-fueled and noisy with laughter, it's no cringe-worthy poetry slam.

WINE & SPIRITS

SAMBUCA
909 TEXAS *at Travis*
☎ (713) 224-5299
sambucarestaurant.com
F6

UPPER CLUBS AND MANDATORY COCKTAIL attire are largely remnants of a bygone era. But during nights at Sambuca, you might still be asked to dance the old-fashioned way. The sultry tone is set by dark woods and white linens and though there is a per person minimum at dinner, the food is consistently well prepared. Of course, you can simply enter for a cocktail on the rare moments you aren't on the dance floor. Musical genres vary widely, from R&B to Latin, though Sambuca is mostly known for live jazz and very talented musicians, including our favorite, Yvonne Washington.

UNDER THE VOLCANO
2349 BISSONNET *at Morningside*
☎ (713) 526-5282
underthevolcanohouston.com
E7

ALCOLM LOWRY'S *UNDER THE VOLCANO*, the literary namesake for this tiki bar, is brutally depressing. Luckily, the bar is more about the Day of the Dead theme than mescal-soaked purgatory (though that really depends on what you did last night). People come to enjoy the excellent classic cocktails and Monday steak night, which offers a three-course spread for $12. The frothy piña colada, *not* produced from a machine, comes with a giant wedge of pineapple on the rim, cucumber chunks bob in the Pimm's Cup and a single Singapore Sling will knock you flat. The crowd is laconic around happy hour. But give it a few more frozen screwdrivers, and you could very well find yourself in Mexico by the end of the night.

WARREN'S INN
307 TRAVIS *at Congress*
☎ (713) 247-9207
F6

HERE'S SOMETHING DIFFERENT ABOUT drinking in a place with history. All the first dates, last dates, bad decisions and wild nights that have gone on in a room leave behind a trace, and Warren's has seen a lot of those in the decades it's been open. Perched on Market Square, the legendary bar's oversized mirrors and dark wood belie the casual expectations. One of the best jukeboxes in town sits in a corner, loaded with music by Sam Cooke, Dr. John and Lightnin' Hopkins. You come here to drink, plain and simple, and pours are generous. The inevitable old drunk will be seated at the bar, and judges, hipsters and club babes wander in and out. They're all just contributing to the history.

ZIMM'S MARTINI & WINE BAR

4321 MONTROSE *at Richmond*

☎ **(713) 521-2002**

zimmsbar.com

E7

IMM'S IS A BAR FOR ADULTS. ADULTS THAT enjoy mint chocolate chip martinis, but still, the ample leather seating and voices chatting at a low register are perfect for people who are comfortable with the choices they've made in life. The walls function as a gallery for featured local artists and the low light lends a romantic bent to every conversation. The wine list urgently needs updating, but they do warm the brandy snifter, and the more classic cocktails are executed to perfection. It's a class act that draws in folks who have plenty of money for a bar-night splurge.

{ *Beer Bars* }

ALICE'S TALL TEXAN

4904 N. MAIN *at Walling*

☎ **(713) 862-0141**

E5 🖐

LICE'S IS AN OLD-FASHIONED TEXAS BEER joint. It's as simple as that. There are a few beers by the bottle, but if you're not ordering the 20-ounce schooners of Lone Star or Shiner then you're doing it wrong. The fishbowl-sized goblets are kept chilled in a refrigerator in back, and Alice herself will frequently be the one behind the counter doling out refreshments. If she doesn't recognize you, she'll ask who you are, and many of the blue-collar regulars will greet you or ask you to dance as well. The jukebox is loaded with country new and old, from Taylor Swift (surprisingly popular) to Patsy Cline. Some might call Alice's a dive bar, but it's really too clean and friendly for that.

BONEYARD DOG PARK & DRINKERY

8150 WASHINGTON *north of I-10*

☎ **(832) 494-1600**

boneyardhouston.com

D6

OST OF THE REAL ESTATE AT THE BONE-yard is dedicated to an enclosed puppy play area. This is excellent news for dog owners who are tired of missing out on happy hour because of pet duty, but this laid-back watering hole holds a lot of attraction for the dogless as well. Picnic tables offer seating outside the dog park, and the industrial interior of the bar offers additional space. The beer selection and daily specials are the major draws, with every Abita and Shiner variety available, plus a few brews from New Belgium and Southern Star. Expect to drink cheap because

WINE & SPIRITS

happy hour is all day during the week. Bonus: A food truck is often parked nearby.

BREWERY TAP
717 FRANKLIN *at Milam*
☎ **(713) 237-1537**

 HUNDRED YEARS AGO THE NOW-DEFUNCT Magnolia Brewery mixed its barley and hops in the exact location that currently houses this scruffy but amiable corner bar on Market Square. It's a favorite post-work spot and long-time regulars bring stories from the good ol' days and occasionally that special dart for competing in the Wednesday-night tournament. There's a full bar, but the 35 brews on tap make it a destination for beer lovers. You'll find a range including Spaten Optimator, Saint Arnold, Maredsous and Fat Tire, to name a few. As the contemporary nightlife scene moves towards expensive shoes and Kobe beef sliders, it's nice to just sit a while in a place that actually has some history.

FLYING SAUCER DRAUGHT EMPORIUM
705 MAIN *at Capitol*
☎ **(713) 228-9472**
beerknurd.com

 URE, THE BUXOM "BEER GODDESSES" AND FREE popcorn have pretty universal appeal, but you should probably only come here if you like beer. There are around 80 beers on draft and 100 more by the bottle, and the folks manning the counter can out-geek any beer nerd. It's the nice stuff, too, such as Chimay Grand Reserve and Left Hand Milk Stout. Despite two levels of seating, the bar is often overcrowded during happy hour and weekend nights. When there's a free table, we like to retire to the cozier upstairs with a basket of chili cheese fries. The demographic is a little male heavy, but that just means that women in the bar get their pick of trivia teams, which all seem to take the Tuesday night proceedings pretty seriously.

THE GINGER MAN
5607 MORNINGSIDE
north of University Blvd.
☎ **(713) 526-2770**
gingermanpub.com

 OMETIMES WE GET TIRED OF LIVING IN THE

CRAFT BEER SPOTS

DRINKING YOUR DINNER IS MADE FAR MORE RESPECTABLE IF THE BEER IS CRAFTED WITH care and not advertised along the freeway. Clean taps, full kegs, can't lose.

THE GINGER MAN
5607 MORNINGSIDE
☎ (713) 526-2770
This Rice Village mainstay is a beer lover's paradise with nearly 80 beers on tap and an emphasis on Belgian varieties. Oh, and there are pretzels.

FLYING SAUCER
705 MAIN
☎ (713) 228-9472
It's not Houston-born, but you can't deny that this craft-beer emporium knows what it's doing. There are some mass-produced beers, but almost everyone here is a like-minded microbrew purist.

PETROL STATION
985 WAKEFIELD
☎ (713) 957-2875
This neighborhood bar makes up for its reduced selection by having a curated list of exciting microbrews and an obsessed staff. Glass half-gallon growlers labeled "Badass Mother******" are also available.

LIBERTY STATION
2101 WASHINGTON
☎ (713) 640-5220
The beer selection here is small, but locally focused. If Southern Star and Independence Brewing don't get your friends excited, there are cocktails and Cornhole for the haters.

ANVIL BAR & REFUGE
1424 WESTHEIMER
☎ (713) 523-1622
Yes, the heart of Houston's cocktail culture also offers an impressive list of craft brews, meticulously tended to. Look for co-owner Kevin Floyd's pet project beer bar Hay Merchant to open Fall 2011.

BREWERY TAP
717 FRANKLIN
☎ (713) 237-1537
There are 35 beers on tap on the former site of the Magnolia Brewery. You'll find Maredsous and Fat Tire, to name a few.

capitol city's shadow so we're just going to take a moment to firmly declare that the Ginger Man began in Houston—not in Austin and not in Dallas, either, where there are other locations. It's understandable why others would try to claim it as their own. A fixture in Rice Village since 1985, it boasts an entire wall of draft beer, from fine Austin porters to the best of Belgium, and the beer menu constantly evolves as new or seasonal brews become available. Even on the warmest days, the front and back patios are crowded, but the best time to visit is Wednesday, when the purchase of a particular beer comes with a free logo pint glass.

HANS' BIER HAUS
2523 QUENBY *at Kirby*
☎ **(713) 520-7474**
hansbierhaus.com

H ANS' POSSESSES ONE OF THE FEW BOCCE courts in town, though no amount of dirty looks will convince other parties to take leave of it once it's been claimed. Luckily, there are nearly 60 beers from around the world on tap to keep you amused. The inside of this creaky old house is nothing special, but the sprawling back patio is lovely when a breeze blows through. Though some complain that the taps could be cleaned more frequently, we've never had a problem with our Zei-

genbock. It's the last place you'd think to be involved in drama, but Hans' has been embattled with the neighboring high-rise about noise complaints for over a year now and the squabble has gotten dirty. But that needn't concern you, because the pizza-delivery guy is on his way.

THE HARP
1625 RICHMOND *near Dunlavy*
☎ **(713) 528-7827**
theharphouston.com

I F YOU LIKED THE PUB SCENES SEEN IN THE JOHN Wayne film *The Quiet Man*, you will love The Harp. Step inside a somewhat renovated house that's punched down on the nose of the Montrose area and don't expect fancy—there is nothing slick about this hangout. Dimly lit and as comfy as your 10-year-old bathrobe, The Harp welcomes dogs to wander in if they bring along a customer. No food, but on hand are a bevy of menus from nearby restaurants for ordering in a delivery. There's a wee bar from which you might request a Guinness, or call for the namesake brew, Harp Lager, on tap. Trivia night is Tuesday at 8, league darts on Wednesday. Be careful where you park: Many have been towed from the parking lots of inhospitable businesses that rub up against the tavern.

THE HAY MERCHANT
1100 WESTHEIMER *at Waugh*

E6

NVIL'S BOBBY HEUGEL AND KEVIN FLOYD HAVE announced the beer counterpart to their cocktail sanctuary. With as many as 80 beers on tap, Haymarket is set to open in late Fall 2011 in the space where famous lesbian bar Chances used to be. What the neighborhood mourns in the loss of a neighborhood institution is made up for in anticipation. Physics PhD students don't put as much study into their subject matter as Floyd has into beer technologies. The bar will feature two coolers so that different types of beer can be stored at the right temperature and rare, hand-pumped cask offerings will regularly be on hand.

PETROL STATION
985 WAKEFIELD *east of Ella*
☎ **(713) 957-2875**

E5

HIS MODEST GARDEN OAKS FAVORITE GAINED a citywide reputation for possessing an amazing microbrew selection, and suddenly people from all over Houston began to trek here to have a pint for themselves. Beat-up wooden tables inside are fully occupied during meal times because Petrol Station, a converted gas station, is also known for its huge,

juicy burgers. During the afternoon, local families come to fuel up, and by happy hour, the demographic skews older male (something about beer nerds). It is truly a beer mecca, with rare cask ales and locally brewed beers on tap. The bartenders definitely know what they're talking about but don't judge if you don't—just ask for a recommendation.

YARD HOUSE
800 W. SAM HOUSTON PKWY.
in CityCentre
☎ **(713) 461-9273**
yardhouse.com

B6

S A CHILD, YOU LIKED TO DRINK OUT OF curlicue straws. As an adult, you prefer half-yard-long beer receptacles. Don't worry; it's part of your natural development. This California-based bar chain is right at home in CityCentre, where hordes settle in at the stroke of 5 pm for "the world's largest selection of draft beer" and almost as many food items. We drink too much to be good at math, so we can't refute or prove the claim about the number of taps, but it's safe to say you'll find pretty much anything you could possibly want. Lindemans Framboise and ahi tuna sashimi? Available. Buffalo wings and Amstel Light? Obviously. Happy hour deals include all beers under $5 (unless you're investing in the half-yard quantity), $5 wells and half-priced appetizers.

{ *Distillery* }

RAILEAN DISTILLERS
341 5TH STREET
near Avenue D, San Leon
☎ **(713) 545-2742**
railean.com
SOUTHEAST OF **19** 🚗

AMESAKE KELLY RAILEAN QUIT THE liquor-distribution rat race and rolled out her micro-distillery just four years ago in 2007. Located in San Leon down on Galveston Bay, the distillery uses only Gulf Coast sugar cane molasses and produces in small batches. Currently three styles of rum are made: white rum, dark rum and aged Reserve Single Barrel Rum. More recently, in 2010, Railean introduced a line of 100% Blue Agave spirits. Yes, others might call them tequila, but Railean respects the rules. These are Texas-made spirits, not Mexican tequila that is bottled in Texas. There are two styles: silver and aged *reposado*. Visitors are welcome by appointment, and tours typically last about an hour. Call before you go to make sure Railean is there and not scouring out a fermentation tank.

{ *Ice Houses* }

BIG JOHN'S ICE HOUSE
12640 BRIAR FOREST
west of S. Dairy Ashford
☎ **(281) 497-3499**
bigjohnsicehouse.com
6A

LAID-BACK, NO-FUSS ESTABLISHMENT IN WEST Houston, Big John's Ice House gradually encloses you in wooden railings and mismatched televisions. At the outermost porch, a wide vista of the western sky lets you bask in the softening light of the evening while keeping one eye on the game. Step down towards the bar through the garage, and the icehouse gains a roof, then walls as the televisions cluster. We appreciate the variety of seats and TV channels. Depending on what you order, there may be no utensils, only a full-sized roll of paper towels. The popular crawfish, available Friday through Sunday in season, crowds a platter that could hold the head of John the Baptist. Steak night comes Wednesday, trivia night comes Thursday, and beer bottles come comfortable in koozies.

STEAK NIGHTS

I F THERE'S ANYTHING A TEXAN LOVES MORE THAN A COLD BEER, IT'S A STEAK. AS IF YOU needed another reason to belly up to the bar, these establishments offer tasty cuts for cheap to get you in the door.

UNDER THE VOLCANO
2349 BISSONNET
☎ (713) 526-5282

Every Monday night, $12 gets you a well-marinated ribeye with a side of chimichurri, a salad and a dessert. Recommended pairing: strawberry basil margarita.

COMMUNITY BAR
2703 SMITH
☎ (713) 526-1576

Chef Bob pulls out all the stops every Tuesday night with a 16-ounce ribeye, marinated and grilled outdoors, and the choice between sides like spicy grilled pineapple and jalapeño mashed potatoes.

SAINT DANE'S
502 ELGIN
☎ (713) 807-7040

At $10 on Mondays, it's probably the cheapest steak dinner in town. And for dessert: fried Oreos.

THE STAG'S HEAD
2128 PORTSMOUTH
☎ (713) 533-1199

This cozy English pub is known for its soccer, ahem, football fans and solid eats. Every Wednesday, a 12-ounce strip goes for $13.

ONION CREEK
3106 WHITE OAK
☎ (713) 880-0706

Not a hump day passes that we don't have a beer. There's no more relaxing place to have one than on the patio of Onion Creek with a ribeye and baked potato, on discount until 10 pm every Wednesday.

COVA
5600 KIRBY
☎ (713) 838-0700

Pair one of the 40 wines by the glass with a classy surf-and-turf: 10-ounce New York strip, grilled shrimp and herbed potatoes, all for $17.99.

BRITTMOORE ICE HOUSE

1535 BRITTMOORE
between Hammerly & Westview
☎ **(713) 932-7797**
partyonbrittmoore.com

 5B

ITTING AT THE BAR AND DRINKING A PEARL AT the Brittmoore Ice House, we could not be any deeper in the heart of Texas. Not that place where everyone wears big hats and hustles cattle, but where the "Folsom Prison Blues" lollops through the air and the man sitting next to you wipes his eyes while listening to the lyrics. There are easily a dozen motorcycles parked inside the hedges, plus one dog tied to a tree stump. Once a transmission shop, Brittmoore's open garage doors and powerful fans make it the ideal cool-down spot. Regular weekday lunch specials range from po'boy baskets to meatloaf for around $7, and steak night, the greatest night of the week, comes on Thursday. Go ahead and enter the Thursday raffle; if you win, you'll get to choose between a bucket of beer and polka-dotted lingerie. And when the band finishes a song, don't forget to give them a "holler and a swaller."

FRONT PORCH PUB

217 GRAY *near Bagby*
☎ **(713) 571-9571**
frontporchpub.com

 6E

COMFORTABLE AFTER-WORK PIT STOP, MANY young professionals on the trek out from downtown might call this Midtown icehouse home. There's no pretension at this abandoned-garage-turned-pub, but there is certainly a crowd to fight on weekend evenings. The old garage door is opened up to the Houston air on fine-weather days, although the namesake front porch is massive enough so that outdoor seating isn't usually hard to find. There are more than 100 varieties of beer on draft and in bottles, from Lagunitas IPA to Boulevard Wheat to Red Stripe, and a full bar complemented by simple bar snacks. Steak-n-Bock Night is every Thursday.

KAY'S LOUNGE

2324 BISSONNET *near Greenbriar*
☎ **(713) 528-9858**

 E7

EEP IN THE HEART OF WEST U, YOU'LL FIND Kay's. It's not technically an icehouse, but it channels an icehouse vibe. A Texas dive bar and landmark for the past five decades, it's a seedy hangout for frat boys and good ol' boys alike. The wise choice would be to stick to beer, as pours are inconsistent, and though it's not as cheap as the dingy surroundings would suggest, there are indeed pitchers. Darts and a pool table provide entertainment and out back a few picnic tables on some grass only technically qualify as a patio. Grab a seat at the Texas-shaped table if you can, though it's very often occupied, and line up a few songs on the jukebox. Otherwise you're going to be hearing a lot of the Allman Brothers Band.

Patio seating at Liberty Station

cribed on a chalkboard menu, and most nights a food truck will be parked outside.

LIBERTY STATION

2101 WASHINGTON *at Henderson*
☎ **(713) 640-5220**
libertystationbar.com
E6

WHILE MUCH OF THE NIGHTLIFE on Washington somehow manages to be both glitzy and generic all at once, Liberty Station retains an authentic personality. Housed in a converted filling station, this open-air watering hole cultivates a laid-back attitude that appeals to all stripes. Flirt over a game of Cornhole or giant Jenga, bring your dog out on the patio or sit inside and watch the game on TV. It stands by its motto "No Crap on Tap," with a lineup of craft beers including options from (512) in Austin and Southern Star from Conroe. A few specialty cocktails, including a strawberry basil margarita, are des-

WEST ALABAMA ICE HOUSE

1919 W. ALABAMA *near Hazard*
☎ **(713) 528-6874**
westalabamaicehouse.com
E7

HERE'S A BIT OF DRINKING TRIVIA FOR you. A boilermaker is a pint of beer with a shot of whiskey poured into it. Technically, with all the proper glassware, you could call it a cocktail, but at the icehouse, you're just pouring your own whiskey into a bottle of Lone Star and at that point it's called an addiction. The open-air bar and its picnic table colony have been around since 1927 and are beloved by many a Houstonian. Bikers and nerdy Rice graduate students alike come for a game of horseshoes and a *lengua* taco from the truck parked out front. The beers could probably be a

WINE & SPIRITS

little cheaper, but patrons are allowed to bring their own liquor if it's kept label down on the table and mixers are purchased at the bar. Of course, hitting the hard stuff is strictly unnecessary when it comes to enjoying yourself here.

ZIMM'S LITTLE DECK

601 RICHMOND *at Jack*
☎ **(713) 527-8328**
zimmslittledeck.com

E6

E DON'T EXTEND THIS COMPARISON often, as it usually rings false, but Zimm's Little Deck does replicate a very New Orleans feel. Something about the sunlight hitting the white marble bar, bistro tables and the petanque court calls to mind spring days in the Crescent City. It bills itself as a "fancy icehouse," but that icehouse pretense is undone by a glance at the price list. Chef Jeramie Robison (who is also helming the kitchen at the Zimmerman-owned Restaurant Cinq a few streets away) has created a menu of po'boys and "rich boys," including a version with duck confit. Our favorite way to experience the Little Deck: Under an umbrella on the patio with raw oysters and a bottle of cold white wine.

{ *Microbreweries* }

8TH WONDER BREWERY

2202 DALLAS *at Hutchins*
8thwonderbrewery.com

F6

YAN SOROKA, ALEX VASSILAKIDIS AND CHEF Matt Marcus—better known in Houston culinary circles as the Eatsie Boys—are diving into the world of craft beer. The team signed a lease in Summer 2011 and have begun repurposing a classic, one-story warehouse building on the east side of the George R. Brown Convention Center to launch 8th Wonder Brewery. They have also brought a new member into the fold, Aaron Corsi, who is in the process of being certified as a Master Brewer by the International Brewers Guild. The brewery is slated for completion during the 2011 holiday season.

KARBACH BREWING CO.

2032 KARBACH *between Mangum & Hempstead*
☎ **(713) 680-2739**
karbachbrewing.com

D5

ARBACH BREWING CO.—WHICH IS LOCATED just blocks from Saint Arnold's original location near the Northwest Mall—released its first beers in early September 2011. The two beers initially available were the Hopadillo IPA and the Weisse Versa Wheat. A third beer, a relatively hoppy lager called Sympathy for the Lager, is slated for future release. City-wide distribution is underway as we go to press. (We spotted Karbach at Rudyard's Pub and The Flying Saucer.) Take a tour of the brewery Friday evening 5 to 7 pm or Saturday noon to 3 pm. Admission is $7 and includes samples.

NO LABEL BREWING
5373 1ST ST.
near Pin Oak Rd., Katy
☎ **(281) 693-7545**
nolabelbrew.com
WEST OF 🚗

O F COURSE THE BOTTLES MUST HAVE LABELS (HOW else would you know which is which?), so the idea behind the name has more to do with being free-spirited. No labels, man. This family operation, run by Brian Royo, his wife Jennifer and parents Gilberto and Melanie, got started in Katy as recently as 2010. By now, they have four beers to their name including the El Hefe, a traditional German Hefeweizen and the Black Wit-O, made more intriguing with a touch of star anise, and at least two more on the way. No Label can be found in bars and restaurants around town includ-

ing El Gran Malo and Firkin and Phoenix, and bottling begins in 2012. Tastings are held at the Katy warehouse 1 to 3 pm every Saturday but the first Saturday of the month.

SAINT ARNOLD BREWING COMPANY
2000 LYONS *east of Hardy*
☎ **(713) 686-9494**
saintarnold.com
 📣

T AKING ITS NAME FROM THE PATRON SAINT OF brewers, Saint Arnold is the oldest microbrewery in Texas. Given the restrictive state alcohol laws, that's only since 1994. Guided by beer lover and former investment banker Brock Wagner, Saint Arnold today brews five beers year round, plus five seasonally, as well as an ever-changing series of extreme single-batch beers called Divine Reserve. Tours take place Monday through Friday at 3 pm and Saturdays 11 am to 2 pm. The $7 admission gets you the tour, a logo tasting glass and several samples. Saturdays are slammed, so arrive as early as possible. Pack snacks and board games and you have yourself a pretty ideal outing, especially for out-of-towners.

WINE & SPIRITS

SOUTHERN STAR BREWING COMPANY

1207 N. FM 3083 RD E.
near Airport Parkway, Conroe
☎ **(936) 441-2739**
southernstarbrewery.com

NORTH OF

THE FIRST THING THAT SETS SOUTHERN STAR apart from most microbreweries is that they can (rather than bottle) their craft beers. The thinking is that the can better protects the beer from light; it's also lighter to transport. The brewery's first product was their signature Pine Belt Pale Ale, which was released in March 2008. This was soon followed by Bombshell Blonde (look for the blue can with the cowgirl riding a bomb) and jet-black Buried Hatchet Stout. All three are available in cans and kegs. Brewery tours are given the first and third Saturday of each month, and hearty German food is provided by The Outlaw Kookers, which uses Southern Star's beers in their mustard and barbecue sauce.

{ *Pubs* }

BAKER STREET PUB & GRILL

5510 MORNINGSIDE *north of University Blvd.*
☎ **(713) 942-9900**
sherlockspubco.com

LIKE STARBUCKS, SOMETIMES DUELING PUBS SIT right across the street from each other (go ahead, raise a tankard to the fellow in the window opposite). Seems to work fine, though, with enough thirsty customers to go around. At this particular spot, the goings-on are lively, the crowds are predominantly Rice University students or doctor types who meander over from the nearby Medical Center, and the draw seems to be the low-priced happy-hour drinks. From 2 to 9 pm Monday through Saturday and all day Sunday, $2 will buy selected drafts and well drinks, $2.50 house wines and $7 selected domestic pitchers. With an interior of low lights and woody aspects, the English pub model is alive and well here.

DOG-FRIENDLY PATIOS

TWO THINGS WILL ALWAYS GIVE YOU COMFORT AT THE END OF THE DAY: YOUR PUPPY AND alcohol. Chocolate cake comes in a close third, but that's less available at Houston area bars for some reason.

DARKHOUSE TAVERN
2207 WASHINGTON
☎ **(713) 426-2442**
The patio behind this low-key, old guard Washington bar is small, but the welcome other dog owners will give you is huge.

WEST ALABAMA ICE HOUSE
1919 W. ALABAMA
☎ **(713) 528-6874**
Sometimes we think the dogs here are having more fun than the humans. The owner's big friendly dog, Tavi, has her own Facebook page.

ZIGGY'S BAR & GRILL
302 FAIRVIEW
☎ **(832) 519-0476**
Ziggy's was approved for a variance to the city's anti-dog ordinance – the city's first such permit – in September 2011. Leashed canines are now legally welcome.

BONEYARD
8150 WASHINGTON
☎ **(832) 494-1600**
Dog-friendly is a bit of an understatement for a bar with a 7,000-square-foot dog park, bagging stations and water bowls. For the humans, there's Abita.

LIBERTY STATION
2101 WASHINGTON
☎ **(713) 640-5220**
The best way to meet adorable women is to have an adorable dog. Or at least that's what we've gleaned from spending time at the picnic tables at this open-air bar.

BIG STAR BAR
1005 W. 19TH
☎ **(281) 501-9560**
It's not so much "a thing" to bring your pet here, but occasionally you'll see a dog on the back patio, warming his backside by a fire pit.

BLACK LABRADOR PUB

4100 MONTROSE *at W. Main*
☎ **(713) 529-1199**
blacklabradorpub.com

HERE ISN'T A MORE IDEAL SPOT IN THE entire Houston metro to hold a cozy English pub than this ivy-covered edifice. Low ceilings, a fireplace and worn wooden floors suggest that it's cold out there on the moors, and no matter the actual outdoor temperature we always feel compelled to order a hot toddy once inside. Bass, Newcastle, Harp, Boddington's and Guinness are all on tap, and there are at least five variations on Irish coffee. The food menu is an assortment of English classics, such as bangers and mash and shepherd's pie, and some Tex-Mex, but eating sometimes results in sticker shock. Outside you'll find a giant chess-playing surface that begs for real people to stand in for bishops and knights.

DOWNING STREET PUB

2549 KIRBY *at Westheimer*
☎ **(713) 523-2291**
downingstreetpub.com

F YOU'RE THE KIND OF PERSON WHO PREFERS the feel of leather on your skin and the caramel notes of fine scotch on your tongue, there is only one place to be. Downing Street attracts a certain clientele who may be known for muttering, "There's no accounting for taste," from time to time, and they're happy to find a place as discerning as themselves. The walk-in humidor that dominates the bar is enjoyable to tour just for the mingling scent of cigars. The staff knows how to cut and light a cigar properly with the cedar strip and will be happy to advise even the most rudimentary beginner. The scotch, bourbon and port selection is excellent and reasonably priced (given retail prices), though by no means inexpensive.

KENNEALLY'S IRISH PUB

2111 S. SHEPHERD *at Indiana*
☎ **(713) 630-0486**
irishpubkenneallys.com

HERE'S NOT AN IRISH EYE IN THE HOUSE THAT forgets to smile when throwing back a draught or two of Guinness at this jolly neighborhood bar. Folks of other persuasions are wont to grin widely, too, when visiting proprietor John Flowers' well-established pub (circa 1983 and counting). The tired façade has the look of shabby Ireland before the Celtic Tiger roared. Surprisingly enough, the outstanding feature of this pub is the Chicago-style (yes, Chicago) thin-crust pizza, including the corned-beef-topped Shamrock Special. What won't surprise you is that the bar and the surrounding block turn into a green drunken monster come March 17.

McGONIGEL'S MUCKY DUCK

2425 NORFOLK
between Kirby & Morningside
☎ **(713) 528-5999**
mcgonigels.com

HE MUCKY DUCK'S BUSI-NESS MODEL IS UNIQUE to Houston. It's a supper club that boasts a full schedule of some of the best barely-under-the-radar country and folk performers in the U.S. James McMurtry, James Blake and Bob Schneider are the musicians you can experience here in an extremely intimate setting, always for less than $30 cover. The food is traditional English pub fare, from shepherd's pie to fish and chips. It's actually tasty, though we wouldn't come just for that. Instead, it's the friendly faces and cozy quarters that define the experience. That and a few pints of Smith-wick's and the discovery of a new favorite singer-songwriter.

RED LION PUB

2316 S. SHEPHERD *at Fairview*
☎ **(713) 782-3030**
redlionhouston.com

T RED LION, YOU'LL FIND AUTHENTIC ENG-lish fare and prices similar to their English originals as well. Just as often as people praise the curry, roasted Brussels sprouts and roast beef and Yorkshire pudding, you'll find someone to complain about the prices. The beer, from Old Speckled Hen to Fuller's ESB, is a little pricier than Houston's average, too, which may explain why so many men who can afford nice suits dine here. Owner Craig Mallinson, a native of England, has recreated the neighborhood pub of his youth with a cozy wood-paneled sitting area and a fireplace burning in the winter, even outdoor dining under willow trees. It's a grown-up pub—few frat boys here—with attention to detail. (Even the bawdy cartoons in the men's room are regularly changed out.) Overall, people who spend time here—and there are more than enough of them—agree that it's worth a bit of extra coin.

RUDYARD'S BRITISH PUB

2010 WAUGH *at Welch*

☎ **(713) 521-0521**

rudyardspub.com

 UDYARD'S IS PRETTY MUCH EVERYTHING YOU could want in a Montrose bar. Live shows on the second floor several nights a week feature some of Houston's most interesting bands plus touring indie acts from all over. The darts boards are always being taken advantage of, and there's pool and shuffleboard in the back. But if the sporting life is not for you, Rudz is also known for having a delicious burger. The beer selection includes its fair share of local and craft but the staff will just as willingly shake up a fruity shot. Monthly beer dinners from chef Joe Apa bring gourmet food (think truffle egg toasts and lamb shank) to what is, aesthetically speaking, a pretty grubby location. But like we said, this is the perfect Montrose bar, not the perfect Washington Avenue bar.

{ Sports Bars }

CHRISTIAN'S TAILGATE

7340 WASHINGTON

just north of I-10

☎ **(713) 864-9744**

multiple locations

christianstailgate.com

 EOPLE SAY THAT CHRISTIAN'S HAS ONE OF THE best burgers in town. It's definitely good, the meat ground and formed in house. But come on, we all know that's the booze talking. The original Washington Avenue location was at one time a seedy sports dive but since the expansion to two other locations, even the flagship has taken on a bit of a soulless shine. Then again, your definition of soul probably depends on your opinion of college nights, karaoke and Jaeger bombs. If you're a fan of the latter, then you'll more than likely enjoy yourself. Between the dozens of flatscreen TVs and shuffleboard, all your sporting needs should be met.

GRIFF'S SHENANIGANS CAFE & BAR

3416 ROSELAND *at Hawthorne*
☎ **(713) 528-9912**
griffshouston.net
E7

HAT IS THE DISTINCT SMELL OF SPILLED BEER you're smelling. It has pervaded Griff's as long as it's been open, which is since 1965. The oldest surviving sports bar in Houston looks grungy, with plastic cups strewn haphazardly across the floor and back porch. But Griff's is practically an institution for sports fans who come to watch and holler at the television collectively. On certain game days the bar hosts a party bus that will shuttle inebriated fans around town. As a testament to its Irish flair, Griff's also boasts "Texas' largest St. Patrick's Day festival," a multi-day event with live music, cook-offs and, of course, drinking. On normal weekends, however, customers will find the usual suspects just hanging out enjoying the 25 varieties of beer.

{ *Retailers* }

FRENCH COUNTRY WINES

2433 BARTLETT *just east of Kirby*
☎ **(713) 993-9500**
frenchcountrywines.com
E7

F BEING A WINE SHOP WAS NOT SPECIALIZED enough, French Country Wines trades only in French wines, importing them from small family-owned, estate-bottled and (often) organically grown vineyards throughout France. Curious? Plan to come to one of the free tastings from noon to 6 pm on Saturdays. Buy a case and receive a 10 percent discount.

HOUSTON WINE MERCHANT

2646 S. SHEPHERD *at Westheimer*
☎ **(713) 524-3397**
houstonwines.com
E6

VERYONE FROM THE EXTREMELY KNOWLEDGE-able to the woefully uninformed can be grateful for owner Scott Spencer and his staff. Ask a simple question (How do you pronounce Pouilly-Fuissé?) or a more complicated one (What is a high-quality but affordable Lambrusco?) and you'll receive the same friendly accommodation. Believing it only wise that we taste before we buy,

WINE & SPIRITS

Spencer offers free wine tastings every Friday 5 to 7 pm and every Saturday 2 to 4 pm. Tastings are usually themed and run from staff favorites to "over the top reds," from Champagne to the mouth-watering wines of Louis Latour. Fine liquor is also available, but wine is center stage here.

RICHARD'S LIQUORS & FINE WINES

2124 S. SHEPHERD *at Fairview*
☎ **(713) 529-4849**
multiple locations
richardsliquors.com

E6

SINCE 1949, RICHARD'S HAS BROWN-BAGGED booze for your father and your father's father. As the business grew, its stock and trade became more diversified with fine wines, fine cigars from the Dominican Republic and upscale gift items being added to the shelves and bins and humidors. The staff, knowledgeable and eager to offer recommendations, shares a commendable professionalism at all five locations. Offering in-store specials every day, the wine is always premium quality, whether modestly priced or rare vintage. Customers in neighborhoods surrounding each of the locations can call for home delivery.

SPEC'S WINES, SPIRITS & FINER FOODS

2410 SMITH *at McGowen*
☎ **(713) 526-8787**
multiple locations
specsonline.com

F6 ✍

NO ONE IN HOUSTON EVER SAYS THEY'RE

Wine shopping in Spec's

CLASSIC COCKTAILS

A CLASSIC IS A HISTORICALLY MEMORABLE STANDARD OF EXCELLENCE. SO THAT'S A no-go for you, appletini. These bars, on the other hand, respect traditions and sometimes even improve upon them.

SIDEBAR
807 TAFT
☎ **(713) 522-0995**
The extremely competent bartenders at Gravitas' pocket-sized bar can surely make a classic, but we love their take on the Texas mojito with the zing of habanero syrup.

ANVIL BAR & REFUGE
1424 WESTHEIMER
☎ **(713) 523-1622**
Some of the greatest innovations in cocktail flavor technology have been created here. But order anything from a pisco sour to a classic Hemingway daiquiri and you'll be served the definitive version.

BEAVER'S
2310 DECATUR
☎ **(713) 864-2328**
Beaver's may like to play it crass with playful names and obscenely large cuts of meat, but it shows a real delicate side at the bar. Best gin gimlet in town.

HEARSAY
218 TRAVIS
☎ **(713) 225-8079**
Housed in the second-oldest commercial building in town, Hearsay's soaring ceilings and twinkling lights are the perfect setting to sip a stiff Sazerac or French 75.

UNDER THE VOLCANO
2349 BISSONNET
☎ **(713) 526-5282**
An icy cold Singapore Sling and the English-born Pimm's Cup are best enjoyed while sporting a Hawaiian shirt on this tiki-fied patio.

BRANCH WATER TAVERN
510 SHEPHERD
☎ **(713) 863-7777**
Known for its impeccable selection of American whiskey, this inviting tavern offers a different whiskey cocktail special every day at happy hour. Come Fridays for a classic Manhattan.

going to the liquor store. They say they're going to Spec's, just like everyone says they need a Kleenex or a Band-aid. At the mothership location on Smith, there are close to two acres of store to wander through, stocked with some 40,000 labels of wine, spirits, liqueurs, beer and gourmet food. Walk right into the humidor to peruse 900 cigar varieties, and follow your nose over to the huge deli to paw through some cheese. Overwhelmed? Over-excited? That's typical. The staff is sometimes a little less savvy at satellite locations, not to mention the diminished selection, but all will get the job done. Cash purchases receive a 5 percent discount.

{ *Wine Bars* }

13 CELSIUS
3000 CAROLINE *at Anita*
☎ **(713) 529-8466**
13celsius.com

E6

1 3 CELSIUS, NAMED AFTER THE IDEAL TEMPERATURE to store wine, is Houston's defin-itive wine bar. The vintage 1927 building, once the site of a dry-cleaner, is now outfitted with leather sofas, a 40-foot white mar-ble bar and an inviting candlelit courtyard. The industrial feel and low lighting makes you feel hip even if you aren't, and, thankfully, you don't have to know anything about wine to enjoy yourself. The bartenders aren't pretentious in the least and will recommend a delicious wine based on your ex-tremely vague description of your preferences and budget. On Sun-days, enjoy all open bottles at 50 percent off, and every Tuesday come for the cupcake-and-wine pairing. The baked goods are from Jody Stevens, who just so happens to make the city's definitive cupcake.

COVA
5600 KIRBY *at Nottingham*
☎ **(713) 838-0700**
multiple locations
covawines.com

E7

THIS BOUTIQUE WINE SHOP AND BAR FUNC-tions as a retail store during the day with almost 1,000 available bottles. In the evening, Cova be-comes a sultry bar and restaurant when the kitchen begins to pro-duce hot and cold tapas, including house-cured salmon with shallot crème fraîche, artisan cheeses, beef tartare and osso buco. At that point, there are 40 wines offered by the glass and live jazz on occa-sion. Tuesdays are steak night, when a steak and shrimp go for $18.

D'VINE WINE BAR

25202 NORTHWEST FWY.
at Skinner, Cypress
☎ **(281) 213-4656**
dvine-winebar.com
NORTHWEST OF A2 🚗

TUCKED INTO A CORNER OF THE SPRAWLING Metro mixed-use development in Cypress, D'Vine Wine Bar is a hidden gem in the northwest suburbs. D'Vine pours some unusual (but tasty) wines by the glass, and also has an extensive list by the bottle, with fair pricing on both. However, the real surprise is the food. Chef Clarence Alexander dishes up lamb chops, seafood dishes, great pizzas (wild boar sausage with pepperonata, anyone?) and much more. The staff is especially friendly.

LA CARAFE

813 CONGRESS *at Milam*
☎ **(713) 229-9399**
F6

BE CAREFUL WHOM YOU BRING TO LA CARAFE. Between the candlelight, a few glasses of wine and the dark nooks and crannies, you'll inevitably feel the pull of romantic attraction to your companion, no matter your personal history. Speaking of history, La Carafe is housed in a building more than 160 years old and listed on the National Register of Historic Places. Twenty-five years of candle wax formations transition from charcoal gray to white, a visual indicator of the institution of the smoking ban. The bar is beer and wine (and cash) only and sometimes the wine is a little warm, but we don't mind. A seat on the second-floor balcony gazes out over the most beautiful twinkling horizon and downtown at twilight.

PLONK BEER & WINE BISTRO

1214 W. 43RD *at Ella*
☎ **(713) 290-1070**
plonkbistro.com
E5

GARDEN OAKS IS FAST BECOMING THE PLACE to be for good food and drink. Intimate spots like Plonk that are favorites among the locals and manage to produce a high-quality product without losing their homespun charm are more and more common in this part of town. Wander up the bar to place your order. There may be some misses on the menu but the burger piled high with caramelized onions and the muffaletta are spot on. Owner Scott Miller was once the wine director at Pappas Bros. Steakhouse, so while cheap glasses of wine abound, if you move up the price ladder just a little, you'll find some truly interesting options to explore. It's not a very romantic venue, with eclectic decorative choices and the football game on TV, but you have

WINE & SPIRITS

The burger at Plonk

the capacity to make of it what you will just like everybody else.

SIMONE ON SUNSET
2418 SUNSET
between Kirby & Greenbriar
☎ **(713) 636-3033**
simoneonsunset.com

MALL, EFFORTLESSLY URBANE SIMONE BOASTS polished concrete floors and exposed filament light bulbs that make this wine bar's interior both sophisticated and cozy, but on nice nights the brick-paved patio is where people gather. A mix of older couples from the West U mansions nearby and a well-dressed happy-hour crowd descend for Thursday's $15 steak night. Two pages of wines are supplemented by a serviceable cocktail menu and dozens of beers by the bottle. The selection

won't inspire a true oenophile, but there are enough good choices to satisfy most.

SONOMA RETAIL WINE BAR & RESTAURANT
2720 RICHMOND *west of Kirby*
☎ **(713) 526-9463**
sonomahouston.com

HIS COMFORTABLE WINE BAR IS A GREAT CHOICE for a glass of wine and late-night bite, such as sliders, Caprese salad, cheese and meat platters and hand-tossed thin-crust pizza. (By the way, on Thursday, that pizza is half price.) Unlike many of Houston's drinking spots, the atmosphere is quiet, and you can sit outside on a crisp evening for conversation. Be sure to try the house sangria in the summer; it has a cult following.

Daily happy hour 3 to 7 pm always has something on offer. *Note:* A second Sonoma at 801 Studewood in The Heights is already on the drawing board and should be ready in the first half of 2012.

THE TASTING ROOM

1101-18 UPTOWN PARK
at S. Post Oak Blvd.
☎ **(713) 993-9800**
multiple locations
tastingroomwines.com

 D6

 ROM THE SAME OWNERS AS MAX'S WINE DIVE, branches of this sleek, airy wine bar have extended to three neighborhoods across Houston. .The CityCentre location is by far the biggest, clocking in at 11,000 square feet with an open kitchen, several bars and a wrap-around patio. The food at each is well regarded and TTR is especially renowned for its thin crust pizza (possibly because it came free with a bottle purchase for a time at the River Oaks location). Nowadays, the locally sourced cheese plate is a good bet, and the wine selection is meticulous, even if the pretty young things who drink here occasionally have other things on their minds. A fourth Tasting Room is in the works for Kingwood.

VINE WINE ROOM

12420 MEMORIAL
west of Gessner
☎ **(713) 463-8463**
vinewineroom.com

C6

ROPRIETOR JOE PIPPEY MAKES FRIENDS OF HIS customers with his personal easy-going amiability and his public-pleasing fine taste in wine. This is, literally, the coolest wine bar in Houston—the temperature inside is set to baby the stock—so our host has several shawls on hand should a bare-shouldered lady's teeth start clacking. There are about 200 wines from small and unique estates around the world to buy by the bottle. Per glass the wine choices run from $5 to $36, and the imported beer goes for $5. Inside the setting is Old World charm, with antiques and artwork to accentuate the style. Outside you can participate in the "Pairings on the Patio" event every Tuesday, with wine, pizza and live jazz, 6 to 9 pm, $20 per person.

WINE & SPIRITS

{ *Wine–Related* }

NOS CAVES VIN
2501 WROXTON
between Morningside & Kirby
☎ **(713) 524-2554**
noscavesvin.com

SERIOUS WINE COLLEC-
TORS WHO BUY CASES
at a time often need a safe, temperature-controlled place to rest
and age their wines. That is the
mission of Nos Caves Vin, a private,
members-only wine venue in Rice
Village. It's a beautiful little facility that not only provides custom
lockers, 24/7 security and refrig-
eration, but also has a private
lounge that members may use for
entertaining, even hosting a wine
dinner for up to 24 guests. Imagine serving your own wine in your
own luxury wine-storage facility at
your next board meeting.

VINTNERS OWN
3482 W. 12TH *west of Ella*
☎ **(713) 880-3794**
vintnersown.com

HOW MUCH INTO THE
WINE-MAKING PRO-
cess do you want to get? Want to
start with the crush? Serious wine-
lovers can come to Vintner's Own
for the specialized custom crush
facility that focuses on small-lot
barrel production. You choose how
much or how little you want to
be involved in the crushing,
blending, aging, bottling and
labeling process. The grapes are
shipped from California, and you'll
make a barrel (about 24 cases).
Your wine stays in the barrel in
the Vintners Own warehouse for
aging, but you can visit and taste
as often as you like. When it's time
to bottle, design your label, too.
Note: Some Houston restaurants

Wine barrels in Vintners Own

have begun bottling their own house wines here.

WATER 2 WINE

3331 WESTPARK
just west of Buffalo Speedway
☎ **(713) 662-9463**
water2wine.com

IF YOU LIKE FRAME-IT-YOURSELF SHOPS AND The Mad Potter, you'll love this place. This "custom winery" is an actual wine-making operation that invites customers to blend their own wines and design their own labels. Everything can be tasted, so you are able to find just the right balance of fruit and acid to suit yourself. The staff experts will help you through the whole process, and you are welcome to bring in your own food and make a party of it. (Sounds like a fun bachelorette party, no?) They have all kinds of related activities, too, such as movie nights, chair massages, wine-and-food pairings and book-signings.

{ *Winery* }

HAAK VINEYARDS WINERY

6310 AVENUE T
1.8 miles south of Hwy 6, Santa Fe
☎ **(409) 925-1401**
haakwine.com
SOUTHEAST OF

LOCATED JUST 10 MILES FROM THE GULF OF Mexico, this three-acre vineyard comes with a 11,000 square-foot, gray stone winery where scores of events take place—some on a grand scale, like their Greek Festival, their sumptuous feast nights and their summer concert series, and some on a more casual note, like the pruning day that's paired with an oyster fry or tapas served with toe-tapping music. A dream brought to fruition by owners Raymond and Gladys Haak, the vineyard started in 1969 when Raymond began experimenting with grape varietals that might grow well in our humid coastal Texas climate. They have had particular success with the lesser-known hybrid, Blanc du Bois, and today they produce several styles from this grape. Summer and winter hours for tours and tastings differ, so check times on the website.

WINE & SPIRITS

RESTAURANTS

As you use this book, you will discover intriguing food markets, perhaps snack on something you've never eaten before or finally join friends for a round of longnecks at that icehouse you've driven past a thousand times. But only now, in this outsized chapter, do we approach mealtime. Houston's restaurant scene is ready for its close-up.

So just how spirited is the local restaurant scene?

The office where this book was edited is in an older Houston neighborhood inside Loop 610. Within five miles are first-rate French, Vietnamese, pan-Latin American, Thai, Belgian, Spanish, Cuban, Chinese, Jewish deli, Moroccan, Japanese, Mexican, Italian, Greek, English pub food, "head-to-tail" cooking and American cuisine of every variety, including barbecue, Gulf Coast seafood, burgers, health food, soul food and big-ticket steaks. Even as this book was being readied for the printer, several more "important" restaurants were coming online. (Yes, we've included them.)

More than 380 restaurants are included in this chapter and are listed in alphabetical order. Use the indexes to narrow your search by location, type of cuisine and special features.

As you will notice, this guidebook does not score restaurants with a numeric or letter grade. We think the simplified shorthand of scoring shortchanges both restaurants and diners. Restaurants do not operate in a clinical vacuum, and every meal is a little different. What we've tried to do is give you a summary of our experiences. If a place is included in the book, you may assume there are reasons we find it worthy, even if a few blemishes give character to the overall quality.

So please be seated, pick up a fork and get ready to dig in. ★

KEY TO PRICES		
Y = CHEAP	YY = MODERATE	YYY = EXPENSIVE

X *17

1117 PRAIRIE at San Jacinto,
in the Alden Hotel
☎ **(832) 200-8888**
17food.com
🍴 **F6**

SINCE ITS LAUNCH IN 2004, ALDEN HOTEL has been home to one of the most beautiful modern dining rooms in Houston, with red brocade walls, white wingback dining chairs and glimmering chandeliers. It's the perfect backdrop for an elegant meal but small enough to take the edge off its formality. In recent years, TV monitors have been added to allow for business meetings. The hotel has changed management and chefs many times since its inception; it even changed ownership in 2010. So *17 has had a challenge gaining traction in this food-besotted city. David Coffman (he's spent time at Voice, Rainbow Lodge and Benjy's) is running the kitchen as of August 2011. The menu plays it safe, with crab cakes, Gulf Coast snapper, strip steak and pork tenderloin, along with some of the enduring favorites of earlier chefs (e.g. English pea and ricotta ravioli). The lunch menu has a good-value-deal "Sam Saddle Bag" for $17. It includes your choice from three entrees, plus soup, salad and dessert.

III FORKS

1201 SAN JACINTO
at Dallas, in the
Houston Pavilions
☎ **(713) 658-9457**
3forks.com
🍴 **F6**

TEXAS MAY KNOW ITS STEAK, BUT DALLAS knows its steakhouses. So by the time this Big D restaurant made its way down south, Houstonians couldn't have been more excited. The dining room itself is breathtaking, full of white wood paneling and brass bead chandeliers. Order the bone-in ribeye but save room for the bread pudding, which gets rave reviews. The wine selection is particularly noteworthy, with more than 1,500 bottles housed in a temperature-controlled glass cellar. All in all, it's a restaurant well-suited to its downtown location: plenty of private rooms for business events, impeccable service and refined Texas fare for client meetings, and a weekday happy hour for those who want to soak in the surroundings while sampling bar bites and martinis with a bit of a discount.

RESTAURANTS

✗ 51 FIFTEEN

. . . .

5115 WESTHEIMER *inside Saks Fifth Avenue, in The Galleria*
☎ **(713) 963-8067**
51fifteen.com

🍴 **D6**

I F YOU WERE EVER TO SIT DOWN TO DINNER INSIDE A flute of Champagne, it would look a lot like this: All gold, taupe and rich, dark brownish yellows. The mobiles and undulating artwork at the back of the restaurant even suggest Champagne bubbles. But maybe that's just our imagination working overtime after a glass or three of bubbly. This is the old Ruggles Grille 5115, originally launched by Ruggles' chef/owner Bruce Molzan back in the 1990s. (Frédéric Perrier also put in time here as chef.) It remains a favorite, if somewhat secret, spot for a ladies lunch (we love the pianist) while doing heavy-duty Galleria shopping. But it's also lovely at dinner, with a sexy vibe. The menu, by chef Pedro Silva, reworks many familiar options: lamb chops, bacon-wrapped filet, salads, ceviche, pasta, seafood bisque. Not earth-shaking, but nicely done. Plans call for a balcony dining area to be built out over the valet parking area in early 2012.

✗ 59 DINER

. . . .

3801 FARNHAM *between S. Shepherd & Greenbriar*
☎ **(713) 523-2333**
multiple locations
59diner.com

 E7

F ROM THE ICONS OF THE EISENHOWER YEARS TO the blue-plate specials, everything under the purview of your vinyl booth is exactly what you'd expect of a traditional American diner (except for the free WiFi). Waitresses with old-school sass sling milkshakes at the soda counter and a jukebox awaits near the entrance. Breakfasts of eggs, pork chops and biscuits draw huge weekend crowds of families, and sloppy burgers fuel revelers and students 24 hours a day with the exception of the Missouri City location, which closes at midnight. There are some lighter options on the menu, such as egg white omelets, but the kitchen is really best at the unhealthy stuff—the curly fries are habit-forming.

100% TAQUITO

......

3245 SOUTHWEST FWY.
at Buffalo Speedway
☎ **(713) 665-2900**
100taquito.com
🍴 **E7**

THE QUESTION OF WHY A DECORATIVE GREEN taxicab is parked in the middle of this quirky strip center Mexican joint remains unanswered. But whereas 100% Taquito fails to conjure up the authenticity or festivity of an outdoor Mexican market (as intended), it does succeed in having air conditioning and no flies. Messy street food items, including two-bite tacos and *elotes* of corn, crema, queso fresco and chile are served a la carte. A hefty *torta de tinga* of spicy brisket piled high with chopped lettuce, onion and avocado makes an inexpensive lunch and, on a summer day, ideal with one the fruity *aguas frescas*. For the adults, margaritas are available by the pitcher and for the tykes, a kiddo taco menu.

A MOVEABLE FEAST

9341 KATY FWY. *at Echo Lane*
☎ **(713) 365-0368**
amoveablefeast.com
🍴 **C6**

IT'S A GOOD NAME, FOR THIS HEALTH-FOOD-STORE-and-restaurant hybrid really has moved around since its founding in Montrose back in 1971 by John Fain. Trans-fat-free snacks, vitamins and supplements, aromatherapy and teas line the shelves of the store half, while Suzanne Fain's rustic counter-service restaurant serves nothing fried. The entrees display a smattering of Mediterranean, Asian and Southwestern influences—try the quesadillas—and some are gluten-free or vegan. In the grab-and-go section of the store, several of the kitchen's creations, such as chicken salad and tabouli, are sold in bulk, as are frozen organic meats. Nothing here will absolutely change your life, but having a quick, no-hassle resource for simple, good-for-you eats will very likely improve it. After shopping, make time for a smoothie on the front patio behind the landscaped screen of plants and wildflowers.

ABDALLAH'S BAKERY

......

3939 HILLCROFT
at Westpark
☎ **(713) 952-4747**
🍴 **C7**

THE PITA BREAD AT THIS HIDDEN GEM IS SO GOOD, it's sold citywide at Whole Foods and other Middle Eastern spots. There are a few very good reasons to buy it straight from the source, though, starting with the daily steam-table lunch buffet.

RESTAURANTS

The modest but cozy dining room begins to fill up around 11:30 am every weekday with people seeking tender shawarma sandwiches, zesty tabouli and *kibbe* pie. The other lure is the array of Lebanese baked goods. Trays of barely sweet baklava, delicate bird's nests and shortbread cookies filled with nuts are a huge hit at the office or parties. And while you're availing the bakery, you might as well stock up on bulgur, hookah supplies and the owner's Old Country olive oil available in the grocery section.

AL'S QUICK STOP

. . . .

2002 WAUGH *at Welch*
☎ (713) 522-5170
🍴 E6

I T MAY NOT BE MUCH TO LOOK AT, BUT THIS CONvenience store is known throughout Montrose for its falafel. Open until 3 am on weekends for the hungry revelers coming out of Rud-

Exterior of Al's Quick Stop

yard's Pub next door, the deli produces an interesting assortment of tacos and Middle Eastern cuisine. And while the falafel is what headlines, for our money (and once at the cash register, not much of it at that), we'll pick the gyro sandwich any day. A mountain of tender, moist lamb is piled high on soft pita and crowned with the requisite tomatoes, onion and tzatziki. Bonus points if you talk to Al, who is a total sweetheart.

ALADDIN

. . . .

912 WESTHEIMER *at Montrose*
☎ (713) 942-2321
aladdinhouston.com
🍴 E6

I T MUST BE ROUGH SITTING IN THE SHADOW OF all the big names along Restaurant Row, but Aladdin holds its own with piping hot pita and mountains of fresh Lebanese food served cafeteria-style. The lentil salad is a favorite, as is the vegetarian sandwich popping with every available non-meat side. Moist chicken shawarma and tender lamb shank are both excellent choices, but if you're having trouble deciding, combination platters allow for broad sampling. Mediterranean touches such as ornate chandeliers and feet-high glass vases spiff up the informal dining room and diners are welcome to linger over some baklava and any wine or beer they've brought

BYOB SPOTS

BYOB—BRING YOUR OWN BOTTLE—GETS US ESPECIALLY EXCITED. IT COULD BE THE anticipated savings, the feeling of complete control or just the alcohol-induced buzz talking. These restaurants offer the best food to pair with that bottle.

HUYNH
912 ST. EMANUEL
☎ **(713) 224-8964**

The dumpy strip mall exterior belies the coziness inside this cafe, which serves some of the best Vietnamese food in town. Start with the pulled duck salad.

DRY CREEK
544 YALE
☎ **(713) 426-2313**

Between the avocado-coiffed burgers and sleepy patio, the only thing necessary to complete the idyllic picture is a frosty beer. In this dry area of The Heights, you'll need to bring your own.

LA GUADALUPANA
2109 DUNLAVY
☎ **(713) 522-2301**

This Mexican cafe excels at a number of things, including hearty Mexican breakfasts and enchiladas verdes. Feel free to bring your own beer, which is handily sold at the adjacent convenience store.

LATIN BITES
1302 NANCE
☎ **(713) 229-8369**

This tiny Peruvian restaurant manages to pull off a lot given its limited confines: cheerful energy, a modern interior and superlative eats. Go with the theme and bring a South American wine.

HIMALAYA
6652 SOUTHWEST FWY.
☎ **(713) 532-2837**

Long heralded as one of the best Pakistani restaurants in town, Himalaya draws huge crowds. Come with beer or wine and order the biryani.

TWO SAINTS
12460 MEMORIAL
☎ **(713) 465-8967**

The Memorial area's neighborhood restaurant is both romantic and accommodating. Forgot your wine? Lucky that owner Joe Rippey also runs the Vine Wine Room in the same strip center.

with no extra corkage fee. This little gem may be unassuming, but should never be underestimated.

ALEXANDER THE GREAT

· · · · · · · · · · · · · · · ·

3055 SAGE *at Hidalgo*
☎ **(713) 622-2778**
alexanderthegreat.cc
🍴 **D7**

THE EXTERIOR SIGNAGE IS A BIT KITSCHY, BUT looks can be deceiving. What actually awaits indoors is a rather upscale Greek dining experience. Meals begin with feta cheese and olives and end with sludgy Greek coffee. In between there are excellent moussaka and gyro plates to be had and seafood dishes that shine. Whole grilled snapper served bone-in and octopus are extremely well done. As in Europe, the pace might be slower, but there will plenty to enjoy in exchange for patience. Live music and belly dancers on the stage area make for a lively weekend evening.

ALTO PIZZERIA

2800 KIRBY *at Westheimer (upstairs), in West Ave*
☎ **(713) 386-6460**
avaalto.com/alto

ALTO PIZZERIA (UP-STAIRS) AND AVA Kitchen (downstairs) are linked not only by their West Ave location and ownership (the Schiller-Del Grande restaurant group) but also share a sort of fictitious back-story on their *joint* website. This is chef Robert Del Grande's interpretation of a pizza joint, though clearly joint is the wrong noun. Here are striking design-it-up interiors and high-end tabletop superfluities. Thin-crust pizza is presented chicly on your table on tall metal stands along with little porcelain bowls of spices like crushed red pepper. A dozen or so 10-inch pies fill the menu. A few include Italian sausage with broccoli rabe and garlic, little neck clam, and a terrific gorgonzola, mission fig, arugula and bacon number, which are cooked in a massive wood-burning pizza oven. On our visit, the kitchen was still struggling to get the crust cracker-crisp. Nice cocktail menu and lots of big TVs for watching sports.

AMAZON GRILL

· · · · · · · · · · · · · · · ·

5114 KIRBY
between Hwy. 59 & Bissonnet
☎ **(713) 522-5888**
cordua.com

RESTAURATEUR MICHAEL CORDÚA (OF AMÉRICAS, Churrascos and Artista fame) took his pan-Latin cuisine and went fast-casual with Amazon Grill. The self-service cafe strikes a chord with West U families looking for a crowd pleaser, and it has the noise levels to match. Take solace in a happy hour mojito while tucking into a savory empanada. The puffy chicken tacos are simultaneously light and rich with sour cream, and the tabletop s'mores are always a hit with the kids and kids at heart. Plantain chips and chimichurri sauce, a Cordúa restaurant staple, are available at a bar for the taking and practically ensure oversnacking before the meal arrives. Breakfast is served Saturday and Sunday mornings.

to expose Houston to South American flavors and in recent years has groomed his son David (who won the 2010 Houston Culinary Award for Up-and-Coming Chef of the Year) to take the reins. But as the multi-concept empire has expanded, there have been a few hiccups, such as delayed openings. Still, when things are on point, a flight of ceviches, crawfish taquitos, tender churrasco and a slice of milky *tres leches* cake are an essential Houston meal. Don't forget the tender-sweet *maduros* (fried plantains), either.

AMÉRICAS

. . . .

2040 W. GRAY *at S. Shepherd*
☎ **(832) 200-1492**
multiple locations
cordua.com
🍴 **E6**

⌐T WOULD BE SAFE TO SAY THAT THE CORDÚA FAMILY doesn't believe in minimalism. The dining rooms of these Houston landmark restaurants are a fantasia of color and swooping surrealist shapes. (The much-loved Post Oak Blvd. original, alas, recently closed when its lease expired in August 2011.) The menus, originally built around the signature churrasco—a butterflied and grilled beef tenderloin with chimichurri sauce—exhibit bold pan-American flavors. Way back when, chef/owner/impresario Michael Cordúa was the first

AMERIGO'S GRILLE

. . . .

25250 GROGANS PARK
off Sawdust, The Woodlands
☎ **(281) 362-0808**
amerigos.com
🍴 NORTH OF **D1** 🚗

⌐HE NORTHERN ITALIAN CUISINE SERVED UP at this family-run steakhouse by executive chef Arturo Osorio commands a fervent following. When owners Casey and Nancy Kosh opened the doors in 1994, Amerigo's was the most elegant restaurant in The Woodlands. Today, a host of similarly upscale restaurants (e.g. Américas, Jasper's) round out what is now an expansive adult playground, but everything at this local business feels a bit more authentic. Near-perfect dishes include the beef carpaccio, *pappardelle capesante* with sea scallops and tomato mint sauce, and even the occasional game dishes. You basically can't go wrong ordering seafood, and Amerigo's wine list was named one of the best in the world by *Wine Spectator* in 2007 and 2008. The bar up front, complete with piano, is often packed with happy-hour enthusiasts.

ANDALUCIA TAPAS

....

1201 SAN JACINTO
at Dallas, in the Houston Pavilions
☎ **(832) 319-6673**
andaluciatapas.com
🍴 **F6**

THIS ISN'T RESTAURATEUR YOUSSEF NAFAA'S FIRST round with Spanish food (he founded Mi Luna in Rice Village before selling it a few years ago), and everything about this tapas joint shouts authentic *taverna*. Dim lighting, wrought iron details and a matador mural set the mood for the array of hot and cold small plates from sweet piquillo peppers stuffed with salmon tartar to *tortilla española* (something like an omelet) and larger entrees including paella and lamb tangine. If you've never tried fresh sardines, these deboned, grilled versions sprinkled with onions, peppers and garlic are the exactly right place to start. Late weekend hours and

flamenco dancers complete the European dining experience.

ANTICA OSTERIA

....

2311 BISSONNET *at Greenbriar*
☎ **(713) 521-1155**
anticarestaurant.com
🍴 **E7**

SOME SAY THAT COMING UP WITH ROMANTIC SURprises is difficult, but the existence of flowers and restaurants like Antica Osteria render moot such complaints. Dining areas ramble throughout this old house, both upstairs and downstairs, and between the candlelight and gracious service a meal here will help set the mood. The menu is more Italian than Italian-American—a couple of the highlights are the braised lamb shank and sautéed chicken breast with prosciutto in wine sauce. There are always a few nightly specials that are likely to entice, plus classics such as spaghetti alla carbonara, veal Milanese and eggplant parmesan. The food may not be bold, but the whole package is easy to fall into and very appealing. The wine list is not extensive, but there are some well-priced bottles. Dinner only.

ARCO SEAFOOD
9896 BELLAIRE BLVD.
at Beltway 8
☎ **(713) 774-2888**
🍴 **B7**

OUT OF THE INNUMER-ABLE RESTAURANTS TO choose from in Chinatown, Arco distinguishes itself by offering a slightly more upscale setting and tanks of live seafood. It's nothing you have to dress up for, but upholstered seating and an opulent chandelier provide a feast-worthy setting for groups large and small (but usually large). And a feast it will be, with a menu of Cantonese classics: clay pots, lobster with chives and garlic, and walnut shrimp. Fresh—as in just-swimming-before-hitting-the-wok fresh—seafood like razor clam and grouper that you can personally select from the tanks is considerably more expensive than the other menu items, but you could not pick a more impressive entree.

ARCODORO
5000 WESTHEIMER
at Post Oak Blvd.
☎ **(713) 621-6888**
arcodoro.com
🍴 **D6**

THE LONG-NEGLECTED ITALIAN OUTPOST OF Sardinia gets all the loving attention it deserves in this pretty setting—all earthy tones of gold, brown and russet—popular with a well-attired Galleria crowd. Owned by Efisio and Lori Farris (who also have Arcodoro & Pomodoro in Dallas), Arcodoro emphasizes grilled meat and seafood, simply prepared. Excellent dishes such as linguini *su Barchile* with fresh clams, skinless tomatoes and *bottarga* (salted, pressed and dried gray mullet roe) and handmade semolina dumplings tossed with braised lamb ragu aren't readily found anywhere else in the city. The simple pizzas are also excellent, and brunch is especially fun with its unique Sardinian touches. Efisio's 2007 cookbook, *Sweet Myrtle and Bitter Honey: The Mediterranean Flavors of Sardinia,* is one of the standards on this lesser-known cuisine. The couple also operates Gourmet Sardinia, which sells Sardinian food products (e.g. olive oil, rice, honey) online.

ARGENTINA CAFE
3055 SAGE *at Hildago*
☎ **(713) 622-8877**
🍴 **D7**

SINCE OPENING A LITTLE OVER A YEAR AGO, THIS cozy family-run spot near the Galleria has grown popular with transplanted Argentines and area office workers who swarm the counter for quick and satisfying workday lunch. The concise menu offers a few different sandwiches, salads and hot plates plus an array of house-made pastries. The most popular items

RESTAURANTS

include full-blown steaks gilded with fried eggs, a spicy *choripan* (sausage sandwich) with perfectly snappy casing and beef empanadas with robust and generously portioned but not overwhelming filling. Excellent coffee is an unexpected perk, all the better to wash down a *dulce de leche* cake roll gleaming with caramel.

ARIRANG KOREAN RESTAURANT

· · · · · · · · · · · · · · ·

9715 BELLAIRE BLVD.
at Corporate
☎ **(713) 988-2088**
🍴 **B7**

HE MAJOR DOWNSIDE TO THIS KOREAN BARbecue restaurant is that you'll leave smelling of smoked meats. White people's problems, right? During dinner hours, tabletop grills are lit and diners can choose from a menu of marinated meats including sliced beef, pork ribs and prawns, so it's always more fun to bring a large group to experiment with more items. The crispy, pizzasized seafood pancake is an excellent way to fuel up before the work of cooking begins. Table grilling isn't an option during lunch, but the bento boxes are both delicious and inexpensive. Unlike every other Korean restaurant in the area, side dishes, or *banchan*, such as kimchee are not complimentary, and that's a sticking point with a lot of patrons.

ARMANDOS

· · · · · · · · · · · · · · ·

2630 WESTHEIMER *at Kirby*
☎ **(713) 520-1738**
armandoshouston.com
🍴 **E6**

OU MIGHT SAY THAT IT'S UNNATURAL TO serve Tex-Mex on white tablecloths, but a very successful restaurateur would disagree with you. The original Armandos was a notable fixture on Houston's culinary landscape back in the 1980s with the eponymous owner Armando Palacios serving up "River Oaks Tex-Mex," as it was described affectionately by some and dismissively by others. Since its 2007 reopening in plush digs after a seven-year hiatus, Armandos has begun to cultivate a younger and trendier crowd, complete with the occasional celebrity cameo. Notable menu items include the *queso flameado* (a sizzling plate of melted cheese), fajitas, chicken mole and, of course, the legendarily potent margaritas. Despite the plush surroundings, the food is simply and authentically done, and that's a good thing.

ARPI'S PHOENICIA DELI

·················

12151 WESTHEIMER
west of S. Kirkwood
☎ **(281) 558-0416**
phoenicia-deli.com

🍴 **B7**

ARPI IS THE MATRIARCH OF THE TCHOLAKIAN family, owners of both massive Phoenicia Market locations. And even though the cuisine is over-seen by her knowledgeable eyes, the dining experience is more modern and sleek than it is any-thing "like grandma used to make." The massive cafeteria set-up is all gleaming surfaces and, like the supermarket next door, offers a pure smorgasbord of edible delight. Point and choose whatever small teardrop-shaped dishes of salads and dips (such as *muhammarra*, the roasted red pepper, pomegran-ate and walnut dip) from the line-up you like or opt for a heartier entrees such as the Armenian-style lamb shank or chicken shawarma. Choosing the cardamom Turkish coffee gelato from among the many enticing flavors will be the last of many difficult decisions you'll have to make before digging in.

ARTISTA

·················

800 BAGBY
at Rusk, in the Hobby Center
☎ **(713) 278-4782**
cordua.com

🍴 **F6**

IT MAKES SENSE THAT A CORDÚA RESTAURANT would be installed inside the Hobby Center of Performing Arts, as the restaurateur always likes to make an elegant statement. The interior of Artista is, like all Cordúa establishments, a visual stunner. Seating is luxurious, and the giant windows show off a truly spectacular view of downtown, exceeded only by the panorama from the patio. The menu retains some of the South American favor-ites from the other restaurants, such as the churrasco steak with yuca, crawfish taquitos and *tres leches*, but also has more global touches, including a miso soup with avocado and lamb osso buco with saffron risotto. Service at lunch can sometimes be iffy, but the staff is skilled at timing your dinner before a theater performance so you don't miss the curtain.

RESTAURANTS

ARTURO BOADA CUISINE

....

6510 DEL MONTE *at S. Voss*
☎ **(713) 782-3011**
boadacuisine.com

🍴 **D6**

FTER A DRAMATIC DEPARTURE FROM Arturo's Uptown in early 2011, chef Arturo Boada wasted no time opening the doors to his newest venture. Fans of his previous work will find similar appeal in the menu here: the same wood-oven pizzas, pastas and steaks are served in a casual, bistro setting complete with saffron-colored walls and white tablecloths. Tapas-style dishes including tuna tartare and ceviche are welcome additions. The *camarones hennessy en hamaca* (sautéed shrimp with hearts of palm, tomato and cilantro in a thick soy-ginger sauce over a bed of plantains) demonstrates the chef's playful side, and the crème brulée is an especially nice rendition. The simple, satisfying cooking is perfectly suited to the expectations of the locals who crave it regularly, and so the neighborhood vibe runs strong.

ARTURO'S UPTOWN ITALIANO

....

1180-1 UPTOWN PARK
at Post Oak Blvd.
☎ **(713) 621-1180**
arturosuptown.com

🍴 **D6**

INCE NAMESAKE AND FORMER EXECUTIVE chef Arturo Boada left to open his own restaurant, the kitchen, led by Seles Romero, has sailed on valiantly without him. The product remains largely unchanged, but then again, the menu was never one to break new ground. Almost everyone starts with the fried calamari, and the yellow bell pepper soup is a fun and unusual appetizer. From there, the veal scaloppini and ravioli stuffed with chicken and mushrooms and topped with white wine sauce and jumbo lump crabmeat make for classic Italian-American cuisine served with enthusiasm and hospitality. The wine list is made even better by knowledgeable waiters who offer spot-on suggestions. On a pretty day, Arturo's outdoors really does seem like a slice of Tuscany, with the stately porch perfect for a languorous afternoon of wine and conversation.

AU PETIT PARIS

. . . .

2048 COLQUITT
just east of S. Shepherd
☎ **(713) 524-7070**
aupetitparisrestaurant.com

🍴 **E7**

I N MANY WAYS, DINING AT THIS LITTLE FRENCH RES-taurant, founded in 2007 by Eric Legros and Dominique Bocquier, is approximate to dining in France itself, although you are in a Montrose bungalow. The technical skill of the kitchen can occasionally be breathtaking, and likewise the presentation. High points on the ambitious menu include the house-made foie gras terrine, slow-braised beef cheeks and any of the well-prepared fish entrees. The lunch selection is pared down, with a range of tempting salads and sandwiches such as salad Lyon-naise topped with a poached egg and bacon and a classic croque madame. Burnished wood in a warren of intimate dining rooms, blurry Impressionistic cityscapes, shiny copper pots and colorful posters advertising absinthe are the final touches to a restaurant that is just oh-so-French.

AURA

. . . .

3340 FM 1092 *between Cartwright and Hwy. 6, Missouri City*
☎ **(281) 403-2872**
aura-restaurant.com

🍴 **A9** 🚗

W E'RE NOT IN THE SUBURBS ANY-more, Toto. Well, we are, but the pedigreed French fare at this Missouri City mom-and-pop would have you think otherwise. Frédéric Perrier, who used to helm Cafe Perrier and functioned as opening chef at Ruggles Grille 5115, and wife Michelle have fashioned a modest but modern cafe with an ambitious menu. Do try the sandwich de St. Jacques, a take on surf and turf with meltingly soft short ribs and diver scallops. Buffalo bison sliders are the glaringly American note, but they're given such a refined treatment, with seared foie gras and a brioche bun, that they're signature Perrier. If that's not tempting enough, there's also a $50 three-course prix fixe that allows the chef to send out whatever his mood dictates. Service has been known to lag, but that shouldn't dissuade you from staying for one of the excellent desserts.

RESTAURANTS

AVA KITCHEN & WHISKEY BAR

....

2800 KIRBY _at Westheimer,_
in West Ave
☎ **(713) 386-6460**
avaalto.com/ava

🍴🍷 **E6**

AVALON DINER

....

2417 WESTHEIMER
just east of Kirby
☎ **(713) 527-8900**
multiple locations
avalondiner.com

🍴 **E6**

THERE IS A BIT OF FINE PRINT TO READ BEFORE visiting this restaurant: Although it is from acclaimed chef of the Southwest Robert Del Grande, it isn't exactly chef-driven or food-focused. A gorgeous contemporary interior features ceiling-high windows—gazing out on Kirby, you'll feel like you're dining on a boulevard in a European capital—gunmetal grays and bold reds. Look up at the stunning Möbius-strip light fixtures. The setting is almost as fabulous as the glitzy crowd that gathers here for chic cocktails and the much-touted whiskey. The truth is, this Spanish-French-Italian-American restaurant is a scene. But the menu isn't a total wash. Though some consistency would be nice, the squid stuffed with shrimp sausage and blanketed in Mediterranean _salsa verde_ is a brilliant concept, and the skirt steak with herb butter is a worthwhile indulgence. Pastry chef Ryan Savoie's desserts, however, get unswerving full marks and the caramel-drenched tarte tatin alone warrants a visit.

A DINER WITHOUT HISTORY ISN'T A DINER; it's just a restaurant with bad service. But Avalon Drug Co. has been around since 1938, and despite the fact that it has moved from its original drug-store location, it's still the real deal. Poached eggs and grits, fluffy pancakes, pecan waffles and a tart greeting from the ageless waitresses who staff the counter have made this River Oaks institution a longtime favorite among the city's movers and shakers, many of whom grew up at the Avalon and today use it as a second office. Blue-plate specials such as roasted turkey with dressing and chicken pot pie with corn-

Inside Avalon Diner

bread muffins round out the nourishing greasy-spoon pickings. The River Oaks location on Westheimer has the *best* made-to-order chocolate milkshakes.

AZUMA

. . . .

5600 KIRBY *south of Sunset*
☎ **(713) 432-9649**
multiple locations
azumarestaurant.com
🍴 **E**

INCE THE ORIGINAL KIRBY LOCATION OF AZUMA opened, regard for it has seen its highs and lows, and owners (and brothers) Yun and Hubert Cheng have opened two more Azuma locations, plus Soma on Washington Avenue and critical darling Kata Robata up the street on Kirby. But they've recently turned their attention back to their flagship restaurant and it shows. Executive chef Masa Wakatsuki, who trained at a culinary school in Osaka, Japan, is simultaneously returning to more traditional Japanese roots while aiming for innovative highs. Call a day in advance for the special live lobster sashimi or come by for tender, crispy pork yakitori. If you can afford it, order the chef's-pick *omakase* to experience a dazzling array of the day's best. Sugar Land's Azuma on the Lake location couldn't be more scenic.

BABA YEGA

. . . .

2607 GRANT *at Missouri*
☎ **(713) 522-0042**
babayega.com
🍴 **E6**

OMETIMES YOU DON'T WANT TO EAT YOUR burger inside; you just have to eat it outside. And the lush back patio of this neighborhood favorite, adjacent to fragrant gardens and a decorative pond, is the perfect spot to do so. Of course, many of the burgers served at this bohemian landmark are of the veggie variety. Meat-free fare is the draw here, with faux bacon sandwiches and veggie loaf just two highlights of almost a full page of vegetarian options. There are also plenty of items for omnivores as well, because Baba Yega is, above all, a crowd pleaser. Friendly service and quirky indoor decor complete the picture at this eclectic eatery ideal for its eclectic clientele.

BACKSTREET CAFE

. . . .

1103 S. SHEPHERD
between W. Dallas & W. Gray
☎ **(713) 521-2239**
backstreetcafe.net
🍴 **E6**

RACY VAUGHT'S LONG-POPULAR RESTAURANT —it celebrated 28 years in 2011—

RESTAURANTS

is hardly French, to be sure. Chef Hugo Ortega's menu is filled with items like jalapeño fettuccine, shrimp cheesecake and red corn chicken enchiladas. But by serving creative and well-made takes on up-market comfort food, coupled with somm Sean Beck's intelligent wine list, all in a refined but relaxing setting, Backstreet Cafe is a classic Houston bistro. Another highpoint: Chef Ortega is one of the few chefs in town to put extra effort into creating an appealing vegetarian and vegan menu. Every summer, for example, there is a special menu devoted entirely to tomatoes. Ease into Saturday or Sunday brunch with a watermelon mimosa on the plant-edged brick patio with the splashing fountain, located just on the cusp of River Oaks. We'll have the crispy lobster sandwich on toasted brioche, please.

BANANA LEAF

. . . .

9889 BELLAIRE BLVD.
at Beltway 8
☎ **(713) 771-8118**
bananaleafhouston.com
 B7

ANANA LEAF IS THE MOST PROMINENT MA-laysian restaurant in Houston (although we'd be hard pressed to name a single other one). That isn't meant to be a backhanded compliment; staples of the cuisine, such as *roti canai* (the fluffy flatbread accompanied by curry dipping sauce) and sambal shrimp, are extremely well done. Other must-tries include the Hainanese chicken and brothy rice, laksa noodle soup and the whole flounder wrapped in banana leaf. The semi-open kitchen allows a view of the cooks as they toss roti. Alongside the learning experience of adventuring into new terrain like crispy pork intestine, a trip to this bamboo-lined restaurant is always a full entertainment experience. Just beware of the long wait for a table during peak hours and plan accordingly.

BARBECUE INN

. . . .

116 W. CROSSTIMBERS *at Yale*
☎ **(713) 695-8112**
🍴 **E5**

MORE APPROPRIATE NAME FOR THIS RES-taurant would be Fried Shrimp Inn. A ridiculous name to be sure, but that's the dish to order rather than the barbecue, which is decidedly subpar. This Southern diner has been open since 1946, and its birth date is evident the moment you walk in the door. (Peruse the framed newspaper clippings and old menus while you wait for a table.) The waitresses call everyone "honey," and everyone sits down to a basket of crackers with butter. Many a loyal Houstonian first started dining here as a kid and continue to do so today,

DINER BREAKFASTS

IT'S IMPORTANT TO START THE DAY OFF RIGHT, WHETHER THAT MEANS A POWER JAM WITH THE shower radio or a plate of sausage and eggs. These no-frills breakfasts will fuel you up without a drop of béchamel in sight.

TRIPLE A
2526 AIRLINE
☎ (713) 861-3422

Never veering off course from the Southern diner classics, Triple A always seems to have what we're hungry for, plus waitresses who still call you "darlin.'"

TEL-WINK GRILL
4318 TELEPHONE
☎ (713) 644-4933

Like all good diner breakfasts, this one is served all day. This landmark gem fries up a hefty plate of hash browns and eggs for a blue-collar crowd.

AVENUE GRILL
1017 HOUSTON
☎ (713) 228-5138

The best seat at this historic greasy spoon is without a doubt at the counter. Rub elbows with an eclectic mix of Houstonians chowing down on bacon and omelets.

AVALON DINER
2417 WESTHEIMER
☎ (713) 527-8900

Avalon is no longer in its original 1938 location, but the drugstore counter meals are largely the same. Wash down your pecan waffles with one of the delicious milkshakes for a true breakfast of champions.

DOT COFFEE SHOP
7006 GULF FWY.
☎ (713) 644-7669

This diner may no longer be independently owned, but it's still got the heaping piles of fluffy biscuits and beautiful Art Deco elements in the dining room.

BUFFALO GRILLE
4080 BISSONNET
☎ (713) 661-3663

Families flock here for a casual, down-home breakfast. The apple pancakes are as big as hubcaps, and the pork chop special is an equally generous affair.

seeking house-made tartar sauce for the fried shrimp, plus piping hot fried chicken and chicken-fried steak. Fried entrees are cooked to order, so be prepared for a slightly longer wait. It's one you won't mind.

✕THE BARBED ROSE STEAKHOUSE AND SEAFOOD CO.

. . . .

113 EAST SEALY
east of N. Gordon, Alvin
☎ **(281) 585-2277**
barbedrose.com
🍴 SOUTH OF **G9** 🚗

E'D BE LESS THAN HONEST IF WE didn't admit to a streak of skepticism when this Alvin restaurant first opened. It seemed way too ambitious for such a podunk town. We're happy to have been wrong: This is one place that lives up to its hype, with terrific food and friendly, casual hospitality. Chef Jason Chaney (previously at The Houstonian, Commander's Palace in New Orleans and Hilton Americas) and his team practice from-scratch cooking and make artisanal-handcrafted foodstuffs such as sausages, cheeses and breads. Oh, and there are the big Texas-style steaks, of course. Among our favorite dishes: country-fried oysters, BBQ shrimp and grits, Wagyu hot dog on a pretzel bun and smoked pepper steak.

Owner Joe Schneider has plans to add a freestanding bakery and butcher shop in the cluster of old buildings he has bought up in downtown Alvin.

BARNABY'S CAFE

. . . .

604 FAIRVIEW
east of Montrose
☎ **(713) 522-0106**
multiple locations
barnabyscafe.com
🍴 **E6**

HIS CALIFORNIA-TINGED COMFORT FOOD CAFE has spread its wings throughout River Oaks and Montrose (and now even to Tanglewood) but the original hippie location on Fairview with its rainbow chimney remains the most loyal to its funky roots. While each has its own vibe, menu items like a slightly sweet Doctor Gale's meatloaf and a range of hamburgers, sandwiches and salads (try the Lebanese *fattoush* salad) make them all popular neighborhood spots for easy, crowd-pleasing dinners. The restaurant is well known for its uncommonly friendly service, especially at breakfast-only Baby Barnaby's, where you're sure to be called "sweetheart" with every coffee refill. Speaking of breakfast, that's where Barnaby's truly shines. Though every location serves breakfast on weekends, Baby is the only to serve it exclusively and every day. On weekends the line for green eggs and chicken apple sausage can be an hour long.

BB'S CAFE

. . . .

2710 MONTROSE
just north of Westheimer
☎ **(713) 524-4499**
multiple locations
bbscafe.com

🍴 **E6**

THIS REVIEW MIGHT GET A LITTLE VULGAR, BUT given the extremely drippy nature of some of the sandwiches at this Cajun spot, it can hardly be avoided. Both the Heights and the Montrose locations are perfectly poised to serve the post-last-call crowds, and the grub at the downtown spot is good for those who only wish they'd been drinking. The expected fried seafood po'boys and red beans and rice are menu staples, but a few

BB's specialties are the work of an especially sick and indulgent mind. The Tex-Cajun Virgin, for example, is owner Brooks Bassler's version of Canadian poutine, with shoe-string fries sopping up queso, gravy and roast beef.

✓BEAVER'S ICE HOUSE

. . . .

2310 DECATUR
south of Washington
☎ **(713) 864-2328**
beavershouston.com

🍴 **E6**

BEAVER'S DRAWS STRONG REACTIONS. SOME PEOPLE can't get enough of executive chef Jonathan Jones' silly, sometimes crass, style and elevated Texas grub, while others gripe about the misplaced hype. The setting is casual, but the food is chef-driven with a local ingredient focus. Barbecue anchors the menu and oth-

RESTAURANTS

Outdoor seating at Beaver's

{ 143 }

er indulgences, including braised beef tacos and bacon-wrapped meatloaf, round out the meat worship. Meat is *big* here, including the Spam-Wow Sandwich, which features two eggs, several slices of bacon, nearly a quarter pound of pulled pork and half a loaf of Spam. Exceptions to the meaty stuff include exemplary fried pickles and some surprising vegan items, such as the Beaver Nut Burger. The excellence of the bar program, on the other hand, requires no debate and even if the food doesn't draw you in, there is every reason to come for some of the best cocktails in town. A classic gin gimlet will be perfectly made, but for some fun, try the Smoky Julep with house maple-smoked rye whiskey.

BECKS PRIME

. . . .

2902 KIRBY *between W. Alabama & Westheimer*
☎ **(713) 524-7085**
multiple locations
becksprime.com
🍴 **E6**

IKE ANYTHING ELSE THAT'S BEEN AROUND long enough, this Houston burger chain draws as much criticism as it does praise. The praise: Real, ground-in-house burgers and real fries—none of it prefab, all of it fairly exemplary in the field. For the more highbrow, there's even

ahi tuna salad and center cut filet on the menu (although why you'd want to eat a steak in surroundings that are still of the fast-food aesthetic is beyond us). The criticism: A meal of a burger and fries pushes (and often exceeds) $10, and that is simply too much for a restaurant that still has a drive-thru. It's all about priorities. *Note:* The Augusta Drive and Memorial Park locations are especially nice for outdoor dining, while the Sportatorium at Memorial City Mall is also a huge sports bar.

BENJY'S

. . . .

2424 DUNSTAN *east of Kirby*
☎ **(713) 522-7602**
multiple locations
benjys.com
🍴 **E7**

Y NOW, WE ALL KNOW NEVER TO JUDGE A book by its cover. Of course, Benjy's has a beautiful cover—the newer Washington location is lush and botanical, and the original Rice Village Benjy's is contemporary and chic—but in the restaurant world that can mean less attention to the food quality. Benjy's excels at both, however, and while the happy hour scene is constantly buzzing with well-dressed 20- and 30-somethings raising decibel levels, things are kicking in the kitchen too. Both executive chef Mike Potowski at Washington and executive chef

Joseph Stayshich on Dunstan have put together modern American menus that are fresh and satisfying. Scallops on forbidden black rice sounds like a familiar dish but the execution keeps things interesting. Three-course meals of comfort food every Sunday add to the fun. Note: Benjy's Washington location won *My Table*'s Houston Culinary Award for Best New Restaurant in 2009.

BERRYHILL BAJA GRILL

· · · · · · · · · · · · · · · ·

2639 REVERE at *Westheimer*
☎ **(713) 526-8080**
multiple locations
berryhillbajagrill.com

🍴 **E6**

A LL ACROSS HOUSTON, BERRYHILL IS PRACtically synonymous with fish taco. Before it found its widespread fame, it was but a tiny, blue-collar taqueria with a wonderfully hideous Elvis painting and a roll of paper towels on each table. The original location on Revere still retains most of that charm, but now people are chowing down on catfish tacos as far out as Sugar Land. With chicken tenders for the kids and a Baja Burger now added to the menu, the owners are hardly keeping things authentic. Yet the fish tacos, whether fried or grilled, heaped with cilantro and the thinnest red cabbage,

are still fantastic, and the tamales— the chain was originally called Berryhill Tamales—hold their own as well. The Montrose location is (in)famous for raucous patio parties, which can be heard in passing cars on the street.

THE BIRD & THE BEAR

· · · · · · · · · · · · · · · ·

2810 WESTHEIMER *west of Kirby*

🍴 **E6**

L LOUISE ADAMS JONES, PROPRIETRESS OF Ouisie's Table, is opening this new restaurant in Fall 2011. In announcing the new venture, Jones said The Bird & The Bear will give her much-appreciated eclectic tendencies even more freedom. It's expected to be more casual, with lots of Southern flair in both menu and décor. Long-time Ouisie's Table GM Wafi Dinari is managing partner.

BISTRO ALEX

· · · · · · · · · · · · · · · ·

800 W. SAM HOUSTON PKWY.
in the Hotel Sorella
☎ **(713) 827-3545**
bistroalex.com

🍴 **B6**

T HE NEWEST REST-AURANT FROM ALEX Brennan-Martin and the main in-house restaurant in the Hotel Sorella is a credit to the family name. The small but gorgeous dining room is done up in mirrors and panels of wavy rough-cut mesquite. Rolando Soza mans the kitchen stove, putting out the famous Brennan's turtle soup alongside his own versions of Tex-Creole cuisine. House charcuterie is a must-try, as is molasses-painted quail. Brunch is a lavish affair. After a turn at the make-your-own Bloody Mary Bar, the duck debris and butternut waffle, a tasso ham flatbread and heavenly white chocolate bread pudding, you'll be nearly unable to walk to your car. There is some closer seating by the hotel pool if you need to rest a while.

BISTRO DES AMIS

. . . .

2347 UNIVERSITY *at Morningside*
☎ **(713) 349-8441**
bistrodesamis.com
🍴 **E7**

THE MODEST AND QUAINT SETTING OF THIS SMALL cafe is exactly the kind of dining room in which one should eat rustic French fare, at which owners Odile de Maindreville and Bernard Cuillier excel. Well-executed Gallic classics such as garlic butter escargot, vegetable potage redolent with thyme and perfectly braised beef bourguignon make up a large part of the menu, but are served up without any of the pretense or formality sometimes associated with French restaurants. For lunch, there are lighter options, including quiche, crêpes and open-faced sandwiches. Set two-course lunches and dinners Monday through Thursday allow diners to save a little money. Don't pass up on the baked goods, which are made in-house.

BISTRO LE CEP

. . . .

11112 WESTHEIMER *at Wilcrest*
☎ **(713) 783-3985**
bistro-lecep.com
🍴 **B7**

HERE YOU CAN ENJOY SUCH TIME-TESTED and rich dishes as duck pâté, poisson meunière, coq au vin, pot-roasted rabbit, steak au poivre, pan-roasted calf liver with apples, onions and bacon, plus tarte tatin and strawberries Romanoff. Oh, a French farmhouse, you say? Close enough.

Inside Bistro Le Cep

Aging pine floors and a rooster theme set a decidedly rustic tone well matched to the hearty cuisine. This homespun number is actually an offshoot of chef/restaurateur Joe Mannke's much-admired Rotisserie for Beef & Bird (now long closed) and quite different from its grand progenitor. The wine list is moderately priced, offering most bottles below $50, as well as a remarkable 50-plus selections by the glass that are served in generous 8-ounce pours.

BISTRO PROVENCE

. . . .

13616 MEMORIAL
between Wilcrest & Kirkwood
☎ **(713) 827-8008**
bistroprovence.us
🍴 **B6**

IN A CULINARY WORLD WHERE "FUSION" IS THE point of so many menus, it's refreshing to find a kitchen that glorifies tradition. Old-fashioned, homey Provençal meals start with *fougasse* (a crusty twist of warm bread) and olive oil, then proceed to such resolutely old-time bistro dishes as *confit de lapin* (rabbit confit with prunes), pig's feet in white wine, mustard, garlic and parsley sauce, grilled sausages and *boeuf cocotte* (beef stew with black olives). There are more than a few places in Houston that call themselves bistros. *This* is a bistro.

Between the open kitchen and wood-beamed ceiling, the dining room is warm and inviting, if a bit snug. And even though people hover around the front door waiting for a table, owners Jean-Philippe and Genevieve Guy seem able to move everybody along with a minimum of discontent.

BLOCK 7 WINE COMPANY

. . . .

720 SHEPHERD
south of Washington
☎ **(713) 572-2565**
block7wineco.com
🍴 **E5**

THERE ARE MANY WINE BARS IN THIS CITY, BUT very few exhibit the knowledge and passion that the folks at Block 7 do. As if that wasn't enough, bottles are sold at retail prices (the actual retail store adjoins the restaurant-bar), the menu is extremely delicious and well executed—e.g. roasted butternut squash ravioli, roasted chicken—and it's all done in a sleek refurbished appliance store. Just as many people sit down for a full meal as they do to mingle over a glass or two, and it's easy to see why. The smoked pork chop is prepared perfectly and the tangy cauliflower with preserved lemon is our favorite side. Low bottle prices allow oenophiles to experiment with wines that would be out of their price range in another restaurant. Juggling its roles as store, bar and restaurant, Block 7 manages to accomplish all three very well.

BLUE FISH HOUSE

· · · · · · · · · · · · · · · ·

2241 RICHMOND
between Greenbriar & Kirby
☎ **(713) 529-3100**
multiple locations
bluefishhouse.com

🍴 **E7**

HOW AUTHENTIC YOU PREFER YOUR SUSHI is an important metric when considering Blue Fish because while this restaurants puts out some tasty and popular eats, the cuisine is hardly straight Japanese. In fact, most of the menu items tilt Thai, which can lead to some fresh, fun takes like the mango and snow crab roll, if you're amenable to that sort of thing. As for the entrees, the katsu curry with deep-fried pork cutlet and the red curry udon noodles are hearty and satisfying. Though the exterior of the Richmond location reads ramshackle hut, the inside is rather sleek, with leather banquettes mostly populated by younger couples. The newer Sugar Land and The Woodlands locations are even more chic and extremely popular during happy hour.

BLUE NILE ETHIOPIAN RESTAURANT

· · · · · · · · · · · · · · · ·

9400 RICHMOND
between Fondren & S. Gessner
☎ **(713) 782-6882**
bluenilerestaurant.com

🍴 **C7**

WASHING YOUR HANDS IS ALWAYS a good idea, but it's definitely a must before entering Blue Nile, where eating with your hands is part of the fun. Use spongy *injera*, the traditional Ethiopian flatbread, to scoop up spicy, bite-size portions of *yemissir wot* (a red lentil stew) and *gomen besiga* (a mixture of collard greens and cubed beef). Vegetarian items make up a large portion of the menu and a number of combination platters piled high with all manner of legumes are perfect for sharing. The dining room is equipped with white tablecloths and cloth napkins, so don't come expecting a hole in the wall. Another unique draw is the traditional coffee service, in which coffee is served with frankincense, popcorn and a great deal of gravity.

BODARD BISTRO

. . . .

9140 BELLAIRE BLVD.
at Ranchester
☎ **(713) 541-5999**
🍴 **C7**

FIRST THE CONS: ONCE YOU FIND BODARD lurking in a corner of one of the older strip malls in Chinatown you'll have to contend with parking. The two-hour time limit on the already largely unavailable spots is closely patrolled by the police at the station next door. And certain items are not worth your time: noodle soups such as pho or *bo bun hue* are better elsewhere. Truly great, however, are the pork meatball spring rolls with an added crunch from the addition of wonton crisps, and the turmeric-tinged rice flour pancake stuffed with pork, shrimp and bean sprouts, the latter being an architectural as well as culinary wonder. Those two items alone are worth the visit and can be had for a song.

BODEGAS TACO SHOP

. . . .

1200 BINZ *in Park Plaza Professional Bldg.*
☎ **(713) 528-6102**
bodegastacoshop.com
🍴 **E7**

THE MUSEUM DISTRICT'S ONLY MEXICAN REST-aurant is not what you might expect from the name—it's not in a rustic little bungalow or old convenience store, for example. It's located in a busy medical building. Still, it's a welcome addition to the neighborhood and just a short walk from the museums and Hermann Park. Owners Ryan and Josephine Granger have installed a build-your-own tacos or burritos concept (think Chipotle or Mission Burritos). Meats include fajita beef, spicy ground beef and rotisserie chicken, plus there are 10 house-made salsas. Free WiFi for customers, margaritas and live music on the weekends, too. Open every day for lunch and dinner.

BOHEMEO'S

. . . .

708 TELEPHONE *at S. Lockwood*
☎ **(713) 923-4277**
bohemeos.com
🍴 **F7**

THIS EAST END GEM IS LIKE YOUR HIPPIE younger brother all grown up: After years of marijuana abuse he really learned how to cook. Bohemeo's is housed inside the neon-painted Tlaquepaque Market, and the inside is a small, cozy space scattered with couches and tables occupied by "mobile office" workers, artist types and a downtown lunch contingent. Outside there are still some vagrant cats roaming around the fountain, but inside the healthy food

RESTAURANTS

is well done: Satisfying fish tacos, simple but tasty salads and inexpensive sandwiches round out the menu. Lattes and cappuccinos are made to order as expected, but so are mugs of fresh brewed coffee. At night, Bohemeo's functions more as a bar, with patrons sipping cold beers on the patio during all-Beatles open mic night.

BOILING CRAB

....

8300 W. SAM HOUSTON PKWY. at *Beechnut*
☎ **(281) 988-4750**
theboilingcrab.com

🍴 **B8**

VERY YEAR AS THE CLOUD OF CAJUN spice descends over the city during crawfish season, mudbug fans basically enter a frenzy trying to locate the plumpest, freshest and cheapest per pound offerings across town. Boiling Crab, even with its kitschy nautical theme, is always at the top of the list. This California-based chain was founded by Vietnamese fishermen from Seadrift, Texas, and now enjoys popularity with a wide demographic. People wait in lines for up to two hours for crawfish with Cajun, lemon pepper or garlic butter flavors and a range of heat options (warning: even mild is fiery). Other seafood options include blue crab, snow crab, lobster, shrimp

and Dungeness crab that come either boiled or fried. The major disappointment is that sides like corn and sausage must be ordered as extras.

BOMBAY PIZZA COMPANY

....

914 MAIN at *Walker*
☎ **(713) 654-4444**
bombaypizzaco.com

🍴 **F6**

HE LATEST IN THE LONG LINE OF WACKY culinary pairings that actually work—after French fries and chocolate milkshakes—is Indian food and pizza. Menu items at this downtown pizza joint include the Gateway of India (a thin sesame crust topped with cilantro-mint chutney, tandoori chicken, crabmeat and artichoke hearts) and non-pizza items like curried mashed potatoes and filled *kati* rolls. There really isn't anything not to like about the concept—why wouldn't you enjoy eating any type of savory food piled high on a carbohydrate? It's a favorite stopover among the downtown lunch crowd, and delivery is available within a 10-block radius.

BRANCH WATER TAVERN

....

510 SHEPHERD
south of Washington
☎ **(713) 863-7777**
branchwatertavern.com

🍴 **E6**

ATING AT BRANCH WATER TAVERN IS A culinary experience akin to being warmed by the fire. Gorgeous flocked forest-green wallpaper and exposed brick surround you in this former pool hall while you sup on chef David Grossman's composed comfort food, such as chicken-fried oysters with celery root slaw and Berkshire pork chops with succotash. The Kobe burger has a passionate following and the breakfast sandwich of cheesy, soft-scrambled eggs and thick-cut bacon during Sunday brunch is outstanding. The long wine list is dense with affordable bottles, but BWT specializes in notable and explor-atory American whiskeys. A daily whiskey cocktail is only $3 during happy hour, which also features cheap snacks like duck fat popcorn and reuben sliders that draw good-looking crowds.

BRASIL

....

2604 DUNLAVY *at Westheimer*
☎ **(713) 528-1993**
brasilcafe.net

🍴 **E6**

S MUCH AS EVERYONE LOVES BRASIL, it doesn't always love you back. Between the tree-shaded front and back patios and the roomy, industrial-chic interior, Brasil is definitely the coolest cafe in Houston and the kind of place the city could use more of. Artsy-intellectual types are drawn here and the food, lo and behold, is actually good. Salads and sandwiches get little gourmet touches like roasted beets, pumpkin seeds and jicama, and weekend

Inside Brasil

brunch is swarmed. A full coffee menu is complemented by beer and wine, and movie nights on the patio or live music make Brasil an adorable date spot. But there are consistently never more than five of the homemade chips sent out on your plate. The staff, though not rude, is never friendly, and if a mistake has been made with your order, well, godspeed. And yet, we return; we need this to be good so badly.

BRASSERIE 19

. . . .

1962 W. GRAY *at Driscoll*
☎ **(713) 524-1919**
brasserie19.com
🍴 **E6**

THIS NEWCOMER (MAY 2011) TOOK OVER THE space that used to house Tony Mandola's Gulf Coast Kitchen. New owners Charles Clark and Grant Cooper have replaced the dark, clubby feel of the erstwhile Gulf Coast Kitchen with a simple, bright look of whitewashed walls, globe lighting, marble tables and faux wicker chairs. The atmosphere is brisk and bustling, with a small army of white-shirted, aproned waitstaff that occasionally seem so numerous they get in each other's way. An unavoidable by-product of this popularity, combined with the restaurant's open, undressed design, is a tendency to be noisy, even raucous at times. In its early weeks Brasserie 19 went through two high-profile chefs, and it's taken some time for the kitchen to stabilize. The fare is traditional French-meets-Gulf Coast, and the prices are high. The wine list, by the way, is presented via an iPad

Oysters on ice at Brasserie 19

EATING GREEN

MAYBE ONE DAY ENVIRONMENTALLY RESPONSIBLE DINING WILL SIMPLY BE ASSUMED. But for now, a few local eateries are making that extra effort to be earth friendly.

PAULIE'S
1834 WESTHEIMER
☎ (713) 807-7271

Paul Petronella is taking his parents' business and introducing local produce and meats to the menu. The locally grown (some of it even grown on site) salads are among our favorites.

✗ RUGGLES GREEN
2311 W. ALABAMA
☎ (713) 533-0777

Ruggles is a little green around the seams and by seams we mean hemp empanadas. It's the first (and only) restaurant in Houston that is a three-star Green Restaurant certified by the Green Restaurant Association.

HAVEN
2502 ALGERIAN WAY
☎ (713) 581-6101

Today chef Randy Evans harvested vegetables from his restaurant garden and turned them into a torn-greens salad with fried green tomato croutons. What did you do? One of the most sustainable restaurants in Houston, Haven is a shrine to LEED.

T'AFIA
3701 TRAVIS
☎ (713) 524-6922

Chef-owner Monica Pope was using local produce and talking up Texas wines before anyone knew what the word "locavore" meant.

RADICAL EATS
3903 FULTON
☎ (713) 697-8719

The greatest way to reduce your carbon footprint is to cut out the animal-related products. This vegan cafe serves up vegetable-centric Tex-Mex.

REEF
2600 TRAVIS
☎ (713) 526-8282

Not only is chef Bryan Caswell a co-founder of Foodways Texas, his seafood restaurant is all about locally sourced fish.

brought to your table. Some patrons may find this delightful. Some may consider it one of the seven signs of the Apocalypse. We are left wondering which Houston restaurant will be the first to let diners tweet their orders directly to the chef?

BRASSERIE MAX & JULIE

. . . .

4315 MONTROSE
south of Richmond
☎ **(713) 524-0070**
maxandjulie.net
🍴🍴 **E7**

AFE RABELAIS GOT A YOUNGER SIBLING WHEN owners Laurence and Chris Paul opened this white linen- and lace curtain-bedecked restaurant in lower Montrose. The cooking is hearty and not terribly dissimilar from its predecessor, but it includes more traditional brasserie favorites, such as chilled shellfish platters and *choucroute*, that Alsatian sauerkraut favorite. Other menu possibilities: sautéed sweetbreads, bone-in ribeye, foie gras and cassoulet *Toulousain*. Chris Paul also happens to be a well-informed oenophile and offers an extensive French wine list, including many by-the-glass selections and Champagne splits. The treetop balcony upstairs is the perfect place to enjoy a weekend brunch of crêpes and omelets. Delivering

the check in a beer glass is a nice tip of the hat to brasseries' beginnings as breweries.

BRC GASTROPUB

. . . .

519 SHEPHERD
south of Washington
☎ **(713) 861-2233**
brcgastropub.com
🍴 **E6**

HEN THE COMFORT FOOD TREND BLEW through Houston in 2009, quite a few restaurants popped up offering artery-clogging "gastropub" food. But irreverent BRC (which stands for Big Red Cock, represented by a proud rooster statue out front) has staying power thanks to the strong menu of founding chef Lance Fegen. There's very nearly nothing on the menu that's good for you, from the daily mac 'n' cheese flavor to the "burger bowl" filed under salads. But the blue cheese potato salad and bacon and cheddar biscuits are exceptional, and you can wash away your feelings of shame with a pint from the well-curated craft beer menu. Mondays are an excellent time to drop in because a juicy, thick-cut bacon-topped burger and fries are discounted to $7.

THE BREAKFAST KLUB

. . . .

3711 TRAVIS *at Alabama*
☎ **(713) 528-8561**
thebreakfastklub.com

🍴 **E6**

THE GRUB AT THE BREAKFAST KLUB IS top-notch, but you don't really need to hear it from us. Just look at the line streaming out past the front doors every morning of the week. This soul food spot from owner Marcus Davis is a Houston classic, deeply loved for its fried chicken and waffles and catfish and grits (or "katfish & grits," as it's referred to on the menu). The French toast is some of the best on the planet—we suspect foul play or at least the use of a deep fryer—and while less popular, the lunch plates such as crawfish fettuccine and red beans and rice, wouldn't be a mistake. Arrive earlier in the morning to avoid the crowd. But if you arrive during the rush, take heart in the fact that the line moves quickly, and service is most gracious.

BRENNAN'S OF HOUSTON

. . . .

3300 SMITH *south of Elgin*
☎ **(713) 522-9711**
brennanshouston.com

🍴 **E7** ✍

THIS BELOVED HOUSTON RESTAURANT, first opened in 1967, took a long sabbatical after 2008's Hurricane Ike when it was badly damaged by fire. When Brennan's finally reopened on Fat Tuesday 2010, the public could not have been hap-

The Breakfast Klub's fried chicken and waffles

pier to discover that the rebuild had only made Brennan's more beautiful and the kitchen under chef Danny Trace is still producing the same award-winning Texas-accented neo-Creole cuisine. The restaurant is justly famous for a few things: the turtle soup with a splash of sherry and bananas Foster flambéed tableside. Long-time New Orleans classics continue to evolve a bit due to the availability of fresh fish and game. Meanwhile, beef and poultry also make an appearance, though seafood seems to always reign. Add to that some of the city's best shrimp and grits and gumbo, and brunch on the charming patio, and it is easy to understand why Brennan's is an institution and the grand quintessence of all the elegance of the Old South.

BRENNER'S

. . . .

10911 KATY FWY.
between Brittmoore & Wilcrest
☎ **(713) 465-2901**
multiple locations
brennerssteakhouse.com
🍴 **B6**

THE STORY OF BRENNER'S IS VERY HOUSTON-specific, in a way. The rustic original Brenner's first opened in 1936 and served only USDA prime beef from early on. When Mrs. Lorene Brenner retired in 2002, Tilman Fertitta's Landry's Restaurant Group purchased the landmark. But from there the tale is less typically Houston. Instead of razing the decrepit building, Fertitta invested more than $1 million in refurbishing it and brought it back to life. Besides its prime beef, Brenner's was known for crispy German-style potatoes and wonderful blue-cheese dressing, both of which are still on the menu. Steaks are wet-aged and served in a puddle of *jus*, which makes for a very moist and tender mouthful. The second location, Brenner's on the Bayou, was once the original Rainbow Lodge. Again, the Landry's group rescued a landmark. (Donnette Hansen took her Rainbow Lodge to a new location on Ella, where it's all good.) Brenner's on the Bayou, as it's known, is breathtakingly scenic with meticulous landscaping and a view of the water, although the attached Blue Bar does its best to drown out nature sounds with techno beats.

BROKEN SPOKE CAFE

. . . .

1809 WASHINGTON *at Sabine*
☎ **(713) 863-7029**
brokenspokecafe.com
🍴 **E6**

AS YOU DRIVE EAST TOWARDS THE MORE tattered end of Washington, you could easily drive right past the

Exterior of the Broken Spoke

BROWN BAG DELI

. . . .

2036 WESTHEIMER
just east of S. Shepherd
☎ **(713) 807-9191**
multiple locations
thebrownbagdeli.net

🍴 **E6**

squat building that houses the Broken Spoke. But inside these sunshine yellow walls and a wonky, half-finished ceiling mural is one of the city's primary purveyors of *moules frites*, or steamed mussels served with fries. There are a number of preparations from curry to Roquefort mussels, but the *marinière* version prepared with white wine and butter rules. A number of other Brussels classics are also available, starting with Chimay and ending with the *croque madame*. While the restaurant is well known for its mussels, it also deserves some kind of city-bestowed medal for its apple crêpe—more of a thick, caramelized pancake than apple taco. It's the stuff sugar plum dreams are made of.

THIS HOUSTON-GROWN MINI-CHAIN FROM THE brain behind Barnaby's is simple but good at what it does. Place your order by marking down preferences on the eponymous brown bag checklist with standout offerings such as pimiento cheese, hummus and jalapeño cheddar bread. Basics like chicken salad are fresh and tasty and worthwhile because the support ingredients—snappy, naturally tinted pickles and soft, slightly sweet bread—are good. Sides include dilled red potato salad, a soup of the day and coleslaw. The exceptional chocolate chip cookies are a secret too well kept, being hefty but tender on the inside with melted chips. Spread the word.

RESTAURANTS

THE BROWNSTONE CAFE & CRÊPERIE

....

2736 VIRGINIA
just south of Westheimer
☎ **(713) 446-7690**
cafebrownstone.com
🍴 **E6**

THE BROWNSTONE IS BACK—IT OPENED WITH a new look and menu in early July 2011—and it's not anything like you remember from Beau Theriot's previous incarnation. This cafe/crêperie is casual, with mismatched furniture put together in a way that seems both careless and charming (We love the faux-croc banquettes!) The very French menu by partner/chef Olivier Ciesielski (formerly exec chef at Tony's) includes both sweet and savory crêpes, quiche, hot and cold sandwiches, omelets and pizza. There's a full bar, and the patio is being rehabilitated. Prices are very reasonable.

BUBBA'S TEXAS BURGER SHACK

....

5230 WESTPARK *at S. Rice*
☎ **(713) 661-1622**
bubbastexasburgershack.com
🍴 **D7**

ALL FIRST-TIME VISITORS TO THIS CITY, please head to Bubba's. Its location under a freeway is so very Houston and its weathered shack and super friendly (if slightly gnarled) staff is so very Texas. The burgers themselves—there's a choice of beef and bison but the leaner buffalo is the specialty—are not the best the city has to offer, but tasty enough, especially when combined with the atmosphere. Our tip is to get the double patty, which makes for a juicier burger experience. Fries are, sadly, not on the menu but in their place are Zapp's chips and baked potatoes and Shiner and Saint Arnold beer to wash it all down. Pick a seat inside, surrounded by various "Get ye to Texas" memorabilia, or grab a picnic table outside for the breeze and incomparable view of aggressive Houston driving.

THE BUFFALO GRILLE

....

4080 BISSONNET *at Weslayan*
☎ **(713) 661-3663**
multiple locations
thebuffalogrille.com
🍴 **D7**

IT'S NOT QUITE BIG ENOUGH TO SHATTER WORLD RECORDS—that would be unreasonable—but the pancakes at this rustic neighborhood favorite are at least hubcapsized. The medley of American and Tex-Mex grub here is well loved by families and an elderly contingent, the line to the cash register often snaking out the door on weekend mornings. The aforementioned pancakes, studded with bananas, apples or chocolate chips at your request, and the ludicrously portioned pork chop and egg plate are an ideal way to start your day. Pecan-crusted chicken and a side of jalapeño cornbread makes for a hearty Southern meal, all the better in the pure Texas surroundings, complete with self-serve soda and wooden tables. Breakfast is served every day.

BURGER GUYS

. . . .

12225 WESTHEIMER
west of S. Kirkwood
☎ **(281) 497-4897**
theburgerguys.com
🍴 **B7**

IT'S DIFFICULT FOR A RESTAURANT TO DISTINGUISH itself in the Houston burger wars, but the brains behind the Burgers Guys pulled out all the stops. Each burger is named and themed after a city, so the Houston gets onion bacon jam and Fancy Lawnmower Ale mustard while the Saigon is topped with pâté, pickled carrots and jalapeño. Fat-marbled Texas Akaushi beef ensures dripping down the forearms, and everything is sourced with exacting foodie nerdiness. The pâté is the same used at local Vietnamese joint Thien An and the soda fountain is stocked with real sugar (*not* HFCS) drinks. The milkshakes are also worth making room for, especially the caramel or "Ten Cup" chocolate. It's all very

extravagant and you'll more than likely need to be rolled out of the dining room—but don't pretend like you don't like that.

BURNS BAR-B-Q

. . . .

7117 N. SHEPHERD
just South of W. Little York
☎ **(713) 692-2800**
multiple locations
🍴 **E4**

THE ORIGINAL BURNS BAR-B-Q WAS A DILAPIDATED frame house on DePriest street in Acres Homes. There was no eating-in; it was strictly carry-out, although you could sit just outside at a picnic table near fly-infested garbage cans. It was a hard-core old-school smokehouse that had a moment of national fame when Anthony Bourdain did a Travel Channel feature on it several years ago. In 2010, following the death of clan patriarch Roy Burns Sr., the place was closed down by the health department. A few weeks later, it reopened at this new address in a much-improved building under the direction of Burns' daughter Kathy Braden. The specialty, as at the original, is African-American East Texas barbecue (as opposed to German-Czech Central Texas barbecue), with an emphasis on brisket, pork ribs and, especially, hot links. Shortly before we finished this book in 2011, Burns' son (and

Braden's brother) Gary Burns opened his own Burns Old-Fashioned Pit Bar-B-Q at 6314 Antoine between W. Tidwell and W. Little York.

CADILLAC BAR

. . . .

1802 SHEPHERD
just south of I-10
☎ **(713) 862-2020**
multiple locations
cadillacbar.com
🍴 **E6**

SOME THINGS, HAPPILY, NEVER CHANGE. AT THE Cadillac Bar (inspired by the Nuevo Laredo original) that list includes awesome margaritas and the noise of very happy dudes and dudettes reverberating off the walls. The Tex-Mex food is above average, with good mesquite-roasted pork carnitas, smoked pork ribs, bacon-wrapped stuffed shrimp and milk-fed cabrito (baby goat) among the traditional offerings. Even after all these years, it remains a lively spot

Exterior of the Cadillac Bar

to take good-sport friends who can handle the sensory overload. In a hurry? Check out the tortas-to-go menu; pre-order by phone or online for pick-up. Also, note: Breakfast is served on Saturday, brunch on Sunday.

√CAFE BENEDICTE

. . . .

15455 MEMORIAL
between Eldridge & Hwy. 6
☎ **(281) 558-6607**
cafebenedicte.com
🍴 **B6**

SPORTING A GREEK-SPANISH-FRENCH-North-African menu, Cafe Benedicte features broadly Mediterranean items bolstered by some all-American beef-hearty dishes to appeal to the globe-trotting energy-industry workers of west Memorial. It appears right on the mark for the area, as the bright blue dining room is usually packed during peak hours. In an airy and comfortable setting looking out onto a green belt, dine on mussels, foie gras, paella, entree-sized salads, gyros, a popular lasagna and grilled items such as lamb and Chilean sea bass. A well-attended brunch is also thrown into the mix.

FOOD FESTIVALS

ARK YOUR CALENDARS FOR THESE ANNUAL CELEBRATIONS IN HOUSTON FOOD AND culture. Don't forget to wear comfortable shoes and, preferably, an elastic waistband.

GREEK FESTIVAL
first week in October
greekfestival.org
Every year the delicious aroma of gyros descends upon Montrose signaling the arrival of Greek Fest. Eating is pretty much the main activity. We recommend the fried honey balls.

CAESAR SALAD COMPETITION
mid-October
caesarsaladcompetition houston.com
My Table's own annual toss-up brings together 20 of Houston's finest restaurants to compete in four categories. Our all-time favorite entry: Caesar salad lollipops.

GRAND WINE & FOOD AFFAIR
last week in April
thegrandwineand foodaffair.com
HEB presents five days of wine luncheons and cooking demos. GW&FA culminates in the Grand Tasting, featuring bites from big-name Houston chefs and wines from around the world.

RODEO UNCORKED: BEST BITES COMPETITION
mid-February
hlsr.com/events/wine/ best-bites.aspx
A ticket grants access to hundreds of stands filling up the ground floor of Reliant Stadium, each showcasing its culinary wares. Hundreds of wines are available to wash it all down.

CHINESE NEW YEAR
early February
All of Chinatown comes out to celebrate the Lunar New Year with dragon dances, community programs and, of course, tons of food.

SOS/TASTE OF THE NATION
early May
houstontaste.org/ Houston
Some 50-plus Houston restaurants offer bites and wineries send out wine for this annual fund-raiser extravaganza held on the meadow of The Houstonian Hotel. Live music and silent auction, too.

Pizza dough is rolled out at Phoenicia Specialty Foods

• CAFE CASPIAN

. . . .

12126 WESTHEIMER
between S. Kirkwood &
S. Dairy Ashford
☎ **(281) 493-4000**
cafecaspian.com
🍴 **B7**

THE WARM *TAFTOON* FLAT-BREAD THAT ARRIVES AT your table with a plate of feta and herbs is the first sign that the meal ahead will be a good one. From there, enjoy all the Persian classics from ground beef *kubideh* kebabs to saffron-tinged lamb shank. *Fesenjan*, a chicken, pomegranate and walnut stew, is also a high point. Almost every dish is served with long-grain basmati rice, but variations include rice mixed with barberries or sour cherries and pistachios. Portions are quite large and leftovers are inevitable, but you can always soothe your overextended gut with some hot tea while quietly admiring the ceilings painted light blue and white to mimic clouds.

CAFE CHINO

. . . .

3285 SOUTHWEST FWY. *at Edloe*
☎ **(713) 524-4433**
cafechinohouston.com
🍴 **D7**

THIS IS A VERY INNER LOOP CHINESE RESTAU-rant. Sesame chicken, wonton soup and fried cheese wontons are served up in a well-appointed dining room. Blueberry bread pudding has nabbed a spot on the menu, and there's even a full bar. At lunch, inexpensive specials draw nearby Greenway Plaza workers, and at night families order takeout or come in for some slightly more upscale offerings such as five-spice quail and Chilean sea bass with Asian pesto. Owners May and Eddie Chan have been pleasing local palates since 1988—the restaurant was originally located not too far away in Rice Village.

• CAFE EXPRESS

. . . .

1422 W. GRAY *west of Waugh*
☎ **(713) 522-3100**
multiple locations
cafe-express.com
🍴 **E6**

"PALATABLE" AND "FAST CASUAL" ARE NOT mutually exclusive terms, it turns out. These yuppie, counter-service operations originally, from the Schiller Del Grande Restaurant Group, were briefly owned by Wendy's before being rescued by the original owners. After some dark days, Cafe Express is again one of the city's better choices for a quick and easy meal. Each location comes with a full bar and patio and begins serving food (under the direction of chef Greg Martin) at breakfast time. Pleasing entrees include the pasta amore tossed with olive tap-enade, roasted garlic and sun-dried tomatoes, photogenic sandwiches and the generously portioned chicken Caesar salad. We are especially fond of the lavish condiment bar, the "oasis table," where diners help themselves to salad toppings, dressings, grated cheese, olives, cornichons, sun-dried tomatoes, breadsticks and more.

CAFE LILI

. . . .

5757 WESTHEIMER
west of Chimney Rock
☎ **(713) 952-6969**
cafelili.com
🍴 **D7**

EVERYONE IS ALWAYS TALKING ABOUT HOW good for you the Mediterranean diet is. But then you go and eat an entire sampler plate of hummus, kibbe and spinach pie, and it's not so healthful anymore. That's just how tasty all the offerings are at this Lebanese mom-and-pop—you are driven to hoover. Expect the standards: shawarma sandwiches, fried cauliflower and falafel. The lentil, rice and caramelized onion dish *moujadara* is especially addictive. The line to order at the counter during lunchtime is long with Galleria-area office workers, but if you have time to spare, the cups of Turkish coffee are bottomless.

CAFE MOUSTACHE

. . . .

507 WESTHEIMER *west of Taft*
☎ **(713) 524-1000**
cafemoustache.com
🍴 **E6**

WHEN THIS RESTAURANT OPENED in Montrose in 2010, moustaches were at the peak of their tight-pants hipster fame. We can probably assume, however, that that's just lucky coincidence as owner Manfred Jachmich had opened a Cafe Moustache once before in the 1980s. This, then, is a bit of a rerun, not cutting edge. The food served on the deep blue tablecloths is more broadly Continental than French and a bit reminiscent of days gone by as well: Butter-slicked trout meunière is garnished with old-fashioned parsley sprigs, and romano-crusted chicken breast seems similarly out of step with modern culinary times. There's still a fairly loyal River Oaks crowd that leaves the keys of their various luxury vehicles to the valet for happy hour; this seems to be the best time to come in for truffle fries and a few glasses of well-chosen wine.

CAFE PIQUET

. . . .

5757 BISSONNET
west of Chimney Rock
☎ **(713) 664-1031**
cafepiquet.net

🍴 **C7**

THE CLOSEST WE'VE ACTUALLY BEEN TO Cuba is through the transportive effects of *Dirty Dancing 2: Havana Nights,* but, from what we understand, Cafe Piquet is very authentic. The restaurant is clean and modern with walls covered in photos of Cuban movie stars. Well-made Cuban favorites include *yuca frita* (lightly fried yuca), *papa rellenas* (balls of mashed potatoes stuffed with ground meat, then fried), empanadas, *picadillo* (seasoned ground beef), *masitas fritas* (fried pork chunks), *ropa vieja* (shredded seasoned beef) and *pargo entero frito* (whole fried snapper). Obviously the deep-fat fryer sees a lot of action, but our bodies also receive a lot of action from fried foods, so we approve. Check the website for special events, such as salsa classes.

CAFE PITA+

. . . .

10890 WESTHEIMER
at Lakeside Estates Dr.
☎ **(713) 953-7237**
cafepita.weebly.com

🍴 **B7** 🖐

SUPERLATIVE *CEVAPCICI* IS ONLY THE BEGINNING at this modest Bosnian mom-and-pop on the west side. What is *cevapcici*? Why, it's the Bosnian national dish, a seasoned hamburger made to look like a hot dog and served with fluffy *lepinja* bread and *ajvar,* a bright red bell pepper and eggplant spread. Beyond that, the menu offers earthy bean soup, a generous *mezze* plate of cured meats and pickled vegetables, fried anchovies, stuffed cabbage, lamb shank and, interestingly enough, some popular pizza—all hearty fare that tastes as if your Bosnian mama made it. Despite the slightly shabby appearance of the place, cornered in a typical West Houston strip mall, Café Pita+ is a food lover's paradise. The offerings never fail to pique curiosity and are unique to this one restaurant in all of Houston. Note: The name of the restaurant is left over from an earlier tenant.

RESTAURANTS

CAFE RABELAIS

· · · · · · · · · · · · · · · · ·

2442 TIMES *between Kirby & Morningside*
☎ **(713) 520-8841**
caferabelais.com

🍴 **E7**

FOR A COUPLE IN LOVE, EVEN MUNDANE HAND-holding at the grocery store can be romantic. But for a night out, this is the restaurant you want to inch closer in, over candlelight and Provençal-inspired fare. Quaint and often boisterous (despite its small size), this French restaurant from Laurence and Chris Paul serves robust peasant-style dishes along-side a surprisingly lengthy and award-winning wine list. Although the mood is refined, there's noth-ing uppity about the food. Try the lamb sausage and fries or the steamed mussels, considered some of the best in town. The chalk-board menu also lists *boudin noir* with apples, veal sweetbreads and duck breast with strawberry bal-samic reduction. Rabelais is a favor-ite among the neighborhood, and though they're probably not all there for the romance, patrons always return for a consistently good meal.

CAFE RED ONION

· · · · · · · · · · · · · · · · ·

3910 KIRBY *at Richmond*
☎ **(713) 807-1122**
multiple locations
caferedonion.com

🍴 **E7**

OWNER RAFAEL GALINDO NOW HAS A STRING OF popular Latin American restaurants, most emphasizing seafood. The names vary—e.g. Cafe Red Onion, Red Onion Seafood & Mas, Red Onion Mexican Grill—but if it con-tains the words "Red Onion," it belongs with the group. The food can loosely be characterized as Lat-in fusion. Galindo himself is from Honduras, but Mexico is obviously a part of the mix here, as is Peru and the Caribbean. All of the res-taurants provide a festive atmo-sphere and good values. Among the attractions: pineapple salsa with the tortilla chips to begin, "Latino sushi" creations and 100-plus kinds of tequila.

CAFE TH

· · · · · · · · · · · · · · · · ·

2108 PEASE *at St. Emanuel*
☎ **(713) 225-4766**
cafeth.com

🍴 **F6**

THE OLD, RUN-DOWN THIEM HUNG BAKERY took a dip in the fountain of youth and came out as a revived Cafe TH. Minh Nguyen, a former patron of the bakery, took matters into his own hands and purchased the restaurant, recipes and all, and reinvented the place as a cool, modern cafe. The menu has more than doubled in size, and rich broth soups are the centerpieces. It's obvious after a sip of pho that time went into stewing the beef bones, and the pork meatball soup is thick, fatty and spiked with tomato. Though most dishes are exceptional in their authenticity, there is also the surprising addition of vegan pho and superior vegan curry. Normal business hours are limited, but Nguyen will occasionally open the doors on a weeknight for a "chef's choice" prix fixe of sorts.

CALLIOPE'S PO-BOY

....

2130 JEFFERSON *at Hutchins*
☎ **(713) 222-8333**
calliopespoboy.com
🍴 **F6**

HOUSTON HAS AUTHENTIC FOOD FROM PLACES a lot farther away than New Orleans, but Louisiana natives just never seem satisfied with our city's Cajun offerings. To those complainers, we suggest Calliope's, the source for the best po'boys Houston has to offer. The roast beef is slathered in gravy, and the oyster version also gets suitably juicy. Aside from

sandwiches, crawfish are available seasonally and there are also an intriguing number of Asian side dishes. As it turns out, owner Lisa Carnley is a Vietnamese American from New Orleans. Depending on how you calculate these things, this makes her very qualified to produce excellent po'boys as well as shrimp fried rice. Judging by taste, we'd have to agree.

CANDELARI'S PIZZERIA

....

6002 WASHINGTON
east of Westcott
☎ **(832) 200-1474**
multiple locations
candelaris.com
🍴 **E6**

THE "KING OF SAUSAGE" HAS COME A LONG WAY from its founding by two Bellaire High grads. Now this pizzeria has five locations across the city and is well known for its Italian sausage (although the traditional pork version is worlds away from the low-fat turkey jalapeño, in our opinion). These are neighborhood joints with the typical drawbacks—sometimes noisy, sometimes crowded, spotty service—but great food. Our favorite pizza is the Salsiccia, topped with Italian sausage, roasted grape tomatoes and goat cheese, but there's also a deep dish pie called the Wrigley (also loaded with Italian sausage) and a meat-heavy option called the Gunslinger. At lunch every day, the format turns buffet.

CANOPY

················

3939 MONTROSE *at Sul Ross*
☎ **(713) 528-6848**
canopyhouston.com
🍴 **E6**

THE VERDANT INTERIOR IS THE FIRST THING you'll notice. Photo murals of tree branches wrap around the walls and wood beams crisscross above the main dining room for a lush effect. It's all in keeping with the theme that chef-owner Claire Smith began with her Heights restaurant Shade, and the food at both is similarly nourishing and fresh. There's a Houston eclecticism to the menu, with room for both duck confit enchiladas and flour-crusted calamari with wasabi aioli. The buttermilk-fried pork loin is a crowd favorite, served with jalapeño andouille gravy. Both cocktails and dessert are also worth your time— the lemon icebox pie in particular should not be missed. The valet situation is slightly irritating, as cones block off all available spots in front of the restaurant, but that tends to be standard practice in fine dining these days. Fine baked goods and breakfast are also available. A new patio draws us outside on fine days.

CANTINA LAREDO

················

11129 WESTHEIMER *at Wilcrest*
☎ **(713) 952-3287**
cantinalaredo.com
🍴 **B7**

PART OF DALLAS-BASED CONSOLIDATED RESTAURANT Operations, Inc.—it also has El Chico Cafe, Good Eats, III Forks, Lucky's Cafe and others— Cantina Laredo is an upscale Tex-Mex that's done a good job of not feeling corporate. The menu includes several kinds of hand-rolled enchiladas (our pick: Veracruz, with chicken, spinach and Monterrey jack), "top-shelf guacamole" that is made tableside, tacos al pastor and bacon-wrapped shrimp. *Mole* dishes, daily fish specials and grilled items set this apart from your standard Tex-Mex. It's more like Mex-Mex. There's also an appealing Sunday brunch menu. A live band plays on weekend nights, so if it's quiet conversation you want, stick to lunch or weekdays.

CAPITAL GRILLE

················

5365 WESTHEIMER
between Sage & Yorktown
☎ **(713) 623-4600**
thecapitalgrille.com
🍴 **D7**

CLOSE YOUR EYES AND VISUALIZE A GRAND,

beautifully appointed bastion of Republican dining featuring expensive steaks, expensive side dishes and expensive wine. In fact, it's reported that the Capital Grille has the highest check average of any restaurant chain in the country. It's the kind of restaurant that is often described as "a man's restaurant": clubby dark wood, cushy Oriental carpeting and hunting trophies on the wall. Everything is crisp white napery, heavy flatware and good wine glasses. You will eat a meal built around excellent meat cut into obscenely thick hunks and an award-winning wine list. You will also be cosseted by polished service and so pampered into submission that, by the time you're ready for a cigar you won't think twice about dropping $40 for a good smoke.

CARMELO'S
. . . .

14795 MEMORIAL
west of Dairy Ashford
☎ **(281) 531-0696**
carmelosrestaurant.com
🍴 **B6**

UCH OF THE MENU AND PRESENTATION at Carmelo Mauro's white-tablecloth stalwart follow a timeworn model, but the kitchen can shine with its more soulful Southern Italian creations. Of all the Sicilian-infused Continental dishes, a lunch special of an eggplant stuffed with quickly sautéed seafood, then baked, seemed straight from a fine *ristorante* in the *mezzogirno*. Pastas, veal and steaks will satisfy most diners, and fresh fish, including salmon with Champagne sauce and grilled swordfish, make this as much a seafood as Italian destination. Carmelo's is very often availed of for large banquet dinners and by West Houston teens before prom. The setting is comfortable and unpretentious and the service eager to please.

CARRABBA'S ITALIAN GRILL
. . . .

3115 KIRBY *south of W. Alabama*
☎ **(713) 522-3131**
multiple locations
carrabbas.com
🍴 **E7**

ARRABBA'S ORIGINAL KIRBY LOCATION IS still owned and operated by cookbook author and PBS cooking show host Johnny Carrabba and remains hugely popular after 25-some years. This homegrown chain—with locations now all over the country, thanks to OSI, the parent company of Outback Steakhouse—helped define the exuberant Sicilian-rooted Gulf Coast cooking that is today one of the best-loved staples of the Houston dining scene. The kitchen perpetuates its *nuova rustic* reputation with well-tended grills and some of the best filled pastas intown. Don't

FRIED CHICKEN

FOR DOWN-HOME COOKING, A PERFECTLY FRIED BIRD IS AWFULLY DIFFICULT TO ACHIEVE. Luckily, Houston has a team of professionals on the case.

BARBECUE INN
116 W. CROSSTIMBERS
☎ (713) 695-8112

It's not the barbecue that has made this restaurant a legend in Southern cooking. Fried chicken is its hallmark. The cooked-to-order chicken is simply floured and fried...which makes us wonder, Why can't everybody do that?

SUPER H MART
1302 BLALOCK
☎ (713) 468-0606

A stand in the food court of this Korean supermarket is poised to change your life with its tender, garlicky brand of fried goodness and a side of pickled daikon.

ZELKO BISTRO
705 E. 11TH
☎ (713) 880-8691

All the food coming out of chef Jamie Zelko's kitchen is hearty and Southern. The boneless Captain's fried chicken is moist enough without the shallot jam, but we wouldn't have it any other way.

MAX'S WINE DIVE
4720 WASHINGTON
☎ (713) 880-8737

The fried chicken is buttermilk-marinated and served with old-fashioned sides of mashed potatoes, collards and Texas toast in a heaping Max's-style portion. Go ahead and order a glass of Champagne, too.

PONDICHERI
2800 KIRBY
☎ (713) 522-2022

The Tuesday night special is a feast for two, and thanks to a chickpea-flour batter, gluten free. Cilantro-spiked yogurt sauce adds to the appeal.

DAILY REVIEW CAFE
3412 WEST LAMAR
☎ (713) 520-9217

Add the black pepper-studded gravy to this already perfectly crisp and juicy rendition of Southern fried chicken and you have a food revelation on your hands.

overlook the surprisingly good pizzas on chewy, slightly charred crusts, either, or the seafood salad that is a smartly dressed toss of bitter greens, grilled shrimp and scallops. These restaurants may not be so trendy anymore, but there's still always a crowd. Always.

CARTER & COOLEY
....

375 W. 19TH *at Ashland*
☎ **(713) 864-3354**
carterandcooley.com
🍴 **E5**

HOUSED IN AN OLD DRUGSTORE OUTFITted with bentwood chairs, pressed tin ceilings and antique scales for weighing deli meat, C&C is so perfectly quaint that it ought to be the setting for some Hollywood meet-cute between a BLT and your mouth. The long menu describes it as having "lots of crisp bacon" and it's definitely not lying about that. From there, there's also a

Exterior of Carter & Cooley

classic reuben, plus liverwurst and pimiento cheese. Sides are limited to potato salad or chips, but there is always a soup of the day. The staff is exceedingly accommodating, so if you don't see what you want, just ask. The only downside is that the doors close in the middle of the afternoon.

CHARIVARI
....

2521 BAGBY *at McGowen*
☎ **(713) 521-7231**
charivarirest.com
🍴 **E6**

SMACK IN THE MIDDLE OF THE SWIRL OF NIGHTLIFE that keeps Midtown overpopulated with tight T-shirts and velvet ropes, this representative of Old World Europe stands sentinel. Under the watchful eye of Transylvania-born chef/owner Johann Schuster, Charivari (French for "beautiful good mix") serves a seasonal menu of European classics. The restaurant celebrates white asparagus, for example, every spring but evergreen appetizers include a "Dracula" garlic soup, escargot, beluga blinis and "Budapest-style" foie gras. Entrees encompass such fascinating choices as Transylvania pork filets, wienerschnitzel, spätzle with wild mushroom sauce, seafood *choucroute* and a ribeye "Cafe de Paris" that is dry-aged for 20 days. Presentation is very nice, albeit old-fashioned, with silver domed

RESTAURANTS

dishes placed before diners in unison, and service is impeccable. Charivari attracts a power lunch crowd by day and a more mature set at night.

CHEZ NOUS

·················

217 S. AVENUE G
just south of Main, Humble
☎ **(281) 446-6717**
cheznousfrenchrestaurant.com
🍴 🅖🅘 🚗

ERARD BRACH OPENED THIS LITTLE FRENCH country inn in a former Pentecostal church in 1984. Since then, longing for retirement, he has brought in some co-owners, currently executive chef Stacy Crowe-Simonson and husband/maître d/sommelier Scott Simonson. Even without Brach's hands-on management everything has remained pretty much the same over the past decades. Situated in a modest residential neighborhood in Humble, a few blocks off Main Street, this is the kind of place you'd brag to your friends about discovering on a trip through Napa Valley, say, or Vermont. It's a French restaurant of decades past, so full of charm you almost expect the bartender to wear a straw boater. Most of the menu's offerings are sturdy, classic dishes with good sauces, and there's a generous wine list. Recommended: house-made charcuterie, steak marchand de vin, shrimp Provençal

and snails sizzling in thick garlic butter. Here's everything you love about French restaurants, but without the hauteur.

CHEZ ROUX

·················

600 LA TORRETTA
at Del Lago Blvd., Montgomery
☎ **(936) 448-3020**
latorrettalakeresort.com
🍴 NORTH OF 🅒🅘 🚗

IT'S HARD TO BELIEVE, BUT SOME OF THE BEST food to be had in the Houston area—some would argue that it's some of the best in Texas—is actually an hour outside city limits in little old Montgomery, right on Lake Conroe. The principal restaurant at the La Torretta Resort is powered by chef Albert Roux, who was voted one of the most influential chefs in the U.K. in 2003. His

Lake views at Chez Roux

hands-on executive chef, Matthew Gray, earned a Michelin star while in Scotland. All that talent has not gone to waste. The Texas cheddar soufflé is a specialty, light and airy but with a satisfying savory flavor and delectably creamy. Many of the dishes make use of regional ingredients (e.g. wild boar chops, Gulf fish and shrimp) that are prepared with classic French technique. Portions are modest and prices are high, but you'll leave satisfied. Try to organize your reservation to coincide with sunset over the lake. At the end of the evening, a golf cart will scoop you up and deposit you at the resort's front door. Note: Occasional prix-fixe meals and cooking classes are a fun way to cop a deal.

CHILOSO'S TACO HOUSE

. . . .

701 E. 20TH *west of N. Main*
☎ **(713) 868-2273**
🍴 **E5**

COMPOSING A BREAKFAST TACO IS A VERY simple thing, but it is indeed a craft. Ask anyone in the long line of people queuing outside Chiloso's on a Saturday morning, and they'll tell you that this modest neighborhood joint is the very best place to get them. Thick flour tortillas stuffed with eggs, potatoes and bacon or chorizo nest in steam table trays that separate the din-

ing room from the kitchen, and though that sounds less than ideal in terms of quality, you don't hear a peep of complaint from the loyal regulars. The restaurant closes around three but if you make it before then, the carne guisada and chicken fajita tacos are also solid options. The vibe is homey and the front porch is packed during tolerable weather.

CHURRASCOS

. . . .

2055 WESTHEIMER
at S. Shepherd
☎ **(713) 527-8300**
multiple locations
cordua.com
🍴 **E6**

THESE POPULAR EATERIES, NOW 20-PLUS years old, are the foundation of Michael Cordúa's restaurant empire, and it was the namesake churrasco that started it all. It's a flavorful quick-grilled cut from the tenderloin that is perfect for a city that loves beef. Here it's lavishly basted with garlicky chimichurri sauce. We also love the addictive plantain chips that start every meal; this Churrascos habit has spoiled us for every Latin restaurant to follow in its footsteps. You will also like the rich and soft *maduros*, yucca fries, variety of ceviches, corn-smoked crab fingers, variously filled empanadas, bacon-wrapped shrimp and the famous *tres leches* for dessert. The excellent beef, sexy Latin flavors, festive atmosphere, earnest service, good drinks and value-priced Chilean wines make this pair of restaurants well suited for our city.

CHUY'S COMIDA DELUXE

. . . .

2706 WESTHEIMER
just west of Kirby
☎ **(713) 524-1700**
multiple locations
chuys.com

🍴 **E6**

THE TELLTALE SIGN THAT ANY GIVEN RES-taurant is from Austin? Knick-knacks. They cover the wall here, ranging from hubcaps to a shrine to Elvis Presley. There's always a long wait, and it's a favorite among youngsters who love to drink. Enchiladas are a specialty, as are crispy flautas and Big As Yo' Face burritos. The addictive ranch-based creamy jalapeño dip (or "Creamy J") used to be only available to regulars in the know, but now it comes standard with the chips alongside a chunky pico de gallo. Portions are huge, which is just part of the appeal of a campy joint offering fairly typical Tex-Mex food. Chile-heads: Watch for the Hatch chile promotion every August.

CIAO BELLO

. . . .

5161 SAN FELIPE *at Sage*
☎ **(713) 960-0333**
ciaobellohouston.com

🍴 **E6**

THE VALLONE NAME HAS STATURE IN THIS CITY. It sometimes conjures up feelings of intimidation associated with the imposingly expensive Tony's. Luckily, Ciao Bello is a more casual, neighborhood affair with Italian food that lives up to its reputation for authenticity. The pizza is

Grilled shrimp and goat cheese salad at Ciao Bello

{ 174 }

considered some of the best in the city and, by some wonderful mistake, is given away free during happy hour. The thin-crust pies are as simple as the classic margherita but we love the *fresa al solare* with goat cheese, roasted garlic and shaved pear. Other specialties include osso buco ravioli and their grilled shrimp and goat cheese salad, but there's a section of more familiar fare including spaghetti and meatballs and lasagna as well. All in all, it's a restaurant well suited to its Tanglewood location, and families of excellent zip codes come to relax over a satisfying meal.

CIRO'S ITALIAN GRILL
. . . .

9755 KATY FWY. (I-10 WEST)
between Bunker Hill & Gessner
☎ **(713) 467-9336**
ciros.com
🍴 **C6**

THIS USED TO BE LITTLE HIDEAWAY IN SPRING Branch. But expansion of I-10 forced it to move farther west and across the freeway, and a glossy expansion came with that. Ciro Lampasas' Italian-American menu includes a number of heart-healthy selections as well as good seafood. The variety of breads for the table earns raves, and the lasagna, pork chop, calzones and seafood pasta are particularly good. Try the grilled sausage

and peppers, penne with crawfish and eggplant parmigiana. We like that many of the pasta dishes are available as regular or large portions (for table sharing). Ciro's is always noisy and crowded, but you can now buy the restaurant's various sauces to prepare similar meals at home. Up to a bit of exercise? There's a bocce court outside. Perhaps "Pappa C" will be there to give you a brief lesson.

CLEBURNE CAFETERIA
. . . .

3606 BISSONNET *at Edloe*
☎ **(713) 667-2386**
cleburnecafeteria.com
🍴 **D7**

THE BEST WAY TO DESCRIBE MOST CAFETERIA food is often "boring," but that's definitely not so at this popular, non-chain cafeteria known for fresh, made-from-scratch squash casserole, broiled fish, carrot salad and turkey with dressing. Cleburne's is popular among an older set, of course, but also much liked by West U-area families. It's also a good lunch spot with its proximity to Greenway Plaza, but go early because the line often is out the door. It burned down several years ago, much to the despair of its loyal clientele. But the Mickelis family rebuilt it better than ever, and so Cleburne (named for the downtown street where it first originated) endures. Word to the wise: Bring your checkbook, it's cash or check only. Credit cards are not accepted.

COLLINA'S ITALIAN CAFE

. . . .

3835 RICHMOND
just east of Weslayan
☎ **(713) 621-8844**
multiple locations
collinas.com

🍴 **D7**

THIS *PIZZERIA E RISTOR-ANTE* IS A LONGSTANDING neighborhood choice for casual Italian cuisine and meeting friends. But what it's best known for is a long-standing BYOB policy, which makes it a popular gathering spot for serious winos to share and taste their prized bottles. Yes, you can bring your own wine to drink with their pasta, calzones or pizza. All pies have yeasty dough, puffy edges and crisp bottoms, and whole-wheat crust is also available. Our favorite: the Mona Lisa with roma tomatoes, mushrooms, spinach and feta. Retro selections include a Hawaiian pizza with Canadian bacon.

CONSCIOUS CAFE

. . . .

2612 SCOTT *south of I-45*
☎ **(713) 658-9191**

🍴 **F7**

THE COPY OF ELIJAH MUHAMMAD'S *HOW TO Eat to Live* prominently displayed in this humble but comfortable cafe is the first clue that this is a Nation of Islam restaurant. What that means is that the food is in accordance with Muhammad's rather particular dietary restrictions, but the dishes on the short menu are so fresh and lovingly made that they have appeal for everyone. The wild-caught salmon burger is the most popular item, but the eggplant hoagie on lightly toasted wheat bread dressed with tomatoes, olives and a smidge of Veganaise will also appeal. For dessert, be sure to get a slice of nutmeg-scented bean pie. It's a take on Southern sweet pota-to pie, a forbidden foodstuff that is subbed here with navy beans.

COPPA RISTORANTE ITALIANO

. . . .

5555 WASHINGTON
at T.C. Jester
☎ **(713) 426-4260**
copparistorante.com

🍴 **E6**

OWNERS CHARLES CLARK AND GRANT COOPER HAD

a critically loved success on their hands with Catalan. But once chef Chris Shepherd departed for his own project, rather than attempt to imitate his style in his absence, Clark and Cooper transitioned over to a more rustic Italian concept in the same space. Coppa opened just before we went to press with this book..

CRAPITTO'S

2400 MID LANE
north of Westheimer
☎ **(713) 961-1161**
crapittos.com

THIS ITALIAN-AMERICAN RESTAURANT STANDS apart from its glitzy Galleria neighbors, housed in a remodeled 75-year-old farmhouse that's full of charm and liked by an older crowd. Regulars rave about the crabcakes, lasagna, pan-sautéed snapper, salmon florentina and cheesecake. The eating here is not light, and even the lunch menu has a full selection of veal, beef filet and seafood-stuffed portobello. Large groups can snag the table inside the clubby wine cellar, but the deck makes for a beautiful dining experience under the fine old live oaks. Prices are on the expensive side, but service is quite personable—it's not unusual to see owner Frank Crapitto greeting diners.

CRAWFISH & BEIGNETS

11201 BELLAIRE BLVD. *at Boone*
☎ **(281) 498-5044**

THE VIETNAMESE-CAJUN BOILED CRAWFISH IS excellent, but best enjoyed during crawfish season. Expect frozen mudbugs in off months. Stockpile the various condiments available and take advantage of their cheap beer prices. Want your crawfish spicy? Just say so. Note that this is not the place for germ-phobes, as it's pretty scruffy. And don't expect to find beignets: No one ordered them, so the proprietor took them off the menu.

CRICKET'S CREAMERY & CAFFE

315 W. 19TH *at Rutland*
☎ **(713) 869-9450**
cricketscaffe.com

RIGHT AT HOME ON THIS FUNKY, WALKABLE street in The Heights lined with antique stores, this eclectic lunch spot and gelato bar is the perfect resting point during an afternoon of shopping. Open for breakfast and lunch only, all the menu items are vegetarian and fairly light. Try the portobello mushroom with mozzarella and pesto mayonnaise for a heartier option or a half goat cheese and tomato sandwich with a bowl of tomato basil. Don't leave without a scoop of gelato, the blackberry and Nutella being our favorites. There are plenty of coffee drinks and magazines to linger over and a corner of kids' books, making this a welcoming spot for a few hours respite.

CULLEN'S UPSCALE AMERICAN GRILL

....

11500 SPACE CENTER BLVD.
between Genoa Red Bluff & Hwy. 3
☎ **(713) 481-3463**
cullensgrille.com
🍴 SOUTHEAST OF **19**

HE WORD "UPSCALE" IS IN THE RESTAURANT name, so it only makes sense that all 37,000 square feet of Clear Lake's poshest restaurant would be outfitted with a state-of-the-art kitchen visible from the main dining room and done up in marble and limestone touches. Cullen's menu, designed by executive chef Paul Lewis, is American with a twist. The Frito pie-style starter, for example, boasts Berkshire pork in the chili, toasted tortilla chips, Texas goat cheese, two kinds of cheddar and crème fraîche. You'll also find prime rib, steaks and chops, seafood,

chicken, duck, homemade pizzas and sandwiches. The wine list is very 21st century with a computerized wine tablet that allows patrons to search wines by type, vintage, region and price. Even with all this fussy refinement, the attached bar is very laid-back, kid-friendly and even houses a game room.

CYCLONE ANAYA'S

....

309 GRAY *at Bagby*
☎ **(713) 520-6969**
multiple locations
cycloneanaya.com
🍴 **E6**

IKE THAT ONE COOL KID IN HIGH SCHOOL, Cyclone Anaya's is known for its great parties. Once a popular, down-home Tex-Mex joint owned by a former wrestler (the Cyclone himself), now this Houston chain is rather upscale and popular as much for its margaritas and pick-up scene as any of the food it has to offer. Still, under the direction of chef Jason Gould, the guacamole is fresh and the enchiladas, no mat-

Patio dining at Cyclone Anaya

ter the filling, are excellent, classic interpretations. Refried beans are loaded with lard, but we think that's a good thing, and the salsa is very good. Noise levels can get irritatingly loud, but that's expected at a restaurant where brunch isn't just breakfast, it's part of "Sunday Funday."

D'AMICO'S ITALIAN MARKET CAFE

. . . .

5510 MORNINGSIDE
between Rice & University
☎ **(713) 526-3400**
multiple locations
damico-cafe.com
🍴 **E7**

'AMICO IS AN OLD NAME IN HOUSTON eateries, going back to the 1970s. Nash D'Amico closed all his restaurants in Houston and Galveston to concentrate on this concept, a combination Italian grocery store, deli and cafe all in one. You eat at tables near cases of wine and bottles of olive oil; a few feet away, folks are buying hunks of cheese to take home; over there, cooks are preparing a dish. It's crowded but full of energy. Daily lunchtime steam-table specials are popular and quite a bargain, but we're a fan of the pastas—try the mushroom and walnut tortellini or penne with grilled chicken and asparagus—which are mostly made fresh in

house. The cheesecake, though made by an outside company, is the ricotta variety and perhaps the best in town. Note that a second location of D'Amico's Italian Market Cafe in The Heights opened Fall 2011.

DA MARCO

. . . .

1520 WESTHEIMER
between Waugh & Mandell
☎ **(713) 807-8857**
damarcohouston.com
🍴 **E6**

ARCO WILES' FLAGSHIP IS CONSIDERED by many to be the best Italian restaurant—nay, the best restaurant, period—in Houston. And not just by easily impressed Houstonians: In *My Table*'s special Italian issue (April-May 2011), we asked four Italian expats to tell us where, if money were no object, they would go in Houston for an authentic Italian meal. Three of the four listed Da Marco as their first choice. From this converted house on busy Westheimer comes food that spans regions of Italy with far more than a dash of creativity and talent. It is appealing and eclectic, sometimes sublime. Here you are expected to dine in the Italian fashion with an *antipasto* like artichoke *alla giudea,* which is softened in chicken broth, fried and served with a lemon sauce, followed by a *primo* pasta, risotto or gnocchi course, then a *secondo* of meat or fish and

RESTAURANTS

finally a *contorno* of a separate vegetable side dish. Look to the chalkboard menu for specials, but be warned: Prices can be quite high. In the fall, during white truffle season, come here to have a blizzard of naughty truffles shaved over your pasta.

DAILY REVIEW CAFE

. . . .

3412 W. LAMAR at *Dunlavy*
☎ **(713) 520-9217**
dailyreviewcafe.com

🍴 **E6**

OR WELL OVER A DECADE NOW, THIS tucked-away spot just south of Allen Parkway has been dishing up Southern-inflected modern comfort food that suits keen local sensibilities desiring healthy or hearty. The peaceful patio is eminent among its peers for obscuring the urban surroundings and it's a wonderful place to indulge in a fennel-accented chicken pot pie and a good bottle of wine. Other Houston-attuned dishes include a lobster taco with yellow tomato salsa, pan-seared tilapia with corn masa spoonbread and ahi tuna with wasabi mashed potatoes. For those going low carb, a special menu allows diners to mix and match a protein with vegetable sides. There's often a wait for a table in the small space, so it might be best to avoid peak hours.

DAMIAN'S CUCINA ITALIANA

. . . .

3011 SMITH at *Rosalie*
☎ **(713) 522-0439**
damians.com

🍴 **E6**

HIS MIDTOWN CLASSIC HAS BEEN A WELL-WORN stop for downtown businesspeople since it opened in the 1980s. Owned by the affable Frankie Mandola and Bubba Butera—it was founded by their relative Damian Mandola—Damian's does not quite excite as it once did, but it remains a fine-dining Houston favorite. The cooking might be described as upscale Gulf Coast Southern Italian-American, and flavors and portions are both generous. In a dining room made cozy by low ceilings and lights, you can enjoy specialties such as thick veal chops, braised pork shank over cannellini beans, and linguine with a medley of seafood in a piquant marinara sauce. The robust food and snappy waiters wending their way through the dining room make an absolutely comfortable environment, and the convenient shuttle service to downtown establishes it as a go-to for pre-theater dining.

DANTON'S GULF COAST SEAFOOD KITCHEN

·················

4611 MONTROSE
just south of Hwy. 59
☎ **(713) 807-8883**
dantonsseafood.com
🍴

⌐T IS A SUBLIME PLEASURE
└─TO SIT AT A TABLE IN DAN-
ton's bar with a dozen raw oysters,
a martini and the view of the tree-
lined streets of Montrose outside.
The atmosphere is a mix of sophistication and easy charm. just as
the menu is a perfect Houston
confluence of Texas Gulf seafood
with generous Cajun and Mexican
influences. Chef-owner Danton Nix
is an alumnus of Goode Co. Seafood and Joyce's and his experience is evident. Grilled items are

The bar dining area in Danton's

woodfired over oak and hickory,
and the gumbo is cooked for up
to 18 hours to get its signature
flavor. Danton's is also a top pick
for crawfish once they are in season.
The Sunday blues brunch is straight
out of New Orleans.

DARBAND SHISHKABOB

·················

5670 HILLCROFT
between Harwin & Westpark
☎ **(713) 975-5670**
multiple locations
🍴 C7

⌐─┐HE ORIGINAL DARBAND
└─┘ IS LOCATED AMONG
the many Middle Eastern, Indian
and Pakistani shops and cafes
that line multicultural Hillcroft,
but its namesake is all the way
back in Tehran, a special-occasion
restaurant in a parklike setting. The
Hillcroft Darband is a much more
modest (some would say dumpy)
affair, with out-of-season Christmas lights wrapped around the
counter, but the food is something
the kitchen can take pride in. The
kubideh, tubes of spiced ground
beef, and turmeric-tinged lamb
shank are among the most popular and best in the city. The fresh,
hot flat bread and grilled tomatoes
crushed into white rice are beautifully simple sides. The newer
Darband Bar & Grill on Fountain
View is a dressier affair, but the
menu is similar.

RESTAURANTS

DEL FRISCO'S DOUBLE EAGLE STEAK HOUSE

....

5061 WESTHEIMER in *The Galleria*
☎ **(713) 335-2600**
delfriscos.com

🍴 **D6**

EQUALLY WELL-LOVED BY FOOD CRITICS AND the city's businessmen and their wives, The Galleria location of this national steakhouse boasts luxurious interiors, including a hand-painted Italian glass ceiling and light fixtures and 40-foot windows with striking skyline views. The sizzling bar is packed nightly with professional athletes and their hangers-on, to the point where the two-story space can get quite noisy, and the layout is certainly more about see-and-be-seen than an intimate dinner. Speaking of dinner, the kitchen is known for its USDA prime beef, classic steakhouse sides like oversized onion rings, one of the city's best crab cakes and an enormous (if pricey) wine selection. Whether in spite of or because of the hubbub, Del Frisco's is a beautiful location for a martini and a salad or a quick prix-fixe business lunch.

Prime-beef steak with wine at Del Frisco's

DENIS' SEAFOOD HOUSE

....

9777 KATY FWY.
west of Bunker Hill
☎ **(713) 464-6900**
denisseafood.com

🍴 **C6**

THIS NOISY MEMORIAL SPOT IS A MIX OF LAS Vegas style, courtesy the lurid exterior paint job, and New Orleans flavors. The blackboard lists the catches of the day, and your choice is then served grilled, sautéed or blackened (though the latter option tends to be over-seasoned and overcooked to our taste). For a bit more coin you can also add one of seven seafood sauce toppings like the Florentine, a delicious shrimp, scallop and crawfish-laden spinach cream sauce. The slightly upscale interior—there are beautiful mosaic walls with tile work by noted Houston artist Dixie Friend Gay—is not always matched by the level of service.

DHARMA CAFE

. . . .

1718 HOUSTON *at Crockett*
☎ **(713) 222-6996**
dharmacafehouston.com
🍴 **E6**

OUSED IN THE HISTORIC KESSLER BUILDING, John Gurney and Susan Ralph's cozy little spot only has a few tables but it makes up for it with a big, freewheeling spirit. There's a hippie vibe to the place, aided by its shelf of poetry by Allen Ginsberg and books on Buddhism, and the menu is vegan- and vegetarian-friendly, with tempting salads, pizza and sandwiches along with entrees of cedar-planked salmon and blueberry chicken breast. The dining room can be quite romantic at night, but the West Coast-with-French-flair-style brunch is probably the most popular offering. The buffet includes scones, pancakes, pasta dishes and eggs cooked to order, plus the first mimosa comes free.

DIM SUM KING

. . . .

9160 BELLAIRE BLVD.
at Ranchester
☎ **(713) 270-6788**
🍴 **C7**

OU'D IMAGINE THE KING OF ANYTHING to be rather grandiose and despite the tradition of dim sum halls being larger than life, this modest little hole in the wall is exactly the opposite. Instead of the usual pushcarts loaded with plates and steamers, diners simply order from a checklist and picture-book menu. Some of the fun of dim sum is lost, but also the hassles—all the food comes out piping hot and there's no neck craning to see what's headed your way. The selection is fairly standard, with the usual lineup of pork *shu mai* dumplings, red bean paste, sesame balls and chicken feet, but it's one of the few places to offer dim sum all day (except Tuesdays, when it's closed).

DIVINO

. . . .

1830 W. ALABAMA
near Woodhead
☎ **(713) 807-1123**
divinohouston.com
🍴 **E6**

OW A DECADE OLD, THIS IS A COMFORTable neighborhood eatery rather than the fine-dining establishment its prices might suggest. And if you go in with those reined-in expectations, you'll do just fine. In the *osteria* and *enoteca* tradition, Divino features a small menu of items mostly from the Emilia-Romagna region, where executive chef and co-owner Patrick McCray trained. Though not terribly ambitious, you will find straightforward and usually satisfying renditions of dishes from this region, such as Emily's

RESTAURANTS

GRILLED CHEESE, PLEASE

THE HUMBLE GRILLED-CHEESE SANDWICH, A CHILDHOOD FAVORITE, HAS BEEN ELEVATED to gourmet stature and value at some Houston restaurants. Here are a few of our favorites.

GRAVITAS
807 TAFT
☎ (713) 522-0995

Pungent gruyère cheese oozing from perfectly buttered and crunchy, thick grilled sourdough bread makes this an addictive indulgence for the grilled-cheese purist. Served with a lovely side of fresh tossed salad greens.

MAX'S WINE DIVE
4720 WASHINGTON
☎ (713) 880-8737

Everything's big at Max's, and this grilled cheese is constructed on artisanal organic Texas toast with local Veldhuizen Farms gruyère and provolone, and then dusted with piquillo peppers. Decadent with a tangy pimiento cheese effect.

OUISIE'S TABLE
3939 SAN FELIPE
☎ (713) 528-2264

"The Best Ever Grilled Mozzarella Cheese Sandwich" comes on sourdough with Paula's snowy white mozzarella, sliced tomatoes, fresh basil leaves and anchovy butter brushed on the bread. Olives come on the side. Super fresh and original.

TINY BOXWOOD'S
3614 W. ALABAMA
☎ (713) 622-4224

Pity, ladies who lunch probably avoid this caloric yet delish crispy gouda grilled cheese on white pagnotta bread with basil-garlic pesto. The precious price tag includes the huge sandwich and side salad. Split it with a garden-gabbing friend and enjoy the view.

59 DINER
3801 FARNHAM
☎ (713) 523-2333

The "Texas Grilled Cheese" sandwich sports both baby Swiss and cheddar cheese, plus sliced tomatoes on grilled jalapeño cheese bread. Love the reasonable price and the undeniable layers of zesty flavor.

goat cheese ravioli in sage brown butter sauce. Neighborhood regulars love it, and there is a decent, frequently updated wine list.

DOLCE VITA PIZZERIA ENOTECA

500 WESTHEIMER *at Taft*
☎ **(713) 520-8222**
dolcevitahouston.com
🍴 **E6**

IZZA DOWN SOUTH CAN BE TRICKY BUSINESS, but this pizzeria and wine bar from Marco Wiles actually does the genre justice. The thin and slightly scorched wood-fired pies are appropriately crackly, the *robiola* (mixed-milk cheese), leeks and pancetta pizza being our favorite. Other items, including spaghetti *cacio e pepe* (with pecorino and black pepper), calamari with mint, oranges and olives and a side dish of shaved Brussels sprouts with pecorino, are also excellent and perfect for sharing with a group. The converted house is trendy and casual, perfect for boisterous get-togethers and, being dark and rambling, also romantic enough for dates. The under-sized bar area can be a bit of a scene and peak hours are a mess, but it's made up for by more than hype.

DONERAKI

2836 FULTON *north of Quitman*
☎ **(713) 225-1243**
multiple locations
doneraki.com
🍴

HE ORIGINAL FULTON STREET DONERAKI IS still the place to go for an authentic Tex-Mex experience. The suburban locations, though less distinctive (and less grimy) than their forebear, bring in droves of fajita-loving customers to noisy, festively overwrought cantina settings. The service is hit or miss, but the free queso with the chips is a nice touch. Enchiladas, especially those with the kicky tomatillo sauce, are always tasty, plus the margaritas are decent—why not order a pitcher? A live mariachi band on the weekends is fun for those who want the full-sensory experience, but it does make conversation almost impossible.

DOOZO DUMPLINGS & NOODLES

1200 MCKINNEY *at Lamar in Houston Center*
☎ **(713) 571-6898**
🍴

VERY DAY AT NOON, DOWNTOWN WORKERS flock to the food court at the Shops

Inside Down House

at Houston Center for their sandwiches, salads and sodas. Many of them end up in the long line at Doozo, aka "The Dumpling Nazi." Move along quickly and obediently and decide what you want before you get to the counter: (1) a full order of 10 or a half order; (2) pork, chicken or veggie; (3) spicy or extra spicy sauce. Dumplings are steamed fresh and come out piping hot. They're also inexpensive but be sure to have your payment in hand to pay for them—otherwise you'll suffer the consequences.

DOWN HOUSE
. . . .

1801 YALE *at W. 18th*
☎ **(713) 864-3696**
downhousehouston.com
🍴 **E5**

EVERYONE INVOLVED IN THE OWNERSHIP AND planning of this cafe is from Austin

and Down House exhibits all the best and worst traits of that city. It's flagrantly hip, with a vintage bike hanging from one wall and the checks delivered in old hardcover books. It's a nice change of pace for Houston but can feel a bit show-offy. Luckily, it's backed up with serious coffee and cocktail programs (yes, here, they're programs) and fantastic food that owes as much to its quality ingredients as its preparation. Local ingredients are a priority here, with sources including Pola Artisan Cheeses and Atkinson Farms listed at the bottom of the menu. For breakfast, order the decadent croissant sandwich of fried eggplant, spinach and a farm-fresh egg, and at lunch the five-spice pork belly sandwich.

DOWNTOWN AQUARIUM

410 BAGBY at *Memorial*
☎ **(713) 223-3474**
aquariumrestaurants.com
🍴 F6

NY SERIOUS HOUSTON DINER CAN RATTLE off a dozen seafood establishments that have better food than the Downtown Aquarium. At none of those places, however, will they try to guess your weight for an extra couple of bucks—and award you a plastic fish if they fail. Granted, many patrons would gladly pay *not* to have their avoirdupois evaluated. But these are probably not Downtown Aquarium kind of people. Such people are equally unmoved, no doubt, by hearing that they are mere minutes from leaving their table and climbing aboard a miniature train headed on a Shark Voyage, pausing within a tunnel where the creatures swim in a see-through tank above them. And no amount of oohing and aahing about the beckoning Ferris wheel will melt the cold hearts (and gourmand bellies) of the anti-Aquarium elitist. On the other hand, your kids and grandkids will probably love this place. More than $38 million was spent by Tilman Fertitta's Landry's Restaurants, Inc. to redevelop two city-owned downtown structures into a six-acre theme park that includes a public aquarium, seafood restaurant, white tigers, ballroom, casual cafe, lounge, midway, Ferris wheel, train and carousel. The Aquarium Restaurant offers a variety of seafood dishes, including coconut shrimp, grilled mahi-mahi, crab salad and fried calamari, and enormous desserts at prices that admittedly outpace the quality of food. But this impressive Disney-esque restaurant—stunning architecture, a well-stocked 150,000-gallon aquarium right in the dining room—is definitely a scene.

DRY CREEK CAFE

544 YALE at *W. 6th*
☎ **(713) 426-2313**
drycreekcafe.com
🍴 D5

HE SUN NEVER SETS ON THE CREEK EMPIRE, now four locations deep and all in The Heights. This refurbished 1930s gas station is the smallest and most food-focused. It's located in a dry part of The Heights, so you'll have to bring in any alcohol and you'll pay a corkage fee. Simple California-style grub includes ahi tuna salads laced with avocado, Swiss and mushroom burgers and veggie quesadillas. Nothing is bold or innovative, but with half the seating outdoors under old pin oaks, it's an ideal pick for an easy spring dinner.

⌕E TAO

....

5135 W. ALABAMA *in The Galleria*
☎ **(713) 965-0888**
etaoasian.com

🍴 **D6**

⌐I⌐ N HOUSTON, IT USED TO
└─┘ BE THAT FOR A GOOD
soup dumpling, you'd have to venture outside the Loop and into the
heart of Chinatown. But that was
before this unassuming restaurant
opened in 2011 in The Galleria on
the second floor a few doors down
from Nordstrom. You may have
walked by E Tao without noticing,
but if you happened to take a look
inside, you'd see a clean, bright
open kitchen with several white-
clothed, hat-wearing Chinese chefs
making everything from fresh dim
sum like *har gow* shrimp dumplings
to stir fry, roast pork and lobster
four ways. It's a scene straight off
of the streets of Hong Kong. But
we go first and foremost for the
soup dumplings, beautifully constructed with 25 pleats that end in a
pinch at the top. Dip the bun in the
soy-vinegar-ginger dumpling sauce
and revel in the deliciousness.

•EDDIE V'S PRIME SEAFOOD

....

12848 QUEENSBURY
in CityCentre
☎ **(832) 200-2380**
multiple locations
eddiev.com

🍴🍴 **B6**

⌐I⌐ S IT TOO MUCH TO ASK
└─┘ THAT THE MAN SERVING
your Chilean sea bass wear a white
waistcoat? Absolutely not, according to this Scottsdale steak and
seafood chain. Between the two,
the seafood is stronger—note the
massive raw bar near the entrance
—and flown in three times a week
from the East Coast and Hawaii.
Spending big? Order the dramatic seafood tower and a bottle of
Chablis to share as a starter. There's
an Asian element to many of the
dishes, from the crab fried rice side
dish to the ginger-soy jus that
bathes the ahi tuna steak, and the
Maryland-style crabcake and lemon sole in parmesan crust you
ordered will be delivered to your
pristine table by the impeccable
wait staff. The refined lounge features live music every evening and
practically ripples with retro mas-
culine energy.

EL HIDALGUENSE

. . . .

6917 LONG POINT
between Silber & Antoine
☎ **(713) 680-1071**
🍴 **D5**

GETTING RIGHT TO THE POINT: THE THING TO come here for is the cabrito. This modest Spring Branch restaurant —it shares the strip center with Vieng Thai—is probably about as close to Hidalgo (a city south of Mexico City) as you will get within the state of Texas. Walk in, and the open kitchen is directly ahead. There's an odd-looking waist-high brick structure in it. If you go over to take a look, you'll see roasting kid goats and lambs. Just go with the flow, and order the cabrito. If you get a nice chunk, you'll have crisp skin and succulent rib meat to fold into your tortillas. Other notes: The owners have only a beer/wine license, so the margaritas are not the real thing—no tequila. Sometimes, however, they pass out little tequila shots to their guests for free. There's also lively mariachi music on the weekend. Finally, it may seem like this is going to be a cheap meal, but the cabrito and extras can quickly add up.

EL MESON

. . . .

2425 UNIVERSITY
at Morningside
☎ **(713) 522-9306**
elmeson.com
🍴 **E7**

THE ECLECTIC BLEND OF CUBAN, TEX-MEX and Spanish cuisine at Peter Garcia's longtime Rice Village institution can come off as confused or brilliant, depending on whom you're talking to. For some, cozy El Meson is a perennial favorite. Those looking for authentic Cuban will be disappointed that each meal begins with chips and salsa regardless of dinner intentions, but you will be perked up by the tender *ropa vieja,* or garlicky shredded beef. The selection of Spanish tapas is traditional and includes *patatas bravas* (fried potatoes with spicy tomato sauce) and serrano ham with manchego, and all go down better with some of the popular sangria. You'll also find a Caesar salad, seven varieties of paella (including one made with cuttlefish ink, squid and shrimp), whole roasted baby pig (call ahead) and enchiladas verdes on the menu. And an award-winning wine list. We did say it's eclectic.

RESTAURANTS

EL PUEBLITO PLACE

. . . .

1423 RICHMOND *west of Mandell*
☎ **(713) 520-6635**
elpueblitopatio.com

I F YOU ASK FANS OF THIS QUIRKY OASIS WHAT THEY like about the place, odds are they'll rave about the patio before getting around to the food. And usually they like the food well enough, too. Owners Eduardo and Monica Lopez specialize in Mexican and Guatemalan cuisine. Tucked into an intimate cabana surrounded by palm trees wrapped in fairy lights, practically anything will taste good. The cilantro-heavy salsa also makes anything taste good, from the fish tacos to the platter of grilled chicken and black beans served over fried plantains. There are quite a few bargain seafood dishes, such as salmon piled high with scallops and snapper marinated in achiote sauce. These days, the patio is heavily populated with the stiletto-shod who enjoy the tropical resort feeling, but otherwise everything remains modest and inviting.

EL PUPUSODROMO

. . . .

5802 RENWICK
between Hwy. 59 & Gulfton
☎ **(713) 661-4334**
multiple locations

THOUGH THEY STILL SEEM TO OPERATE BELOW THE radar, in some parts of Houston *pupuserias* are as common as taquerias. The namesake *pupusas* of Salvadoran cuisine are fluffy maize pancakes redolent with lard and stuffed with cheese, meat or beans. Be sure to spoon on some *curtido*, the pickled cabbage condiment that comes on every table, before chowing down. Tamals are similar to their Mexican cousins, though lighter, and fresh juices and beer are also available. Another odd but winning combination is *yuca con chicharrones*, which is boiled or fried yucca dressed and then sprinkled with crunchy bits of pork. Of the three locations around town, the converted Taco Bell on Renwick is our favorite. Call us crazy.

EL REAL TEX-MEX

. . . .

1201 WESTHEIMER
west of Montrose
☎ **(713) 524-1201**
elrealtexmex.com

W HAT KIND OF MEXICAN FOOD WOULD

you expect from the pedigree of chef Bryan Caswell and Bill Floyd of Reef and food critic Robb Walsh as the owners? If you guessed a nostalgic tour through historic Tex-Mex, then you'd be correct. Almost every piece of décor and all the menu items have history—greasy puffy tacos dripping with picadillo beef were born in San Antonio, and the stacked enchiladas *borunda* smothered in guajillo chili are a West Texas phenomenon. Our favorite menu item: cheese enchiladas #7, with exactly the right chile con carne gravy. Inhabiting the massive two floors of the restored Tower Theatre, the festive interior complete with Western films projected on the wall attracts everyone from foodies to Montrose hipsters looking for a late-night solution to too many beers.

EL REY TAQUERIA

. . . .

910 SHEPHERD *at Washington*
☎ **(713) 802-9145**
multiple locations
elreytaqueria.com
🍴 **E6** ✏️

RIVE-THRU FAST FOOD OR NOT, EL REY IS ONE of our favorite places in town. If you choose to go inside, overlook the blue cafeteria trays and plastic utensils because everything from the first cup of coffee of the day to the last late-night taco before you go to bed is done well.

Golden rotisserie chickens spin on spits behind the counter, making it difficult to stick with your original order of tender fish tacos or stew-like *ropa vieja* cut with sticky sweet plantains and rice. (Speaking of plantains: You must try the Cuban taco with fajitas, smoky black beans, plantains and a schmear of *crema*.) Breakfast tacos aren't quite as good as the lunch and dinner versions, but otherwise most everything is stellar.

EL TIEMPO

. . . .

3130 RICHMOND *between Kirby & Buffalo Speedway*
☎ **(713) 807-1600**
multiple locations
eltiempocantina.com
🍴 **D7**

OR TEX-MEX WITH A SIDE OF BEAUTIFUL PEOple, head here for often excellent and relatively expensive takes on the humble fajita and chalupa. The raucous crowds begin to pour in starting at happy hour and don't let up until the doors close. Rare is the person not holding a margarita or *cerveza*, and they know that to build a solid drinking base, one should try the famous stuffed and fried avocado or the more delicate shrimp and mango campechana. All the main courses are gussied up a little; enchiladas can come stuffed with filet and crab and fajita plates are piled high with sizzling lobster and quail as often as they are beef or chicken. All three locations—the one on Montrose is called 1308 Cantina, El Tiempo—of this well-appointed cantina are festive, but at the Washington location you know everyone is only beginning their wild night.

EMPIRE CAFE

....

1732 WESTHEIMER *between Dunlavy & Woodhead*
☎ **(713) 528-5282**
empirecafe.com
🍴 **E6**

VERY NEIGHBORHOOD NEEDS ONE. A COZY gathering place that offers both bustling brunch on Saturday morning and a quiet, candlelit table to savor a glass of wine on a Thursday night. Empire is just that place for Montrose, and people find the unpretentious setting well suited for most purposes, be it a latte and a book or a simple, hearty bowl of pasta with a friend. The food won't blow anyone away but it more than gets the job done. The draw of half-priced cake night every Monday is almost as huge as the slices of cake themselves—Tollhouse, peanut butter chocolate and hummingbird are all good. The line at the counter is epic during breakfast and cake hours, but it usually moves quickly.

EMPIRE TURKISH GRILL

....

12448 MEMORIAL
just west of Gessner
☎ **(713) 827-7475**
empiretrgrill.com
🍴 **C6**

HIS RESERVED LITTLE SPOT BRINGS A TASTE of authentic Turkish flavor to suburban Memorial. Though the white tablecloths seem a bit formal, the dress code is strictly T-shirt and jeans—all the better to eat hummus in. A variety of kebabs get top billing on the menu but the yogurt grills, in which fried bread cubes are covered in yogurt and topped with grilled meat, are the most intriguing. All the Turkish all-stars are available, from falafel to a half dozen preparations of eggplant to grape leaves. The *imam bayildi* (cold roasted baby eggplant with onions, tomato, parsley, garlic and olive oil) in particular is splendid heaped on the warm flat bread that accompanies every meal. For a little more challenging fare, try the tripe soup with vinegar dressing, fried liver or *tarama*, a red caviar spread.

ERIC'S RESTAURANT

4800 CALHOUN
in the University of Houston's Hilton Hotel (entrance 1)
☎ **(713) 743-2513**
hrm.uh.edu/the-college/ Our-Hotel/Erics-Restaurant
🍴 **F7**

IN THIS FOOD-MAKING AND FOOD-SERVICE LABoratory you will find breakfast, lunch and dinner served seven days a week by the students of the UH Conrad N. Hilton College of Hotel and Restaurant Management. Go in knowing there will be hits and misses because, while their hearts are in the right place, their heads aren't quite filled as yet with seasoned restaurant savvy. Although the menu items change frequently, they generally tend towards stiff-collar American cuisine like salmon medallions (any meat in medallion form, really), crabcakes, entrée salads at lunch and shrimp scampi. Oddly enough, breakfast is twice as expensive as any fully actualized restaurant in town, but it's nice to give the kids some encouragement. The name? Eric Hilton is school namesake Conrad N. Hilton's youngest son.

ESCALANTE'S

4053 WESTHEIMER *at Drexel*
☎ **(713) 623-4200**
multiple locations
escalantes.net
🍴 **D6**

VALET AT A TEX-MEX JOINT? WHAT IS THIS? Dallas? Turns out people in this city like to dress up, too, and the snazzy, colorful interiors of this mini Houston chain provide great backdrops for looking ones best. Once inside, you'll find top-shelf margaritas, made-tableside guacamole and classic enchiladas verdes. There are some highly inauthentic items as well—Pat's Mexico City salad with mango chipotle dressing and pine nuts? Hmm. But the women out for ladies' night don't mind one bit, and who wants to spoil their fun? We would, however, like to issue a formal complaint with whoever invented the concept of fat-free refried beans. That's just wrong.

FACUNDO CAFE

3103 ELLA *at W. 34th*
☎ **(713) 880-0898**
facundocafe.com
🍴 **E5**

ASK NOT WHAT YOUR BURGER CAN DO FOR your stomach, but can your burger come with a car wash. The same family who owns the auto shop next door also operates this no-frills cafe that, as our quirky city might have it, manages to turn out some fairly impressive grub. Both the breakfast and lunch dishes are simple American fare. For breakfast, get a bacon and egg sandwich to go or settle down for French toast. The extensive burger menu utilizes sourdough buns, thick, juicy beef patties and a wide range of toppings from mushrooms and Swiss to house-made salsa. Even though your floor mats are getting a scrubdown a few yards away, the granite countertops and open kitchen ensure the experience is anything but auto shop.

FADI'S MEDITERRANEAN GRILL

....

8383 WESTHEIMER *at Dunvale*
☎ **(713) 532-0666**
multiple locations
fadiscuisine.com

🅛IKE PUPPIES AND 70-DEGREE WEATHER, FADI'S is pretty universally loved. Between consistently good Mediterranean food, heaping portions at affordable prices and a family-friendly environment, it's easy to understand why. Grab a blue cafeteria tray and head down the line of handsomely displayed hills of *fattoush* (Lebanese salad), tabouli and lentil salad that lead to cumin-rich lamb shank

and fried cauliflower. It's a great resource for vegetarians, but the kebabs and roasted meats are also very well done. Just-out-of-the-oven pita bread comes with every meal, and baklava awaits at the end of the line. The interior is actually quite regal, with pretty lanterns dangling from the ceiling, but the atmosphere is casual enough for potentially fussy tykes and loud groups.

FALAFEL FACTORY

....

914 PRAIRIE *at Travis*
☎ **(713) 237-8987**
🍴 **F6**

🅣HE NAME SUGGESTS THAT A CONVEYOR BELT is involved in the falafel production at this downtown lunch spot. If that were so, we wouldn't mind having our open mouths at the end of it. But as it turns out, the crisp chickpea patties are simply fried to order in a tiny shotgun kitchen. There's not much eye candy in this dim, closet-sized establishment but for office workers on the run, it's a reliable addition to the rotation. There's the falafel, of course, which is both hot and almost creamy in the center, hummus and shawarma, which comes with either salad or fries. Finding cold water and a ketchup bottle can be a bit of a chore, but there's always take-out.

FEAST

. . . .

219 WESTHEIMER
between Bagby & Taft
☎ **(713) 529-7788**
feasthouston.com
🍴 **E6**

WHEN THIS ADVEN-TUROUS NEO-BRIT restaurant from Richard Knight and James and Meagan Silk burst onto the scene in 2008, it garnered praise from local and national publications alike. Diners were both amazed and frightened by the prospect of nose-to-tail dining. (What exactly is civet of wild boar?) Now, things have settled into routine and those who can't stomach blood sausage can rely on constants like fish and scallop pie and crispy pork belly from the "Feast Favorites" section of the menu, while daring foodies can dine off of the seasonal, rotating half. All that bubble-and-squeak and cock-a-leekie is presented on small, wooden tables packed tightly into a rustic, converted house and can be washed down with any number of classic cocktails. Happy hour and the Saturday prix fixe lunch (two courses for $15) are outrageous bargains.

FELIX 55

. . . .

5510 MORNINGSIDE
north of University
☎ **(713) 590-0610**
felix55.com
🍴 **E7**

NESTLED BETWEEN D'AMICO'S AND BAK-er St. Pub, this newcomer featuring chef Michael Kramer (formerly at Voice here and McCrady's in Charleston, S.C.) opened August 2011, the week before we finished up this book. The space was still waiting for its permanent custom high-end furnishings. But the modest rental tables and chairs didn't diminish an early brunch. We loved our food—grilled steak with hollandaise-gilded poached eggs, roasted potatoes and arugula for him, shrimp and grits for us, and apple-ricotta fritters for the table. Our service was just the right mix of familiarity and snap-to attention. Felix 55 serves lunch, dinner and brunch: bourbon-brined pork chop, fried chicken and waffles, mesquite-smoked duck, flat-

Dining room at Feast

breads and, at lunch, sandwiches and salads. There are also late-night and happy-hour menus.

FIELD OF GREENS

....

2320 W. ALABAMA *east of Kirby*
☎ **(713) 533-0029**
fieldofgreenscuisine.com

🍴 **E6**

NO MATTER YOUR DIET-ARY RESTRICTIONS, Field of Greens can feed you. Vegetarian, vegan, macrobiotic and low-carb dishes all have a place on the menu. Wild field pockets are stuffed with soy ham and chicken, shiitake mushrooms, sprouts and guacamole. Layers of roast vegetables make up the vegan lasagna, and gluten-free spinach salad is dressed with feta, pecans and a bright vinaigrette. As a concession to the pescatarians, there are also grilled Alaskan salmon and a tuna salad sandwich with a zing of curry. It is a wee short on ambience, those stark green walls being reminiscent of an elementary school cafeteria and it's just as educational—piles of alternative-lifestyle reading material are available near the entrance.

FLEMING'S PRIME STEAKHOUSE

....

2405 W. ALABAMA *east of Kirby*
☎ **(713) 520-5959**
multiple locations
flemingssteakhouse.com

🍴 **E6**

THE DEEP LEATHER BAN-QUETTES, DIM LIGHTING and wood-paneled walls all point to one thing: old-fashioned steak house. But Fleming's is not the stuffy men-only lounge of mounted hunting trophies. Of course, the wet-aged, hand-carved USDA Prime bone-in ribeye and porcini-rubbed filet in gorgonzola sauce will do even the most traditional meat-eater right. But the deconstructed salmon Niçoise salad with truffled deviled egg and flirty 99-calorie cocktails draw in abundant female crowds as well. A long bar prides itself on offering 100 wines by the glass and is a congenial place to gather for the noisy and extremely well-priced happy hour. As a classic with a few curveballs, Fleming's gives a modern twist to conventional steakhouse dining.

FLOR DE CUBA

. . . .

16233 CLAY *near Hwy. 6*
☎ **(281) 463-8611**
flordecuba.com
🍴 **B5**

CUBAN FOOD ISN'T TERRIBLY PREVALENT IN Houston, but the almost endless list of choices at this authentic family-run restaurant helps make up for that. For breakfast there's a fried plantain omelet, and for lunch the ubiquitous pressed Cuban sandwich. Then there's the falling-off-the-bone *pollo asado*, perfect with black beans, though you should also keep an eye out for pigeon peas and icy cold *limonada*. If you're dining with a large group, indulge in the *parrillada Cubana* family-style meal, which includes massive portions of pork chops, *vaca frita* (fried shredded beef), fried yucca and much more. The bakery portion produces a variety of *pastelitos* (traditional Cuban puff pastries filled with sweet or savory fillings), *tres leches* and custom cakes.

FLORA & MUSE

. . . .

12860 QUEENSBURY
at Beltway 8, in CityCentre
☎ **(713) 463-6873**
floraandmuse.com
🍴 **B6**

THE CHARMING STREETS OF PARIS AREN'T ENclosed by interstates and parking garages, but this aspirational European-style cafe in CityCentre does its best to conjure the Continental experience. It's a lovely space, bedecked with tufted banquettes, sparkling chandeliers and gilded mirrors. Half of Flora & Muse is dedicated to coffee, pastries and flowers, and the other is a full-service restaurant and bar. Needless to say, there's a lot going on. The menu is quite long as well. Of all the options, we've found the stone-oven flatbreads topped with cured salmon and capers or pear and gorgonzola, expansive "rustic" pancakes and wild mushroom ravioli to be the most consistently delicious. Open for business late into the night, Flora does a nice service for the community, allowing you to drop in any time for day for an inventive cocktail, afternoon tea or whatever would sustain you at the given moment.

FOGO DE CHAO

. . . .

8250 WESTHEIMER
between S. Voss & Fondren
☎ **(713) 978-6500**
fogodechao.com
🍴 **C7**

MANKIND HAS EVOLVED TO THE POINT WHERE one can chow down on unlimited amounts of Brazilian-style grilled meat practically any time one wants, in any number of restaurants. But

{ 197 }

there was a time about 10 years ago when this *churrascaria* was the only one in town. Fogo de Chao set the standard for rodizio service in Houston and continues to maintain it. Waiters roam the dining room with enormous skewers of grilled meat they're looking to unload, and you're only job is to turn your table token green side up. Do so, and waiter after waiter will stop to dispense meat onto your plate. This might be any of some 15 various cuts of beef, lamb, pork and chicken. Don't overlook the 30-plus-item vegetable bar, which is loaded with such fine choices as salads, artichoke hearts, cheeses, prosciutto and potatoes, or the surprisingly enchanting lemonade. It's all presented in a handsome room suitable for impressing visiting corporate bigwigs or treating the family.

FOUNTAIN VIEW CAFE

. . . .

1842 FOUNTAIN VIEW
south of San Felipe
☎ **(713) 785-9060**
🍴 **D6**

WHAT AVALON IS TO RIVER OAKS AND the Buffalo Grille is to West U., the Fountain View Cafe is to Tanglewood—that is, a diner in the neighborhood. Businessmen leave their jackets in the car and line up along with ladies in their workout togs. On Saturday sweaty soccer team kids cram in for thin, buttery pancakes and bacon, lone white-haired gents eat reubens while perusing the newspaper and quartets of golfing buddies sit out front telling fishing stories. Moms with strollers stop by for the daily blue-plate lunch specials and thick pineapple shakes. Open only for breakfast and lunch, many a hungry local has peered past the closed sign into darkness at 6 pm and wept. The one unneighborly note is the guy at the cash register. He's been taking our money for years, and we've never had so much as a smile. We don't take it personally.

FRANK'S CHOP HOUSE

. . . .

3736 WESTHEIMER *at Weslayan*
☎ **(713) 572-8600**
frankschophouse.com
🍴 **D6**

TWO FRANKS—FRANK CRAPITTO (CRAPITTO'S Cucina Italiana) and Frank Butera (who helped open Carrabba's so many years ago)—partnered to open this spot for an older, posh River Oaks clientele. Butera has since moved on, but his country club menu remains. In addition to steaks and chops, the restaurant has a fine chicken-fried steak, maple-brined double pork chop, shrimp and grits and fried chicken. The emphasis here is on meat and potatoes dishes that satisfy, not challenge. The beef isn't

Kobe or dry-aged USDA Prime or anything like that. Expect many locally sourced vegetables, including Crapitto's own famous home-grown tomatoes. The dining room provides a hefty dose of mahogany and a clubby atmosphere, which is perfect if you are the targeted clientele. We are not the first to observe that this is a great place to take your grandparents.

FRATELLI'S

················

10989 NORTHWEST FWY.
near W. 34th
☎ **(713) 957-1150**
multiple locations
fratellishouston.com
🍴 **D5**

NOTHING ABOUT THIS RESTAURANT'S STRIP center location says "authentic Italian," but that's what it is indeed and such is the reality of dining in Houston. Chef and owner (with her husband Bob) Teresa Tadeo Whitman plates fresh, handmade pasta and some of the best thin-crust, charred bubble pizza in town from their wood-burning oven. The spaghetti Bolognese is a fan favorite, and it's the homey dishes and the personal touches that make the place. More upscale entrees include veal with prosciutto and sage and pork chops stuffed with spinach and gorgonzola. The wine list is short but heavy on inexpensive bottles. Service is friendly in a neighborly way.

FRENCHIE'S

················

1041 NASA ROAD 1
at El Camino Real
☎ **(281) 486-7144**
frenchiesvillacapri.com
🍴 SOUTHEAST OF **19**

FRENCHIE'S ISN'T FRENCH, BUT THEN again, neither is French Stewart and no one tells him to change his name. This Clear Lake restaurant is actually Italian, which a passerby might assume if the place had been named after brothers/owners Frank and Giuseppe Camera. The food has been a favorite of astronauts since 1979 and by now the walls are covered with NASA memorabilia and photos of celebrities posed with the Cameras. During the day Frenchie's is a hectic counter-service spot that serves heaping bowls of manicotti and plump sandwiches. It settles down a bit at night when table service puts people in their seats, but expect a lengthy wait, especially on weekends. This place isn't fine dining, but it's loaded with character and local Clear Lake color.

√FRENCHY'S CHICKEN

....

3919 SCOTT *at Wheeler*
☎ **(713) 748-2233**
multiple locations
frenchyschicken.com
🍴 F7

OPULAR WITH THE STU-DENTS AT NEARBY UH and TSU because of its late-night hours, cars are lined up through the drive-thru line at midnight. The Frenchy's on Scott Street is also slammed on Sundays with people picking up the best part of their Sunday dinner. And good luck getting some chicken before you tailgate at Robertson Stadium. (It pairs just perfectly with a cold beer.) Frenchy's specialty, if you don't yet know, is Southern-style fried chicken that leans heavily

Fried chicken at Frenchy's Chicken

Creole with addictive cayenne-laced spiciness. Gathering legions of fans since the late 1960s, this walk-up/drive-thru shack has long lines (although this just ensures fresh, hot chicken) and an aversion to credit cards (take cash to be safe). Don't miss the dirty rice, collard greens with bacon or buttery biscuits.

FUFU CAFE

....

9889 BELLAIRE BLVD.
at Beltway 8
☎ **(713) 981-8818**
🍴 C7

S IF THINGS IN CHI-NATOWN WEREN'T confusing enough, what with the dozens of "sterling" this and "golden" that, there is the added disorder of both a Fufu Cafe and, around the corner, a Fufu Restaurant. Assuming accurate navigation, this unadorned cafe is one of a hand-ful of places in Houston to find *xiao long bao*, or soup dumplings. Con-taining hot broth as well as meat, soup dumplings are made by filling the purse-shaped pouches with aspic that liquifies when cooking, then splashes out and burns your tongue if not eaten with careful technique. (Use a spoon and chop-sticks.) Several other things are done very well here, too, including the steamed and fried pork dumplings, *ma po* eggplant and the spicy beef noodle soup layered with pickled mustard greens. Certain amenities like polite service must be given up to dine here, but for the unafraid the food is certainly worth it.

FUNG'S KITCHEN

....

7320 SOUTHWEST FWY.
*between Bellaire Blvd.
& Fondren*
☎ **(713) 779-2288**
fungskitchen.com
🍴 **C7** ✍

![F]UNG'S KITCHEN IS A FLAGSHIP OF AUTHENTIC Cantonese dining in Houston. Weekend mornings are bustling with casual dim sum service and in the evening the rather formal, gilded dining room is often home to celebratory banquets. Chef and owner Hoi Fung has put together a menu of hundreds of items, from softshell crabs served in a blizzard of golden minced garlic to claypots brimming with oysters. Fish tanks along the wall are stocked with oceanic creatures live and fresh from around the world and destined for the table. Seafood is what you come here to eat. Try the sautéed lobster spiked with chives and steamed scallops still in their shells. Of course, all that cooked-to-order seafood isn't cheap, but there's hardly anything quite as impressive. Keep an eye for the Chinese Lunar New Year banquet held every winter.

GATLIN'S BARBECUE

....

1221 W. 19TH *at Bevis*
☎ **(713) 869-4227**
gatlinsbbq.com
🍴 **E5** ✍

![T]HE KINDS OF THINGS WE WOULD NEVER accept from, say, an Italian restaurant, we gladly seek in a barbecue joint. The Styrofoam plates instead of ceramic, long waits and minimal outdoor seating make eating properly smoked meats even more

Gatlin's brisket with a side of dirty rice

RESTAURANTS

enjoyable. That's largely the experience at Gatlin's, widely considered to serve up the best ribs in town and some extremely well done, moist and smoky brisket as well. Spicy, house-cased sausage is further perked up by the zest of vinegary sauce, well served by being piled onto white bread with a ring of onion or pickle. Even the sides, especially the dirty rice, are exemplary. The tidy converted house in The Heights has limited hours and, with only three tables, is mostly for takeout, which is all the better for unbuttoning your pants after you eat.

GIACOMO'S CIBO E VINO
. . . .

3215 WESTHEIMER *west of Kirby*
☎ **(713) 522-1934**
giacomosciboevino.com
🍴 **E6** ✍

WNER LYNETTE HAWKINS WANTS YOU TO DROP IN any time of day to hang out like a Venetian. That, of course, means with food and wine. During lunch, when food is served cafeteria-style at the counter, a variety of tempting *cicchetti*, or small plates, like marinated peppers and spicy lamb meatballs, are on display and additional large plates, including tortelli richly stuffed with chard and goat cheese, are described on chalkboards hanging above. At dinner, the lights dim and waiters hustle

to serve simple grilled rainbow trout made even better by one of the inexpensive, drinkable wines. The mosaic of colorful, asymmetrical tiles on the main wall creates a casual, cheerful environment that makes you want to stay a while, as does a very pleasant vine-lined patio. Giacomo's is proof that a cafe can be both casual and terrific.

GIGI'S ASIAN BISTRO & DUMPLING BAR
. . . .

5085 WESTHEIMER
near McCue, in The Galleria
☎ **(713) 629-8889**
gigisasianbistro.com
🍴 **D6**

OCATED NEXT TO DEL FRISCO'S, THIS GORgeous restaurant with a sultry vibe is the work of Gigi Huang, whose family long had Hunan in The Pavilion. You can enter from the street or from inside The Galleria, and if with a group, ask for a table in the "Alley," where each cubbyhole is curtained off from prying eyes. Samplings from the dinner menu include tamarind-glazed short ribs, green curry chicken and crispy whole fish with Thai basil sauce. There's a major yum factor in the house-made table condiments, too, including plum sauce and chile oil. Unlike so many Asian restaurants, the dessert menu here is worth the calories, so save room for a post-

HAMBURGERS

IKE POLITICS AND RELIGION, YOU PROBABLY SHOULDN'T BRING UP THE CITY'S BEST burgers around polite company if you want to avoid a heated argument. Here are our favorites, but shhh...Keep it to yourself.

BRC GASTROPUB
519 SHEPHERD
☎ **(713) 861-2233**

Not only is this burger a model of perfect construction, juicy but not falling apart and topped with thick-cut bacon, it's super cheap on Monday discount.

NINFA'S ON NAVIGATION
2704 NAVIGATION
☎ **(713) 228-1175**

You wouldn't expect a Tex-Mex institution to make a top-rated burger (and if it did, probably not so good as the Tex-Mex?). Wrong. The new bar menu's fajita burger is a slippery beast topped with avocado, melted white cheese and roasted poblanos.

HUBCAP GRILL
1111 PRAIRIE
☎ **(713) 223-5885**

Come lunchtime, this downtown hole-in-the-wall has lines snaking out the door for hand-formed patties and gluttonous toppings. The new Heights location also serves beer.

BERNIE'S BURGER BUS
@BerniesBurgers on Twitter
☎ **(281) 386-2447**

This mobile burger school bus produces grass-fed Angus burgers with an excellent char. Get the "Substitute" topped with mushrooms, caramelized onions and blue cheese.

THE BURGER GUYS
12225 WESTHEIMER
☎ **(281) 497-4897**

Globally themed Akaushi beef burgers topped with everything from foie gras to papaya salad and paired with caramel shakes are almost excessive. Almost.

BUBBA'S TEXAS BURGER SHACK
5230 WESTPARK
☎ **(713) 661-1622**

Not only are the double-patty buffalo burgers juice-down-your-forearms good (and done Texas-style with yellow mustard), they come with a side of full-on Texas charm.

prandial sweet. For a more casual dining experience, sidle up to the Dumpling Bar for cocktails and a dim sum snack.

GLASS WALL

·················

933 STUDEWOOD *at E. 10th*
☎ **(713) 868-7930**
glasswalltherestaurant.com
🍴🍴 **E5**

THERE WAS A TIME WHEN THE GLASS WALL WAS A preeminent restaurant, particularly within its neighborhood. But since then, The Heights has been a magnet for Houston chefs and their pet projects and Shepard Ross' establishment isn't quite as unique. The food from executive chef Jorge Rodriguez displays a playful mix of influences, from comfort food to Southwestern flair, and changes regularly to reflect seasonal ingredients. A wine pairing is denoted next to each entree courtesy of Ross, who is extremely knowledgeable and passionate on the subject. Beer options are limited in comparison, but a bar menu of indulgent chef-driven junk food is available until 10 pm. Warning: The noise level inside the sparkling dining room crescendos with the influx of beautiful people around 8 pm every night.

GOLD RIBBON BAKE SHOP

·················

2416 WEST HOLCOMBE
between Morningside & Kirby
☎ **(713) 665-6464**
🍴 **E7**

THERE AREN'T TOO MANY SPOTS IN HOUSTON TO find Filipino food, but this slightly run-down restaurant is where homesick families and Med Center workers flock with their families to feed the craving. While the buffet won't win any awards with its 12 or so items and oftentimes absent or aging rice, it does serve up decent home cooking. Pork adobo, a stew of tender meat, soy sauce, vinegar and peppercorns, is a must-try, and the sinful, crispy pork belly was on the line long before foodies were asking for its autograph. Just watch out for the *dinuguan* (pork-blood stew). Be sure to peruse the bakery items and pick up a pack of chewy coconut *pitchi-pitchi* before leaving.

{ 204 }

GOODE CO. TAQUERIA & HAMBURGERS

. . . .

4902 KIRBY *at Westpark*
☎ **(713) 520-9153**
goodecompany.com

🍴 **E7**

OVER ON ITS INTERSECTION OF KIRBY, GOODE Co. has covered a lot of real estate and several food genres but funnily enough, none of the restaurants tout breakfast in their names. And that's one of the best offerings (along with the chocolate cinnamon milkshakes) at this hybrid restaurant. Old-fashioned country breakfasts, served seven days a week now, are supplemented with wild game meats, including venison sausage and quail, and Mexican elements such as tortillas, chorizo and beans. In the afternoons and evenings, grab a longneck and settle down on the popular patio for a mesquite-tinged burger that you can opt to slather with chili con carne. The restaurant is a longtime Houston favorite, and the interior is just kitschy enough to inspire nostalgia that would make the food taste even better if it weren't so good already.

GOODE CO. TEXAS BAR-B-Q

. . . .

5109 KIRBY *at Westpark*
☎ **(713) 522-2530**
multiple locations
goodecompany.com

🍴 **E7**

AN ENTIRE BLOCK OF KIRBY IS PERFUMED with Texas barbecue mesquite smoke, luring huge crowds of visitors and local fans alike into Jim Goode's barbecue mecca, opened way back in 1977. The brisket doesn't hold a candle to the Central Texas standard (it's not fatty or tender enough), but Czech sausage, peppery chicken and sauce-slathered pork ribs will do you right. When scooting down the cafeteria-style line in the midst of all the kitschy Texas paraphernalia, be sure to ask for the duck, which is moist, well flavored and not too lean. Whole pecan pies are highly valued gifts come holiday season and devotees of the jalapeño cheese bread are legion. The Kirby location especially has a nice atmosphere, with lights strung on tree branches dangling above picnic tables; the Katy Freeway spot looks like an old-timey saloon.

RESTAURANTS

GOODE CO. TEXAS SEAFOOD

. . . .

2621 WESTPARK *west of Kirby*
☎ **(713) 523-7154**
multiple locations
goodecompany.com

🍴 **E7**

ON A FRIDAY NIGHT AT GOODE CO. SEAFOOD, you'll arrive to find hordes of anxious-looking Houstonians packed into the bar area waiting for their chance to snag a table or stool at the counter. Crowds are not much reduced on weeknights either, but everyone makes the most of it with a glass of wine or one of the strong frozen margaritas. No competitor has ever been able to equal Goode's sundae-glass campechana, boosted with cubed avocado and chopped onion. Then there's a wide selection of fresh filets that are offered fried or mesquite grilled (a cooking technique perfected across Goode restaurants) and generously stuffed fried seafood po'boys. The original location on Westpark is partially constructed out of an old train car, but both spots are a true-life tribute to Gulf Coast fishing.

GORDITAS AGUASCALIENTES

. . . .

6102 BISSONNET
between Renwick & Hillcroft
☎ **(713) 541-4560**
multiple locations
gorditasaguascalientes.com

🍴 **D7**

THE REALITY IS THAT THE *BARBACOA* SERVED at certain local restaurants—and the schnauzer-sized *barbacoa* burritos made from it—isn't true barbacoa, which is the meat from the cow's head. Gorditas serves the real deal, of course, like everything else on the menu. What comes from these Houston kitchens is more working-class Mexican than Tex-Mex, and standouts include tortas, the namesake gorditas and tacos stuffed with *nopales* (prickly pear cactus), *rajas* (poblano strips) and *chicharrones* (fried pork skin). Mornings mean a host of breakfast tacos that can be washed down with hot *atole*—a drink that mixes masa, cinnamon and chocolate. Homemade tortillas, huge bowls of grease-beaded chicken soup and the holy grail of salsa verde round out the attractions. Checkerboard tiles and a few neon signs define the otherwise simple dining rooms.

GRAPPINO DI NINO

....

2817 W. DALLAS
between Waugh & Montrose
☎ **(713) 528-7002**
ninos-vincents.com

🍴 **E6**

HE MANDOLA FAMILY HAS MADE THIS MONTROSE-area enclave into a mini and extremely well groomed empire with Grappino di Nino and big sister restaurants Vincent's and Nino's surrounding it. What was first simply a patio bar now has an abbreviated dinner menu and is an idyllic location for intimate dinners, special occasion gatherings or ordering a few small plates or flatbreads, a bottle of wine and making of the place what you will. Pink flowers dangle from the wooden beams overhead, and a live band installed on most nights serenades you as you snack on a plate of stuffed pasta or calamari. Linger over a glass of grappa or an espresso before heading home and ponder the advantages of an unhurried life.

GRAVITAS

....

807 TAFT
just south of Allen Parkway
☎ **(713) 522-0995**
gravitasrestaurant.com

🍴 **E6**

HERE WAS AN UGLY AND VERY PUBLIC DUST-UP at Gravitas in 2009 that resulted in chef Jason Gould leaving and owner Scott Tycer going it alone. Many foodies commenced an informal boycott of the restaurant in sympathy with Gould, and Gravitas limped along until 2011 when it was finally sold to an entirely new team, Liquid Gold Hospitality Group. With Tycer out, the new owners have plans to warm up the barebones dining room, adding savvier signage and a sexier, more intimate banquette area. They're leaving the menu—bistro food with designer touches—pretty much alone, though we're told there may be some light editing. We look forward to Gravitas getting back on track.

GRIMALDI'S

....

20 WATERWAY
at Timberloch, The Woodlands
☎ **(281) 465-3500**
multiple locations
grimaldispizzeria.com

🍴 NORTH OF **D1** 🚗

HE TEXAS GRIMALDI'S ARE SIMILAR TO THE

famous Brooklyn original only in name, which has been licensed by the owners of what is now a mini Southwest chain. There's no two-hour wait for a pie (thankfully), and while there are coal-oven pizzas at both The Woodlands and Sugar Land locations, the traditional char on the bottom of the crust is often absent. Of course, you may very well prefer it that way. The toppings, from the lively tomato sauce to the rough-textured pepperoni, are top-notch. Menu options are limited—only pies with two types of sauce (red or garlicky white) and a few starter salads—but we support the idea of sticking with what you know. The two-story Woodlands branch includes a bar that overlooks the Waterway, and both locations are kid-friendly.

GROTTO

. . . .

4715 WESTHEIMER
just inside Loop 610
☎ **(713) 622-3663**
multiple locations
grottorestaurants.com
🍴 **D6**

THIS HOMEGROWN ITAL-IAN SPOT, FOUNDED BY restaurateur Tony Vallone as a major hotspot in the 1980s and now a part of the Landry's restaurant group, has expanded to locations in The Woodlands and even Las Vegas. The sprawling dining room enclosed with vibrant murals reaches stadium-concert noise levels at full capacity, which usually is on weekends. The menu is just as expansive, with an impressive antipasti bar and Neapolitan-inspired selections built with from-scratch pastas. Try the *pappardelle alla campagnola* with chicken and zesty *sugo rosa* sauce, or come for brunch. Service is extremely accommodating with substitutions. Business lunch specials feature an entree plus salad or soup for about $16.

THE GROVE

. . . .

1611 LAMAR *at Crawford,*
on Discovery Green
☎ **(713) 337-7321**
thegrovehouston.com
🍴 **F6**

DURING THE DAY, A SEAT ON THE PATIO OFFERS a view of lively Discovery Green and at night, things turn sparkly as downtown's high-rises come into focus. The Schiller Del Grande group scooped everyone in 2008 by getting the contract to operate this gorgeous high-profile spot in front of the George R. Brown Convention Center. The menu is the now-classic influence medley, Gulf Coast-New American. But with no executive chef to helm the kitchen since the departure of opening chef Ryan Pera (now at Revival Market), reports on the food have been mixed. Slow-roasted pork ribs rest on hominy and cactus salad, and grilled salmon salad comes with Mediterranean chickpea salad. There are quite a few nice specialty cocktails, such as the Cucumber Rose, made with gin and Texas cucumbers, and discounted snack items make happy hour the perfect time to drop by.

GUADALAJARA BAR & GRILL

......

2925 SOUTHWEST FWY.
between Kirby & Buffalo Speedway
☎ **(713) 942-0772**
multiple locations
guad.com
🍴 **D7**

THIS BIG, BOISTEROUS CHOICE FOR TEX-MEX food promises all the Anglo favorites—*margaritas*, bottomless baskets of chips and salsa and fajitas. There's a sizable bar that offers the requisite *margaritas* and *cervezas* along with a happy-hour appetizer menu. *Favoritos de la casa* include seafood enchiladas, bacon-wrapped Pacifico shrimp, grilled South Texas quail and snapper Veracruz. The fajitas have a menu all their own. The atmosphere is festive, and the West Houston and Inner Loop locations do a steady business with families and large parties while the downtown Del Centro spot feeds office workers with speed.

HARRY'S

......

318 TUAM *at Bagby*
☎ **(713) 528-0918**
harrysrestaurantcafe.com
🍴 **E6**

THE 2003 REMODEL ERASED SOME OF ITS more visible history, but this notable diner has been serving blue-plate specials since 1948. In its current form, the menu is an amalgamation of Greek and South American cuisine with excellent breakfast plates thrown in for good measure. Blueberry pancakes and fresh-squeezed orange juice in a sunny, lively dining room make for a classic Saturday morning, but there are also some more experimental items, such as the bacon waffle, pancake omelet and waffles with buffalo chicken strip combo. During lunch, which ends at 2:30 when the restaurant closes, steam-table offerings include both moussaka and chicken-fried steak. Feta-and parsley-dotted thick-cut fries are crave-worthy.

HAVEN

......

2502 ALGERIAN WAY
east of Kirby
☎ **(713) 581-6101**
havenhouston.com
🍴 **E7**

BY NOW, LOCAL AND ENVIRONMENTALLY

responsible dining is de rigueur, but when chef Randy Evans first opened his LEED-certified fine dining establishment with a garden out back in late 2009, he was a Houston pioneer. The cuisine leans toward hearty Southern with gourmet and ethnic inflections that are truly of Houston (wild boar chili, peanut-crusted softshell crab), and the menu reads like a who's-who of Texas farmers, ranchers and artisans. Favorites include the fried green tomatoes and shrimp corndogs with Tabasco mash remoulade as starters and the Akaushi steak with crescenza cheese grits to follow. The white tablecloths denote special-occasion dining, but the lush patio and affordable wine list make snacking on pan-roasted Gulf oysters a happily affordable activity. Lunch specials five days a week—chicken potpie on Wednesdays, fried chicken on Thursdays—are a ridiculous bargain at $10. Haven won *My Table*'s Houston Culinary Award for Best New Restaurant in 2010.

HEARSAY GASTRO LOUNGE
....

218 TRAVIS *at Congress*
☎ **(713) 225-8079**
hearsayhouston.com
🍴 **F6**

THE TERM "GASTRO-LOUNGE" WILL ALWAYS sound like a mildly disgusting diges-

tive experiment to us, so maybe it's a good thing that Hearsay's designation as one isn't entirely accurate. It's more of an upscale comfort food restaurant with a nice cocktail program. And while it's perfectly acceptable to belly up to the bar for a post-work drink, most patrons tend to enjoy full meals. The bacon burger with rosemary fries is the most popular item, and well done mahi-mahi tacos and the Kobe beef dog round out the classed-up menu. Housed in the second-oldest commercial building in town, Hearsay is really rather grand, with soaring ceilings, exposed brick and a twinkling chandelier. The mood is kept low-key, however, with some help from the TVs over the bar playing sports and the friendliness of the wait staff.

HIMALAYA
....

6652 SOUTHWEST FWY.
just west of Hillcroft
☎ **(713) 532-2837**
🍴 **C7** 🖐

CHEF AND OWNER KAISER LASHKARI IS A HOUSTON food celebrity. Not the kind you'd find at the judge's table on reality TV, but the way he presides over his Pakistani restaurant has made him somewhat famous. The experience can be a funny one when he's barking orders from his desk smack in the middle of the dining room or encouraging you to eat more in his hospitable way. The lunch platter is a good place to start, as the compartments of the old-school cafeteria trays are filled with a variety of dishes to try— sometimes a tomato-rich chicken *tikka masala* and often *chopli kebab*, which is a spicy meat patty delicious with cool raita. Otherwise, almost everyone orders the mountainous lamb biryani. The fluffy naan is some of the best in town, and the flan, a bit thicker than the Mexican version, is also a surprising treat. Himalaya is in the same strip center as India Grocers and London Sizzler.

HOBBIT CAFE

. . . .

2243 RICHMOND
between Greenbriar & Kirby
☎ **(713) 526-5460**
myhobbitcafe.com
🍴 **E7**

WE'VE SPENT MANY NIGHTS AT THE Hobbit pondering whether the plastic bags of water dangling overhead actually manage to repel mosquitoes or merely add to the funky hippie aura, only to be distracted by bowls of guacamole or melty tuna sandwiches. When the Hobbit Hole first opened in the 1970s, it was truly for the granola-and-sprouts crowd. Now a swarmed Sunday brunch and several meat items have detracted a bit from its purity, but it's still a favorite for

vegetarian fare and its laid-back mood. The Tolkien theme is evident in some frames hanging around the creaky converted house and in the entree names. The Dwalin, or chicken curry sandwich, is one of the best, as is the salmon burger doused in creamy dill sauce. Our main complaint is with the sides: Shredded carrots and black beans as default options are much-too-earnest holdovers from the spot's health-food days.

HOLLISTER GRILL

1741 HOLLISTER *at Long Point*
☎ **(713) 973-1741**
thehollistergrill.com
🍴 **C5**

ONE OF THE BEST BYOB RESTAURANTS IN HOUSTON, this little Spring Branch restaurant is off most foodies' radar —and its many neighborhood fans like it that way. Shoehorned into a dreary strip center, there's no impressive interior design either. It's all about the food and friendly service. The menu has two speeds. At lunch it's a casual burger-salad-pasta spot with a daily blue-plate special. In the evening the lights are lowered and the dining room is transformed into a fine-dining venue with dishes such as shrimp and scallop risotto, steaks, a grilled veal chop and excellent crabcakes. You might not think it, but this place really bustles in the evening, so be sure to make a reservation.

RESTAURANTS

GET YOUR HOT DOGS HERE

IF YOU CAN'T GRILL YOUR OWN HOT DOGS, HIT THE TOWN—SOME OF THESE PUPS WILL LEAVE you panting for more.

BARNABY'S
1701 S. SHEPHERD
☎ (713) 520-5131
Naturally, dog-themed Barnaby's has hot dogs. Come hungry because the all-beef one-foot kosher dog is large enough to feed two. The semi-chewy sourdough hot dog bun and homemade chili, cheese, onions and/or relish make this marvy.

MOON TOWER INN
3004 CANAL
☎ (832) 266-0105
Yes, beef and pork hot dogs are on offer here, as well as an ever-evolving line-up of unusual wild-game hot dogs, all served on Slow Dough pretzel buns. Definitely a hipster scene.

JAMES CONEY ISLAND
3607 S. SHEPHERD
☎ (713) 524-7400
The skinny tender frank tastes a little saltier and the chili gravy a little oilier than when we were kids. But the bun is still super soft and fresh, and we love the sweet minced onions. The New Yorker with sauerkraut is doggone good.

KAHN'S DELI
2429 RICE BLVD.
☎ (713) 529-2891
The All-American is excellent with a hefty grilled knockwurst (all-beef hot dog) nestled in a soft French roll that's been slathered with mustard and Russian dressing. Chopped tomatoes and purple onions crown this masterpiece.

MAX'S WINE DIVE
4720 WASHINGTON
☎ (713) 880-8737
For a mere (gulp!) $14, you get this astonishing Texas 'Haute' Dog: grass-fed all-beef kosher hot dog on Kraftsmen artisan bun with house-made St. Arnold's sauerkraut or Broken Arrow venison chili, topped with jalapeños and fried onion strings. Plus, crisp frites.

HOLLYWOOD VIETNAMESE & CHINESE

. . . .

2409 MONTROSE
just south of Fairview
☎ **(713) 523-8807**
hollyviet.com
🍴 **E6**

YOU WILL EAT BETTER VIETNAMESE FOOD IN your life, but let's keep in mind the limited dining options at 3 am on a Friday and the fact that you're coming from a costume party. There actually are a few quite good highlights on the elephantine menu, including black pepper tofu and the Vietnamese fajitas (their words, not ours), which are simply grilled meats wrapped in rice paper. Avoiding the Chinese entrees would be advisable but we appreciate the come-as-you-are, whoever-you-are attitude. The patio, festooned with colorful adornments and semi-screened from the boulevard by plants, has become a Montrose landmark.

HONDURAS MAYA CAFE & BAR

. . . .

5945 BELLAIRE BLVD. *at Renwick*
☎ **(713) 668-5002**
hondurasmayacafebar.com
🍴 **C7**

IT'S UNLIKELY THAT YOU WILL VISIT ANOTHER HOUston restaurant where you are served as many black beans as at this mom-and-pop Honduran restaurant. Every meal begins with a basket of chips and cistern of black bean dip sprinkled with salty cheese. Traditional breakfast, which is served all day, comes with slices of fresh avocado, plantains, eggs and refried black beans. *Baleadas*, fluffy, thick tortilla pockets, are smeared with, yes, more refried black beans and stuffed with cheese, beef or eggs. For dinner, try the *lomito de res*, a platter of steak and sautéed peppers, or the *camarones Maya*, shrimp in lemon butter sauce. The margaritas are well crafted and easy to enjoy in the tidy dining room of granite tabletops and beautiful tiling behind the full bar.

HOT POT CITY

. . . .

8300 W. SAM HOUSTON PKWY. S. *at Beechnut, in Hong Kong City Mall*
☎ **(832) 328-3888**
hotpotcityhouston.com
🍴 **B7**

THERE ARE A FEW HOT POT RESTAURANTS across the city, but this one is perhaps the most popular with quite a line during peak winter hours. There are five types of broth to choose from, spicy Mongolian and subtle Japanese shabu being our two favorites. Use the checklist menu to mark what items you would

RESTAURANTS

like to cook in the broth. Split pots allow for two broths per pot, which is pretty neat, and there is a huge selection of proteins (e.g. lamb, pork, head-on shrimp, fresh cuttlefish), noodles (udon, vermicelli, "Canada noodles") and vegetables. There will be rising steam aplenty and probably some sweating, which makes the dish a favorite in cold weather. It's all part of the fun of interactive dining.

HOUSE OF PIES

. . . .

3112 KIRBY *between Richmond & W. Alabama*
☎ **(713) 528-3816**
multiple locations
houseofpies.com
🍴 **E7**

THERE ARE THE DINERS WITH THE JEWEL-TONED vinyl seats and nostalgic Coke wall art...and then there are the real diners. This is the real deal: shabby, brusque and open 24 hours. It's a mainstay for families in the daytime, students and a ravenous post-party clientele in the nighttime. Breakfast is serviceable and popular and, of course, there are the pies. The Bayou Goo, which involves a pecan crust with layers of sweet cream cheese and vanilla custard swirled with chocolate chunks, is a signature flavor. Honestly, though, we prefer the plain chocolate cream. All pies may be purchased whole to take home, and the line on Thanksgiving is madness. This is *not* the place to lounge for hours with coffee and a laptop—there is a minimum charge per hour for sitting at a table if you don't order.

HUBCAP GRILL

. . . .

1111 PRAIRIE *at San Jacinto*
☎ **(713) 223-5885**
multiple locations
hubcapgrill.com
🍴 **F6** 🖐

SURROUNDED BY THE 40-STORY BUILDINGS OF downtown Houston, this squat broom closet of a building liberally appliqued with hubcaps produces some of the best burgers in the city. The hand-formed patties provide the juicy, perfectly seared base for some inventive topping options. Our favorite is the muffaletta burger, layered with housemade olive mix and Swiss cheese.

A slice of banana cream pie at House of Pies

The Triple Heart Clogger comes with a sliced hot dog, bacon and cheese, and the Sticky burger receives a dollop of peanut butter. Arrive early to avoid the disappointment of the kitchen selling out. The lunch rush is so intense that owner Ricky Craig has expanded with a roving burger truck and second location in The Heights (it opened Summer 2011), which offers a bit more seating in a Texas beer garden setting.

HUGO'S

....

1602 WESTHEIMER *at Mandell*
☎ **(713) 524-7744**
hugosrestaurant.net
🍴 **E6** ✍

HOUSED IN A NICELY RESTORED 1920S building, Hugo Ortega's eponymously named citadel of regional Mexican cuisine has been a hit since opening day. Don't dare to think of this place as Tex-Mex; the menu has gone far south of the border to introduce Houstonians to the distinctive flavors of places such as Oaxaca (the birthplace of *mole*) and Puebla (the birthplace of Ortega himself). Octopus al carbon, pork cooked in banana leaf and even fried grasshoppers are on the menu. The boozy Sunday brunch, complete with a Mexican band up on the mezzanine, is a lavish affair with a large buffet spread including an epic dessert table (Ortega's brother Ruben is pastry chef) complete with *tres leches*, thick hot chocolate (the chocolate nibs are ground in house) and more. Other attractions include a serene high-walled patio and mixologist extraordinaire Sean Beck.

HUYNH

....

912 ST. EMANUEL *at Walker*
☎ **(713) 224-8964**
huynhrestauranthouston.com
🍴 **F6** ✍

LIVE IN HOUSTON LONG ENOUGH, AND YOU'LL start to develop some very particular criteria for pho. And in the noodle soup hierarchy, the version here is king, thanks to a complex broth and generous portion of both noodles and meat. Tucked away among the shabby, closed-down storefronts of east downtown, Huynh is cute, modern and a poorly kept secret. There's hardly a miss on the multi-page menu, but since you must eventually choose, we recommend the pulled duck salad, the Phoenix chicken served with a fried egg and spicy-sweet dipping sauce and the fried noodle pancakes. The iced coffee is also exceptional, and the owner will tell you with pride that she imports the beans from Vietnam. For something stronger, feel free to BYOB wine or beer—most people do.

IBIZA

. . . .

2450 LOUISIANA *at McGowen*
☎ **(713) 524-0004**
ibizafoodandwinebar.com
🍽 **F6**

ALTHOUGH HE LOST BY ONE POINT TO CHEF Mario Batali on *Iron Chef*, Ibiza chef/co-owner Charles Clark scores a win with his Spanish-inspired restaurant, now a decade old. With business partner Grant Cooper, the duo stays on point delivering all that's tasteful to a consistently packed house. It's all noisy sophistication here, with spirits high and happy thanks in part to the reasonably priced wine list. High notes include fantastic french fries, grilled shrimp with smoked jalapeño butter resting on crabmeat cornbread and six-hour lamb shank laced with Spanish mint oil and pan-seared foie gras. We also love the pork rib roast, succulent and juicy, with luxurious foie gras blackberry butter atop spicy mashed potatoes, and the mocha bread pudding is famous.

INDIKA

. . . .

516 WESTHEIMER *west of Taft*
☎ **(713) 524-2170**
indikausa.com
🍽 **E6**

CHEF/OWNER ANITA JAIS-INGHANI'S COOKING STYLE is marked by innovation, evident in dishes like sea bass in coconut kari leaf broth and fish in coconut, mint and cilantro marinade. This is progressive Indian cooking, and vegetarians will be pleased with cauliflower kofta or stuffed eggplant. (Meanwhile, the goat brain masala is legendary among adventurers.) Sunday brunch is a good time to pay a visit, when $25 garners unlimited access to a *chaat* bar, small plates from the kitchen such as Parsi soft-scrambled eggs and desserts. Speaking of dessert, Jaisinghani began her career as a pastry chef, so the sweets should not be skipped. The interior is almost as stunning as the food. It has a simultaneously high-tech and medieval feel, in soothing apricot, persimmon, orange and caramel tones that stimulate the appetite. Jaisinghani also conducts cooking classes at the restaurant the fourth Sunday of the month.

IRMA'S

. . . .

22 N. CHENEVERT *at Commerce*
☎ **(713) 222-0767**
🍽 **F6** ✍

FOR FIRST-TIMERS, PLEASE KNOW GOING IN THAT THE menu at this breakfast/lunch spot is speed-recited in Spanish—and since it's understood among gentle folk that mentioning the price is tacky, meal prices aren't mentioned. It might help push you toward a visit to know that the James Beard Foundation named Irma's one of five

The spinach enchiladas at Irma's

2008 "American Classic" restaurants. The over-stuffed decor—full of hundreds of campaign posters, photos and weird gewgaws—is dubiously "classic," but the Mexican home-cooking is not. Owner and *capitán general* Irma Galvan (she's in the safari shorts and combat boots) always oversees front and back of the house with a strong and colorful character: She will pour your lemonade (a miraculous concoction) while barking orders to those in service. Bigwig downtowners love her and love tucking into chicken and spinach enchiladas and pork ribs in tomatillo sauce. The guacamole and charro beans are stuff to write home about, and so is just about everything else. Irma's is also open evenings when the Astros play at nearby Minute Maid Park.

ISTANBUL GRILL
. . . .

5613 MORNINGSIDE
just north of University
☎ **(713) 526-2800**
istanbulgrill.com
🍴 **E7**

THE MAIN AND UNFORTUNATE DIFFERENCE between the delicious *pides* at Istanbul Grill and pizza is that there is no *pide* delivery service that we know of. The thick *pide* dough stuffed with a number of possibilities, including cheese, Turkish sausage and eggs, are pure carb heaven, and we crave them often. The *iskender kebab*, thin-sliced *doner* on buttered *pide* bread, is another winner, though none of the kebabs will do you wrong. Sandwiches accented with red cabbage make for an inexpensive lunch, perfect for a break from shopping in

Rice Village. The small restaurant, decorated with all sorts of beautiful Turkish curios, is also popular with Rice University folks and groups fueling up before a Village pub crawl.

JANG GUEM TOFU HOUSE

. . . .

9896 BELLAIRE BLVD.
at Beltway 8
☎ **(713) 773-2229**
🍴 **B7**

JUST ONE OF THE MANY RESTAURANTS IN THE EVER-multiplying Chinatown strip centers, this Korean cafe's generic "Tofu House" signage does little to attract attention. But the interior's warm yellow wallpaper, adorned with lacquered tree branches, invites you to a comfortable meal. The specialty is tofu soup, which comes to the table bubbling out of its stone bowl, with a serving of rice, varying levels of spiciness and a massive quantity of replenishable sides including kimchee and a small fried fish. Quick and friendly servers whisk away empty dishes and are more than willing to help you decide between other menu items such as Korean barbecue platters and a tasty fried seafood-and-green-onion pancake.

JASMINE ASIAN CUISINE

. . . .

9938 BELLAIRE BLVD.
at Beltway 8
☎ **(713) 272-8188**
🍴 **B7**

TO THE UNINITIATED, SEVEN COURSES OF beef sounds like a dare, but that (and seven courses of fish as well) is a favorite tradition in Vietnamese dining. Jasmine offers both beef and fish cooked seven ways, as does its sister restaurant Saigon Pagolac, and they are quite an undertaking. A portion of the meal requires you to cook the food yourself tableside, while other courses are simply brought from the kitchen alongside the ubiquitous fish sauce, rice paper wrappers and pickled vegetables. If you have enough people in tow, do order the whole fried catfish that comes with maraschino cherry eyes. The dining room is quite refined, with dark wood and paper fans hanging from the ceiling. Lately bills have been upped on weekend nights to account for the live music.

JASPER'S

·················

9595 SIX PINES
at Lake Woodlands Dr.,
The Woodlands
☎ **(281) 298-6600**
jaspers-restaurant.com
🍴 NORTH OF **D1** 🚗

 FTER CONQUERING THE FOOD SCENES IN Dallas, Austin and Plano, restaurant impresario Kent Rathbun brought his "backyard gourmet" to The Woodlands and plopped his sophisticated setting and American comfort food menu down on Market Street overlooking the square. Promising diners the experience will be "like eating at my house," Rathbun stimulates appetite with fall-off-the-bone baby-back ribs (a house specialty), rotisserie-roasted prime rib and fantastic house-made potato chips with blue cheese. The smoked bacon cheeseburger comes with onions braised in Shiner Bock and, by request, can be made with Kobe beef.

JAX GRILL

·················

1613 SHEPHERD
between I-10 and Washington
☎ **(713) 861-5529**
multiple locations
jaxgrillhouston.com
🍴 **E6**

HE FOCUS AT THESE ROADHOUSE DINERS IS definitely the spirited fun and neighborhood atmostphere more than the food. There's a Cajun focus on the fare, with gumbo and bacon-wrapped shrimp with a jalapeño kick and a surprising oyster hidden in the wrap. Your best bet will be the fried catfish, although many patrons of the Bellaire location stick to the not-so-diet-friendly salads during lunch. Burgers are pretty sad and dry. The party is boosted on Friday and Saturdays at the Shepherd location when live zydeco gets everyone out of their seats and dancing. The big space seems much smaller once the crowds roll in, and newcomers are often scooped up as dance partners. Kids are certainly welcome at Shepherd but, in general, the Bellaire location is more family-oriented.

JEANNINE'S BISTRO

·················

106 WESTHEIMER *at Bagby*
☎ **(713) 874-0220**
jeanninesbistro.com
🍴 **E6**

NE OF THE GREAT THINGS ABOUT A GOOD FRENCH fry is that it's so versatile. It can come with a nasty back-alley hamburger or with a side of mussels on a white tablecloth. It's the latter here—whew!—and the fries are among the best. While items like salade Niçoise, creamy chicken *a la reine* in puff pastry and a seafood

RESTAURANTS

omelet please French palates, the specialty is mussels, specifically *moules marinieres*. Plump, astonishingly large bivalves swim in a buttery white-wine broth loaded with chopped celery and onions, which is perfect for dipping rolls and the super crispy *pommes frites*. The tiny, eight-table room is dark and refined, which may explain the mature clientele, but you'll feel perfectly cozy sipping a Belgian ale in the light of a flickering candle.

JIMMY G'S CAJUN SEAFOOD RESTAURANT

. . . .

307 N. SAM HOUSTON PKWY.
EAST *east of I-45*
☎ **(281) 931-7654**
jimmyg.com
🍴 **E2**

IND OF STUCK OUT IN NO-MAN'S-LAND ON THE highway to Bush Intercontinental Airport, Jimmy G's takes advantage of the executive airport business in terms of pricing and cursory (but adequate) service. It's more of a convenient stopover for semi-desperate, stranded travelers than anything else but there is one bright spot: the grilled oysters. They're really just blazed on the gas grill and bathed in garlic butter and parmesan, but they're tasty. Fried oysters are similarly reliable and when in season, order the fried crawfish po'boy.

JONATHAN'S THE RUB

. . . .

9061 GAYLORD *at Corbindale*
☎ **(713) 465-8200**
jonathanstherub.com
🍴 **C6**

HEF/OWNER JONATHAN LEVINE JUST WANTS TO cook you a spice-rubbed salmon or a nice black pepper-encrusted steak au poivre. No, really, he wants to cook it with his own hands, on the line at his clubby (but recently expanded) neighborhood joint. Some still recall the infamous incident with the jettisoned food critic, but overall a cozy, simple meal is the most frequent outcome here. Every meal begins with cheesy bread and most of the menu is simple, rustic fare such as a nicely brined pork chop, the burger on a slightly sweet but sturdy bun and macaroni and five cheeses. There are some Brooklyn-Italian touches (e.g. pasta and meatballs, seafood fra diavolo), and in the grand Houston tradition, portions are over large, which to a certain extent makes up for the high prices. BYOB for a $7 corkage fee.

JOYCE'S SEAFOOD & STEAKS

....

6415 SAN FELIPE *at Winrock*
☎ **(713) 975-9902**
joycesseafood.com
🍴 **C6**

THE EXTERIOR DOESN'T LOOK LIKE MUCH, AND the inside is so excessively nautical that Joyce's could easily be mistaken for a Galveston seawall tourist trap—that or the live action set for "Spongebob Squarepants." But that just makes it more fun to eat in one of Houston's best-kept secrets. Joyce's blends culinary traditions of the Gulf Coast, Southern Louisiana and Mexico and the result is blackened catfish enchiladas and oyster shooters on tortilla chips with chipotle aioli. Raw oysters, grilled fish tacos, gumbo, crabcakes with a sauce of poblano peppers and New Orleans-style barbecued shrimp made with Shiner Bock beer all seem to be menu naturals. If you're unfamiliar with the location, know that this reliable Tanglewood eatery is set back from its San Felipe address on Winrock.

JUAN MON'S INTERNATIONAL SANDWICHES

....

1901 TAFT *at W. Webster*
☎ **(713) 528-5826**
juanmons.com
🍴 **E6**

HOUSED IN A RENOVATED GAS STATION and painted a garish green in the sleek, modern interior, Juan Mon's physical qualities only hint at the shop's quirky character. Each of the 17 sandwiches on the menu were inspired by owner Juan Montero's travels—the Venice is stuffed with spaghetti, salami and grilled onions, and the Mexico City houses breaded beef milanesa, avocado and jalapeños in a fresh, chewy bolillo roll. The fun is in choosing which monstrous sandwich or city personality matches your own, while the food itself is fresh and indulgent. We do find ourselves choosing the Mexico City most often and wondering why we don't just go get a real torta, but Juan Mon's is awfully loveable. Montero recently added a full bar so similarly goofy cocktails like the Moscow (a white Russian) are also available.

RESTAURANTS

{ 221 }

JULIA'S BISTRO

....

3722 MAIN *at Alabama*
☎ **(713) 807-0090**
juliasbistro.com
🍴 **E7**

SLEEK AND VIBRANT DECOR WITH SUPER-saturated colors of magenta, ruby and red-orange, complemented by spanking white tablecloths, fresh flowers and candles, sets up this ultra-urbane dining room for high expectations. The MetroRail whizzes by outside on Main Street, concrete floors guarantee it will get noisy, and it isn't cheap. This Nuevo Latino eatery is the inspiration of restaurateur Carmen Vasquez, and the menu is as vibrant as the dining room. Try the chipotle Caesar topped with manchego cheese, pulled pork taquitos or pork sandwich with avocados and plenty of a spicy mustard sauce. Julia's isn't as trendy as it was in its heyday and can be ghostly empty, but we're rooting for the restaurant to soar again.

JUS' MAC

....

2617 YALE *at E. 26th*
☎ **(713) 622-8646**
jusmac.com
🍴 **E5**

THE QUESTION IS: HOW MUCH DO YOU LIKE MAC 'n' cheese? You have to love it a lot to like Jus' Mac. Apparently many people do, so 17 varieties plus fried mac 'n' cheese balls and a mac 'n' cheese soup can only be a good thing. Not only is there the expected four-cheese mac, but brazen toppings like roasted poblano peppers, buffalo chicken and taco fixings get mixed in for diversity. The counter-service dining room is tiny (so is the parking lot) so you'll probably have to jockey for a table or order to-go. But pass the time until your personal-sized skillet of noodles arrives with a glass of wine and you'll do just fine. The owners recently added a few paninis to the menu, and there are a couple salads as well.

KAHN'S DELI

....

2429 RICE BLVD.
between Kirby & Morningside
☎ **(713) 529-2891**
kahnsdeli.com
🍴 **E7**

BEING A FAN OF KAHN'S IS A LOT LIKE BEING A fan of the Astros; there's a lot of mourning. Many a Houstonian was still wet behind the ears when they first visited Alfred's in the Village and tasted their very first reuben. Then, Alfred's closed and we mourned until his son carried on the deli tradition, albeit in a tiny Village hole-in-the-wall. Now, the deli has changed hands once again and given the location a shiny re-do, complete with flat-screen TVs and a

MUSEUM DISTRICT LUNCH

LOOKING AT NEOCLASSIC NUDES ALWAYS MAKES US HUNGRY. HERE ARE SIX CLOSE-BY spots for refreshment and a meal.

DANTON'S GULF COAST SEAFOOD KITCHEN
4611 MONTROSE
☎ **(713) 807-8883**

Finish up a day of art-gawking with a dozen oysters (in season), bowl of gumbo or a po'boy at this New Orleans-style restaurant a few blocks north of the Contemporary Arts Museum.

CAFE EXPRESS
5601 MAIN *(downstairs)*
☎ **(713) 639-7370**

You don't even need to step outside the Museum of Fine Arts-Houston in order to dine at Cafe Express. It's located on the lower level of the Beck Building. Open for breakfast, lunch and dinner—and MFAH members receive a discount.

BOCADOS
1312 W. ALABAMA
☎ **(713) 523-5230**

A short walk from the Menil Collection, Rothko Chapel, Dan Flavin Installation and Houston Center for Photography, Bocados specializes in Mexican seafood dishes.

MONARCH
5701 MAIN *in Hotel ZaZa*
☎ **(713) 526-1991**

The poshest of this group of restaurants, the Monarch offers splendid outdoor seating and a beautiful view of the Mecom Fountains. It's just a block from the MFAH.

BODEGAS TACO SHOP
1200 BINZ *(entrance faces Caroline)*
☎ **(713) 528-6102**

Bodegas, not far from the Houston Museum of Natural Science, will inspire your own inner culinary mad scientist with an extensive mix-and-match menu of tortillas, fillings and salsas.

RAVEN GRILL
1916 BISSONNET
☎ **(713) 521-2027**

Straight west of the MFAH and handy to Rice University Art Gallery, this neighborhood spot serves up traditional American food with some great Mexican dishes.

* Visit houstonmuseumdistrict.org for a list of Houston's many museums.

few reuben variations on toasted French rolls. The history is no longer there, but the sandwiches are still huge and a good value. The amount of knockwurst in particular is almost obscene.

KANEYAMA

. . . .

9527 WESTHEIMER
east of S. Gessner
☎ **(713) 784-5168**
kaneyama-houston.us

🍴 **C7**

T HERE'S NO NAKED SUSHI OR SAKE BOMB shooting going on at this traditional Japanese staple in west Houston. The focus is instead on the authentic food, which the restaurant has been producing steadily since 1994. There's no shabbiness to be seen, either: The dining room is well lit, and the hostesses wear kimonos. Private tatami rooms are beautiful, but unless your group wants privacy, we recommend a seat at the sushi bar. Larger entrees like tempura, soba noodle and pork katsu are quite good, but the raw fish preparation is remarkable. Owner Keeper Lin describes the sushi preparation as "art for consumption," and the fresh king crab, sea urchin and deliciously oily salmon prove the point.

KANOMWAN

. . . .

736½ TELEPHONE
near S. Lockwood
☎ **(713) 923-4230**

🍴 **F7**

T WAS A SAD DAY IN THE HOUSTON FOOD WORLD when Darawan Charoenrat, the gruff owner of this longtime favorite, passed away in 2010. He had presided over the dining room with a commanding bark, but like the gritty location on Telephone Road, it was all part of the experience. Never shying away from the big heat, the kitchen has a liberal hand with the chilies (and lemongrass and basil). It's BYOB until 8:30 pm, so bring your own cooler stocked with beer or wine to put out the fire. Try the deep-fried pork toasts, the whole fried snapper with chile sauce and, if you have an iron palate (because it's fiery hot), the green curry with chicken.

KASRA PERSIAN GRILL

. . . .

9741 WESTHEIMER *at Gessner*
☎ **(713) 975-1810**
kasrahouston.com

🍴 **C7** 🔖

MEAL AT KASRA BEGINS WITH PIPING HOT FLATbread, feta and fresh herbs and should ideally continue on with the garlicky hummus, fork-tender lamb shank in sour cherry sauce and gently spiced *kubideh* kebabs on a heaping pile of dill rice. The fried eggplant is stellar and, if available, order *tahdigh*, the "bottom of the pot" crispy rice starter. Leftovers are highly likely. The food is maybe the best in town as far as Persian restaurants go, which is why the spare, but rather elegant dining room is packed with both families and foodies during prime hours. Tucked into the corner of a nondescript strip mall in Westchase, Kasra is easily bypassed by the uninformed but a destination for those in the know.

KATA ROBATA

3600 KIRBY *at Richmond*
☎ **(713) 526-8858**
katarobata.com
🍴 **E7** ✍

KATA ROBATA IS THOUGHT BY MANY TO BE THE best sushi restaurant in the city. But to truly take advantage of what it has to offer, it helps to have an adventurous palate. Bypass the California rolls and such on the menu and test the skills of sushi master Manabu Horiuchi, ideally by ordering the *omakase* (chef's choice tasting menu) if your bank account allows. The sushi—a sliver of fresh fish subtly dressed with a crunch of salt and tart *yuzu* or a bolder pat of foie gras—is world class. Hot meals, ranging from Kobe short ribs to

sake-steamed mussels, are also exquisite. A seat at the sushi bar affords a view of the action and the small back patio outfitted with a robata grill is popular for happy hour. Be sure to also take advantage of the sake list.

KATSUYA BY STARCK

2800 KIRBY *at Westheimer in West Ave*
🍴 **E6**

THIS GLAM WEST COAST JAPANESE RESTAURANT— a high-powered, high-dollar collaboration between sushi chef Katsuya Uechi and design impresario Philippe Starck—is set to open in the West Ave development in Spring 2012.

KENNY & ZIGGY'S

2327 POST OAK BLVD.
between Westheimer & San Felipe
☎ **(713) 871-8883**
kennyandziggys.com
🍴 **D6** ✍

THEY SAY EVERYTHING IS BIGGER IN TEXAS and that's true even of our out-of-state imports. Everything in this New York-style deli—from the dining room (still always packed) to the sandwiches to the éclairs in the old school glass pastry case to owner Ziggy Gruber's personality—is outsized. Breads and cakes are baked

RESTAURANTS

in-house, and meats are cured and pickled on site. The smoked fish is overnighted from New York, and the chicken matzo ball soup is widely believed to cure colds. If you dare the $38 eight-decker sandwich (The Zellagabetsky) and can finish it all alone, free cheesecake is your reward. (A regular pastrami sandwich is a mere three inches thick.) Try also the cheese blintzes, fried *kreplach* (filled dumplings), cold beet borscht, whitefish salad and chopped liver.

KHUN KAY THAI-AMERICAN CAFE

. . . .

1209 MONTROSE *at W. Clay*
☎ **(713) 524-9614**
khunkaythaicafe.com
🍴 **E6**

CO-OWNERS/COUSINS SUPATRO YOOTO (FRONT of the house) and Kay Soodjai (chef), proprietors of the late Golden Room in the same location, reopened in 2008 with this fast-casual concept where all their customers' Thai favorites are still available. Walk-up counter-service inside the sunny yellow dining room guarantees a quick lunch or dinner. Entrees tend to run a little sweet, but that can be combated by upping the spiciness level (choose from the five available levels), and the *tom yum* soup in particular is a nice balance of sour and spicy. Vegetar-

ians will find a whole menu devoted to them: Tofu and imitation duck can be substituted for meat in nearly every curry or stir-fry. Limited free delivery is available in the neighborhood, and the food is nicely packaged.

KHYBER NORTH INDIAN GRILL

. . . .

2510 RICHMOND *east of Kirby*
☎ **(713) 942-9424**
🍴 **E7**

THE FIRST THING YOU'LL NOTICE ABOUT THIS restaurant is the signage outdoors. Whoever chooses the wording on the marquee has a playful sense of humor and if you don't spot an odd, altered aphorism, then look for a sassy retort to the nearby Pappadeux marquee. Inside, there is an attractive exposed-brick interior with lots of tree-sized plants and Oriental carpets. Even though the kitchen has its good days and its bad days, most who try the lamb *korma* come away routinely satisfied, and the hot, buttered naan is quite good. Owner Mickey Kapoor's lunch buffet still keeps them coming in, but it seems sometimes like the place is running on auto pilot. Or maybe it's just that there are so many newer, more authentic places in town that have diminished our admiration for this golden oldie.

KILLEN'S STEAKHOUSE

2804 S. MAIN
south of CR 518, Pearland
☎ **(281) 485-0844**
killenssteakhouse.com
🍴 SOUTH OF **G9** 🚗

I N TRUE COWBOY STYLE, OWNER/CHEF RONNIE Killen doesn't ask you to dress up even if he's serving Allen Brothers USDA Prime beef. Located more or less in the middle of nowhere between Pearland and Alvin, in a low-ceilinged building with a Western theme, one wouldn't expect this to be one of the best steakhouses in greater Houston. But that it is and overall, the menu is simple and very well executed. Draped over the edge of a stemmed cocktail glass filled with crushed ice, the five plump shrimp are served with a splendid homemade tartar sauce or rémoulade. The steaks (including a 32-oz. dry-aged Kobe long bone-in ribeye) come to the table all alone on a plate, seasoned ever so gently and grilled exactly as ordered. Among the sides, there are steak fries, sensational creamed corn, sweet potato fries and haricots verts with shallots. Save room for Killen's signature dessert, the crème brûlée bread pudding.

KIM SON

2001 JEFFERSON *at Chartres*
☎ **(713) 222-2461**
multiple locations
kimson.com
🍴 **F6**

"MAMA LA" (AKA KIM SU TRAN LA), HER husband and seven kids fled Vietnam in 1980, came to Houston and opened a modest spot where she set about cooking selections from the 250 recipes memorized from the culinary repertoire of her mother-in-law. Thirty-one years later, numerous restaurants, cafes and banquet halls all over town relate quite a success story. Each location retains its own personality. The Bellaire location is a buffet at both lunch and dinner, with a huge spread of Vietnamese delights, including spring rolls, snails, stir fried crabs and even hot pot. The Stafford spot has Americanized lunch specials during the

Exterior of Kim Son

weekdays and is popular for dim sum on the weekends. The original Jefferson Kim Son is still a favorite for Vietnamese families celebrating with banquets. Be sure to order the seafood birds nest.

KIRAN'S

4100 WESTHEIMER
east of Mid Lane
☎ **(713) 960-8472**
kiranshouston.com

🍴 **D6**

WNER/CHEF KIRAN VERMA HAS TWO PASSIONS: reimagining traditional Indian cuisine and providing diners with urbane tasteful surroundings. Her namesake restaurant responds to both. The main dining room, with its sophisticated burgundy furnishings and abundant orchids, gives way to a second equally elegant dining space also used for private parties and business groups. Try Kiran's tandoori portobello mushroom stuffed with creamy paneer or her roasted red snapper in *ajwain* sauce to sample her approach to contemporary Indian cuisine—and pair them with a wine from her smart collection. Don't be surprised if you're waitlisted to attend her popular wine dinners and scotch dinners. Kiran's monthly high tea, India-style, has also developed its own devoted following of ladies who lunch and sometimes their guys, too.

KUBO'S SUSHI BAR & GRILL

2414 UNIVERSITY BLVD.
(upstairs) at Morningside
☎ **(713) 528-7878**
kubos-sushi.com

🍴 **E7**

BOVE THE HUBBUB OF RICE VILLAGE, THIS minimalist-chic sushi spot could easily be dismissed as another glam restaurant with no real heart. But despite the crowds and their shopping bags, Kubo's has consistently won raves from critics and customers alike. Chefs come and go, but the currently installed mind in the kitchen belongs to chef Kiyoka Ito, and he has turned Kubo's into a top-notch restaurant. Begin the meal with braised pork belly and move to market-fresh fish, including delicate mackerel and sweet scallops. A current house speciality is *kaiseki*, an eight-course chef-designed meal that celebrates the current season. Call a week in advance to make a *kaiseki* reservation and be prepared to shell out around $100 per person.

LA GRIGLIA

....

2002 W. GRAY *at McDuffie*
☎ **(713) 526-4700**
lagrigliarestaurant.com
🍴 **E6**

THIS IS THE RESTAURANT THAT INTRODUCED HOUSTON to shrimp and crab cheese-cake. Once a shining light in Tony Vallone's now-gone collection of restaurants (there's a historic collection of signatures from another generation of Houston society captured in the cement floor from the 1991 opening night), the place is now a part of the Landry's restaurant empire. The noisy see-and-be-seen aspect remains, however, and the kitchen is steady, the service polished and the food better than it needs to be. Murals, tiling and carpet are all a riot of color and mis-matched patterns, which could potentially work as an appetite stimulant for seafood tortellini or a veal chop with crimini mushrooms. The tucked-away patio, complete with a splashing fountain and fire pits, is a nice respite from the bedlam inside.

LA GUADALUPANA BAKERY & CAFE

....

2109 DUNLAVY
north of Fairview
☎ **(713) 522-2301**
🍴 **E6**

THERE ISN'T MUCH CURB APPEAL TO THIS MEXI-can hideaway, but the food served in snug booths and its convenient BYOB policy has made Guadalupana a low-key neighborhood favorite. Breakfast draws in a hung-over crowd craving the fragrant, house-roasted cinnamon coffee, sizeable and sloppy breakfast tortas and *machaca norteña*, a migas alternative made with scrambled eggs and dried beef. For lunch and dinner, the *sopes* topped with tender *barbacoa* and queso fresco are exceptional, as is the first-class *mole*. If you pass on bringing beer (which you can buy in the adjacent convenience store), order a tumbler of layered orange, beet and carrot juices known as the Vampiro. Owner Trancito Diaz was once a pastry chef at the Houston Country Club, so diners would be remiss in passing up on the various baked goods in the case in front.

Flour tortillas are rolled out at Ninfa's

LA MEXICANA

....

1018 FAIRVIEW *at Montrose*
☎ **(713) 521-0963**
lamexicanarestaurant.com
🍴 **E6**

NOWN AS "LA MEX" TO ITS FANS, MANY of whom have been dining here for more than 20 years, this sprawling restaurant is another Montrose favorite for filling breakfasts. The *huevos rancheros* with a side of excellent, spicy tamales makes for a huge spread and there are a number of breakfast taco options as well. The fajitas are pretty standard fare, but the *taco de guisado de puerco* (a handmade flour tortilla with cubes of pork in red sauce) will do you better. The soups, either *caldo de pollo* (chicken) or *sopa de fideo* swimming with skinny fideo noodles, are also good choices. Service is hit or miss, but the colorful paper flags hanging from the ceiling along with the margaritas keep things festive.

LA VISTA

....

1936 FOUNTAIN VIEW
at San Felipe
☎ **(713) 787-9899**
fatbutter.com
🍴 **D6**

HIS SOMETIMES COMFORTABLE, SOMETIMES cramped, neighborhood joint is known for two things: its BYOB policy (one of the earliest BYOB advocates in Houston) and the addictive bread that comes complimentary before every meal. If you don't completely spoil your appetite, there are a number of grilled entrees that read more American than Italian ahead of you. Shrimp and grits shares menu space with gnocchi, but the pizzas and steamed mussels are the reliable options. There's nothing wasted on pretense at La Vista, including the "vista" that can range from a street-side view of clogged traffic to sweating delivery people at nearby places of business. But the atmosphere is nice and the food can be surprisingly good.

LANKFORD GROCERY

....

88 DENNIS *at Genesee*
☎ **(713) 522-9555**
lankfordgrocery.com
🍴 **E6**

OUSTON HAS MORE THAN ITS SHARE OF burger dives, but Lankford has the distinction of having been featured on the Food Network's *Diners, Drive-ins and Dives*. The little old white house with red trim (and undulating floorboards) was originally a grocery store when it opened back in 1938, but has since become famous for good old-fashioned breakfasts and sloppy, non-artisan hamburgers. The ooze factor on the hand-formed, coarse-ground patties is high, especially if you order the Grim, which is layered with an egg, bacon and macaroni 'n' cheese. The Firehouse is legitimately spicy from chopped habanero, so beware if you're dainty. Lankford is usually packed at lunch; you may have to jostle for service. Breakfast and lunch only; credit cards are not accepted.

LAREDO TAQUERIA

· · · · · · · · · · · · · · · ·

915 SNOVER at Washington
☎ **(713) 861-7279**
🍴 **E6**

HY BYPASS OTHER, FANCIER TEX-MEX joints in the area to stop at this goofy-looking orange and yellow building? Well, the long line for breakfast tacos on weekend mornings indicates the kitchen is doing something right. The owners appear to be Texans fans, if you're into that. And things are certainly inexpensive, with a rich chicken *mole* taco ringing in under $2. There are also *nopales* (cactus), *barbacoa*, *chicharrones* (fried pork rind) and *fideo* (noodle) tacos, and larger combo plates with beans and rice sides or tamales if you're extra hungry. It's a no-frills operation, with neon signs and red vinyl seating, but Laredo's cult following finds it more than worth it.

LAST CONCERT CAFE

· · · · · · · · · · · · · · · ·

1403 NANCE west of McKee
☎ **(713) 226-8563**
lastconcert.com
🍴 **F6**

OU'D IMAGINE THAT THE KIND OF BUSINESS where you have to knock to get in speakeasy-style would have a strict dress code and celebrity DJ spinning inside. That's certainly not the case at this hippie haven. No, the knocking probably has more to do with the fact that everyone in the back courtyard is engaged in, *uh*, certain activities—at least when they're not participating in the drum circle, sipping on slightly overpriced bottles of cheap beer or scarfing down a plate of quesadillas and guacamole. The Tex-Mex here really isn't particularly good, but the this-is-what-I'd-make-at-home quality to the stewed beef tacos sprinkled with shredded cheese and black bean tostadas is certainly never offensive. Last Concert will surely provide a bit of local color, and if you're already here enjoying a Beatles cover band, a bowl of the potato and green chile soup will probably hit the spot.

LATE NITE PIE

....

302 TAUM *at Bagby*
☎ **(713) 529-5522**
🍴 **E6**

A FTER THIS LATE-NIGHT PIZZA PLACE moved from its original converted garage location (now St. Dane's), it lost some of its edge. Known for the world's slowest service and a too-cool-to-care tattooed and tired crowd, the restaurant had long been appreciated for serving middling-quality pies to people coming down from one too many. Or maybe it lost its edge after we turned 21. Either way, the pizzas are the same, with a doughy crust and frat-boy names like the Italian Stallion (Italian sausage, pepperoni, roma tomatoes and Italian dipping sauce) and the Stanky Whore (with anchovies, roasted garlic and goat cheese). Now there are more well-dressed Midtowners than bikers pouring in just a little before 2 am and some arcade games in the back.

LATIN BITES CAFE

....

1302 NANCE *at Richey*
☎ **(713) 229-8369**
latinbitescafe.com
🍴 **F6** ✍

T HE FACT THAT STUNNING, CHEF-DRIVEN CUISINE can be served in a teeny dining room surrounded by abandoned warehouses is just part of the beauty of this city. Driving up to it, you wouldn't expect much from Latin Bites. But once inside this Peruvian spot, you'll come to love the Mid-Century style wall hangings, the exposed brick and, of course, chef Roberto Castre's food. Start with the *tacu-tacus*, three mini rice and bean cakes topped with pork adobado, lamb cilantro stew and shredded beef that arrive looking very stately on a clean white plate. You can't go wrong with one of the ceviches (which change frequently and range in style from Japanese to traditional Peruvian), the tender churrasco steak with chimichurri and the *seco de cordero* (slow-cooked lamb stew). Bring your own wine ($5 wine corkage fee) and be sure to make reservations.

LAURENZO'S PRIME RIB

....

4412 WASHINGTON
at Patterson
☎ **(713) 880-5111**
laurenzos.net
🍴 **E6**

T HIS NEWCOMER FROM THE NINFA LAURENZO family had a bit of an identity crisis when it first opened in 2010. First it was an upscale sports bar; now it's a prime rib house with a sporty feel and an emphasis on the margaritas. The menu still shows signs

RESTAURANTS

of a schizophrenic personality, with shrimp scampi, burgers and quesadillas all offered, but most of it is well done and served in heaping Texas-style portions. Specialties include the French dip sandwich, house-smoked salmon and, of course, prime rib. Another interesting component is the sustainable garden in the back, watered with rain and fed with compost scraps from the kitchen, then turned into incredibly fresh eats back in the restaurant.

LAURIER CAFE

. . . .

3139 RICHMOND
east of Buffalo Speedway
☎ **(713) 807-1632**
lauriercafe.com
🍴 **E7**

INING AT GARY FULLER'S LAURIER CAFE IS a distinctly adult experience; there are no toys to sweeten your Happy Meal deal. Minimalist red, white and blue décor set the tone for simple, well-executed fare. The short and tight French-American menu adapts traditional bistro classics with a modern, local sensibility. Salads like the leek and asparagus with a poached egg truly let the ingredients shine while the scallops served on a bed of sliced beets get a very Houston touch of Thai chili glaze. A savory vegetable tart made with expert pastry crust is crowned with bite-size pieces of eggplant, artichoke and fennel in

a cloud of goat cheese. The wine list is very reasonably priced (so yes, this is still a happy meal), and the patio is screened by greenery from the noise of passing traffic.

LE MISTRAL

. . . .

1420 ELDRIDGE *near Briar Forest*
☎ **(832) 379-8322**
lemistralhouston.com
🍴 **A6**

UT IN THE WEST SIDE OF HOUSTON, WHERE European oil executives are all too eager to patronize the several French restaurants, Le Mistral's Provence-inspired cuisine still manages to stand out. Its newer digs a parking lot away from the original location are very swank and outfitted with a bar area and its own bar menu. Despite the fancy surroundings and food presentation that utilizes more than its fair share of swoops and dabs of sauce, the menu is rife with hearty, soul—warming fare. The escargot and seared foie gras are excellent places to start, and the duo of duck leg confit and seared breast in orange sauce is gorgeous. We also like the onion tart, seared scallops, mussels and wild mushroom soup. Brothers David Denis (chef) and Sylvain Denis (front of the house) run Le Mistral, which was named as having the Best Food in Houston by Zagat 2010.

YOU SAY TOMATO

HOW DO YOU LIKE YOUR TOMATO SOUP? CHUNKY WITH GARDEN FRESH TOMATOES and basil, or smooth and light as silk? Rich with cream or just clean? Here are five versions to try.

BROWN BAG DELI
2036 WESTHEIMER
☎ (713) 807-9191
Thick and dazzling red, with naturally tart fresh-pureed tomatoes, lots of refreshing basil, a touch of pepper and a buttery mouth-feel (no cream). Satisfying and warming, right down to your toes.

EPICURE CAFE
2005 W. GRAY
☎ (713) 520-6174
Light, silky and drinkable with blended tomatoes and tasty fresh basil slivers. Delivers a super tangy flavor and makes the ideal partner for a sandwich or quiche.

LA MADELEINE
6205 KIRBY
☎ (713) 942-7081
This locally beloved creamy tomato basil soup is so popular it's even sold in take-home jars. Thick with cream, flecks of basil and sweet-tinged pureed tomatoes, this luxurious bisque verges on cream sauce.

PALAZZO'S TRATTORIA
2620 BRIAR RIDGE
☎ (713) 784-8110
Chunky, rustic cream-based version with tomato pieces, seeds and lots of fresh basil shredded on top tastes tart and opulent all at once. Toasted herb crouton garnish is a nice touch.

RUGGLES CAFE BAKERY
2365 RICE BLVD.
☎ (713) 520-6662
"Mr. Clark's" tomato basil soup is a beautiful coral color with a bright flavor to match. Expect thick and soulful soup with the right balance of cream and fresh-tart tomato puree, green basil flecks and a whisper of garlic.

LEE'S SANDWICHES

....

11210 BELLAIRE BLVD. at Boone
☎ **(281) 933-9988**
multiple locations
leesandwiches.com
🍴 **B7**

Dining room at Les Givral's

THE MCDONALD'S OF VIETNAMESE SAND-wiches touched down in Houston in 2006 with all the corporate trappings that Houstonians aren't used to getting with their $2.50 lunches—a drive-thru, clean and ample seating, and even a little showmanship. Turns out, the sandwiches themselves aren't very good but there are still a few good reasons to drop by. The Vietnamese iced coffee will do you right, and the pastries are even better. Ogle the baguette production line on display behind glass and pick up a *pâté chaud* (a stuffed flaky pastry) and a cream puff. Then head elsewhere for your *banh mi*.

LES GIVRAL'S

....

2704 MILAM at Drew
☎ **(713) 529-1736**
multiple locations
lesgivrals.com
🍴 **F6**

LES GIVRAL'S IS A PROM-INENT NAME IN HOUS-ton quick Vietnamese, which makes distinguishing which of the locations belong to the original owning family and which were started by disgruntled relatives all the more confusing. The Milam location has the best food of all of them, this much we know. The one on Congress is rather sorry and the Les Givral's Kahve on Washington a complete departure from the seeming hole-in-the-wall imperative of the others with a full bar and soaring architectural detail. The menu at all locations hits the basic categories: *banh mi* sandwiches, *pho* and rice plates. The sandwiches are the most reliable, whether chargrilled pork, tofu or the head meats, but the *pho*, while not bad, is easily outshone by versions at other nearby restaurants.

LITTLE BIG'S

....

2703 MONTROSE at Westheimer
☎ **(713) 521-2447**
littlebigshouston.com
🍴 **E6**

BIG NAME CHEF BRYAN CASWELL (OF REEF,

Stella Sola and El Real) went down-home with this sliders joint on a busy nightlife intersection. The brief menu includes four burger options: beef with caramelized onions, fried chicken, pulled pork and black bean. (The removal of the cheese-stuffed mushroom cap slider from the menu was met with a picket-sign protest.) The delectable hand-cut fries with sriracha remoulade have soaked up many a pint of beer out on the spacious deck, and almost as many booze-laced milk-shakes like the Dude have done work in the opposite direction. Open until 3 am on the weekends and equipped with a jukebox with EPs from local bands, Little Big's is perfect for the neighborhood, especially late night.

LITTLE BITTY BURGER BARN

. . . .

5503 PINEMONT *east of Antoine*
☎ **(713) 683-6700**
littlebittyburgerbarn.com
🍴 **D5**

"LITTLE BITTY" REFERS TO THE SIZE OF THE trailer dining room rather than the burgers, which are full-sized. If you do love miniature food, there are sliders as well as a number of sand-wiches, including a patty melt, French dip and double-decker BLT. Of course you're probably only here for the burger, so you should know that the rather thin patty is

touted for being never frozen and it's evident in the taste. Each comes on a toasted bun with lettuce, pickle and onion and the condi-ments of your choosing—a line-up of bottles on the counter indicates they are serious about their hot sauce—and hand-cut fries cooked to a deep brown. This is America in the year 2011, so there's also a Double Dare burger challenge should you be so bold.

LOLA

. . . .

1102 YALE *at E. 11th*
☎ **(713) 426-5652**
eatlola.com
🍴 **E5**

WITH TWO INTER-ESTING RESTAU-rants—Pink's Pizza and Dragon Bowl—under his belt, restaurateur Ken Bridge strikes again with a crowd-pleasing diner concept. Situ-ated on a busy intersection in The Heights, the cheery, retro interi-or is spacious and buzzing. Cute touches include a blue telephone-booth door and chartreuse walls. Familiar but well-executed menu items that are varied enough to keep customers interested should be ordered at the counter. Break-fast is enjoyed all day long by late-risers, and the "Day After Thanks-giving" sandwich—a combo of tur-key, cranberry sauce, dressing and gravy—is good any time of year. Some complain that prices are a little too

RESTAURANTS

HOTEL RESTAURANTS

THEY SAY EATING WHERE YOU SLEEP WILL GIVE YOU INSOMNIA, BUT IN THIS CASE WE'LL MAKE an exception. These hotel restaurants are good enough to visit whether you're an out-of-towner or simply a savvy Houston food-lover.

BISTRO ALEX
Hotel Sorella
800 W. SAM HOUSTON PKWY.
☎ **(713) 827-3545**
The Brennan family expanded to the west side of town with this stunning, mesquite-planked restaurant with a must-visit Sunday brunch and the signature turtle soup. Chef Rolando Soza runs the kitchen.

VALENTINO
Hotel Derek
2525 WEST LOOP SOUTH
☎ **(713) 850-9200**
Restaurateur Piero Selvaggio (who has Valentino in Santa Monica, Calif.) has utterly revamped this trendy restaurant and ramped up the wine list. Chef Cunninghame West executes it all.

OLIVETTE
The Houstonian
111 N. POST OAK LANE
☎ **(713) 685-6713**
Whether you're coming off an indulgent day at the hotel's gorgeous spa or just looking to meet friends for lunch, the Mediterranean-accent restaurant in the Houstonian is a pretty and dependable choice.

RESTAURANT CINQ
La Colombe d'Or
3410 MONTROSE
☎ **(713) 469-4750**
Throwing off the hotel reputation for boring standards, chef Jeramie Robison is producing some of the most interesting cuisine in the city.

RISTORANTE CAVOUR
Hotel Granduca
1080 UPTOWN PARK
☎ **(713) 418-1104**
The lush, regal surroundings are one of a kind in Houston, and the upscale Northern Italian dishes are equally memorable.

QUATTRO
The Four Seasons
1300 LAMAR
☎ **(713) 650-1300**
Young chef Maurizio Ferrarese runs the kitchen, which has a bold Italian accent. Great wine list, too.

high for what's offered, but we just consider it The Heights cool factor premium.

LONDON SIZZLER

....

6690 SOUTHWEST FWY.
at Hillcroft
☎ **(713) 783-2754**
londonsizzler.com
🍴 **C7**

SURPRISINGLY, THIS IS *NOT* THE PLACE TO GO if you want an overcooked English breakfast. Instead you'll find top-notch British-style South Asian cuisine with a bit of North African flair thrown in. The bar is well stocked with English beer and popular enough in the evenings and during football games, and the rest of the dining room is rather nondescript if you don't count the built-in fish tank. The food, however, is quite remarkable with a splendid array of tandoori, kebab and masala-style meats, poultry and seafood. Try the crispy *mogo* (cassava sticks with hot red chili dip), meat sizzlers and vindaloo. The naan is both fluffy and crisp and there's a generous portion of the menu dedicated to vegetarian dishes, the masala *bhindi* (okra stir-fried with spices) being our favorite.

LOPEZ MEXICAN RESTAURANT

....

11606 S. WILCREST
at Southwest Fwy.
☎ **(281) 495-2436**
vivalopez.com
🍴 **C8**

THERE'S A LOT OF TEX-MEX TO CHOOSE FROM in the suburbs of Sugar Land and Stafford, but if we had to choose between a restaurant with a children's sandbox and margaritas the only good things to its name and this family-run establishment, we'd choose Lopez every time. The menu has all the usuals: fajitas, gooey enchiladas and guacamole. The chile rellenos is our regular order, the two poblano peppers stuffed with ground beef and cheese, battered and fried. The noise level gets up there as it can when families and margaritas mix, but service is fast and friendly and you'll surely leave with your fix.

LOVING HUT

....

2825 S. KIRKWOOD
north of Richmond
☎ **(281) 531-8882**
lovinghut.us/Houston
🍴 **B6**

CULTS ARE GREAT AT TWO THINGS: BRAINWASHING and cooking vegan food. Or so we learned upon visiting this nation-

RESTAURANTS

al vegan chain now with a location in West Houston. The Supreme Master Ching Hai International Association based in Taiwan is responsible for the plates of animal-product-free Exquisite Curry and Wonton Harmony. But if you have no pressing ethical objections, many of the items on the menu are satisfying, healthful and served with haste. Several different Asian cuisines are represented, from Japanese "sushi" to Vietnamese meatless soy protein *banh mi*, although not are all equal in flavor. The spring rolls are enjoyable, as is the Silken Moonlight fried noodle plate. There's even a freezer case full of entrees to take home for later, all of them made in the factory in Taiwan to ensure their vegan purity.

LUCIO'S

. . . .

905 TAFT *near W. Dallas*
☎ **(713) 523-9958**
luciosbyob.com
🍴 **E6**

THE WORD FOR THIS BYOB MONTROSE SPOT is "quirky." The interior is modest, some might even say cozy, with tile floors and mismatched local art hanging from the walls. The dated menu seems as though it might have been conceived in 2000, pulling together crabcakes, beef carpaccio, sesame-crusted ahi tuna and moussaka all in the same list. Still, some of those items can be

very well-executed, and a steady, stylish crowd appears every weekend ready to hand their keys over to the valet and devour some spinach and artichoke dip (the best of the starters). The prosciutto-wrapped pork chop and seared scallops served on butternut squash risotto are consistent favorites, and for dessert, try the bread pudding.

LYNN'S STEAKHOUSE

. . . .

955 ½ DAIRY ASHFORD
south of I-10
☎ **(281) 870-0807**
lynnssteakhouse.com
🍴 **B6**

FOR 26 YEARS, PEOPLE FROM ALL OVER THE Houston area have had a beef or two with this understated steakhouse in West Houston. That's because since opening in 1985, the place has been consistently named among the best steakhouses in the city. The original Lynn is long retired, but Loic and Benedicte Carbonnier carry on her tradition: a New York strip, brushed with salted butter and seared on a 1,600-degree grill to give it a savory crust, and worthy side dishes that include fat onion rings, rich spinach casserole and steamy-soft baked potatoes wrapped in gold foil. The award-winning wine list is unusually deep: Cabernet Sauvignon is king and usually found in verticals of at least five deep. The decor hints of the restaurant's age, but a little life experience never hurt anybody.

MADRAS PAVILION

. . . .

3910 KIRBY *north of Hwy. 59*
☎ **(713) 521-2617**
multiple locations
madraspavilion.us
🍴 **E7**

WHAT THIS SOUTH INDIAN SPOT LACKS in style (the maroon tablecloths are the one nice touch), it makes up for in willingness to please and friendly service. At the Kirby location, which also happens to be kosher (the Sugar Land location is not), a varied crowd passes through for the daily lunchtime steam table. The vegetarian offerings change regularly, and on any given day might include soup, *channa masala* (with chickpeas), *palak paneer* (homemade cottage cheese cubes cooked with seasoned spinach), *medhu vada* (rather bland unsweet doughnut, good for mopping up sauces), fried veggie cutlets, vegetable *korma* (simmered in coconut cream), filled samosas and much more. An enormous cooked-to-order *dosa* (kind of like a crêpe) is included in the lunch buffet price.

MAI'S RESTAURANT

. . . .

3403 MILAM *south of Elgin*
☎ **(713) 520-5300**
maishouston.com
🍴 **F6**

BEFORE THE CALAMITOUS FIRE IN FEBRUARY 2010, Mai's had been a late-night stand-by for hungry folks winding down from a night out. There was some warranted suspicion that the only thing the well-worn restaurant (it opened in 1978) had going for it was the human desperation for sustenance of any kind once 1 am rolls around. But since the post-fire rebuild, Mai's is a completely different animal. First of all, owner Mai Nguyen remade the grub-by bare-bones dining room with sea-foam green walls and bamboo accents. Second, there's a full bar. Third, the very, very long menu has been sharply edited down to a manageable length. As for the food, it remains largely the same. Though we wouldn't necessarily come here for the pho, the rice plates, vermicelli bowls and tofu dishes are filling and offer the expected flavors. Among the starters, the eggrolls, summer rolls, stuffed "crêpe" and *xoi chien thit nurong* (sticky rice patties and grilled pork) are all good. We also recommend the house signature dish *bo luc lac* (garlic beef stir-fried with jalapeños and onions).

MAMA'S CAFE

....

6019 WESTHEIMER
between Fountain View & S. Voss
☎ **(713) 266-8514**
mamascafe.net
🍴 **C7**

MAMA'S LOOKS AND FEELS LIKE A WELL-used country cafe, something most people get to study while waiting in line Sunday morning to get a seat at one of the booths or tables. The breakfast menu includes Mexican-style *migas*, biscuits and sausage gravy, eggs, grits, pancakes and cinnamon coffee. Sit and read the papers—no one will bother you. Lunch and dinner menus include burgers, chicken-fried steak, baby back ribs, fried catfish platter and our favorite, the messy and delicious bean burger. Yes, you'll sleep alone, but it's worth it.

MANENA'S PASTRY SHOP

....

11018 WESTHEIMER *at Wilcrest*
☎ **(713) 278-7139**
manenaspastry.com
🍴 **B7**

GIVEN THE OFTEN TRY-ING NATURE OF ADULT life, it's nice to fall back on the childlike pleasure of pressing your nose against a pastry case. Gaze in wide-eyed wonderment at some beastly large *alfajores* (caramel sandwich cookies) at this Argentine bakery and maybe even opt for dessert before your breakfast, lunch or very early dinner (doors close at 8). The empanadas are the stars of the show, and out of the half-dozen available fillings the *de humita*, with creamy corn and red peppers, is a favorite. The milanesa sandwiches are hefty and surprisingly greaseless, but the sandwiches *de migas* built with crustless white bread and interesting fillings like blue cheese, celery and walnut are very traditional. The line for sandwiches during lunch hour is long, but service is brisk and friendly, as you would expect from people working in this sun-dappled room.

MARIA SELMA

....

1617 RICHMOND
between Mandell & Dunlavy
☎ **(713) 528-4920**
mariaselma.com
🍴 **E7**

THIS RESTAURANT FROM JOSEPH VARON (MARIA Selma is his mother) and Rene Hidalgo is a bit different from the typical Houston Tex-Mex cafe. The menu touches down in many parts of Mexico and includes weekend breakfasts of *chilaquiles* and *huevos rancheros*, as well as a generous lunch/dinner slate of *sopas* (soups), *tortas* (sandwiches), enchiladas and seafood. Yes, there are chips and salsa, but the chips are thicker and rougher than you find at most Tex-Mex cafes in town. (We like them.) There's *mole* on the menu, plus crab-stuffed avocado and some tropical touches, such as pineapple grilled with the roasted pork, as well as an extensive tequila collection. The large palapa out front, complete with ceiling fans, makes dining out on the patio as pleasant as can be.

MARINI'S EMPANADA HOUSE

....

10001 WESTHEIMER
near Briarpark
☎ **(713) 266-2729**
multiple locations
🍴 **C6**

G O WEST, YOUNG EMPA-NADA HOUSE. THE 1970S Montrose empanada house, which burned in 1985, has had several incarnations since then, always moving steadily west it seems. The two current locations in the Carillon Center and in Katy are beloved for their savory and sweet Argentine turnovers, of which there are many to choose from. The Gaucho is a classic, stuffed with beef, boiled eggs, olives and onions, while the Demichelli with avocado, tomato, bell peppers, cheese and mushrooms is perfect for vegetarians. For dessert, upgrade to the "specialty" varieties like fig, mozzarella cheese and walnuts. There's usu-ally a lunch rush and wait times for the empanadas to appear can be a bit long, but patience is a rewarded virtue.

MARK'S AMERICAN CUISINE

....

1658 WESTHEIMER
east of Dunlavy
☎ **(713) 523-3800**
marks1658.com
🍴🍴 **E6**

I N THE MIDST OF TATTOO PARLORS, ANTIQUE SHOPS and vintage clothing boutiques, there stands Houston's quintessence of fine dining. Chef-owner Mark Cox's food is innovative and refined and, yes, it is expensive and, yes, you should wear a jacket. It offers the kind of exciting upscale dining that is evermore rare in a city full of chef-driven comfort food and persistent denim. Mark's is located in a former church, and rather than try to decorate that fact out of sight, Cox and wife Lisa have done a splendid job of incorporating the theme throughout. There's dining in the choir loft and even a post-church addition given over to the architecture and subsequently called the Cloister. It's beautiful. The menu is often artfully surprisingly and never allowed to get old, with changes made almost daily.

RESTAURANTS

MARY'Z MEDITERRANEAN CUISINE

. . . .

5825 RICHMOND
east of Fountain View
☎ **(832) 251-1955**
maryzcuisine.com
🍴 **C7**

WE'D LIKE TO BUY THE WORLD A hookah and keep it company. The handsome glass tobacco pipes draw in all manner of customer—from 20-somethings in tight T-shirts to elderly men with long white beards— to this expansive Lebanese restaurant. More than half of the seating is on the two patios, where it's easy to laze away hours with one of the many odd flavors of tobacco (the Incredible Hulk, anyone?) and a mezze combination platter that could feed five. The kibbi are particularly good, as is the *foul moudammas* (seasoned fava beans). The chicken shawarma sandwich, stuffed with all the necessary pickles and tahini, is exemplary in its field, but generally the vegetable dishes outshine the rather lean meats. An accommodating spot for large groups, it's one of our favorites for celebrations in spite of the modest decor.

MASRAFF'S

. . . .

1753 POST OAK BLVD.
south of San Felipe
☎ **(713) 355-1975**
masraffs.com
🍴 **D6**

OPULENCE, THY NAME IS MASRAFF'S. THE NEW location of this restaurant from father and son owners, Tony and Russell Masraff, could not be more different from the original lodge-like setting. A faux tree log runs across the ceiling in the dining room emitting blue flames and glass light fixtures give off a frosty light. We think that Gordon Gekko would be very happy here, and there are indeed many men in nice suits in attendance. The food is just as fancy, if a little evocative of the 1980s thanks to familiar Asian touches and an abundance of salt. Still, there are some high moments, including the seared foie gras with pears, the ahi tuna salad with an unreasonable amount of bacon and the housemade chips. Just don't dribble any soy glaze on your extremely expensive shirt.

FOOD BLOGS

HOUSTON MAY NOT ALWAYS GET MUCH NATIONAL RECOGNITION AS A FOOD CITY, but within city limits its proponents are fervent. These local food bloggers are the ones to consult to get the scoop on the latest restaurant opening or best cardamom short-bread recipe.

BLUE JEAN GOURMET
bluejeangourmet.com
Nishta Mehra is the source for said cardamom short-bread recipe and touching anecdotes that connect the kitchen to experiences outside it.

HOUSTON FOODIE
jcreidtx.com
J.C. Reid is an expert in Texas barbecue, where to find the best crabs in Galveston and the well-timed joke.

COOK'S TOUR
29-95.com/alison-cook
Houston Chronicle food critic Alison Cook details her adventures around town in exquisite detail.

TEXAS EATS
robbwalsh.com
Former *Houston Press* food critic Robb Walsh explores the food scene (he has a special fondness for barbe-cue and Tex-Mex) with an eye towards regional history.

EATING OUR WORDS
blogs.houstonpress.com/eating
One of the city's top re-sources for food news, the troupe of *Houston Press* food bloggers is never afraid to stir the pot.

GUNS & TACOS
gunsandtacos.com
Jay Rascoe is continuously on the hunt for underground taco stands. And he knows about guns, too.

DRINK DOGMA
drinkdogma.com
Anvil Bar & Refuge owner Bobby Heugel indulges his nerdy side with how-to's on mustard cocktails, the history of the gimlet and the definition of a Swizzle.

SIDEDISH
my-table.com/sidedish
My Table's twice-weekly newsletter keeps foodies informed on chef shuffles, restaurant openings and upcoming events.

Mussels at Plonk

MAX'S WINE DIVE

. . . .

4720 WASHINGTON *at Shepherd*
☎ **(713) 880-8737**
maxswinedive.com
🍴 **E6**

I N THE INTERVENING YEARS SINCE MAX'S FIRST opened, several restaurants have opened in Houston that specialize in a certain kind of down and dirty, chef-driven comfort food. But this self-identified wine dive was one of the first to pair fried chicken and Champagne, and despite early scoffs of derision, Max's quickly became famous for its $14 Texas "Haute" Dog piled high with onion strings and chili. A simple fried egg sandwich is transformed into something quite different by an addition of truffle aioli, gruyère and even more truffle oil. The small dining room is frequently short on space, and although the tone is casual and even slightly rowdy, diners arrive dolled up. The proprietors are also the owners of the three Tasting Room wine bars, and you'd be hard pressed to find a wine list in town that's any more inviting.

McCORMICK & SCHMICK'S

. . . .

1151-01 UPTOWN PARK
at Post Oak Blvd
☎ **(713) 840-7900**
multiple locations
mccormickandschmicks.com
🍴 **D6**

F OR $3, WE WOULD PUR-CHASE AND EAT A HAM-burger in a lot of rough, verging-on-unsanitary places. But that plan is rendered completely unnecessary by this Portland chain's happy hour menu. Each of the three restaurants almost functions as two separate restaurants: the cheap happy hour spot popular with young professionals and the upscale seafood restaurant suited to professionals used to having money. Happy hour runs 4 to 7 pm as well as 9 to 10 pm on weekdays, so it'd be difficult to miss the opportunity for $2 bruschetta and vegetable tempura. If you're ensconced in one the comfy booths of the main dining room, M&S sells more varieties of raw oysters, harvested in the cold waters of the northern Pacific and Atlantic, than any other Houston restaurant.

The house wine tap at Max's Wine Dive

MEZZANOTTE

· · · · · · · · · · · · · · ·

13215 GRANT
at Louetta, Cypress
☎ **(832) 717-7870**
mezzanotteristorante.com
🍴 NORTHWEST OF **A2** 🚗

YOU WERE PROBABLY ALREADY PLANNING on driving to a strip center smack in the middle of Cypress, right? Just kidding, of course not. But this surprising and imaginative Italian restaurant is a favorite of locals, and should you be so brash as to make the trek, this is the place to stop for dinner. A bold, elegant red paint job and live entertainment are a few of the things that will catch you off guard once you're in the door. Once at the table, beautifully plated lamb chops with mint pistachio pesto and classic pastas such as *bucatini all' amatriciana* (a simple red sauce with pancetta) and carbonara are improved by an intriguing and affordable wine list. It all adds up to the kind of dining experience that would rival any inside Houston city limits.

MIA BELLA

· · · · · · · · · · · · · · ·

1201 SAN JACINTO *at Dallas*
☎ **(832) 319-6675**
multiple locations
miabellatrattoria.com
🍴 **F6**

OWNER YOUSSEF NAFAA HAS THREE INSTALLMENTS (and a fourth coming online Fall 2011) of his Italian-with-a-twist restaurants that offer a little something for every palate. Try the wild mushroom strudel with goat cheese or the ricotta and sundried tomato-stuffed meatballs. Order a full-blown New York strip if you so desire, or stick to four-cheese ravioli. The dining rooms are cozy in a new-rustic sort of way and brunch and happy hour are lively affairs. The original Main Street location offers an extraordinary urban experience if you snag a seat near the tall, near-century-old arched windows, as Metro's modern light rail zips by outside.

MISSION BURRITO

· · · · · · · · · · · · · · ·

2245 W. ALABAMA *east of Kirby*
☎ **(713) 529-0535**
multiple locations
missionburritos.com
🍴 **E7**

IF THIS WERE HOLLYWOOD, CHIPOTLE WOULD BE JULIA Roberts and Mission Burrito would be Connie Britton. Sure, everyone loves Julia and she does a fine job, but just because Connie isn't as famous doesn't mean she wouldn't be better in that lead role. This homegrown mini-chain offers a lot of the same satisfying grub as any other build-your-own burrito joint, but seems to do everything just a smidge better. A wider variety of filling ingredients including fresh corn, cilantro and a number of vibrant salsas are available along the line. The fish tacos and tortilla soup shouldn't be neglected either, the latter a piping hot, cheesy, avocado-buoyed solution to a cold day. The setting is mega-casual with toys on the patio for the tykes.

MO'S A PLACE FOR STEAKS

. . . .

1801 POST OAK BLVD.
south of San Felipe
☎ **(713) 877-0720**
mosaplaceforsteaks.com
🍴 **D6**

FAVORITE IN ITS HOME-TOWN OF MILWAUKEE, Mo's is exactly what it appears. It does indeed serve steak, and the Vegas-style torches aflame near the front door hint at the aesthetic within. The menu exhibits all the steakhouse classics from the crab-cake starter to the filet with a side of creamed spinach, but the dining room has none of the typical stuffy masculinity. Instead, it looks more like a sleek lounge with the short-skirted women to match. The concise steak menu includes a 12-ounce Kobe filet hovering near $100 and the signature bone-in "cowboy cut" ribeye provides big flavor. There's also an assortment of sauces, ranging from chimichurri to brandy peppercorn, if you're not a purist about that sort of thing.

MOCKINGBIRD BISTRO WINE BAR

. . . .

1985 WELCH at *McDuffie*
☎ **(713) 533-0200**
mockingbirdbistro.com
🍴 **E6** ✍

IN THE RESTAURANT WORLD, CROWDS ARE AN ODD THING. They can mean undeserved hype or they can mean collective wisdom. Founded in 2001, Mockingbird has been around long enough that it's stopped appearing on buzzy top-10 lists, and though it's no longer exactly trendy, the dining room enjoys a steady stream of loyal diners. Named for the state bird of Texas, Mockingbird serves "Texas Provence" cuisine that features Texas ingredients with a bistro accent. Standouts from chef/owner John Sheely are killer calamari with two dipping sauces, Texas 1015 onion soup with gruyère crouton, Kobe beef burger with foie gras and truffled frites and warm bittersweet chocolate torte. The interior has lovely gothic touches, such as the medieval-looking chandeliers, and gets downright sexy in the low light of evening. The recently expanded bar is one of the best spots for solo dining in the city and has its own menu. (Try the short ribs.) Excellent service seems to never forget a face.

MOLINA'S

. . . .

4720 WASHINGTON
at Shepherd
☎ **(713) 862-0013**
multiple locations
molinasrestaurants.com
🍴 E6

THE UPSCALE TRAPPINGS (INCLUDING VALET PARKing) of this convivial cantina belie its 70-year history. Part margarita onslaught for the Washington crowd and part bustling family joint, Molina's wears a few different hats. Long-time fans were sad to see the Buffalo Speedway location demolished, but the menu at the other locations still offers customers' favorites, many named after regulars and staff members. Everyone orders Jose's Dip, which is a gooey queso with a dollop of ground beef at the center. The *enchiladas de tejas*, stuffed with cheese and doused in chili con carne in full traditional Tex-Mex glory, are the other must-order item. Other locations, including a new one in Bellaire slated for Fall 2011, are more family-oriented, but service is chipper and helpful all around.

MONARCH

. . . .

5701 MAIN *at Binz, in Hotel ZaZa*
☎ **(713) 526-1991**
monarchrestauranthouston.com
🍴 F6

WHEN HOTEL ZAZA FIRST DEBUTED A couple years ago, the place was mobbed by the posh and the hip. But now that the scenesters have moved on, what's left is a voguish place for Houston to treat itself to a chic evening. (If you're female, uncloset the black pencil skirt and heels.) In the dramatic Monarch restaurant, the menu by chef Adam West is conventionally up-market takes on chicken, seafood (we once had some amazing mussels here) and beef tenderloin, which may seem mildly surprising given the completely unconventional decor of the hotel. Indeed, the aristocratic (if tatty) Warwick Hotel got quite the makeover when ZaZa moved in and upholstered everything in zebra stripes, but the beautiful patio with a view of the Mecom Fountain offers a space as lovely as can be.

MONGOLIAN HOT POT

....

5901-A WESTHEIMER
at Fountain View
☎ **(713) 975-0687**
littlesheephotpot.com
🍴 **C7**

DINING AT MONGOLIAN HOT POT IS A TWO-IN-one deal: A steam facial comes free with every meal. This is one of our favorite spots for this DIY meal, with everything from the spicy broth (a split pot with half mild broth is also an option) to the fresh, verdant vegetables among the best in their class. The specialty here is the sliced lamb, although the selection is extensive. There are at least three types of mushrooms and even more noodles. Be sure to order the fluffy, steaming sesame bread and pickled cucumbers on the side. We recommend coming with a party of at least four to allow for more sampling. Sundays are an ideal time to go because of an all-you-can-eat flat-rate deal.

MOON TOWER INN

....

3004 CANAL *at N. Ennis*
☎ **(832) 266-0105**
damngoodfoodcoldassbeer.com
🍴 **F6** 👆

OWNERS EVAN SHANNON AND BRANDON YOUNG tamed a third of an acre in the Second Ward and turned it into a professional backyard cookout. A rotating cast of game sausages including venison, boar ("Piggie Smalls"), buffalo and lamb are scratched on the chalkboard menu and paired with Zapp's potato chips. The sausages come nestled in sturdy Slow Dough pretzel buns and diners can customize their dogs with different toppings and sauces like black pepper ketchup and stout beer sauerkraut. A selection of melty, indulgent sandwiches was more recently added to the menu,

Wild game hot dogs at Moon Tower Inn

and we enjoyed the oozy, plain grilled cheese the most. Inexpensive craft beer, occasional movie nights and a basketball hoop make the picnic tables a popular hangout for scruffy cyclists late into the night.

MORTON'S

....

5000 WESTHEIMER *(upstairs)*
at Post Oak Blvd.
☎ **(713) 629-1946**
multiple locations
mortons.com
🍴 **D6**

NLIKE SOME OF HOUSTON'S OTHER steakhouses, this one doesn't get a lot of attention. But considering it's within walking distance of a half-dozen large hotels and a national reputation, it doesn't hurt for business whatsoever. If you have ever been to a Morton's anywhere, the drill here will be familiar, with meat and live lobster shown tableside, a dining room decorated with Leroy Neiman prints and photographs of celebrities, and an open kitchen. We would never suggest that ordering steak is just an excuse to devour potatoes. But if carbs are what get your heart racing, Morton's offers four different preparations of spud, our favorite being the hash browns served in a personal-sized skillet.

NAM GANG

....

1411 GESSNER
north of Long Point
☎ **(713) 467-8801**
🍴 **C5**

S IS THE CASE WITH ALL GRILL-IT-YOURSELF Korean barbecue joints, you will leave here smelling like smoky meats and kimchee. We consider it an exceptionally sexy musk. The smell hits you right when you walk in the door, and once seated, your long wooden table will soon be crowded with *banchan*, the various side dishes and numerous types of kimchee that come with every meal. Let the waitress know if you're a newbie to DIY cooking, and she'll be happy to help you grill the meat, deftly snipping the *kalbi* (beef short ribs) and *bulgogi* (thin-cut ribeye) with her scissors. There is a definite language barrier here, so don't expect chitchat while she's doing it. The standard marinated beef and pork is complemented with more adventurous offal and tongue, and though some of the grills are gas-fired, others have coal—a rare find within the city. Put out the fire of the spicy vegetables with some *soju*, a sweet vodka-like Korean beverage.

NARIN'S BOMBAY BRASSERIE

....

3005 W. LOOP SOUTH
at Richmond
☎ **(713) 622-2005**
multiple locations
narinsbombaybrasserie.com
🍴 **D7**

THE MASSIVE CARVED ENTRANCE DOORS TO Narin's shout authentic and they're not lying. The kitchen focuses on North Indian cuisine with a few surprises. A foyer serves as a casual bar, fine for enjoying a cocktail and starter. Try their chicken *pakoras* (deep-fried nuggets) to accompany your gin and tonic. Behind the bar, the restaurant opens into a spacious white-tablecloth dining room starring hand-carved Indian panels. The pan-fried calamari sautéed with hot cherry peppers is a clever

dish that turns the spice up without overwhelming the delicate squid. Ask about their reasonably priced wine dinners, featuring courses such as mussels simmered in a coconut masala. All in all, this is a fine spot for getting your Indian fix and worth investigating if you're ready to expand your horizons a bit, too.

NATACHEE'S SUPPER N' PUNCH

....

3622 MAIN *at Alabama*
☎ **(713) 524-7203**
natachees.com
🍴 **F6**

DOWN-HOME COUNTRY COOKIN' IN THE MIDDLE of downtown, you say? A sign advertising live chickens? The fit seems a little less odd when you consider that this super block of

The dining room in Natachee's Supper N' Punch

Main is populated by other offbeat establishments, from the much-loved Continental Club to Tacos à Go-Go. The menu of diet-busters includes a lot of bacon, and while the macaroni 'n' cheese isn't stellar, the meatloaf and fried pickles are. The chicken on the CBLT is tender and juicy, even better washed down with a sweet, boozy rum punch. While some of Natachee's affectations are a little much (burgers are "hand spanked" daily), the overall effect of sipping a beer and eating something hearty on the umbrella-spiked patio before moving next door to see a local band is pitch perfect.

NELORE CHURRASCARIA

. . . .

4412 MONTROSE
south of Richmond
☎ **(713) 395-1050**
neloresteakhouse.com
🍴 **E7**

THE TASTIEST EXPORT OUT OF BRAZIL AFTER Gisele Bündchen is the nelore, a particular breed of tropics-tolerant humped cattle. Living up to its namesake, this rodizio restaurant serves high-quality meats while distinguishing itself from similar establishments by being cozier, a bit cheaper and having a more intriguing wine list than the national chains. The salad bar is more moderate than the larger opera-

tions, but you don't want to waste stomach space on more than an artichoke anyway, right? Each lance of meat carrying garlicky rump cut or bacon-wrapped filet will be cooked to different levels of doneness, so feel free to be choosy. One unusual offering is the chicken heart. Since it's included in the price of the meal, you might as well try it. What have you got to lose?

NEW YORK BAGEL & COFFEE SHOP

. . . .

9724 HILLCROFT
near S. Braeswood
☎ **(713) 723-5879**
nybagelhouston.com
🍴 **C8**

EVERY MORNING OF THE WEEK, THIS VINTAGE luncheonette bustles with a crowd that feels like family. Elderly ladies on their regular breakfast date, families on the way to soccer practice and everyone else in the city who can appreciate a fine short-order egg plate and bagel gather over the Formica tables for coffee. Most of the smoked fish comes direct from Brooklyn. You can order lox (regular or Nova), chubs, sable, kippered salmon and whitefish salad. The bagels, made and sold in their own adjacent shop, are always fresh and doughy. The matzo ball soup is quite good, and so is the corned beef hash. Portions aren't as massive as some New York-style delis, but they're certainly large enough. Give co-owner Eddie Gavrila a kiss from us.

NIDDA THAI

....

1226 WESTHEIMER
at Commonwealth
☎ **(713) 522-8895**
niddathai.com
🍴 **E6**

PARKING OUT FRONT IN THIS STRIP CENTER PUTS you in close proximity to the Erotic Cabaret next door, so if that bothers you, make a big show of entering the restaurant. Both are Montrose institutions in their own way, Nidda being Westheimer's most reliable Thai spot. A smiling hostess will quickly usher your party to an available table and the rest of the waitstaff tag-teams tasks with eagerness. There are few misses to be found on the menu, but standouts include the *tom yum gai*, a hot and sour chicken soup practically electric with lemongrass, and the sautéed eggplant with Thai chili and basil sauce. The *chu chee* eggplant has gotten a lot of deserved praise, the lightly battered slices arriving perfectly cooked and tender with a coating of red curry bright with kaffir.

NIELSEN'S DELICATESSEN

....

4500 RICHMOND *at Mid Lane*
☎ **(713) 963-8005**
🍴 **D7**

THE FIRST DANISH-ACCENTED NIELSEN'S opened in Highland Village nearly 60 years ago, back when Highland Village would allow such a thing in. Within hours of flipping on the light, the first batch of homemade mayonnaise was whipped up, and success was assured. The much-loved Ellen Nielsen Andersen passed away in early 2008, but her family carries on the Nielsen's tradition. Everything touched with said mayo is a cut above, including Houston's favorite chicken salad, the egg salad and the deviled eggs sold in little paper cups. Sliced meats and cheeses are available by weight, and we love the corned beef-on-rye sandwich with its homemade liver paste. The place is kind of grubby-looking and there are only about five stools, so you'll probably want to take your order to go.

RESTAURANTS

⌡NIKO NIKO'S

·················

2520 MONTROSE
north of Westheimer
☎ **(713) 528-4976**
multiple locations
nikonikos.com
🍴 **E6**

HOUSTONIANS WILL ALWAYS CARRY A torch for this Greek restaurant. Despite traumatic crowds, abysmal falafel and not really being all that cheap, it repeatedly gets voted as the city's favorite by all sorts of media. There are several good reasons for this. The legendary, skinless roasted potatoes and the classic gyro have massive followings, and the pork chop is quite good as well. The bright chicken-lemon avgolemono soup, in our opinion, is the best reason to eat at Niko Niko's and has returned us to full health more times than we can count. Expanded parking has helped the situation at Montrose, but you'll still have to hustle for a seat and your disposable cutlery. Owner Dimitrios Fetokakis is a local hero for his beautiful revitalization of the boulevard's median strip in front of the restaurant. The new Market Square location inside a to-go kiosk is lovely, and the outdoor seating a great gathering place for the downtown community and their dogs in the milder months.

Exterior patio at Niko Niko's

NINFA'S ON NAVIGATION

·················

2704 NAVIGATION
east of the S. Jensen exchange
☎ **(713) 228-1175**
mamaninfas.com
🍴 **F6**

MOST NINFA'S LOCATIONS AROUND TOWN should be avoided. They're not terrible, but it's our job as Houstonians to deride sub-par Tex-Mex. It's the original location that gets all the love, and the onetime hole in the wall has taken all this positive attention as an opportunity for a makeover. A breezy patio was installed in January 2011 with its own bar and a tequila program crafted by Bobby Heugel of Anvil. Who's in the big leagues now? Aside from the bar menu additions (try the amazingly oozy fajita burger), the food sticks to the nostalgic favorites. Order the *queso flameado*

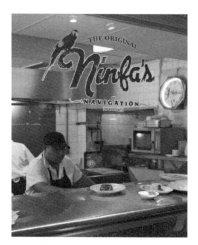

The kitchen counter at Ninfa's

with chorizo to start, and follow that up with the classic beef fajitas. If you don't order a margarita, you're in the wrong place.

NINO'S

2817 W. DALLAS
between Montrose & Waugh
☎ **(713) 522-5120**
ninos-vincents.com
🍴 **E6**

EVERYONE KNOWS THAT ROAST CHICKEN IS SIMPLE in name only. It's the calling card here and reflects what is best about Nino's. The food is straightforward Italian-American but prepared elegantly with quality ingredients. All of the crispy pizzas and pastas are excellent, and the osso buco is some of the city's best. The Mandola family has built their own little universe on West Dallas with cus-

tomers orbiting around upscale Vincent's, more casual Nino's and wine bar Grappino, all on the same campus, for their gustatory needs. When you've finished your meal inside rustic Nino's, exit to the patio for gelato and espresso.

NIPPON

4464 MONTROSE *between Richmond & W. Alabama*
☎ **(713) 523-3939**
🍴 **E7**

SURE, KEEP ON ZOOMING PAST UNASSUMING NIPpon. That way the patrons inside the already-full dining room can keep hold of their hidden gem. The quiet family-owned spot, all dark wood and minimalism with paper lanterns dangling from the porch, is known for its ramen and fresh fish. Houston is woefully short on traditional Japanese ramen, and Nippon offers one of the city's best versions. The broth is always rich and restorative even if occasionally light on meat. As for the sushi, the chefs aim more for consistency than innovation and while basics including hamachi, eel and mackerel will satisfy, sitting at the bar and goading the chef for more adventurous items is a rewarding option. You'll note that many of your fellow diners here are actually of Japanese origin, not Houston hipsters looking for the latest crazy roll.

RESTAURANTS

OCEAN PALACE

....

11215 BELLAIRE BLVD.
west of Wilcrest
☎ **(281) 988-8898**
🍴 **B7**

HOUSTON'S DIM SUM MECCA FUNCTIONS IN the usual Hong Kong fashion. The two cavernous levels are done up in banquet hall style, though the fish tank-lined first floor is only open for dinner. The upstairs is packed every weekend morning with families vying for the desirable dishes off the carts while the food is still warm. Staples include respectable to excellent versions of *ha gao* (shrimp dumplings in delicate wrappers), *shu mai* (pork dumplings), egg custard tarts and puffy fried taro. The pan-fried daikon cake is one of our favorites. Though the adventurous will find the chicken feet and pork blood cubes, most of the vast selection is very accessible. If you're still hungry, take your clipboard to the hot foods bar for some fried noodles or a bowl of congee.

THE OCEANAIRE SEAFOOD ROOM

....

5061 WESTHEIMER
in The Galleria
☎ **(832) 487-8862**
theoceanaire.com
🍴 **D6**

KATE AND LEO WOULD HAVE FELT RIGHT AT home in this dining room that suggests an elegant ocean liner, though shorts-wearing Galleria shoppers won't be turned away. Landry's has purchased this formerly Minnesota-based chain and it's made to feel local by an abundance of Gulf seafood on the changing daily menu. You'll also find Alaskan salmon and ahi tuna from Hawaii and an array of geographically influenced preparations from *moules marinieres* to Chesapeake Bay-style crabcakes. The raw bar at the entrance is great for happy hour, a quick meal or a first stop on the way to the table. Chef Trevor White's oyster list usually features a half-dozen or more, from both the East and West Coasts, and sometimes you'll find littleneck clams, too

HOUSTON INSTITUTIONS

THESE RESTAURANTS ARE DISTINCTLY HOUSTON, AND THE CITY IS MORE DISTINCT because of them.

NINFA'S ON NAVIGATION
2704 NAVIGATION
☎ (713) 228-1175

Mama Ninfa Laurenzo opened this original location of this Tex-Mex joint back in 1973, and Houstonians have been flocking for queso flameado and fajitas ever since.

TEL-WINK
4318 TELEPHONE
☎ (713) 644-4933

If you're coming to this legendary diner for lunch, be sure to arrive by 11:30 at the latest or prepare to wait in a line outside the door before getting your fried chicken fix.

TREEBEARDS
315 TRAVIS
☎ (713) 228-2622

We have dreams about the crispy cheese skin on the grits special at this Cajun restaurant on Market Square. Red beans and rice with cheese and onions comes in a close second.

IRMA'S
22 N. CHENEVERT
☎ (713) 222-0767

Irma's is as famous for not posting prices as she is for her landmark cheese enchiladas and lemonade.

GOODE CO.

The Goode Co. brand is on enough regional cuisines to question it as schizophrenic, but there's no denying its strong presence and, better yet, quality. Whole pecan pies are a hot commodity come the holidays.

MAI'S
3403 MILAM
☎ (713) 520-5300

One of many eateries in Vietnamese-dense Midtown, Mai's gained a reputation for its grimy, late-night appeal. Then it almost burned to the ground, and now locals clutch the rebuilt Mai's even dearer to their hearts.

OISHII

. . . .

3764 RICHMOND *at Timmons*
☎ **(713) 621-8628**
oishiihouston.com
🍴 **D7**

IN CASE YOU HADN'T HEARD, FOOD ISN'T GETTING ANY cheaper. For that, we can blame the world economy. But Oishii is doing its best to keep us well fed with one of the most astoundingly cheap happy hours in town. From 3 to 6 pm on weekdays and 3 to 6 pm on Saturdays, $4 appetizers are buy-one-get-one-free and imported beers, including Kirin, are $1.75. If you're really working to fill your belly, avoid the edamame and opt instead for the vegetable tempura, spicy salmon roll and gyoza. It's not the best Japanese food you'll ever eat but it's fine for the price. The major downside is that this is also one of the city's most popular happy hours, and people are often forced to wait alongside the curb for a table to finally free up. What can we say? Houston is full of cheapskates.

OLIVETTE

. . . .

111 N. POST OAK LANE
between Woodway & Memorial,
in The Houstonian Hotel
☎ **(713) 685-6713**
houstonian.com
🍴🍴 **D6**

LUSH LANDSCAPING WITH WINDING TRAILS, an enchanting entrance and a smiling staff make your arrival feel special, just as one would expect of a posh hotel and spa. Once inside, the charm holds up with a warm Tuscan theme and complimentary bread, hummus and olives arriving promptly on the table. The open kitchen produces American food with a delicate flair evident in the sweet corn soup and crispy artichokes served with the seared scallops. If you haven't already tried it, order the Southwest Caesar Salad, a gazillion-time winner of the annual Caesar Salad Competition held every year in October. The restaurant is no longer allowed in the competition because it wins every year. It's dotted with black beans, corn, *pepitas* and *cotija* cheese. We also love the duck breast with braised cabbage and, after, the strawberry and almond shortcake.

ONION CREEK

· · · · · · · · · · · · · · · ·

3106 WHITE OAK
west of Studewood
☎ **(713) 880-0706**
onioncreekcafe.com
🍴 **E5**

NION CREEK DOES AN ADMIRABLE JOB AT MULTI-tasking, functioning as a coffee-shop, restaurant and bar all at once and like all Creek restaurants, it does its best to channel Austin. Despite that city's total inferiority to our own, the intention translates to an extremely pleasant patio and local beers on tap plus easygoing grub of the sandwich and burger variety. The food won't change your life, but sometimes you just want to eat a really good Frito pie, you know? Doors open at 7 am to meet your coffee needs, and the baristas tend to know their way around a Katz coffee bean. In the evenings, there's often a DJ and if not, the beat-up couches and vintage Pac-Man will keep you perfectly amused.

OPORTO CAFE

· · · · · · · · · · · · · · · ·

3833 RICHMOND *at Weslayan*
☎ **(713) 621-1114**
oporto.us
🍴 **D7**

FTENTIMES, WE FIND OURSELVES BRISTLING at the use of the word tapas, espe-cially when they're used in fussy restaurants to make us order exp-ensive plates of tiny portions. But at Oporto, they actually make sense. The focus during lunch is sand-wiches and salads, which includes some very appetizing grilled pani-ni, even if they cost a little more than we like to spend on a midday meal. At night, the lights dim, and a chic crowd descends to take advantage of the affordable yet serious wine list, including quite a few desirable Portuguese wines. As for eating, the stuffed pequillo peppers and garlicky shrimp in piri-piri oil are very lovable. The choices for both wine and food are limited, but that seems ideal for the setting. Come for a snack with friends, as you might if you were European.

OTILIA'S

· · · · · · · · · · · · · · · ·

7710 LONG POINT
between Antoine & Wirt
☎ **(713) 681-7203**
otilias.com
🍴 **D5**

HERE WAS A TIME WHEN EVERYONE WAS TALKING about Otilia's. Its authentic inter-ior Mexican cuisine was a critical darling, and people couldn't get enough of the *posole*, stuffed pob-lano peppers awash in cream sauce and sprinkled with pomegranate and *cuatros leches*. Since then, the former Whataburger building (any

Texan can recognize that A-frame) has been expanded to more than twice its original size, the prices have risen and very likely all the praise went to Otilia's head. Recent visits haven't been quite the same, with less spice and less zing to our old favorites. The classics are still there, from the limeade to the shredded Yucatan-style pork, and they're by no means bad. They're just no longer our favorites.

OUISIE'S TABLE
. . . .

3939 SAN FELIPE _at Willowick_
☎ **(713) 528-2264**
ouisiestable.com
🍴 **D6** 🔊

OUISIE'S CHICKEN-FRIED STEAK COMES WITH A side of black-eyed peas, corn pudding and serious girl power. Elou-

ise Adams Jones, aka Ouisie, is a local pioneer among women chefs, having opened her first Ouisie's Table in 1973 on Sunset Boulevard. The current location opened in 1995 and has maintained its high standing among Southern and Gulf Coast restaurants in the region. The space is absolutely gorgeous (often rented for weddings), with spanking white tablecloths and a bar bathed in golden light in the main dining room and an idyllic courtyard. Brandied oysters, shrimp and cheese grits, seafood crêpes and pan-roasted chicken are all favorites. So is the raw oyster martini with the cheese-stuffed olive. A favorite memory: Getting up early to watch the April 29, 2011, royal wedding of Prince William and Kate Middleton on a big-screen TV at Ouisie's Table with scores of fellow Houstonians, many in "wedding attire."

PALAZZO'S TRATTORIA
. . . .

2300 WESTHEIMER
between S. Shepherd & Kirby
☎ **(713) 522-6777**
multiple locations
palazzoscafe.com
🍴 **D6**

COME HOLIDAY SEASON, INNER LOOPERS PROBably see a lot of the "Palazzo Pans" of piping hot pasta and salads at parties. That's the kind of restaurant this is—Americanized but sat-

Ouisie's Table dining room

isfying in its own way Italian that's even better in a pinch. Twenty people are coming over? Call Palazzo's. Need to feed the family but you're working late? Do the same. John and Stassa Moore's original Palazzo's at 2620 Briar Ridge has been a popular, if low-key, spot near The Galleria for some time. At the bigger, fancier Westheimer version, the neighborhood feel still runs strong, making dropping by for a cheap bottle of wine more appealing. Pastas and pizzas are fairly standard, but veal dishes—especially the piccata—are delicious.

PAPPADEAUX SEAFOOD KITCHEN

. . . .

2410 RICHMOND *east of Kirby*
☎ **(713) 527-9137**
multiple locations
pappadeaux.com
🍴 **E7**

HERE DO YOU GEAUX FOR SEAfood? Countless locals reply, "Pappadeaux," proving loyalty to the Pappas restaurant empire. This concept is the so-called Cajun branch of the vast Pappas lineup, and if you like themed restaurants, then you'll probably enjoy this place. The seafood is fresh and portions are huge, but we like our Cajun shacks to be a little less staged and a little more authentic. (Our favorite thing on the menu: the gooey

shrimp and crawfish fondeaux.) On the plus side, the staff is accommodating, but the wait for a table can be brutal and the noise level deafening. Success has its drawbacks.

PAPPAS BROS. STEAKHOUSE

. . . .

5839 WESTHEIMER
at Bering
☎ **(713) 780-7352**
pappasbros.com
🍴 **C7**

OU'D THINK THAT BEING A PART OF A chain that includes such goofy name variations as Pappadeaux would take away some of a restaurant's dignity, but you'd be proven wrong by dining at this steakhouse. Cloaked in handsome dark paneling, lined with booths and splendidly decked out from top to bottom, Pappas continues to produce some of the most satisfying steak dinners in the city. This is a great place to celebrate, woo new business or impress a date. The beef is Prime, and the wine list boasts more than 500 entries. Everything is served and priced à la carte, which is a good news/bad news scenario. On the positive, you can order anything you like; on the negative, the check total very quickly reaches stratospheric levels.

RESTAURANTS

PAPPAS SEAFOOD HOUSE

....

3001 S. SHEPHERD
near W. Alabama
☎ **(713)522-4595**
multiple locations
pappasseafood.com
🍴 **E7**

WHAT DO GREEKS KNOW ABOUT GULF Coast seafood? A lot, apparently. Fried calamari, stuffed flounder and all kinds of oysters and shrimp have made this link in the Pappas's chain of restaurants a hit with big appetites. They brag about "portions as big as the ocean," and they are exaggerating only a little. It's a little obscene, to be honest. If you choose not to share, then take leftovers home for a late-night snack or next-day lunch. Softshell crab is a must-try in season (heaven with an ice-cold beer), and the huge Greek salad for two will feed a family. Or try the redfish "on the half shell." Finish with the cheesecake, if you are still vertical.

PAPPASITO'S CANTINA

....

6445 RICHMOND *at Hillcroft*
☎ **(713) 784-5253**
multiple locations
pappasitos.com
🍴 **C7**

HUNDREDS OF PEOPLE TALKING AT PEAK LEVel over "background" music, walls crammed with mounted steer heads, mirrors, posters and more and, all around you, the irresistible aroma of Tex-Mex wafting from passing trays: Pappasito's is a lot to take in. So brace yourself for the noise (watch your waitress strain to read your lips) and, during peak times, a long wait for a table. It helps that the indefatigable young service staff always seems to be peppy, happy to make sure you have a good time. The chips with both red and green salsas are some of our favorites in town—always warm and fresh, and all-you-can-devour. We can barely go a week without stopping in for the Plato Del Mar, a combo of fajitas and bacon-wrapped shrimp on a large sizzling platter. The one weak point has long been Pappasito's margaritas, but the new "Skinny Margarita" made with agave, tequila and lime juice is a big improvement over the icky mix they so often use.

PASHA

. . . .

2325 UNIVERSITY
west of Greenbriar
☎ **(713) 592-0020**
epasha.com
🍴 **E7**

HERE'S A MOMENT WHEN THE FOOD HITS THE table and you know you've ordered best of all your dining companions. That happens to every person who orders the mixed grill plate, an array of *doner* (carved meat, something like shawarma), shish kebab and *adana* (a ground meat kebab) that arrives on a golden platter. There are some lighter Turkish delights, starting with a delectable hummus and including a *doner* sandwich with shepherd salad of cucumbers, tomatoes and feta. All of this goes on in a rather unremarkable looking converted house that's actually quite dressy on the inside, thanks to pomegranate walls and white tablecloths. Still, the attitude at Mustafa Ozsoy's little restaurant is very casual. Try a *gazoz* (Turkish soda) or a glass of Turkish wine, too.

PATRENELLA'S

. . . .

813 JACKSON HILL
south of Washington
☎ **(713) 863-8223**
patrenellas.net
🍴 **E6**

OCATED IN A 1938 HOUSE BUILT BY OWN-er Sammy Patrenella's father, this home-style Italian restaurant had quite the existential crisis as its neighborhood went decidedly younger and upscale with Washington Avenue's boom just a block away. Rising chef Ryan Hildebrand came and went. Now the menu, despite being divided into the traditional Italian *antipasti*, *primi* and *secondi*, has settled back into the hearty Americanized Italian fare that seems to make just about everybody happy. The greatest gem of this quaint 19-year-old restaurant is the one-acre garden just outside the back door. It's not only a beautiful place to drink a glass of wine, but the source of many of the fresh herbs and tomatoes making their way into the kitchen.

PAULIE'S

. . . .

1834 WESTHEIMER *east of Hazard*
☎ **(713) 807-7271**
pauliesrestaurant.com
🍴 **E6**

E'RE THE FIRST PEOPLE TO GET

judgmental about Americanized Italian, but we have to say, Paulie's is delightful. Pesto penne studded with olives and pine nuts is a perfect lunch, and the messy shrimp BLT is famously delicious. The pork tenderloin sandwich and Thursday special osso buco are also recommended. Big windows facing Westheimer make the restaurant a pleasant spot to sit a while, but reasonable prices and quick counter service are also salvation for emergency take-out meals. Owner Paul Petronella recently brought on the crew at Greenway Coffee to start a top-notch coffee program, forever ensuring that Paulie's is just the kind of restaurant you want in your neighborhood.

PEKING CUISINE

. . . .

8332 SOUTHWEST FWY.
at Gessner
☎ **(713) 988-5838**
🍴 **C7**

PEKING DUCK IS THE FEATURED ATTRACTION at this somewhat dingy destination for North Chinese cuisine on the outskirts of Chinatown, and it's the real deal. The extra crispy skin and slow-roasted meat clinging to it comes with crêpes, hoisin sauce and scallions, and you'll find yourself fighting other members of your family for seconds. Make it a duck celebration and have the

duck soup, too. All ducks must be ordered several hours or a day in advance, but if you forget, it isn't an absolute tragedy thanks to a few other worthwhile menu items. There are a number of cold appetizers, including a combination of sliced beef offal and, if you're taken with the crêpe format, a moo shu-style squab dish. Ordering will be made easier by bringing along a Mandarin-speaking friend, as very little English is spoken.

PERBACCO

. . . .

700 MILAM
at Capitol, in the Pennzoil Tower
☎ **(713) 224-2422**
🍴 **F6**

SAY WHAT YOU WILL ABOUT DOWNTOWN HOUSTON, there is a lot of good food to eat. Popular for a quick counter-service lunch and efficient pre-theater dinner, owner Vittorio Preteroti's Perbacco deserves more attention than it gets. The key to good ordering is to look to the whiteboard of specials, which the kitchen seems more excited to prepare. Gnocchi and a salad are a simple pleasure and the portions of baked pasta demand a takeout box. The dining room is very stylish for such a modern operation, with powder-blue walls and high ceilings, though table jockeying can be a competitive sport during the lunch rush.

PERRY'S STEAKHOUSE & GRILLE

. . . .

2115 TOWN SQUARE PLACE
at Hwy. 59, Sugar Land
☎ **(281) 565-2727**
multiple locations
perrysrestaurants.com
🍴 **A9**

IN A LAND FAR, FAR AWAY (CLEAR LAKE), A RESTAUrateur named Chris Perry introduced the monstrous, caramelized pork chop, cheers were heard across the land and a legend was born. Justly famous for this beastly and delicious piece of meat, which just so happens to be on special Fridays at lunch, Perry's has since expanded to several suburbs surrounding Houston and several cities across Texas. Though the pork chop is truly a must, the beef can't be snubbed either. The dry-aged steaks go through a three-step process: caramelizing with signature spices, char-grilling to trap natural juices and finishing with garlic butter. It's like a spa day for your steak. Tableside châteaubriand and flambéed crêpes Suzette are a fun retro touch.

PESCE

. . . .

3029 KIRBY *at W. Alabama*
☎ **(713) 522-4858**
pescehouston.com
🍴 **E7**

PERCHED (GET IT?) CLOSE TO RIVER OAKS, Montrose and West U neighborhoods, this seafood swankienda is a feast for the eyes *and* taste buds. The homegrown white-tablecloth seafood restaurant is known for its center-of-the-action, sexy raw bar and zippy bar area, where singles, couples and expense account spenders pack in like sardines to watch and be a part of the scene. Once seated, there is a lot of pesce (seafood) and some "not pesce" (to quote the menu) from which to choose. Watch for the jaw-dropping Pesce Tower of raw and chilled seafood being delivered throughout the room. Executive chef Mark Holley's smile is as wide and welcoming as the seafood is fresh. His seafood martini is legendary and has spawned countless knock-offs around town. He also has a cult customer following for his monthly fried chicken dinner.

RESTAURANTS

MEXICAN BREAKFASTS

I F YOUR IDEA OF BREAKFAST IS A HARMONIOUS MARRIAGE OF EGGS, TORTILLAS AND SALSA, then join us at one of our favorite Mexican spots.

GORDITAS AQUASCALIENTES
6102 BISSONNET
☎ (713) 541-4560

A side of *chilaquiles* accompanies every breakfast plate. Here the recipe gets a loving dose of chorizo drippings and generous sprinklings of *queso fresco* and *crema* on top.

GUADALAJARA BAKERY
4003 WASHINGTON
☎ (713) 862-0538

When you approach the counter, simply state the total number of breakfast tacos you want. Your flour tortillas will be grilled up while you wait. As for fillings, we recommend *chicharrones* (stewed pork skin) with eggs, as well as the *barbacoa* (steamed cow head).

LOS DOS AMIGOS
5720 WASHINGTON
☎ (713) 862-0462

A cheesy enchilada with a fried egg on top will cure any hangover. Another option is *huevos divorciados*, two eggs over easy, one covered with chunky red ranchero sauce and the other with tangy green sauce.

RUSTIKA CAFE & BAKERY
3237 SOUTHWEST FWY.
☎ (713) 665-6226

The breakfast menu at this Mexican-Jewish bakery boasts a large selection of egg dishes. Start at the top and you'll find meritable *migas* prepared four ways. Chilaquiles are also offered with your choice of red or green salsa.

TEOTIHUACAN
1511 AIRLINE
☎ (713) 426-4420

Breakfast plates start at $3.49 for *huevos rancheros*. These plates come with rice, refried beans, tortillas and your choice of bacon, ham or sausage. A buck and a half ups the ante with a third egg, tamal and roasted potatoes instead of rice.

PHILIPPE RESTAURANT + LOUNGE

. . . .

1800 POST OAK BLVD.
*between Westheimer
& San Felipe*
☎ **(713) 439-1000**
philippehouston.com
🍴🍴 **D6**

CHEF PHILIPPE SCHMIT, WHO PLAYFULLY REFERS to himself as the French Cowboy, successfully brings his classically trained French sensibility to the New American palate, creating dishes that aren't quite comfort food—they're too pretty and refined—but do have that same gratifying emphasis on flavor and impact. Perhaps the most striking dish on the menu is a grilled trout served on a dramatically long, narrow platter. Your initial response is to laugh at the sheer eccentricity of the staging—till you taste the gorgeously subtle, smoky fish. Living up to its ritzy address in BLVD Place, there is a dramatic staircase and dashes of candles and glass to highlight an almost austere setting that's urbane without being imposing. Paper place mats on the tables in lieu of white linen give notice that Philippe may be sophisticated, but it is far from stuffy.

PHO BINH I

. . . .

10928 BEAMER *south of Fuqua*
☎ **(281) 484-3963**
multiple locations
phobinh.com
🍴 **H9**

IF YOU THINK COFFEE OR WINE SNOBS ARE SOMEthing to contend with, try telling a pho snob you eat anywhere other than Pho Binh. This modest trailer is widely considered definitive by those who would stake their family's honor on the matter. The tiny space with extremely limited parking in an easy-to-miss location typifies the best ethnic dining in Houston...and somehow we learned to stop worrying and love the bomb. Undoubtedly it's the reward of food within, where only three cramped tables fit in the front room with a few more in back. Of course, it's the broth that makes the dish, and even without the delicate rice noodles, fatty beef and jalapeño, it's plenty satisfying. Chopsticks fly in ravenous hands, and most diners are in and out in 20 minutes.

PHO DANH

11209 BELLAIRE *west of Wilcrest,*
in Hong Kong City Mall
☎ **(281) 879-9940**
multiple locations
🍴 **A8**

IN A MALL WHERE EVERY OTHER STOREFRONT IS A restaurant, Pho Danh is usually packed. That's because this spotless and efficient space is widely considered to have some of the best pho in town, and though all the tables may be full upon arrival, you'll likely only have to wait a few minutes. The kitchen knows its strength and sticks to it. All you'll find on the menu is noodle soup. The beef broth is layered with notes of beef, onion and star anise. The quality of the sundry meats (e.g. brisket, flank steak, beef tendon, meatball) is relatively high and generously apportioned. For variety, look to the restorative chicken pho or *bun bo hue*, a spicy noodle soup full of shrimp flavor and cubes of congealed pork blood.

PIATTO'S

1925 W. ALABAMA
outside loop 610
☎ **(713) 871-9722**
multiple locations
piattoristorante.com
🍴 **D7**

THE LAST NAME OF PIATTO CHEF/OWNER JOHN Marion Carrabba might ring a bell, as he is a cousin in this first family of Italian restaurateurs in Houston. With that kind of blue blood running through his veins, you can expect large portions of pasta and perfectly grilled meats in a casual but distinctive environment. Everyone begins with the fried asparagus appetizer, lightly breaded, fried and then topped with jumbo lump crabmeat, lemon juice and butter. (That won't be the last you see of butter tonight.) There is a definite buzz in the dining rooms, but it is more bubbly than bothersome and the nice wine list is soothing if that becomes the case.

PICO'S MEX MEX

5941 BELLAIRE BLVD.
west of Chimney Rock
☎ **(713) 662-8383**
picos.net
🍴 **D7** 🚬

ONE TIME SOME FRIENDS ORDERED THE 48-OUNCE *mucho grande* margaritas and ended up in Lake Charles. Okay, not really. But there's a reason Pico's is famous for its margaritas. Aside from getting soused under palapas on the patio, eating interior Mexican cuisine (hence the *Mex-Mex*) usually generates better results. Nachos and quesadillas are tasty enough for happy hour, but if you're going to get serious about it (and what are you really doing with your life?) then stick to one of the three types of *mole* or *cochinita pibil*. The black *mole* with sesame seeds is our favorite. And if you're a fan of *chiles en nogada*, the classic stuffed-chile dish topped with walnut cream sauce made famous by *Like Water for Chocolate*, order it here. Pico's is one of Houston's best spots for soft-shell crabs when they're in season, simply prepared and served with salsa and tortillas.

PIERSON & CO. BBQ

. . . .

5110 T.C. JESTER
north of W. Tidwell
☎ **(713) 683-6997**
🍴 **D4**

TEXAS IS KNOWN FOR ITS BARBECUE AND ITS hospitality, and owner Clarence Pierson is well versed in both. He's happy to show you his hardware, a massive black smoker and firebox burning with mesquite, and newcomers are often offered copious free samples. The brisket is blissfully never dry (though it doesn't maintain much of a crisp outer crust), and ribs are highly lauded for their tender smokiness. The sausage is a divisive issue, but we count ourselves enthusiastically in the "pro" camp when it comes to the links. The sauce is a bit sweet, as are the sides but the homey care put into the potato salad and slaw is evident. Only open 11 am to 7 pm Tuesday through Saturday, Pierson's sells out of certain cuts from time to time. Get your fix while the getting's good.

PINK'S PIZZA

. . . .

403 HEIGHTS BLVD. *at W. 14th*
☎ **(713) 864-7465**
multiple locations
pinkspizza.com
🍴 **E6**

RESTAURANTS

WHAT IS A PERSON TO DO WHEN HE enjoys both sitting on the couch without any pants on but also eating prosciutto, gorgonzola and sun-dried tomatoes? Order a Pink's Pizza from that very spot on the couch. This Houston mini-chain delivers puffy-crust pizza loaded down with fancy toppings. The Deuce comes with goat cheese, spinach, portobellos, roasted garlic and pesto while the Mediterranean-accented Big Sleep gets chicken, feta and artichoke. You can tell by the names that the pizza comes with a side of cool—a hand in the

The Deuce at Pink's Pizza

perience has done wonders for the food, which has gotten consistently good reviews since opening in late 2010 on a walkable stretch of Midtown. The thin, nicely scorched crust of the pizza doesn't sag under the weight of gourmet toppings, such as porcini mushrooms and prosciutto on the Como and smoked salmon and brie on the Copenhagen. In a special that seems almost too good to be true, Piola offers free appetizers with any alcohol purchase during weekday happy hour.

rock-on gesture is printed onto every pizza box—and wait times for delivery are longer than average. But on the whole, Pink's pies are among the most-loved in the city and like we said, sometimes you just don't want to wear pants.

PIOLA

3201 LOUISIANA
just south of Elgin
☎ **(713) 524-8222**
piola.it
🍴 F6

OUSTON HAS BEEN STRUGGLING TO PRO-duce true Italian-style pizza for a while now and finally decided to outsource. Piola is a worldwide chain based in Trevisio, Italy, with locations in Europe and South America as well as big cities throughout the USA. All that ex-

PIZZITOLA'S BAR-B-CUE

1703 SHEPHERD
just south of I-10
☎ **(713) 227-2283**
🍴 E6

S FAR AS WE'RE CON-CERNED, THE MORE humble the exterior of the establishment, the better. Bars on the windows? Pass the potato salad. This little shack has been a barbecue restaurant since 1934 before changing hands to Italian-American Jerome Pizzatola in the 1980s. Now, these ancient barbecue pits are famous for producing some of the best ribs in the city. Seasoned very lightly, they fall off the bone and need no sauce for extra flavor. On the chopped beef and rough textured sausage, you may like some of the thin, vinegary sauce just to get the flavors mingling. Finish up with either a slice of the coconut cake or the banana pudding.

POLLO BRAVO

· · · · · · · · · · · · · · · ·

6015 HILLCROFT *at Hwy. 59*
☎ **(713) 541-0069**
multiple locations
elpollobravo.com
🍴 **D7** ✍

THE LITTLE BIRD MASCOT (WE ASSUME CHICKen, but the beak is oversized) on the Pollo Bravo logo holds both a shopping bag and a telephone in its feathery wings. It's puzzling enough to spend an entire meal pondering the meaning, but it's the hearty Peruvian cuisine that deserves your attention. Rotisserie chicken is the specialty, and it comes out with flavorful, fatty skin and juicy, tender meat. The best way to sample the array of authentic offerings is to go in on the Gordo Combo, which comfortably feeds three. A whole chicken comes with *salchipapa* (a hot dog and frozen French fry combo that's, strangely, kind of good), avocado salad, sweet plantains, rice and pinto beans. Finish with house-made lúcuma ice cream with caramel undertones. We rarely tell anyone to avoid margaritas, but in this case, it's good advice.

POLONIA

· · · · · · · · · · · · · · · ·

1900 BLALOCK *at Campbell*
☎ **(713) 464-9900**
poloniarestaurant.com
🍴 **C5** ✍

OUR ONE MOST SINCERE FOOD WISH FOR HOUSton is to get more central European restaurants. This city could sustain a lot more biergartens. But we're lucky that the one Polish restaurant we have is an excellent one. Despite the mannequins clothed in ancestral dress looming over the sauerkraut and salad bar, the interior is very homey and welcoming. The first thing to do is order a tankard of Pilsner Urquell. Then we recommend the sampler platter for two that's piled high with pierogi, cabbage rolls, kielbasa, meatloaf, duck leg and *bigos*, a Polish hunter stew. It's a tender, fatty smorgasbord of the most comforting flavors—a total sausage fest.

PONDICHERI

· · · · · · · · · · · · · · · ·

2800 KIRBY
at Westheimer, in West Ave
☎ **(713) 522-2022**
pondichericafe.com
🍴 **E6**

ANOTHER IN A CLUSTER OF BIG NAMES bringing their pedigree to West Ave, chef Anita Jaisinghani opened the doors to her second restaurant,

Pondicheri, in early 2011. With an industrial-chic dining room softened by gorgeous orange drapes, and $2 Lone Star on the bar menu, the experience is more casual than at the chef's flagship Indika. The à la carte menu for breakfast, lunch and dinner includes dishes such as a roti wrap with masala eggs and the unctuous beef shank and oxtail curry and is marked by the playful and inventive items like Bournavita ice cream sandwiches and spice-coated "desi fries" that are Jaisinghani's signature. The bakery has been a surprising hit, putting out cardamom-tinged buns and chile-spiked chocolate chip cookies—a toothsome reminder of the chef's early days as a pastry chef.

POSCÓL VINOTECA E SALUMERIA
. . . .

1609 WESTHEIMER *at Mandell*
☎ **(713) 529-2797**
🍴 **E6**

LORIA AND MARCO WILES' POSCÓL TAKES up where Dolce Vita leaves off. There's no pizza, but the genius hinted at with the small plates at Dolce Vita is on full display here, with dozens of little dishes to sample and pass around the table. The name hints at its strengths—wine and house-cured meats—but you'll probably sit at a table for full

dinner. Try the braised octopus with cannellini beans or one of the risottos, never overdone and lush with ingredients. Tables are small and snugly packed, making Poscól the perfect spot for an intimate, grazing dinner but not as ideal for large group celebrations. The early evening is a lovely time to drop by for a half glass of wine, when happy hour prices are a super bargain and small *cicchetti*, or light snacks on toast, are only $2. Sundays feature roast suckling pig.

PREGO
. . . .

2520 AMHERST *east of Kirby*
☎ **(713) 529-2420**
prego-houston.com
🍴 **E7**

ONE OF THE PRETTIEST BARS IN HOUSTON WELcomes as you enter this classic neighborhood favorite. Most diners here are regulars, with favorite tables and servers, greeted with a friendly "welcome back," which creates Prego's neighborhood atmosphere. Try the cornmeal-crusted oysters with pancetta and chive sauce, arugula-radicchio salad with grilled portobello, oranges, peppered goat cheese and apple-walnut vinaigrette, and our very favorite lasagna, made with layers of housemade noodles, veal meatballs, mozzarella, tomato sauce and pesto. We love the casual elegance of this trattoria, as well as chef/co-owner John Watt's dedication to "promoting the marriage and enjoyment of wine and food in the dining ritual." Prego also has Houston's most hidden private room—you have to walk through the kitchen to find it.

PRONTO CUCININO

. . . .

1401 MONTROSE *near W. Gray*
☎ **(713) 528-8646**
multiple locations
ninos-vincents.com
🍴 **E6**

ONE OF HOUSTON'S MOST FAMOUS RESTAURANT families entered the fast-casual dining market a few years ago and found their latest niche. Pronto Cucinino opened on Montrose offering many of the most popular dishes from Vincent Mandola's other three full-service restaurants but without the formality. That meant building a brick-oven rotisserie in Pronto for those beloved

Pronto Cucinino's exterior and patio

fire-roasted chickens. Diners order appetizers, salads and entrees at a counter, and waiters bring the food to the table. Watching the chorus of plump birds turning and spitting while you stand at the counter will either make you hungrier or contemplate Dante. Curbside service is available for takeout orders—just call ahead from your car.

QQ CUISINE

. . . .

9889 BELLAIRE BLVD.
at Beltway 8
☎ **(713) 776-0553**
🍴 **B7** ✍

SIMILAR TO FUFU NEXT DOOR, QQ TRAFFICS IN boldly flavored Sichuan cooking and soup dumplings. There was a time when we were certain the surly waitress was simply refusing to serve us soup dumplings and lying about having run out. But since then we've consumed enough of the rich broth pockets to quell the conspiracy theories for the time being. Gruff service and a no-frills dining room aside, this is one of our favorite spots in Chinatown for the most important reason—the food. Pan-fried pork buns are crisp on the bottom, while a cold celery and tofu skin appetizer and spicy pork belly are both delicious. But the most epic dish of all is the *ma po* eggplant. The three whole eggplants—lightly battered, fried and doused in garlicky sauce—never fail to drop jaws. You know the peppers are the real deal when your tongue goes numb.

QUATTRO

. . . .

1300 LAMAR
*at San Jacinto, in the
Four Seasons Hotel*
☎ **(713) 650-1300**
quattrorestauranthouston.com
🍴 **F6**

THE FOUR SEASONS AND ITS RESTAURANT USED to anchor the east side of downtown, but many competitors have moved in, including the Grove, Vic & Anthony's and all of the Houston Pavilions, and there isn't as much buzz in Quattro's dining room. It hurts, too, that there's been a revolving door of chefs in recent years, but at least for now young chef Maurizio Ferrarese has taken hold of the Italian theme and run with it. There are the requisite hotel standards—a kids' menu, Caesar salad and salmon—but if you look closely enough, there are points of intense interest. Items change seasonally but we've enjoyed the *paccheri* pasta with lamb meatballs and asparagus and pesto pasta. We also recommend a skillet roast duck breast, grilled sea bass and Texas suckling pig. Service is warm and the decor, featuring beaded metal curtains and bright blocks of color, keeps things youthful despite an adult dining experience.

QUEEN VIC PUB & KITCHEN

. . . .

2712 RICHMOND *west of Kirby*
☎ **(713) 533-0022**
thequeenvicpub.com
🍴 **E7** ✍

QUIETLY STANDING SENTINEL ON ITS SHADY patch of Richmond, Richard Di Virgilio's Queen Vic is a modern,

The pukka dog at Queen Vic Pub

comfort pub that's doing wonders for England's food reputation. The concept is simple but tightly executed. Shiva Patel—she is exec chef and Di Virgilio's wife—prepares Indian-accented pub food, much like what you'd find in Britain. An excellent craft beer list plus cocktails with such exotic touches as cardamom, turmeric and jaggery suit both lunches and late nights. Sausage rolls paired with just the right spicy English mustard, the short-rib samosas and Scotch eggs nestled in curry hit all the right spots on the comfort food meter. Adding to the sense of coziness are the pressed-tin ceiling and damask wallpaper, all cast in the dim light of exposed-filament light bulbs. The couple also own Oporto Wine Bar.

RA SUSHI

. . . .

3908 WESTHEIMER
west of Weslayan
☎ **(713) 621-5800**
multiple locations
rasushi.com
‖‖ **D7**

I F WE HAD BEEN ABLE TO INCLUDE A HOTTIE-O-METER in this book (and we certainly tried), Ra Sushi would have scored at least an 8.5. We don't know when the association between sexy happy hours and sushi restaurants began, but things certainly have paid off for the inventor. Ra isn't really for sushi purists—the most popular roll is the "Viva Las Vegas," a flamboyant concoction of crab, cream cheese, sweet eel sauce and tempura bits. But some of the cooked dishes, including vegetable tempura and lobster stir-fry, are delicious and deserving of your attention. None of the young singles crowd lingering over Tsunami Punch under the red globe lights at Highland Village seems too concerned, though, with the food. You'll find a slightly more subdued approach at the City-Centre location.

RAINBOW LODGE

. . . .

2011 ELLA *at T.C. Jester*
☎ **(713) 861-8666**
rainbow-lodge.com
‖‖ **E5**

D ONNETTE HANSEN LAUNCHED THE RAINbow Lodge in 1977 on a sylvan plot bordering Buffalo Bayou. In 2006, the landlord evicted her (taking the restaurant for himself) and Hansen relocated to an equally idyllic 100-year-old log cabin alongside White Oak Bayou. The wealth of fishing and hunting ornamentation will get your stomach growling for game, which the kitchen is conveniently known for. The kitchen's mixed grill includes venison, quail, lamb and a wild boar chop, and a changing Friday burger special often incorporates game as well. Hearty meat dishes like bison brisket pot roast and butter-roasted antelope on vegetable succotash may be reminiscent of the great outdoors, but there is a delicate refinement to each. Don't miss the signature duck gumbo as a starter.

RAGIN CAJUN

4302 RICHMOND
west of Weslayan
☎ **(713) 623-6321**
multiple locations
ragin-cajun.com
🍴 **D7**

HOUSTON'S HOMESICK CAJUNS HAVE long satisfied their cravings at this ramshackle roadhouse. Louisiana paraphernalia decorates everything, and ULaLa and LSU yearbooks are collected in stacks. The TVs are always tuned to a game, and LSU and Tulane alumni naturally congregate at all locations to celebrate Mardi Gras, fall football and March Madness. Many insist that the best crawfish in town are at the Cajun, where two people can quickly go through four pounds of mudbugs, and the potatoes and corn are plentiful. Be prepared to sit at long tables and make new friends, as you'll be forced to sit in close proximity to others from March to late May during crawfish season. Other menu favorites include crab gumbo, po'boys, muffalettas, hot boudin, crawfish pie

and red beans and rice. This is a fun place to bring people visiting from up North who want some local color but aren't interested in Tex-Mex. Put on a bib and get funky, *cher*.

RAVEN GRILL

1916 BISSONNET *at Hazard*
☎ **(713) 521-2027**
theravengrill.com
🍴 **E7**

ON THE GENTEEL, TREE-LINED STREETS OF WEST U sits Raven Grill. Named as a tribute to nearby Poe Elementary, Rob and Sara Cromie's restaurant has been a neighborhood staple since opening in 1998. The drawing card is an always-going green mesquite fire, and the cedar-plank salmon and chipotle-honey glazed pork chops are both first-rate. Many menu items tend towards a Southwestern flair (try the sweet potato-spinach enchiladas) and are more home-style than haute. Start with the tower of onion rings and take advantage of the shady patio when possible. Daily specials— Sunday's chicken-fried steak, Monday's roast chicken, etc.—and reasonable prices keep regulars coming back. Parking can be a challenge, so plan your arrival time accordingly.

AIRLINE DRIVE

A SATURDAY MORNING DRIVE DOWN AIRLINE MEANS LUNCH, ALL THE GROCERY SHOPPING for the week, a mid-afternoon churro and perhaps an impulsive Our Lady of Guadalupe poster purchase.

CONNIE'S SEAFOOD
2525 AIRLINE
☎ (713) 868-2144

Always start with a *michelada*. Once you're well lubricated, it's time to approach the fresh fish resting on ice to choose which particular black drum, red snapper or flounder you'd like cooked
on the spot. Or take it home to cook yourself.

EL BOLILLO
2517 AIRLINE
☎ (713) 861-8885

Grab a set of tongs and a tray and have at the rainbow of baked goods at this fragrant Mexican bakery. Yes, there's such a thing as a *dulce de leche*-stuffed churro.

AIRLINE FARMERS' MARKET
2520 AIRLINE
☎ (713) 862-4027

Stuff your pockets with small bills before coming to this open-air market for bushels of onions, mountains of chiles and buckets of hominy.

FLORES SPICES & HERBS
2521 AIRLINE
☎ (713) 695-8200

Speed-walk past the processed cheese powder and on towards the jagged sticks of cinnamon, dried hibiscus flowers and *mole* paste.

HOUSTON DAIRYMAIDS
2201 AIRLINE
☎ (713) 880-4800

The warehouse where all the cheese for this wholesale operation is stored is open every Friday and Saturday for public tastings.

ASIA MARKET
1010 W. CAVALCADE
☎ (713) 863-7074

Just around the corner about a block off Airline sits the most authentic Thai food in town. Sure, it's in a dingy Thai-food convenience store, but that doesn't stop it from being the best *pad see ew* ("river noodles") in town.

RDG + BAR ANNIE

....

1800 POST OAK BLVD.
between Westheimer
& San Felipe
☎ **(713) 840-1111**
rdgbarannie.com
🍴 **D6** ✍

C AFE ANNIE HAD BEEN A HOUSTON INSTITUTION for more than 25 years. Then one day it was no more, and chef Robert Del Grande and the rest of the Schiller-Del Grande group opened an even swankier restaurant a few hundred feet away. The furnishings at the newish RDG (it opened 2009) are so expensive, it almost hurts to look directly at them. But as the new flagship of the empire, this is the place to feast on the French-inspired Southwestern food that Del Grande is famous for. The rabbit enchiladas in _mole_ sauce are a signature item, and the redfish with cornbread dressing is otherworldly. The long-loved coffee-rubbed filet is no longer on the menu, but ask nicely and the kitchen will prepare it for you. When the weather is fine, reserve a table on the second-floor terrace overlooking Post Oak Boulevard. The downstairs Bar Annie is a more casual setting than RDG, though that term is relative; it's packed constantly with the most glamorous-looking people you will ever see in real life. Most of them are eating the outstanding RDG hamburger.

REEF

....

2600 TRAVIS _at McGowen_
☎ **(713) 526-8282**
reefhouston.com
🍴 **E6** ✍

S UP IN SUNNY AQUATIC-HUED REEF AND YOU'LL understand why chef Bryan Caswell is such a prominent name in Houston dining. Scrolling down the menu, you'll notice a simple, straightforward formula played out again and again—escolar with braised collard greens, triple tail and an artichoke stew, amberjack and asparagus with orange mustard, a seafood "hot pot" served with fingerling potatoes. If you like first-rate (and lesser known) fish expertly prepared and paired with some atypical but rewarding side orders, Reef simply has more choices than any other establishment in town. Preparations stay fairly constant, but the catches

Reef's grilled swordfish

are constantly changing. For cocktails and lighter fare, try Reef's 3rd Bar where sliders and a raw bar are the draw. Note: Reef's wine list is also very good.

REGGAE HUT

....

4814 ALMEDA *at Wentworth*
☎ **(713) 520-7171**
thereggaehut.com
🍴 **E7**

HE PIGEON PEA IS AS DELICIOUS AS IT IS modest. It can be found in massive quantities at the Reggae Hut, Houston's best-known Jamaican spot. Tender goat curry and zesty house-made ginger beer should be ordered at the counter before you find a seat in the colorful dining room. Jerk chicken is smoky, with an alluring aroma and flavor of allspice. Much of the restaurant's business is take-out, we assume because the idea of eating enormous portions of brown chicken stew in front of the TV in your own living room is so appealing. Owner Marcus Davis also runs The Breakfast Klub across town, and the friendliness transferred over. Another Houston fun fact: Notable local artist Tierney Malone is responsible for the murals inside.

RESTAURANT CINQ

....

3410 MONTROSE
south of Westheimer,
in La Colombe d'Or Hotel
☎ **(713) 524-7999**
lacolombedorhouston.com
🍴 **E6** ✎

INQ IS PROOF POSITIVE THAT LIFE IS FULL OF second acts. The stately if stuffy Colombe d'Or—Houston's smallest hotel, with just five rooms—was the location of many Houstonians' anniversaries and business celebrations...20 years ago. Recently young chef Jeramie Robison took over the kitchen and gave the restaurant new life. His food is a dazzling blend of French, Italian, Cajun and mainstream American. His dinner menu is divided into two sections: "Classics" such as filet mignon and rack of lamb for traditionalists or longtime Colombe d'Or diners, and "New Ideas" geared to people willing to eat outside the box. Restraint and creativity are marks of the seasonal and frequently updated menu. The dining room still retains its old-fashioned beauty and is perfect for a romantic occasion, though we recommend dining here for more than just that.

RESTAURANT CONAT

5219 CAROLINE

between Southmore & Oakdale

🍴 **E7**

HOUSTON'S CULINARY ENFANT TERRIBLE, Randy Rucker, announced his new restaurant as we went to press with this guidebook. The name, previously assigned to a Tomball restaurant project, was resurrected for this Museum District restaurant. Pastry chef Chris Leung, who worked with Rucker at Bootsie's Heritage Cafe, will again join Rucker at Conat. It is set to open Fall 2011.

RIO RANCH

9999 WESTHEIMER

at Briarpark, in the Westchase Hilton

☎ **(713) 952-5000**

rioranch.com

🍴 **B7**

FRONTING THE WEST-CHASE HILTON, THIS IS a hotel restaurant with some major differences, such as a pedigree that can trace its heritage to local celebrity chef Robert Del Grande. This was his 1992 take on the perennial Texas ranchhouse theme, and it's still a handsome setting. Del Grande associate and longtime Rio Ranch chef San Hemwattakit, a native of Thailand, has created many dishes that seem

practically iconic for East Texas, among them chicken-fried ribeye steak, tenderloin tip and pork sausage brochette, and wood-grilled mahi mahi. The laid-back setting, an appealing buffet (with omelet and waffle stations) and $4 bloody Marys, bellinis and mimosa make this a top-notch brunching spot on Sundays.

RIOJA

11920 WESTHEIMER

at S. Kirkwood

☎ **(281) 531-5569**

riojarestaurant.com

🍴 **B7**

CHEF IGNACIO FORSECA SENDS OUT HIS FAMOUS paella loaded with squid, mussels, chicken and chunks of house-made chorizo. The short-grain Valencia rice is rife with flavor, and a selection of hot and cold tapas add to the authenticity. Recommended dishes include fried calamari, seared Portuguese sardines (for fish-lovers only), piquillo peppers stuffed with codfish and fried black Spanish sausage. Many of the ingredients such as olives and sardines are imported from Spain and can even be purchased here by the pound. The wine list is all Spanish with quite a few very inexpensive options, and your intrepid waiter will be happy to offer guidance. A three tapas (including paella) lunch is less than $15, and the warm, rustic interior is serenaded with live music Thursday through Saturdays.

RISTORANTE CAVOUR

....

1080 UPTOWN PARK
north of San Felipe, in Hotel Granduca
☎ **(713) 418-1104**
granducahouston.com
🍴 **D6**

IF YOU'VE EVER WANTED TO KNOW WHAT DINING like 19th century Italian royalty feels like, has Houston got the restaurant for you. The Hotel Granduca's tiny jewel box of a restaurant, helmed by chef Renato De Pirro, is bedecked in sumptuous fabrics, golden light bouncing off the jade green walls. The food is traditional to Northern Italy, from pan-seared branzino topped with heirloom tomatoes to unctuous veal osso buco with polenta. Housemade

Ristorante Cavour's exterior

gnocchi with eggplant, a tart tomato sauce and ricotta is simple but bracing in its flavor and improved by impeccable, stately service. Brunch is more typical American, but there's always Prosecco. This is one of Houston's most elegant dining experiences. Please dress appropriately.

RUDI LECHNER'S

....

2503 S. GESSNER
north of Westheimer
☎ **(713) 782-1180**
rudilechners.com
🍴 **D6**

RUDI LECHNER'S IS THE ONE GERMAN restaurant in town and it's not going to let you forget it. The waitstaff and frequent polka bands will be in costume, and people will come in and snap enough photos of their friends drinking beer from boots to fill an entire album. Luckily, the food is not quite so over the top. *Wiener schnitzel* is rushed crisp and golden from the fryer, served with a mound of sauerkraut or red cabbage and Austrian potatoes. Deal of the week is Wednesday evening 6 to 9 when the restaurant offers the German sampler buffet ("Loosen the Lederhosen") for $15.95 per person. Live German music with very long Alphorn is part of the fun. Other recommended dishes: curry wurst, goulash, sauerbraten and beef

RESTAURANTS

rouladen with spätzle. Certain desserts, including *Kaiserschmarr'n* (the emperor's pancakes) and *Salzburger Nockerl* (a meringue dessert), need to be ordered 24 hours in advance.

✗ RUGGLES GREEN

. . . .

2311 W. ALABAMA *east of Kirby*
☎ **(713) 533-0777**
multiple locations
rugglesgreen.com
🍴 **E7**

THE WORD "HEMPANADA" IS ENOUGH TO MAKE any red-blooded Texan cringe, but control your gag reflex long enough and you'll discover truly satisfying eats of the sandwich and salad variety that also up your eco-cred (tallied in reusable shopping bags). Ruggles Green is the first and only restaurant in Houston that is a three-star Green Restaurant Certified by the Green Restaurant Association. (The newer CityCentre location is four-star certified, actually.) The menu is marked with gluten-free, vegetarian and dairy-free indicators, and the quinoa mac 'n' cheese, smoked chicken pizza and grilled egg and cheese sandwich are constructed with a variety of organic, preservative-free and hormone-free ingredients. As for the hempanada, it's stuffed with beef and raisins and surprisingly good. The casual, counter service dining room is always bustling, and the patios at both locations are lovely and tree-shaded. A third location is on its way.

RUGGLES GRILL

. . . .

903 WESTHEIMER
east of Montrose
☎ **(713) 524-3839**
rugglesgrill.com
🍴 **E6**

THIS TRENDY MONTROSE FAVORITE BECAME SO popular in the 1990s and people had to wait so long to have their reservations honored that one might say fame was the root of its once faltering reputation. But 2008's Hurricane Ike wreaked great vengeance on the Houston institution, closing its doors for 18 months. With the reopening came a revitalization of the menu. The robustly seasoned Southwestern American cuisine comes in hefty portions, and since the opening of Ruggles Green, you'll notice the local and green influence bleeding over to this menu, too. The avocado and lump crab tower is a classic, as is the black pepper fettuccine and smoked pork chops in pecan ancho cream sauce. The energy level here is still high, especially on Sunday with the jazz brunch. Professional athletes, friends of Ruggles chef/owner Bruce Molzan, often dine here.

•SAIGON PAGOLAC

. . . .

9600 BELLAIRE BLVD.
at Corporate
☏ **(713) 988-6106**
🍴 **C6**

THERE ARE MANY EXCELLENT VIETNAMESE RESTAURANTS across Houston, but Saigon Pagolac has achieved the rare distinction of being able to draw Inner Loopers out to Chinatown with the siren song of seven courses of beef. Have the whole table order this interactive meal and feel the collective glee as lemongrass-marinated beef is brought to the table to be grilled, followed by a medley of bite-sized beef treats, including meatballs and beef and noodle soup. The whole catfish is another jaw-dropper, served with its haunting eyeballs still intact and a shatteringly crisp skin. Lunch specials provide good value, if not the spectacle.

SALDIVIA'S SOUTH AMERICAN GRILL

. . . .

10234 WESTHEIMER
east of Beltway 8
☏ **(713) 782-9494**
saldivias.com
🍴 **B7**

THE JAR OF CHIMICHURRI SITTING ON EVERY table at this family-run steakhouse begs the question, "What else can we douse with sauce?" The answer is anything and everything—it's just that good. The specialty of the house is the delectable *entraña*, a Uruguayan skirt steak served with Spanish rice and more chimichurri. The *parrillada completa*, or mixed grill, comes with enough meat to feed three people. Feast on *entraña*, beef flat ribs, sausage and sweetbreads and wash it all down with a South American wine. The dining room is rather elegant, making Saldivia's a good choice for romantic occasions, provided your partner finds a post-meal quick change into elastic waistband pants sexy.

SAMBA GRILLE

. . . .

530 TEXAS *at Smith*
☏ **(713) 343-1180**
sambagrillehouston.com
🍴 **E6**

ONE OF THE BEST NEW RESTAURANTS TO OPEN in 2010, this Latin restaurant became a critical darling and proved that not all dining experiences in Bayou Place have to be dour. It originally launched with rodizio service, but eventually dropped that in order to offer a Latin-fusion menu that includes ceviches, paella, sweet-n-spicy scallops and crispy duck carnitas salad. Chef Cesar Rodriguez is sourcing quality meats and searing them to perfection.

Among our favorites are the skewers of grilled beef heart and pan-roasted lamb chops. If you haven't already popped too many of the delicious cheesy rolls, order the earthy empanadas to start. The red-drenched interior is modern and sultry, which makes a caipirinha at the bar and a plate of calamari an appealing option when a full-on meat coma is less so.

✗SANDONG NOODLE HOUSE

. . . .

9938 BELLAIRE BLVD.
at Beltway 8
☎ **(713) 988-8802**
🍴 **B7**

EATING AT THE OLD LOCATION OF SANDONG felt a bit like being transported to China, as you shared cramped bench seating with messy eaters, occasionally splashed with the hot broth of the noodle soup they were slurping. The newer location just down the street is brighter and roomier (though still cash-only), self-serve and fairly heavy on the surliness of the cashier. But suck it up because the perfect, pan-seared dumplings possessing that rare crispy brown bottom and juicy innards are worth it. Mix your own dipping sauce using the soy sauce, hot chili oil and vinegar sitting on each table. Steamed dumplings and beef noodle soup garnished with pickled mustard greens are soul-warming on a cold day.

✗SHABU HOUSE

. . . .

9889 BELLAIRE BLVD.
at Beltway 8
☎ **(713) 995-5428**
🍴 **B7**

LEAVE IT TO THE CREATORS OF HELLO KITTY to give rise to a type of cuisine that translates to "swish swish." Shabu shabu is very similar to Chinese hot pot, in that you'll cook an array of meats and vegetables in broth that is rather delicate and mild. At this pocket-sized restaurant, each person seated at the horseshoe-shaped bar gets their own pot of boiling broth and their own set of ingredients. The loss of the communal aspect is a bit of a disappointment, but not a total letdown. The seafood is obviously previously frozen, so a better bet would be to stick to the beef and vegetables. The meditative act of tending to taro, pale green Napa cabbage and well-marbled beef while a cloud of steam settles over you is one we would return for.

LOWER WESTHEIMER

SOMETHING ABOUT THE SCARY-NARROW TRAFFIC LANES, LACK OF PARKING AND PREponderance of tattoo parlors seems to have drawn the top chefs in Houston to this area. Not only are these the best restaurants on Lower Westheimer, they're some of the very best in the entire city.

FEAST
219 WESTHEIMER
☎ (713) 529-7788

There's no question that this critically acclaimed nose-to-tail kitchen is serving some of the city's most intriguing food. The question is: Do you dare order the Bowl of Necks?

DOLCE VITA
500 WESTHEIMER
☎ (713) 520-8222

This hip spot does right by authentic thin and charred Italian pizza. But that doesn't mean you should skip the *cacio e pepe* (Roman-style cheese and pepper pasta).

INDIKA
516 WESTHEIMER
☎ (713) 524-2170

Chef/owner Anita Jaisinghani has invented some of the most playful and innovative Indian fusion in the country here.

EL REAL TEX-MEX
1201 WESTHEIMER
☎ (713) 524-1201

Former *Houston Press* food critic Robb Walsh and partners Bill Floyd and chef Bryan Caswell serve up old-fashioned Tex-Mex with a side of nostalgia.

DA MARCO
1520 WESTHEIMER
☎ (713) 807-8857

Another Marco Wiles' success (see Dolce Vita, left), the upmarket Da Marco offers Northern Italian dining the traditional way: *antipasti*, *primi* and *secondi*, always with wine.

HUGO'S
1602 WESTHEIMER
☎ (713) 524-7744

Chef Hugo Ortega explores his roots with interior-of-Mexico cuisine. Don't miss the extravagant Sunday brunch.

MARK'S AMERICAN CUISINE
1658 WESTHEIMER
☎ (713) 523-3800

Award-winning chef Mark Cox prepares some of the most creative food in Houston. The "service" is in a beautifully renovated church.

SHADE

. . . .

250 WEST 19TH *near Yale*
☎ **(713) 863-7500**
shadeheights.com
🍴 **E5**

THIS STRIP OF 19TH IN THE HEIGHTS IS ALMOST not of Houston. Walk (yes, walk) past the antique shops and boutiques, soak up the Main Street charm of a past era and duck into lovely Shade for upmarket Southern fare with globetrotting influences. Chef/owner Claire Smith has created such worldly dishes as panko-fried shrimp and bacon cheese grits, fried Texas quail and duck two ways. Though located in a dry part of The Heights, Shade allows diners to partake in one of its playful, inventive cocktails and wine by signing up for the free "Shade Club," which makes the highly evolved urbane dining room a wonderful spot to drop in for a drink, if not a meal, while you're in the neighborhood.

SHAWARMA KING

. . . .

3121 HILLCROFT *at Richmond*
☎ **(713) 784-8882**
shawarmakingonline.com
🍴 **C7**

SHAWARMA KING AL-READY MERITS A HIGH approval rating for its name alone and fully delivers on its promise. The shawarma nestled into fresh pita is moist, slowly roasted and well-seasoned. The necessary accompaniments—shredded lettuce, tomato, pickles and tahini—complete the picture. The falafel, though it doesn't claim to be king, is also quite good and very crispy. All the usual Mediterranean deli suspects are here, including hummus, babaganoush, tabouli, stuffed grape leaves, spinach pies in phyllo and *kibbe* (minced meat and bulgur). But the friendliness of the owner gives this modest shop an edge. Over the lunch hour, the wait can be a little longer than you might like, but it's worth it.

Exterior of Shade

SHIVA INDIAN RESTAURANT

....

2514 TIMES *east of Kirby*
☎ **(713) 523-4753**
multiple locations
shivarestaurant.com
🍴 **E7**

STURDY SHIVA HAS BEEN FEEDING CRAVINGS FOR saag paneer and hot naan in Rice Village for more than two decades. Despite the tidy, if not quite refined, atmosphere created by burgundy tablecloths and cold metal water cups, the invitation is to come as you are and regulars are happy to comply. We consistently order the *gosht dil pasand*, billed as the "perfect lamb curry," though the flavor profile frequently changes. *Gobi alloo*, or potatoes and cauliflower, is another favorite. Vegetarians will be very happy here, with a solid selection of well-spiced dishes that aren't readily available elsewhere. Lunch is buffet format, and the new Sugar Land location has a bit more shine to it.

SICHUAN CUISINE

....

9114 BELLAIRE BLVD.
east of Ranchester
☎ **(713) 771-6868**
🍴 **C7**

THE FIRST TIME WE EXPERIENCED THE NOT exactly spicy, but minty burn of a Szechuan pepper, we had to consult the Internet to make sure we weren't facing early death. But what a way to go! The pepper-spiked food—including blazing hot *ma po* tofu with spicy minced meat, addictive crispy chicken with three chilies and incendiary lamb and celery stir-fry—is nothing short of invigorating. Order the smoked tea duck, which manages to be simultaneously spicy, juicy and smoky, a duck-lover's dream. If you've brought enough people, try the hot pot but ask for the split pot with both spicy broth and the mild to cool things down. Sliced lamb, beef and the usual hot pot vegetables are available. Note: You're not coming to Sichuan Cuisine for the decor; it's your basic starkly decorated Chinese dining hall.

•SINH SINH

....

9788 BELLAIRE BLVD.
east of Beltway 8
☎ **(713) 541-0888**
🍴 **B7**

FACT: IF YOU HAVEN'T BURNED YOUR FINGERtips grabbing hot pork belly out of a Styrofoam container while cruising down Bellaire, you have neither lived nor eaten at Sinh Sinh. Behind the glass of the tiny barbecue counter hang lacquered whole ducks and red-tinged barbecue pork ready to be eaten at a table or taken away by the pound (come early as offerings often sell out by mid-afternoon). Tanks of live sea creatures from succulent shrimp to Dungeness crabs and Maine lobster provide an incentive for dining in. The seafood is pricey, but you get what you pay for. Open until 2 am or later, Sinh Sinh is a top pick for late-night eats. All the best stories unfold, it seems, around a midnight order of geoduck.

SKEWERS MEDITERRANEAN CAFE

. . . .

3991 RICHMOND *at Weslayan*
☎ **(713) 599-1444**
skewerscafe.com
🍴 **D7**

WE NEVER USED TO GIVE MUCH thought to Skewers. But since its recent post-fire renovations, this casual, counter-service cafe has been producing excellent results. All of our Lebanese favorites are here, including creamy hummus, kofta kebabs and lemony stuffed grape leaves. The spinach pies are delicate, and baked chicken is laced with saffron. Skewers is an inexpensive and quick option for weekday lunch, but hookahs and a few Lebanese wines may entice you to stay longer. Belly dancing keeps the weekend crowds entertained, and reverse happy hour from 9 pm until close Monday through Wednesday means $1 off beer and $4 house wine.

SMITH & WOLLENSKY

. . . .

4007 WESTHEIMER *at Drexel*
☎ **(713) 621-7555**
smithandwollensky.com
🍴🍴 **D7**

FORGET THE JALAPEÑO POPPERS AND WAN DRIVE-thru French fries. If you're hungry at midnight, a dry-aged prime steak can be yours, provided you have a robust bank account. This Manhattan-born steakhouse chain keeps late hours and provides the usual elements of luxury, from truffled mac 'n' cheese to the romantic glow of copper lamps. Order the surf and turf, and two minions will appear tableside pushing a silver cart heaving under the weight of a lobster they shell meticulously for your pleasure. We like their wedge salad, impressive shellfish tower and Cajun-marinated ribeye that's both enormous and enormously flavorful. The wine list is all-American (literally) with some 600 selections, and a glass of vino on the large balcony can be a real treat if you get there before the loud scenesters.

SOMA

....

4820 WASHINGTON
between Shepherd & Durham
☎ **(713) 861-2726**
somasushi.com
🍴 **E6**

A S ITS WASHINGTON AVENUE ADDRESS might suggest, Soma is by far the flashiest restaurant to come from the Cheng family, which also owns Azuma and Kata Robata. Well-heeled club-goers feel right at home among the seductive red and black scenery and deafening noise levels. Pomp aside, the kitchen is sending out many reliable dishes, including handmade ramen in fat-dotted pork broth, Wagyu short ribs and tempura-battered rock shrimp. You can also order a five-, seven- or nine-course *kaiseki* (tasting menu). Freshly grated wasabi root is a nice touch, and the sake selection is a serious effort at inclusivity. Recently, the cocktail program has left behind its bubblegum roots and become a darling of mixology fans.

SOPHIA

....

1601 W. MAIN *at Mandell*
☎ **(713) 942-7970**
sophiahouston.com
🍴 **E7**

WHEN THIS SPACE WAS OCCUPIED BY Cafe Artiste, it was a neighborhood favorite for dropping in any time of day. Now that Sophia resides on the lot, it doesn't quite function that way due to high prices. David Alvarado (previously with Shade and La Vista) has opened a very casual eatery serving an upscale menu. The dining room exhibits a budget-minded tastefulness, but the food delivered to the table is uppity: four-cheese ravioli with lobster and brown butter sauce and grilled quail served on a bed of butternut sage risotto. The mussels and blue cheese macaroni are the most touted, and a BYOB policy makes it an attractive option for date night.

SORREL URBAN BISTRO

....

2202 W. ALABAMA *at Greenbriar*
☎ **(713) 677-0391**
sorrelhouston.com
🍴 **E6**

OWNER RAY SALTI AND CHEF SOREN PEDERSEN already had a successful, albeit under-the-radar, restaurant in Fulshear when they decided to open their second restaurant together in Summer 2011, this one in the big city. The space that used to be Ziggy's Healthy Grill has been reborn as a contemporary yet warm dining room with huge photo murals of raw food. The rear wall is a practical wine display case, and the kitchen is not only open but

RESTAURANTS

equipped with closed-circuit TV cameras so that diners throughout the restaurant can watch the kitchen action. With a concept based on "farm to table" devotion and "organically focused" cuisine along with a daily changing menu, Sorrel is inviting high expectations. The menu is printed daily, and there is always a prix-fixe option at lunch and dinner, in addition to the à la carte menu.

SORRENTO

. . . .

415 WESTHEIMER
between Taft & Montrose
☎ **(713) 527-0609**
multiple locations
sorrentohouston.com
🍴 **E6**

ABBAS HUSSEIN (VETERAN OF MICHELANgelo's) and Pedro Castro created an elegant escape within the endcap of this rather suburban-looking strip center deep in the heart of Montrose. Dark woods, handpainted murals, warm lighting and well-appointed tables set the stage for indulgent neo-Italian cuisine. Salads are well dressed and the prosciutto-wrapped scallop is sinfully rich. Seared Hudson Valley foie gras with poached pear is a worthwhile indulgence, and the lobster bisque reminds us why we always perk up when it's on offer. The staff is extremely gracious, which is a good thing considering

the mature crowd and clots of ladies expect it. If you get sticker shock easily, don't say we didn't warn you.

SPANISH FLOWERS

. . . .

4701 N. MAIN *at Airline*
☎ **(713) 869-1706**
spanish-flowers.com
🍴 **E5**

LADY GAGA HERSELF MADE A LATE NIGHT visit to Spanish Flowers after her July 2010 Houston concert. We'll leave it to you to interpret what that means for the restaurant. What we do know is that this 24-hour Tex-Mex legend is a longtime favorite both during the day and late into the night. The cheesier the better when it comes to the food, and we recommend the enchiladas, tostadas de *carnitas* or *mole* poblano above all. Tortillas are served hot, fresh and with a generous hand by the friendly staff. Breakfast is available all day, and though it sounds out of place, the egg-white omelet with jicama is the best in its class. When the weather is mild, ask to be seated outside.

SPANISH VILLAGE

·················

4720 ALMEDA *at Blodgett*
☎ **(713) 523-2861**
spanishvillagerestaurant.com
🍴 **E7**

WHERE DO OLD CHRISTMAS LIGHTS go to die? Spanish Village, that's where. They add a happy sparkle to the cave-like dining room, as do the made-with-fresh-lime margaritas. (But don't come here just for a drink. There's no bar area, and they won't serve drinks without food.) The decor is kitschy and well-worn. (In fact, on our most recent visit, the whole building looked like it was about to tumble down.) Locals like to take out-of-towners to this sentimental favorite for a taste of "the real Houston." There is much here to like—try the *chile relleno*, pork *carnitas* or special enchiladas. And here's a surprise: The Southern fried chicken is some of the best in Houston. Design note: The broken-tile tables were a fixture here long before Williams-Sonoma catalogs began featuring them.

STAR PIZZA

·················

2111 NORFOLK *at S. Shepherd*
☎ **(713) 523-0800**
multiple locations
starpizza.com
🍴 **E7**

STAR PIZZA IS SO BELOVED BY THE CITY THAT we'll forgive it for its temporary foray into the fajita catering business. What it is good at is deep-dish Chicago-style pizza, and the Joe's with garlic and spinach and meat-laden Ben's are our two favorite combinations. (Order half and half.) It's definitely a knife-and-fork kind of pizza. If that's not your calling, thin crust, wheat crust and individual focaccia pies are also available. The menu also includes all manner of sandwiches, but we've never been able to get beyond the pizza options. Both locations are strictly T-shirt and jeans and have a quirky run-down sensibility that's suitable for kids and hungry students. Surprisingly, home delivery can sometimes be faster than table service in the restaurant.

STELLA SOLA

·················

1001 STUDEWOOD *at E. 10th*
☎ **(713) 880-1001**
stellasolahouston.com
🍴 **E5**

BRYAN CASWELL AND BILL FLOYD'S STELLA

RESTAURANTS

Sola—the name means "lone star" in Italian—serves the kind of food that we often want to eat, and we don't mean that as a low-level compliment. The pork-centric menu exhibits the regional flair we love with soul-warming methods of preparation. The food is billed as Texan-Tuscan and you can see both influences in handmade pappardelle with wild boar ragu, the meat market plate of house-cured meats, flatiron steak with cornbread gnocchi and the Gulf snapper in mushroom brodo. But what is genuinely common to most of the dishes at Stella Sola is their heartiness, a characteristic reflected in the restaurant's simple declaration on its signage: Meat & Drink. The restaurant has been a leader in the local charcuterie movement, and you'll see tidy rows of curing sausages hanging in the "pork room." Stella Sola also takes great pride in an economical wine list that routinely charges less than the typical restaurant mark-up.

✗STRAITS

. . . .

800 W. SAM HOUSTON PKWY. NORTH in *CityCentre*
☎ **(713) 365-9922**
straitsrestaurants.com
🍴 **B6**

⌐┰HIS CALI IMPORT SEEMS RIGHT AT HOME IN THE glitzy CityCentre live-play development. The interior is dark and sleek, the kind of place that will impress a date and make older visitors joke about needing a flashlight. (The Atlanta location is co-owned by rapper Ludacris. Luda!) The Singaporean fusion cuisine is meant to be shared family-style, and dishes like sticky tamarind beef and giant crabs doused in chili sauce boast a big wow factor, both visually and flavor-wise. We loved the whole striped bass, fried into a half-moon shape, glossed with chile sauce and filled with Chinese broccoli. You'll also find satay skewers, *roti prata* (griddled flatbread with curry dipping sauce) and long-braised short rib *rendang*. The signature dish, sweet and spicy chicken "lollipops," may not be authentic but please the mojito-sipping crowds that gather on the weekends.

STRIP HOUSE

. . . .

1200 MCKINNEY
at San Jacinto, in the Park Shops Mall
☎ **(713) 659-6000**
striphouse.com
🍴 **F6**

⌐SURE, THE COMBINATION OF STEAK AND HALF-naked women sounds like a winning business proposition, and we might roll our eyes if this bordello-themed steakhouse didn't deliver in the kitchen. The luscious, all-

red interior is enhanced with rosy lighting and cheeky photos of burlesque models, all geared toward working up an (*ahem*) appetite. Meats include wet-aged, crisp-edged, double-cut strip steak, veal T-bone and rack of lamb, and ordering the porterhouse means a showy tableside carving. Our favorite sides include the thick-cut roasted-bacon salad and garlic herb French fries (though some prefer the goose fat potatoes). Save room for the famous 24-layer chocolate cake. It's intensely chocolatey yet light and perhaps more titillating than the showgirl photos.

SUSHI JIN

. . . .

14670 MEMORIAL
west of N. Dairy Ashford
☎ **(281) 493-2932**
🍴 **A6**

A S YOU VERY OFTEN SEEK BUT VERY RARE-ly find, the fish at Sushi Jin is extremely fresh. You can count on this fact because the owner also owns Prime Sales and Trading Ltd., a seafood wholesaler that flies fish in from Japan and elsewhere. The best way to experience the offerings is to sit at the sushi bar and encourage the chefs to challenge you. In our experience, the Canadian salmon alone is worth the trip. Pale orange flesh marbled with creamy stripes of fat creates a rich melt-in-your-mouth experi-

ence. Near raw, barely caramelized scallops are succulent and sweet. Sushi Jin has a full bar and several private dining areas that host everything from gaggles of middle-school girls celebrating birthdays to groups of businessmen from Tokyo closing business deals.

SUSHI RAKU

. . . .

3201 LOUISIANA *at Elgin*
☎ **(713) 526-8885**
sushi-raku.com
🍴 **F6**

R AKU IS BOTH SEXY AND COMPETENT IN the kitchen, just like a Stepford wife. Except instead of apple-pie-and-an-apron sexy, she's tight-red-dress sexy. One wall is draped in 60,000 pounds of red fisherman's rope, and the rest of the elegant dining room is minimalist and swank. Culinary details such as house-made flavored salts, fresh-grated wasabi and fish flown in from Tokyo's famed Tsukiji market will thrill serious foodies. We often find ourselves ordering off the hot menu, which shows an interesting blend of old and new. Sometimes menu items can seem overly trendy (popcorn crabs, Berkshire pork belly roasted until fork-tender), but we love the flavors anyway. A word of advice: Don't even think about parking in the nightmarish 24 Hour Fitness garage. But you can park across the street in the High Fashion Fabrics lot or on the west side of Louisiana.

● SYLVIA'S ENCHILADA KITCHEN

12637 WESTHEIMER
near Dairy Ashford
☎ **(281) 679-8300**
multiple locations
sylviasenchiladakitchen.com
🍴 **A7**

THIS IS A FANTASTIC SPOT TO TAKE OUT-OF-towners to experience the highs of Tex-Mex cuisine in a warm, personal environment. As the name implies, enchiladas rule. There are nearly 20 varieties, from the classic stacked El Paso plate doused in chili gravy to the chicken *mole*. Our favorites include the Mexico City (chicken with *salsa verde* and sour cream) and the Laguna Madre (stuffed with sweet crab). Mesquite-grilled meats are also a hit, and the chocolate cinnamon *tres leches* is extremely lovable. Owner Sylvia Cesares-Copeland may well be on hand to say hello if she's not zooming around town in her new food truck. She also teaches hands-on tamale-making classes at the restaurant.

T'AFIA

3701 TRAVIS
just north of Alabama
☎ **(713) 524-6922**
tafia.com
🍴 **E6**

CHEF/OWNER MONICA POPE DIDN'T INVENT THE word "locavore," but she was Houston's original proponent of the ideal of eating local and eating seasonal. T'afia's menu is built around what local ranchers and farmers raise, as well as some area wines and spirits. Not content with merely dishing out food through a kitchen window, Pope also developed and operates the Midtown Farmers' Market on Saturday mornings to support the growers. How should you cook that weird leafy thing? Pope will show you at her Saturday

The dining room at T'afia

RESTAURANTS

OUTDOOR DINING

S AD BUT TRUE, NOT ALL PATIOS ARE CREATED EQUAL. THERE ARE THE ROADSIDE TABLES under clouds of car fumes, and there are the shady and cloistered respites. Guess which these are.

BACKSTREET CAFE
1103 S. SHEPHERD
☎ **(713) 521-2239**
Secluded from the outside world by a high wooden fence, this brick-paved court-yard is a longtime favorite, especially during brunch with a lobster challah sandwich and pitcher of mimosas.

THE GROVE
1611 LAMAR
☎ **(713) 337-7321**
During the day, a seat at the patio offers a view of vibrant Discovery Green. At night, things turn sparkly as downtown's high-rises come into focus.

BRENNER'S ON THE BAYOU
1 BIRDSALL
☎ **(713) 868-444**
Nestled into the woodsy edges of Buffalo Bayou, Brenner's is true escape. The patio bar is draped with blue canopies and warmed with fire pits when appropriate.

BRENNAN'S OF HOUSTON
3300 SMITH
☎ **(713) 522-9711**
Everything at this Tex-Creole institution is sophisticated Southern, from the turtle soup to the patrons. That grand elegance extends to the back terrace, a veritable secret garden.

ZIMM'S LITTLE DECK
601 RICHMOND
☎ **(713) 527-8328**
Zimm's patio is indeed backed up along busy Richmond, but this little New Orleans-style cafe more than makes up for the nearby roadway with the roomy pétanque court and outdoor TV.

LAS VENTANAS
14555 GRISBY
☎ **(281) 752-6990**
Sprawling and elegant, this family-friendly eatery in the Energy Corridor calls to mind a Mexican resort with its umbrella-shaded garden. Red snapper ceviche for the adults and a playground for the tykes.

morning cooking class during the market; it's free, but you do need to sign up ahead of time as space is limited. Back in the restaurant: The dining room is a study in almost monklike asceticism: Blank brick walls. Concrete floor. Industrial ceiling. Po-mo acrylic tables. And that's about it. All the better to concentrate on the remarkable food, no doubt. Since the menu's ever-changing, it's impractical to start rattling off must-have dishes, which range from antelope chops to quail to buffalo ribeye. It's worth an early visit to T'afia for cocktails and killer lounge food that's free Tuesday through Thursday. Open evenings only, except for a prix-fixe lunch on Fridays.

TACO MILAGRO
. . . .
2555 KIRBY at *Westheimer*
☎ **(713) 522-1999**
taco-milagro.com
🍴 **E6**

IMAGINE A MEXICAN BEACH SHACK RIGHT ON THE trendiest corner in Houston. There's no sand, but the oversized street-side patio is packed on warm weekdays, lazy Sunday afternoons and late summer nights. The Mexican food has never won particularly high praise, even though the concept is the effort of celebrity chef Robert Del Grande (RDG, the Grove, Ava Kitchen). In fact, despite a good soft chicken taco, fish taco and a quesadilla or two, Taco Milagro has become more of a margarita joint than a culinary destination. Still, the salsa bar serves up several excellent varieties to which you may help yourself, the chips are free and the bar is famous for its tequila selection of 150-plus bottles. Inside, expect a lot of noise and stick with the tacos and quesadillas, unless you have had one too many margaritas to care.

TACOS À GO-GO
. . . .
3704 MAIN
just north of Alabama
☎ **(713) 807-8226**
tacosagogo.com
🍴 **E6**

IT'S QUIRKY AND GARISH— LOOK FOR THE LARGE Carmen Miranda head on the front of the building—and it reminds many of Austin. But you have to respect, if not love, a taco joint that serves breakfast tacos all day, stays open until 2 am Friday and Saturday nights, and charges about the same prices as a taco truck. Plus, it's mighty convenient that the always-friendly staff will deliver a late-night order to the Continental Club next door, provided they aren't too busy. Order tacos, gorditas, tostadas and quesadillas with fillings that range from *carne guisada* to lamb *barbacoa* to grilled fish. Vegetarians, don't be shy: There are veggie tacos, too.

TAN TAN

....

6816 RANCHESTER
at Bellaire Blvd.
☎ **(713) 771-1268**
multiple locations
tantanrestaurant.com
🍴 **C7**

MORE SO THAN ANY ASIAN RESTAURANT in town, Tan Tan has perfected the formula for fast, hearty, relatively cheap Asian comfort food. Located on a busy corner, the neon sign to the perennially popular Tan Tan is easy to spot amid a sea of Vietnamese and Chinese signs along Bellaire Blvd. Open until 3 am on weekends, Tan Tan is a favorite among the late-night, after-clubbing crowd for tasty Vietnamese-Chinese dishes such as the *banh bot chien* (fried rice cake), wonton noodle soup, rice plates, pan-fried chow fun noodles and hot pots. During the day, patronage is usually a cross-section of Vietnamese families, couples and groups, while at night, the late hour brings in a diverse crowd that can make for very interesting people watching. Uniformed, English-speaking Asian servers are fast and efficient, calling in orders and requests for drink service or extra utensils over microphone headsets. Large backlit murals of flowing water and flowers adorn the walls, while ample seating in the long main dining area ensures that everyone gets a seat with minimal waiting time. Tan Tan recently opened a second location on Westheimer, but for die-hards willing to make the drive, the original will always reign supreme.

TANGO & MALBEC

....

2800 SAGE *at W. Alabama*
☎ **(713) 629-8646**
tangomalbec.com
🍴 **D7**

LOCATED IN THE SHADOW OF THE GALLERIA, TANgo & Malbec features a wide-ranging menu that has its roots in Argentina and Uruguay—which means enough beef for any Texas cowboy or cowgirl. A meal begins here with a basket of crisp plantain strips, Latin American style. Among the dishes we recommend: slow-poached veal tongue that is sliced thinly and served with a cool vinaigrette; crispy sweetbreads served on a sizzling platter; beef milanesa topped with mozzarella and tomato sauce; and Peruvian-style ceviche. There's a strong Italian influence, too, so don't be surprised to find homemade pasta, an antipasto platter, even vitello tonnato (*vitel toné* on the menu). The place looks great, carefully put together with dark colors, brick and stone. Some might call it romantic. True to its name, management hosts occasional Malbec tastings and wine dinners.

Also check the website for the regularly scheduled tango performances and classes.

TASTE OF TEXAS

. . . .

10505 KATY FWY.
between Gessner & Beltway 8
☎ **(713) 932-6901**
tasteoftexas.com
🍴 **B6**

SINCE ITS FOUNDING IN 1977, THE TASTE OF Texas has grown hu-u-uge. Today it's a sprawling, family-friendly joint for upscale steak dinners with all the trimmings. No clubby Capital Grille this, Taste of Texas opts instead for a casual country feel with vaulted ceilings and a serve-yourself salad bar. Owners Nina and Edd Hendee also step out of the steak box by offering complete meals with each cut of meat (which are available in various sizes to suit your appetite). The red-meat-adverse aren't forgotten, either: There is a grilled-veggie plate, as well as Texas pecan-crusted chicken breast stuffed with goat cheese, grilled onions and roasted pecans. What started as a mom-and-pop steakhouse has turned into an enormous Texas trading post with mail-order steaks and gift boxes, a newsletter, grilling classes and an onsite museum filled with Texana. We give it snaps for having provided free tours of the museum (and lunch!) to several hundred thousand Houston fourth-graders over the decades.

TEALA'S

. . . .

3210 W. DALLAS *west of Waugh*
☎ **(713) 520-9292**
tealas.com
🍴 **E6**

THERE ARE MORE AUTHEN-TIC MEXICAN EATERIES in Houston. But this hideaway is appealing for its fresh fruit-flavored margaritas (don't miss the mango) and warm, wood-lined bar area. If the aroma wafting from diners' dishes has your tummy growling, grab your drink and relax on the welcoming deck on a quiet street. Teala's concentrates on coastal Yucatan dishes, and when ordering, you should too. Don't pass on the *cochinita pibil* with cucumber salad or the chicken in a peanut *mole* sauce. These traditional Mexican dishes outshine the Tex-Mex staples (fajitas, burritos and such) you'll find. It's no wonder Teala's is a neighborhood fave of River Oaksters and nearby denizens.

RESTAURANTS

TEOTIHUACÁN

....

1511 AIRLINE
just north of N. Main
☎ **(713) 426-4420**
multiple locations
🍴 **E5**

WHERE DO HOUSTON'S BEST CHEFS eat? At least one eats here. We were first introduced to Teotihuacán by chef/restaurateur Claire Smith, who eats here with her family when she isn't running the kitchens at Shade and Canopy. The name is a mouthful, but leave room for the delectable and amazingly affordable food at this casual Mexican comfort spot. The exterior is hot pink and hard to miss. Inside doesn't cool off, either, with platters of sizzling chargrilled meats. Whether you choose the chicken, quail, beef, shrimp or all of the above, the grill is the way to go. The basics are done right here: Teotihuacán is known for its fresh corn tortillas, thin-thin chips, bright-flavored salsas, A+ charro beans, even the better-than-average rice. Breakfast scores, too. Servings here are large and so are the crowds. But despite it all, service is quick and friendly.

TEX-CHICK

....

712 FAIRVIEW *east of Montrose*
☎ **(713) 528-4708**
🍴 **E6**

YOU PROBABLY CAN'T GUESS FROM THE NAME what kind of restaurant this is. Surprise: It's Puerto Rican. Actually, this teeny place is so small it hardly can be described as a restaurant. It's more like eating in your grandmother's kitchen. You're sitting here and the cooks are right there, just an arm's length away. The food is very hearty, of course (just like Grandma's) and has a devoted following. Long-time owners Teo and Carmen Gonzales retired a couple years ago and sold Tex-Chick to Carlos Perez, who fluffed up the ambiance a little. But don't worry, it hasn't lost any of its island authenticity. Don't miss the shock-to-the-heart *mofongo* (a fried ball of plantains with garlic and pork rind), *pastel-arroz habichuelo* (similar to tamales), *arroz con granduras* (white rice and pigeon peas), fried pork chop and *carne guisada* (beef stew). Open just until 5 pm.

THAI STICKS

·················

4319 MONTROSE
south of Richmond
☎ **(713) 529-4500**
thaistickshouston.com
🍴 **E7**

MOST EVERYTHING AT THAI STICKS IS DONE with a touch of elegance, and that makes the prices higher than at many local Thai restaurants. We love the curvy hostess stand studded with smooth black river rocks, as well as the clear soup set off with a single wonton-like dumpling. Upscale is spoken in the beautiful plating (e.g. carrots carved into roses) and a more inventive menu than most Thai in town. Take the tamarind mahi mahi topped with grilled scallops, roast duck with vegetables or the lamb chops in a rich brown sauce. Live on the fringe and try *prik khing* with pork or a curry. (The massaman curry, with its hit of tamarind, is particularly nice with chicken.) Thai Sticks is a partnership between Yanee Sornchai Greenwood from Thailand and Mary Varcados from Greece. After all these years, we still don't understand the name.

THELMA'S BAR-B-QUE

·················

3755 SOUTHMORE *at Scott*
☎ **(713) 228-2528**
🍴 **F7**

IT'S A BARBECUE PLACE, SO YOU PROBABLY AREN'T expecting much in the way of decor. That's good, because Thelma's is even less than you expect in terms of interior design. This "new" place is a total dive, just like the Live Oak Street original, which burned a couple years ago. Yet it's a beloved joint that barbecue fans revel in taking friends to. Out-of-towners know it from its appearance on programs like *Sandwiches You Will Like* on PBS. We find the smoked meats and sausage delicious, but the sauce and sides rather over-sugared. But, and here's what you have to know, the very best thing at Thelma's is the fried catfish. It's the most delicious we've ever eaten—smokin' hot from the fryer with a well-seasoned cornmeal crust and tenderest sweet fish. Service? It's as sweet as the sweetened iced tea, so long as you don't rub Thelma the wrong way. So leave your coat and tie in the car, and relax. Warning: Don't even try to place an order while talking on your cell phone. The counter ladies don't like it, and you may just get the boot.

RESTAURANTS

THIS IS IT!

. . . .

2712 BLODGETT
between Alabama & Southmore
☎ **(713) 521-2920**
houstonthisisit.com
🍴 **E7**

HIS IS IT! ABANDONED TRENDY MIDTOWN ABOUT a year ago for a new location nearer Texas Southern University. But don't be alarmed: The ladies at the steam table are still serving up the best soul food in Houston. Open for lunch and dinner, (and breakfast, too, 7 to 10 am Monday through Saturday), This Is It! is owned by Craig Joseph and his wife; Joseph is the grandson of Frank and Mattie Jones, who first opened This Is It! in 1959. The food is pure comfort, with a rotating menu that includes meatloaf, yams, mac 'n' cheese, ham hocks, braised oxtails, chitlins, ribs, smothered pork chops and much more. For around $10, you get three heaping sides, an entree and cornbread, and the ladies who dish it up usually know what you'll like and how much you should have. All you need to see is the overflow of appetites willing to wait patiently in long, after-church-on-Sunday lines to know you're at the right place.

TILA'S

. . . .

1111 S. SHEPHERD
just south of W. Dallas
☎ **(713) 522-7654**
tilas.com
🍴 **E6**

HILE IT MAY BE TRUE THAT NO MAN IS AN island, this Mexican restaurant truly is. It's set on a tiny odd-shaped island of real estate, surrounded on all sides by traffic, on the edge of high-dollar River Oaks. Enter via the driveway right across from Backstreet Cafe. Once inside the golden-lit, quirky joint, it's easy to forget the harrowing Houston traffic. The art-filled dining room feels like Mexico City, and the bar is lined with more than 60 tequilas. Strong margaritas can be ordered straight up and are served in individual carafes nestled in crushed ice. And we love the bucket of warm tortilla chips and plantain chips that arrive at the table with both green and red salsas. The menu is also full of traditional Mexican dishes, including an avocado stuffed with marinated shrimp, roasted corn on the cob slathered with herbed butter, crabmeat tostadas, *milaneza* (breaded cutlet, either pork or chicken) and *chile en nogada* (roasted poblano stuffed with chicken and fruit, topped with a creamy walnut sauce and sprinkled with pomegranate seeds). Breakfast on Saturdays and Sundays.

POTATO SALAD

COOL, CREAMY AND FILLING, POTATO SALAD IS THE MANDATORY SIDEKICK TO SUMMER PICnics, poolside noshing and barbecues.

BROWN BAG DELI
2036 WESTHEIMER
☎ **(713) 807-9191**

Sturdy sliced red potatoes are swathed in a snow-white homemade mayonnaise that tastes of cream. A light hand with salt and a generous sprinkle of fresh dill make this simply sublime.

FOGO DE CHAO
8250 WESTHEIMER
☎ **(713) 978-6500**

Among the beautiful veggies on this spectacular salad bar, there lies potato salad. Firm white potatoes, red pepper slivers, celery, purple onions and a peppery Dijon-mayo dressing make it bursting-fresh.

KENNY & ZIGGY'S
2027 POST OAK BLVD.
☎ **(713) 871-8883**

Tangy-sweet and seasoned right, this Jewish deli-style salad sports diced white potatoes, plenty of mayo, pimiento and relish. Portions are huge.

NIELSEN'S DELI
4500 RICHMOND
☎ **(713) 963-8005**

Tender white potatoes are endowed with chopped eggs and a subtle crunch of scallion, but it's the thick heady homemade mayonnaise that makes this salad justly famous. Note to dieters: It's a tad salty and rich beyond words.

PAULIE'S
1834 WESTHEIMER
☎ **(713) 807-7271**

Skin-on red potatoes are colored with parsley flecks, chopped peppers, scallions and briny black and green olives. Tart, savory and clean with fruity olive oil.

THE FRENCH HOUSE
5901 WESTHEIMER
☎ **(713) 781-2106**

Skinned, rustically cut white potatoes arrive in a shocking shade of green, as they are tossed with a tart parsley and olive oil-vinegar dressing. This refreshing mélange is dotted with crisp celery and tastes oh-so-French.

TINTOS SPANISH RESTAURANT & WINE BAR

. . . .

2015 W. GRAY
just east of S. Shepherd
☎ **(713) 522-1330**
tintosrestaurant.com
🍴 **E6**

ALBERTO ALFONZO, WHO USED TO BE WITH THE Landry's group and The Tasting Room organization, opened this lively Spanish restaurant in the space that was formerly Hunan River/Backdoor Sushi. The kitchen sends out hot and cold tapas (e.g. carpaccio with shaved manchego, the Spanish omelet called *tortilla*, empanadas, sautéed garlic shrimp, Spanish cheeses), as well as paella and traditional soups. There's a great wine list that features Spanish wines, though not exclusively. We like Alfonzo's mission statement: "Eat tapas. Sip Tintos. Purchase retail wines to-go." Check the website for the performance schedule of flamenco dancers.

TINY BOXWOOD'S

. . . .

3614 W. ALABAMA
between Buffalo Speedway & Weslayan
☎ **(713) 622-4224**
multiple locations
tinyboxwoods.com
🍴 **D7**

IT'S AN ODDBALL BUSINESS PLAN: A CAFE squeezed into the design center of chi-chi landscapers Thompson + Hanson. But the ladies-who-lunch adore this place. The handsome, cool interior lends an expansive feel to the dining room, and the outdoor dining has a view of the gorgeous nursery. (You've heard of food pornography? Thompson + Hanson deals in plant pornography.) Chef Baron Doke serves up—let's be honest here—girly food with a French twist. *Le "tiny" dejeuner* is just that, little, *sans* bacon, *sans* pancakes, *sans* hash browns. (Why couldn't we figure out how French women stay thin?) Typical salads such as Cobb and Provençal and a couple of soups play with thin-crust pizza and more interesting sandwiches, like the "Frenchman": crispy wheat bread layered with sliced prosciutto, goat cheese, tomato and homemade basil pesto. A Tiny Boxwood's spin-off called Tiny's No. 5 is opening about the time we go to press with this book; it's at 3636 Rice Blvd. in the old JMH No. 5 grocery store.

TONY MANDOLA'S

1212 WAUGH *at W. Dallas*
☎ **(713) 528-3474**
tonymandolas.com
🍴 **E6**

IF YOU BUILD IT, THEY WILL COME. IN THE SUMMER OF 2011, Tony Mandola's Gulf Coast Kitchen moved into this newly built and much grander restaurant and dropped the "Gulf Coast Kitchen" from its name. When owners Tony and Phyllis Mandola threw open the doors, it launched an opening-night love fest that reminded us of a Hollywood premiere. River Oaksians turned out by the Mercedes-full, as did politicians, judges, media, big-time real estate agents and long-time fans of the old version of the restaurant on West Gray. Oysters are back on the menu: They had been taken off during the restaurant's temporary stay on Westheimer in the old Rickshaw location while this new construction was being completed. It has seafood, pasta and gumbo, just like at the old place, and now pizza, too. In fact, there's even a gumbo pizza.

TONY'S

3755 RICHMOND *at Timmons*
☎ **(713) 622-6778**
tonyshouston.com
🍴 **D7** ✍

WE ONCE ASKED A FELLOW REPORTer at the Houston newspaper where we worked to recommend the city's very best restaurant. We had an out-of-town friend coming and needed to impress. Her answer: Tony's. That was 1982, and many would argue that Tony's is still Houston's very best restaurant— or at least among the top handful. Unctuous, fresh and delicately stuffed pastas, tender veal and impeccable seafood (call ahead for the whole fish baked in salt) are just some of Tony's attractions, not to mention the always excellent service, award-winning wine selection and intriguing setting outfitted with *important* art. The kitchen is a little French, a little Italian, rather like what you might find along the Riviera. Owner Tony Vallone knows better than anyone how to cosset the rich, the famous and the powerful. Current chef Grant Gordon is a 20-something youngster who wasn't even born when Tony's was first launched, but he handles the responsibility well under Vallone's tutelage. In fact, dozens of Houston restaurants are today widely populated by chefs, somms, maitre d's and pastry chefs who learned their skills at, yes, Tony's.

TQLA

. . . .

4601 WASHINGTON
east of Shepherd
☎ **(281) 501-3237**
tqlahouston.com
🍴 **E6**

CHEF TOMMY BIRDWELL ISN'T NEW TO HOUSTON, but TQLA is. (It opened in late 2010.) On Washington Avenue, the restaurant is in the same development as California burger chain the Counter and faces what you might think is a lot of competition: Molina's. But when you walk into TQLA you see that this is completely different in terms of a Mexican cuisine experience. With a Southwestern edge and a slithering bar, the glowing decor does not resemble a family Tex-Mex restaurant. The menu is a combination of traditional coastal Mexican and Southwestern cuisine, with items such as blue corn-crusted oysters with chorizo cream and a wild mushroom tamale with a roasted corn and sun-dried tomato salsa. Tequilier/partner Scott Lindsey has 170 tequilas, including even several on tap.

TRADIÇAO BRAZILIAN STEAKHOUSE

. . . .

12000 SOUTHWEST FWY.
at Dorrance, Stafford
☎ **(713) 339-1122**
multiple locations
tradicaobraziliansteak house.com
🍴 **B8** 🚗

HMM, IN THE MOOD FOR CAIPIRINHAS AND NEVer-ending meat? Try the rodizio service at Tradiçao. In 2011 Tradiçao moved into a new location closer to the prosperous Fort Bend suburbs, and the fancier digs seem to be working for them. This churrascaria—its name is pronounced tra-dee-son and means "tradition"—is a family-friendly Brazilian steakhouse. Expect a never-ending parade of meat (flip your coaster to red or green to indicate when you're ready for the next serving to be brought to your table), those chewy little cheese rolls and a lavish salad bar, but at a lower price point. Lunch is $22.50 per person and dinner is $36.50 per person. Kids age 4 or younger eat free. Very nice service, too. The owner/chef is Vanderlie Bernadi.

TRATTORIA IL MULINO

. . . .

945 GESSNER *south of I-10 in the Westin Hotel*
☎ **(832) 358-0600**
ilmulino.com
🍴🍴 **C6**

Dining at Treebeards

THE ORIGINAL IL MULINO IN NEW YORK IS WORLD renowned for classic Italian food, Abruzzi-style, so it will be interesting to watch how this "lite" hotel version of that restaurant shakes out. (It's the fourth trattoria in the Il Mulino family and opened in this Memorial City-area hotel in Spring 2011.) The setting is very handsome, being richly colored, modern and sexy. Executive chef Michele Mazza recently won the *My Table*-sponsored 1st Annual Meatball Invitational, Italian category. And it's true that his meatballs are extraordinary. Also recommended: the gnocchi, stuffed pasta, pizza, veal and seafood. Note: It can be very loud.

✗ TREEBEARDS

. . . .

315 TRAVIS
between Congress & Preston
☎ **(713) 228-2622**
multiple locations
treebeards.com
🍴 **F6** ✍

IF TREEBEARDS EVER LEFT, DOWNTOWN JUST MIGHT GO with it. And what a shame it'd be to lose Louisiana food of the most remarkable kind—earthy gumbos, red beans and rice with chunks of sausage, duck gumbo, jambalaya and sinfully dirty rice. This lunch-only staple started in 1978 between a peep-show arcade and a rowdy bar in the historic Baker-Meyer Building. It has since flourished into five downtown locations, including the Cloister at Christ Church Cathedral. Lunch is served cafeteria-style and built upon daily specials like etouffee-topped blackened catfish, better than-mom's meatloaf (*My Table* magazine recently gave it a perfect 10) and pot roast. Grab the full deal—an entree and two sides—for cheap or three sides for even cheaper. As one wag observed, the only good thing about jury duty is eating at Treebeards.

TREVÍSIO

. . . .

6550 BERTNER *(top floor)*
at Moursund, in the
Medical Center
☎ **(713) 749-0400**
trevisiorestaurant.com
🍴 **E7**

THIS MAY BE THE ODD-
EST PLACE IN TOWN TO
find a restaurant: On the top floor
of a parking garage. But you can't
miss it. Just look for the 64-foot
waterfall that pours down the
garage exterior. Park your car and
ride the elevator to the top floor
to find a large rambling space with
a spectacular view of the Med
Center on one side and several
adjoining private rooms (for when
the pharmaceutical company reps
come calling) on the other. Chef
Jon Buchanan's contemporary
kitchen rolls out fresh, light Italian
fare, such as chilled arugula soup
and olive oil-poached tuna. Pasta
dishes have flair, like the *strozza-
preti* ("priest stranglers") with calamari, octopus, shrimp and clams,
and meats are all dressed up like
the *fileto*, wood-grilled beef tenderloin with turnip puree, wild
mushrooms, rapini and truffle
demiglace. The rice is especially
nice: Buchanan's lemon risotto
with lump crabmeat won first place
at the International Risotto Festival
in 2010.

TRINITI

. . . .

2815 S. SHEPHERD *at Harold*
🍴 **E7**

THIS LARGE SPACE HAS
BEEN HOME TO SEVER-
al restaurants, including Fox Diner's second incarnation and Los
Tonyos, plus some sketchy night-
clubs. As we put this guidebook to
bed, it's being totally gutted and
readied for an ambitious new spot
from chef Ryan Hildebrand. The
name, Triniti, is a nod to the culinary triad of sweet, savory and
spirits on offer. There are plans
for an onsite garden, too. As it's just
a dinner roll's throw away from
the office, we can't wait.

TRIPLE A

. . . .

2526 AIRLINE *inside Loop 610*
☎ **(713) 861-3422**
triplearestaurant.com
🍴 **E5**

THIS LITTLE OLD-FASH-
IONED SOUTHERN DIN-
er was established in 1942, and
we don't think much has changed
since then—the building, the patrons
or the darn good food. The menu
is pretty standard and includes
eggs, breakfast meats, toast and
biscuits, as well as meatloaf and
chicken-fried steak. The service is
very friendly and they know their
customers—don't be surprised when
regulars walk in and order "the

usual." Predictable menu? Maybe. But sometimes routine and comfort are just what you're hungry for. When you've finished here, stop by Canino's produce market next door to do your fresh-food shopping for the week.

TRULUCK'S

. . . .

5350 WESTHEIMER *west of Sage*
☎ **(713) 783-7270**
trulucks.com
🍴 **C7**

IF YOU ONLY KNOW LOCAL BLUE CRABS, THEN TRU-luck's famous stone crab claws (served in season) will be quite a treat. (Even better, they are a renewable resource, as the claw can be harvested without killing the crab.) But there are other crab options at Truluck's, too, including red king crab and Dungeness crab. On Monday nights, there's always all-you-can-eat Jonah crab from Maine. The ocean is a goldmine for Truluck's, and the menu dances with seafood: crabcake sliders, blackened redfish Pontchartrain (parmesan-crusted redfish with shrimp, crawfish tails and blue crab and a spicy Creole sauce *piquant*), cioppino, seafood Cobb salad, salt and pepper calamari, ceviche and Scottish salmon with béarnaise. The fish is all cut in house, for maximum freshness. Landlubbers are not forgotten, as there are several steak and chop

options. Cocktails and certain appetizers are half-price during the cocktail hour (4 to 6:30 pm) seven nights a week. Outstanding wine list, too.

TWO SAINTS RESTAURANT

. . . .

12460 MEMORIAL
west of Gessner
☎ **(713) 465-8967**
twosaintsrestaurant.com
🍴 **C6**

NESTLED INTO THE CORNER OF WICK LANE Center, Two Saints has a comfortable neighborhood feel with leather couches, comfy chairs and a lively chef's table. The menu offers upscale comfort food, such as parmesan truffle onion rings, piquillo pepper jumbo lump crabcakes, a prime 16 oz. ribeye, Southern red snapper fillet and award-winning pan-seared boneless half chicken. Oh For The Love O Mac-n-Cheese is an elegant twist on the childhood favorite with a four-cheese sauce, fresh jalapeños, thick-cut bacon bits and crisp parmesan bread crumbs. Joe Rippey, owner of the nearby Vine Wine Room, and chef Justin Gasper are co-proprietors. (It makes sense, then, that Two Saints is BYOB.) Two Saints is tucked-away, intimate and sinfully delish. Dinner only Monday through Saturday.

UCHI

904 WESTHEIMER
east of Montrose
🍴 **E6**

ONE OF THE MOST ANT-ICIPATED RESTAURANT openings of Fall 2011 is Uchi, the Japanese import from Austin. Chef Tyson Cole, winner of the 2011 James Beard Foundation Award for Best Chef: Southwest, is in charge of the menu. As with the much-lauded Austin original, the management team is again going for an unexpected setting: They've taken over and are revamping the old Felix Mexican restaurant.

UDIPI CAFE

5959 HILLCROFT
near Southwest Fwy.
☎ **(713) 334-5555**
multiple locations
udipicafeusa.com
🍴 **C7**

THIS UNASSUMING VEG-ETARIAN INDIAN WINS points for its $7.99 lunch buffet (and don't forget to request a fresh *dosa*, a kind of crêpe, for sopping up sauces). To say it's a modest setting would be generous, but the food is hot and flavorful, and exactly hits the spot when you've had too much meat this week. The cooking is mostly South Indian style—hence its name—and is com-

prised primarily of beans, grains, vegetables (no onions or garlic, however) and fruit, but you'll typi-cally find one or more North Indi-an dishes in the buffet or available to order from the menu.

UMAI

8400 BELLAIRE BLVD.
east of S. Gessner
☎ **(713) 750-9222**
theumai.com
🍴 **C7**

THIS IS A DIFFERENT BREED OF JAPANESE restaurant. First of all, it's located on the outskirts of the Bellaire Blvd. Chinatown. However, it's cleaner and less visited than many of the small restaurants in the area. Don't come here expecting a sushi bar. There are a few rolls, but the menu is more about the ramen and udon noodle dishes, tempura, cur-ries, and grilled and steamed fish. (The miso-glazed Chilean seabass is outstanding.) To start, order the tender pan-fried gyoza dumplings. We also recommend the *shiso hasamiage*, minced shiitake mush-rooms and shrimp wrapped in a shiso leaf. Big appetites will want to try one of the Texas-sized bento boxes that come with your choice of entree, soup, salad, tempura vegetables and three appetizers.

OYSTER BARS

THERE ARE FEW FOOD-WINE COMBINATIONS MORE SATISFYING THAN OYSTERS AND A bottle of Chablis. Oysters taste best, of course, when both the weather and seawater are cool.

CAPTAIN BENNY'S HALF SHELL OYSTER BAR
8506 S. MAIN
☎ (713) 666-5469

The kitchen shucks oysters as consistently as a robot right out in the open so there are no mysteries about freshness. Expect just one kind: the fat and juicy Gulf Coast specimen.

DANTON'S GULF COAST SEAFOOD KITCHEN
4611 MONTROSE
☎ (713) 807-8883

Iced-down platters glistening with sweet, plump oysters fly out of the kitchen at record speed. During happy hour, the bivalves are just 75 cents each.

GOODE CO. TEXAS SEAFOOD
2621 WESTPARK
☎ (713) 523-7154

The Westpark location exudes Texas charm in its railroad car where Gulf Coast oysters are served on the half shell.

McCORMICK & SCHMICK'S
1151-01 UPTOWN PARK
☎ (713) 840-7900

This seafood chain prints its menu twice daily and always includes an ever-changing menu of oysters from both coasts.

THE OCEANAIRE SEAFOOD ROOM
5061 WESTHEIMER
☎ (832) 487-8862

Witness dozens of oyster varieties being shucked at the bar daily from Wellfleets to Kumamotos. Feel free to mix and match.

PESCE
3029 KIRBY
☎ (713) 522-4858

Perch at the big marble raw bar and ogle your oysters being shucked. Daily oyster selections are scribbled on the chalkboard.

TOMMY'S RESTAURANT OYSTER BAR
2555 BAY AREA BLVD.
☎ (281) 480-2221

Catching a recent trend, the menu has begun to identify various Gulf oyster appellations so you can taste and compare oysters from various local reefs and bays.

UNDERBELLY

. . . .

1100 WESTHEIMER *at Waugh*
☎ **(713) 523-1622**
underbellyhouston.com
🍴 **E6**

CHRIS SHEPHERD LEFT THE MUCH-ACCLAIMED Catalan in early 2011 to begin work on his first project as chef *and* restaurateur. Shepherd is known for all things pork, and this new spot will provide an opportunity to push even deeper into porcine territory. (It has its own butcher shop.) Underbelly, with its contemporary farmhouse setting and a long community table, is going to be adjacent to Hay Merchant, a new craft beer bar from the Anvil Bar & Refuge team. It is expected to open November 2011.

UP

. . . .

3995 WESTHEIMER *(3rd floor)*
at Drexel, in Highland Village
☎ **(713) 640-5416**
uprestaurant.com
🍴 **E6**

THIS MAY HAVE BEEN THE QUIETEST RESTAURANT opening in town in early 2011, especially given its fancy address (up above the Cole Haan store, hence its name) and obvious ambition. Owner Haidar Barbouti, who also owns the entire shopping center, has created a slick spot with a solidly American menu that ranges from salads and pasta to sautéed shrimp with brown butter sauce, salmon with sorrel sauce to thrice slow-cooked short ribs. On any given night, the place pulsates with the din of Houston's financially confident. Interestingly, the evening crowd is a mix of both young and mature, which is kind of unusual in this city. The setting is coolly contemporary with neutral tones and floor-to-ceiling windows. It called to mind The Four Seasons restaurant in New York City, minus the pool. There's also a balcony for outdoor dining. Nice!

UPTOWN SUSHI

. . . .

1131 UPTOWN PARK BLVD.
north of San Felipe
☎ **(713) 871-1200**
uptown-sushi.com
🍴 **D6**

EIGHT YEARS AFTER ITS 2003 OPENING, VETeran restaurateur Donald Chang continues to lure the young and narrow-hipped to this cosmopolitan Asian-fusion sushi bar. Cocktails are tasty—the restaurant won the 2005 Houston Culinary Award for Best Bar Service—the sushi is fresh and the scene is a real draw. Techno beats bounce as fabulously dressed and yet-to-see-a-wrinkle hipsters circulate through the LA-inspired interior. The dining area is slightly tiered up and around the sushi bar, so it becomes a theater in the round. It has a supper-club crowd that parties late. We once arrived at 10:30 p.m., and the team of five sushi chefs could hardly stay current with the orders that poured in. There are a number of specialty rolls on offer in which the chefs combine a hodgepodge of flavors and textures with surprising success. The Lickety Split roll—"our most popular," affirmed the waiter—tops tuna, crawfish, cucumber and sprouts with spicy tuna, yellowtail, salmon and avocado. The rolls here are sizable, so don't order too much too soon. Many contend this is one of the city's best sushi restaurants.

VALENTINO HOUSTON

2525 W. LOOP SOUTH
at Westheimer, in the Hotel Derek
☎ **(713) 850-9200**
valentinorestaurant.com
🍴 **D6**

HE VALENTINO REST-AURANT GROUP WAS founded in 1972 in Santa Monica, Calif., by restaurateur Piero Selvaggio, who has now taken over and revamped the old Bistro Moderne location in this challenging hotel location. The ambition here is high (as are the prices), and what the restaurant is trying to do is unique for Houston: innovative *modern* Italian cuisine. From chef Cunninghame West's menu we recommend a tartare of marlin with grapefruit, tuna medallions coated with black truffles, tender pasta purses stuffed with lobster and 24-month-old prosciutto di San Daniele. The Italian wine list is brilliantly chosen but, again, you pay for the expertise. The adjacent Vin Bar offers *crudo* (raw fish) and small plates, such as grilled pizza. Dress for dinner: This place is very stylish. Think Giorgio Armani.

VAN LOC

3010 MILAM *north of Elgin*
☎ **(713) 528-6441**
vanlocrestaurant.com
🍴 **E6**

T THE SOUTHERN EDGE OF HOUSTON'S burgeoning Little Saigon in Midtown is Van Loc, where the reliable and affordable Vietnamese fare balances out the cold-shoulder service and a drab environment that is a study in brown. The owners say "van loc" means lots of luck in Vietnamese, and you'll need it to get through the extensive menu. Thankfully, most dishes are under $12, and most are pretty good, if not fantastic. We'll save you the trouble of combing through the menu with a few basic suggestions. For starters, Van Loc makes summer rolls with ideal texture, and they perfectly cook vermicelli in a soup of shrimp and pork. Don't miss the barbecued pork, clay-pot catfish, whole fried fish and the *bo luc lac* (steak with lettuce and tomato). Meatless feasters should try the tofu fried with chile peppers, garlic and scallions. The decades-old debate along lower Milam: Which is better, Van Loc or the nearby Mai's?

VIC & ANTHONY'S

. . . .

1510 TEXAS *at LaBranch*
☎ **(713) 228-1111**
vicandanthonys.com
🍴 **F6** ✍

OWNTOWN HOUSTON'S FIRST MAJOR-LEAGUE steakhouse, located across the street from Minute Maid Park, is the crown jewel of the diverse, publicly traded Landry's Restaurants, Inc. Before its April 2003 debut, much was made of the fact that Landry's CEO Tilman Fertitta traveled the country with his father Vic and cousin Anthony, sampling steakhouses and taking notes. The result of their road trip is this beautiful two-story Craftsman-style setting with fine wood, gorgeous wrought ironwork and over-sized stained-glass chandeliers. Follow a perky hostess to your table, and you'll experience a frisson of anticipation just walking through this lively restaurant. Traditional steakhouse fare (under the direction of exec chef Carlos Rodriguez) is exemplar. The oyster

service, for example, includes a sharp mignonette sauce in addition to the traditional red sauce and horseradish (and the server always knows exactly where the day's oysters are from). A bad-boy bone-in ribeye will be cooked perfectly. Creamed spinach or onion strings or mushrooms as a side? Caviar to start? Carrot cake to end on a sweet note? It's all terrific. Observe the starchy dining room managers at attention, their eyes raking the room as waiters serve and bus people bustle. From the get-go, this steakhouse was conceived to impress, and its award-winning wine list is nothing short of awesome. There are more than 1,000 vintages, including many wines by-the-glass and large-format bottles. Now here's the surprising part: Vic & Anthony's is somewhat less expensive than some other high-end Houston steakhouses, making it a (relative) bargain.

VIENG THAI

. . . .

6929 LONG POINT
between Silber & Antoine
☎ **(713) 688-9910**
viengthai.com
🍴 **D5** ✍

AVE YOU TAKEN ANY OF THE "WHERE THE Chefs Eat" tours sponsored by the Greater Houston Convention & Visitors Bureau? Vieng Thai is one of the chefs' favorite stops. The neighborhood is, *uh*, in transition—it's in the same Spring Branch strip center as the *auténtico* El Hidalguense—but the kitchen dishes up fantastic Thai food, rivaling some of our favorites, including Nidda Thai and Kanomwan. Order anything and, not to be trite, you won't go wrong, from *tom ka gai* coconut milk soup to the beef *panaeng* curry to *pad sar-tor*, which is shrimp sautéed in chili paste with sar-tor (also called "stink beans"). Try the *som tam*, a green papaya salad that includes chilies, palm sugar and tiny dried shrimp. Unlike most local Thai restaurants, Vieng Thai doesn't water down its true cuisine for American palates—the proof is its reputation for funky Thai sausages. Still, we can't have our cake and eat it, too (shucks!). Service is flat, and the atmosphere is nonexistent. Seriously, barebones. This is not a "romantic evening" restaurant but a place to go for darn good food.

VINCENT'S

. . . .

2817 W. DALLAS
between Montrose & Waugh
☎ **(713) 528-4313**
ninos-vincents.com
🍴 **19**

INCENT'S, NINO'S AND GRAPPINO DI NINO, ALL owned by Vincent Mandola, his wife and two daughters, is practically an Italian village unto itself.

Each of the three restaurants in the development has a slightly different role. And Vincent's claim to fame is the best roasted chicken (seasoned with lemon and garlic and pure *amore*) and some of the top mashed potatoes in Texas. The menu has long since moved beyond pizzas and pastas (yet, these dishes are lovely here, too) and today leans on what can only be called home cooking in any language. The Veal Vincent speaks for itself, and a starter of carpaccio will seduce. The service is always dependable, and the surroundings are comfortable. Enjoy live music and a glass of vino in the courtyard that the three restaurants share—evidence that a little sibling rivalry doesn't beat brotherly love.

WILLIE G'S

. . . .

1605 POST OAK BLVD.
north of San Felipe
☎ **(713) 840-7190**
williegs.com
🍴 **D6**

HIS LOCAL SEAFOOD HOUSE, WHICH IS NOW part of the Landry's group, is quintessentially Houston after more than three decades in the Galleria area. Seated in the upscale ocean-liner-like dining room, you'll find the menu to be fairly typical of higher-end Gulf Coast fish joints. But the fish is fresh, and a perk is often a dozen types from which to choose (depending on season): flounder, grouper, golden tile, swordfish, rainbow trout, redfish, etc. A favorite is the snapper Hemingway (breaded in cracker crumbs, topped with lump crab). Other dishes include shrimp remoulade, crabcakes, stuffed bacon-wrapped shrimp, iceberg wedge with blue cheese, an iced seafood tower and softshell crabs (in season). And oysters, of course. We've heard several stories about the kitchen preparing a guest's old favorite that is no longer on the menu, and that should tell you a lot about the level of hospitality here. The service is solicitous, there's a decent wine list, and the energy is high.

XUCO XICANA

. . . .

2416 BRAZOS
between Webster & McGowen
☎ **(713) 523-8181**
🍴 **E6**

IT'S BEEN A LONG AND SOMEWHAT PAINFUL PRO- cess as this middlin' Midtown El Patio has been revamped and re- branded. In early 2011 Beaver's chef Jonathan Jones was hired to shift the menu to a more interior Mexi- can cuisine, and the changes have not been without a great deal of public debate. Many diners appar- ently miss the mediocre Tex-Mex that was previously served here— or was it the atomic-strength mar-

garitas? We visited while the tran- sition was underway and thoroughly enjoyed mushroom enchiladas and tacos made with pork shoulder marinated in pasilla, clove, cinnamon and orange that was velvety, rich and slightly sweet. We even liked a simple dish of tortillas drenched in earthy guajillo and ancho chile and topped with a pile of shred- ded lettuce and queso fresco. As for the future of this restaurant, we think it hinges on the name, Xuco Xicana (pronounced "chuco chicana"). It's hard to set a date to meet friends at a restaurant when you can't pronounce the name.

YELAPA PLAYA MEXICAN

. . . .

2303 RICHMOND *east of Kirby*
☎ **(281) 501-0391**
yelapatime.com
🍴 **E7**

WHEN YELAPA SPLASHED ONTO the scene nearly back in 2009, the Montrose restaurant with the fun- ny name and exotic, beach-based Mexican dishes captured a nota- ble amount of critical attention and customer support. We recall being really impressed during an early visit by a piquant guacamole salad hopped-up with fennel, black olives and mango and a trio of small, succulent lamb tacos. Since then, owner Chuck Bulnes—who has a deep history with Houston's

Mexican restaurants, including Berryhill's, Ninfa's, Joyce's Oyster Resort and Pan Y Aqua—has gone through a couple of high-profile chefs as he's juggled to get the concept just right. What you'll find here is a cantina setting with ambitious Mexican food with Asian touches (e.g. pork belly carnitas served on a green papaya salad with a tamarind dressing). Much of the menu is seafood-based, including ceviches, grilled fish and fish tacos. For vegetarians, depending on the season, you may find quesadillas filled with fresh mushrooms, sweet onions, tasty spinach, poblano strips and melted Chihuahua cheese.

YILDIZLAR

. . . .

2929 SOUTHWEST FWY.
east of Buffalo Speedway
☎ **(713) 524-7735**
🍴 **E7**

AFTER YEARS ON KIRBY IN THE OFFICE DEPOT center, Yildizlar recently moved to this feeder road location, and it's a big aesthetic improvement over the old place. In a city rich with ethnic restaurants of every style, this Lebanese counter-service spot holds its own, dealing in kabobs, falafel, gyros, babaganoush, hummus and such. The real star at Yildizlar is the chicken shawarma sandwich. If you want to try a little of everything, order the

combination plate with bites of 10 different foods. Have a unique experience and sip some of the rose water, but expect a mild perfume taste that lasts for hours. If you hanker for something a little sweeter, try a pastry.

YUM YUM CHA

. . . .

2435 TIMES BLVD.
between Morningside & Kirby
☎ **(713) 527-8455**
yumyumchacafe.com
🍴 **E7**

FLIPBOOKS WITH COLOR PHOTOS OF THE TINY offerings replace the traditional dim sum parlor's pushcarts. Take a look, then check off on the ticket what you'd like to eat. The advantage is that don't have to wait for a cart to wend its way through the crowd and find you. (On the other hand, service is very slow here, so don't plan to order in stages. Your subsequent orders will go to the end of the line.) This is technically the only Inner Loop restaurant that specializes in dim sum,

Yum Yum Cha exterior

FIGURE-FRIENDLY FASTFOOD

A SLEW OF HEALTH-FOOD SHOPS THAT OFFER PRE-PACKAGED GRAB-AND-GO MEALS AS alternatives to fast food and bagged lunches have popped up around town. They all promise to help you lose weight, improve your cholesterol profile, stabilize blood sugar levels and generally improve your life. When you're next in the mood for a week of paleo* dieting, try one of these.

MY FIT FOODS
12 locations in Houston
myfitfoods.com

Although we pre-order online, you can simply stop in and grab something from the glass display cases that line the storefront. Recommended: the tenderloin wrap, which offers a burst of tangy flavor and a savory chew to the wrap.

TRU MEALS
3 locations in Houston, plus outlets
trumeals.com

Glass displays of pre-packaged meals line the wall, and an island of healthful grocery items takes center stage at Tru Meals' Farnham Road location. Try the Thai beef salad, buffalo chili (we like that they cube the meat, rather than grind it) and the soba noodles.

SNAP KITCHEN
3600 KIRBY
☎ **(713) 526-5700**
snapkitchen.com

Fresh-made salads are great at this Austin import, but we're also fond of the gluten-free, dairy-free cheesecake. Satisfying dinners—more kabocha squash, please!—and generous breakfasts are all delicious. A second location is opening soon on Memorial Drive.

REAL MEALS 365
300 SHEPHERD
☎ **(713) 668-7325**
realmeals365.com

Like the others in this list, Real Meals 365 allows you to order via the internet or simply drop in the small storefront. The two best dishes on the menu: the Mongolian rice bowl and chicken couscous.

* The paleo diet is a way of eating that mimics diets of our hunter-gatherer ancestors and includes lean meats, seafood, vegetables, fruits, and nuts. It's sometimes called the caveman diet.

and the food doesn't disappoint. Is it the best dim sum in the city? No. But it's good, and many West University neighbors visit weekly to indulge in the 50-plus regular menu items and additional daily chalkboard specials. Fan favorites include shrimp-and-chive dumplings, turnip cake, steamed buns, sticky rice with sweet sausage and chicken, and the various potstickers. It's BYOB, so bring along a crisp, refreshing Riesling from Pfalz, Alsace or Washington state. Note: Even after all these years of complaint, the AC still hasn't been sufficiently upgraded. Try not to sit by a window.

ZABAK'S

....

5901 WESTHEIMER
at Fountain View
☎ **(713) 977-7676**
zabaks.com
🍴 **C7**

HE STAR HERE: FALAFEL! FRESH, HOT FROM THE fryer, regular or spicy. We once asked co-owner Peter Zabak (he runs Zabak's with sister Sandra and brother Donald) what the heck was in his falafel that makes it so good. Garbanzo beans, jalapeños, onions and a blend of spices—but he didn't specify what spices—are ground together, formed into flattened patties, deep fried and served warm inside a pita or alone with sides. Whatever they're doing,

the result is addictive. This is some of the best falafel we've had in Houston. And we're not the only ones who think so: The *Houston Press* named it No. 85 in the "100 Favorite Dishes" countdown in June 2011. The Zabak siblings opened their minimalist little cafe in 2006, following in the footsteps of their parents, who operated Mama's Po'boy on Hillcroft for 26 years. Besides falafel, try also the Greek chicken salad, tabouli, chicken Caesar pita sandwich or a Mediterranean pizza. Diners (including us) always remark on the hospitality here. Sandra has been known to greet customers at the door, give a quick tour and tell the family's restaurant history, and the siblings make it a point to remember your name.

ZELKO BISTRO

....

705 E. 11TH
west of Studemont
☎ **(713) 880-8691**
zelkobistro.com
🍴 **E5** ✍

AMIE ZELKO, ONE OF THE CITY'S HOTTEST YOUNG chefs—she won the 2007 Houston Culinary Award for Up-and-Coming Chef of the Year—finally has a spot to call her own as of 2010. With experience in some of Houston's best restaurants—Brennan's, Ibiza and Bank at Hotel Icon—Zelko has turned down the flame on high-concept food and has chosen to cook instead fabulous comfort food. Her shrimp and grits are already legend ("an Asian-New England combination of flavors, and it's fantastic!" raved our writer). Other options include corned beef and cabbage, braised short ribs, fish tacos, meatloaf and fried chicken. The wine list is aggressively priced, with few bottles more than $45, and recently Zelko has begun to promote wines from women-owned wineries, as well as sustainably-grown wines. The bistro is in a small house in The Heights, and some complain it's too crowded with diners' chairs bumping up against one another. To us, that's just part of the charm—it's very Portland.

ZIGGY'S BAR & GRILL

· · · · · · · · · · · · · · · ·

302 FAIRVIEW at *Taft*
☎ **(832) 519-0476**
multiple locations
ziggysbarandgrill.com
🍴 **E6**

WHEN ZIGGY'S WAS ON W. ALABAMA, it was Ziggy's Healthy Grill; now it's Ziggy's Bar & Grill. But in truth not much has changed. We think the name change was simply a marketing decision. There's long been (and still is) plenty on the menu here that's not particularly healthful, including three kinds of french fries (sweet potato fries, we love you), Ziggyritas and short-

bread cookies with a spicy zest. This location (there's also one downtown) is housed in a vintage Montrose house, and parking can be a challenge. The food is more healthy-tasting than taste-explosion, but we like it in the same way we enjoy earnest homemade food: spinach-stuffed chicken, vegetable lasagne, buffalo or ostrich burger, white bean soup with pesto. We are also fond of the Tex-Mex dishes, such as quesadillas and enchiladas. Daily breakfast service offers choices for both the healthful and the indulgent, and there are happy-hour specials every day to 6 pm. Leashed dogs are welcome on the patio.

ZIMM'S LITTLE DECK

· · · · · · · · · · · · · · · ·

601 RICHMOND
east of Montrose
☎ **(713) 527-8328**
zimmslittledeck.com
🍴 **E7**

THE MENU AT BROTHERS MARK AND DAN ZIMMERman's newish spot (it opened in late 2010) is New Orleans-inspired and includes chargrilled oysters, crawfish remoulade, gumbo, po'boys and "rich'boys" filled with things like duck confit, harissa-scented lamb or pulled pork. Don't miss the croque monsieur or house-made potato chips, either. Order a glass of wine from those listed on the chalkboard—they're usually a good deal. Inside, the fancy ice-house-slash-seafood bar is cozy and chic; outdoors, there's a fireplace and large flat-screen for watching sports. Or play some: There's an official pétanque court. Jeramie Robison, who runs the kitchen at dad Steve Zimmerman's impressive Restaurant Cinq, also helped con-figure the menu here.

ZYDECO LOUISIANA DINER

....

1119 PEASE *at San Jacinto*
☎ **(713) 759-2001**
zydecolouisianadiner.com
🍴 **F6**

Zydeco's retro sign

NOW APPROACHING ITS 30TH ANNIVERSARY, this Louisiana-accented cafeteria dishes up all the down-home favorites, including fried oyster po'boys, meat-and-three steam-table specials (e.g. stuffed pork chops, jambalaya, chicken fricassee, chicken and sausage Creole), gum-bo and oysters and shrimp every which way. The well-worn restaur-ant reminds us of Poche's in Breaux Bridge, and the setting almost seems to season the food. The crawfish étouffée is one of the city's best versions (tender tails, spicy gravy), and the smothered pork chops and fried chicken aren't too shabby either. The sides can-not be upstaged by the main dish-es because they stand alone: moist cornbread, smoky black-eyed peas, *maque choux*, stewed okra and garlic-mashed potatoes. Just a short distance from South Texas College of Law and many of the city's law offices, we can understand why this is a favorite among Houston's home-sick Louisiana lawyers.

RESTAURANTS

Not just sweets at Raja Sweets

Tafia's kitchen garden

INDEXES

Hot Bagel Shop
Hot Breads
La Victoria Bakery
Moeller's Bakery
Parisian Bakery
Pâtisserie Jungle Cafe
Petite Sweets
Rao's Bakery
Ruggles Cafe
  Bakery
Rustika Cafe &
  Bakery
Six Ping Bakery
Slow Dough
Stone Mill Bakers
Three Brothers
  Bakery

BAR/LOUNGE
*Also see Wine &
Spirits chapter*
Alice's Tall Texan
Anvil Bar &
  Refuge
Barcadia
Big Easy, The
Big John's Ice
  House
Blanco's Bar &
  Grill
Boheme
Boneyard Dog Park &
  Drinkery
Brittmoore Ice
  House
Christian's Tailgate
Continental Club
Flying Saucer
  Draught
  Emporium
Ginger Man, The
Goode's Armadillo
  Palace
Grand Prize Bar
Griff's Shenanigans
  Cafe & Bar
Hans' Bier Haus
Harp, The

Hay Merchant,
  The
Kay's Lounge
La Carafe
Leon's Lounge
Liberty Station
Marfreless
Nouveau Antique
  Art Bar
Petrol Station
Plonk Beer & Wine
  Bistro
Poison Girl
Sambuca
Under the
  Volcano
Warren's Inn
West Alabama Ice
  House
Yard House

BARBECUE
Barbecue Inn
Burns Bar-B-Q
Gatlin's BBQ
Goode Co. Texas
  Bar-B-Q
Pierson & Co.
  BBQ
Pizzitola's
  Bar-B-Cue
Thelma's
  Bar-B-Que

BELGIAN
Broken Spoke
  Cafe
Jeannine's Bistro

BOSNIAN
Cafe Pita+

BRAZILIAN
Fogo De Chao
Nelore
  Churrascaria
Tradiçao Brazilian
  Steakhouse

BREAKFAST
*Many bakeries and
Mexican restaurants
also serve breakfast.*
59 Diner
Avalon
Barnaby's Cafe
Brasil
Breakfast Klub, The
Buffalo Grille, The
Canopy
Down House
Empire Cafe
Fountain View
  Cafe
Flora & Muse
Goode Co. Taqueria
  & Hamburgers
House of Pies
Kenny & Ziggy's
Lankford Grocery &
  Market
Lola
Mama's Cafe
New York Bagel &
  Coffee Shop
Ouisie's Table
Niko Niko's
Pondicheri
Tiny Boxwood's
Triple-A
  Restaurant

BRITISH
Baker Street Pub &
  Grill
Black Labrador
  Pub
Feast
Queen Vic Pub &
  Kitchen
Red Lion Pub

BRUNCH
*Many more
restaurants serve
breakfast or lunch
on the weekend.*
Backstreet Cafe

INDEX

INDEX

GELATO/ICE CREAM/SNOW ICE

Also see Bakeries & Sweets Shops chapter

Amy's Ice Creams
Berripop
Connie's Frozen Custard
Fat Cat Creamery
Gelato Blu
Gelato Cup
Hank's Ice Cream Parlor
La Palatera
Mam's House of Ice
Moreliana Natural Ice Cream
Nundini
Star Snow Ice #1
Star Snow Ice & Teriyaki
Sweet Lola
Swirll
Tampico Refresqueria

GERMAN

Rudi Lechner's

GREEK

Al's Quick Stop
Alexander the Great
Niko Niko's

GROCERY STORE

Also see Markets chapter

Belden's
Central Market
Fiesta Mart
Hubbell & Hudson
Rice Epicurean Market
Whole Foods

GUATEMALAN

El Pueblito Place

HAMBURGERS

Becks Prime
Bubba's Texas Burger Shack
Burger Guys
Christian's Tailgate
Dry Creek Cafe
Goode Co. Taqueria & Hamburgers
Guy's Meat Market
Hubcap Grill
Jax Grill
Lankford Grocery
Little Big's
Little Bitty Burger Barn

HEALTH FOOD

A Moveable Feast
Field of Greens
Hobbit Cafe
Loving Hut
Ruggles Green
Ziggy's Bar & Grill

HONDURAN

Honduras Maya Cafe and Bar

HOT DOGS

James Coney Island
Moon Tower Inn

HOTEL RESTAURANTS

*17/Alden Hotel
Monarch/Hotel ZaZa
Olivette/The Houstonian
Quattro/The Four Seasons
Restaurant Cinq/La Colombe d'Or
Rio Ranch/ Westchase Hilton
Ristorante Cavour/ Hotel Granduca
Trattoria Il Mulino/ Westin Houston Memorial City
Valentino Houston/ Hotel Derek

INDIAN

Hot Breads
Indika
Khyber North Indian Grill
Kiran's
London Sizzler
Madras Pavilion
Narin's Bombay Brasserie
Pondicheri
Queen Vic Pub
Raja Sweets
Shiva Indian Restaurant
Udipi Cafe

ITALIAN

Amerigo's Grille
Antica Osteria
Arcodoro Ristorante Italiano
Arturo Boada Cuisine
Arturo's Uptown Italiano
Carmelo's
Carrabba's Italian Grill
Ciao Bello
Ciro's Italian Grill
Collina's Italian Cafe
Coppa Ristorante Italiano
Crapitto's
Da Marco
Damian's Cucina Italiana
D'Amico's Italian Market Cafe
Divino
Fratelli's
Frenchie's

INDEX

The cupcake display at Crave

Aladdin
Arpi's Phoenicia
  Deli
Fadi's Mediterranean
  Grill
Falafel Factory
Shawarma King
Skewers
Yildizlar
Zabak's

OPEN LATE
Our favorites serving food after 10 pm

13 Celsius
59 Diner
Alto Pizzeria
BB's Cajun Cafe
Baker Street
Black Labrador
Branch Water
  Tavern
Brasil
BRC
Christian's Tailgate
El Real
Frenchy's Chicken
Fufu Cafe
Gorditas
  Aguascalientes
Hollywood
  Vietnamese &
  Chinese
House of Pies
Indika
Kata Robata
Last Concert
Late Nite Pie
Little Big's
London Sizzler
Mai's
Max's Wine Dive
Oporto Cafe
Petrol Station
Piola
Queen Vic Pub
Red Lion
Rioja
Saigon Pagolac
Sinh Sinh

Smith & Wollensky
Soma
Spanish Flowers
Taco's a Go-Go
Tan Tan
Van Loc

OUTDOOR DINING
Our favorites among many:

Américas
Arcodoro
Artista
Arturo's Uptown
  Italiano
Baba Yega
Backstreet Cafe
Becks Prime (The
  Woodlands)
Benjy's
Black Labrador
Brasil
Brasserie Max &
  Julie
Brennan's
Brenner's on the
  Bayou
Cafe Express
Canopy
Chez Roux
Churrascos
Chuy's
Ciro's
Crapitto's
D'Amico's
Daily Review Cafe
Dolce Vita
El Pueblito Place
El Tiempo
Empire Cafe
Giacomo's Cibo
  e Vino
Goode Co.
  Taqueria &
  Hamburgers
Grappino di Nino
Grove, The
Haven
Hugo's
Ibiza

Indika
Kata Robata
La Griglia
La Mexicana
Last Concert Cafe
Laurier Cafe
Le Mistral
Maria Selma
Monarch
Niko Niko's
Ninfa's on
  Navigation
Onion Creek
Ouisie's Table
Palazzo's Trattoria
Pico's Mex-Mex
Pronto Cucinino
Rainbow Lodge
Raven Grill
RDG + Bar Annie
Red Lion Pub
Rioja
Sambuca
Spanish Flowers
Taco Milagro
Teala's
Tila's
Tiny Boxwood's

PAKISTANI
Himalaya

PERSIAN
Cafe Caspian
Darband
  Shishkabob
Kasra Persian Grill

PIZZA
Alto Pizzeria
Bombay Pizza
  Company
Candelari's
Dolce Vita
  Pizzeria
Grimaldi's
Late Nite Pie
Pink's Pizza
Piola
Star Pizza

INDEX

INDEX

ALPHABETICAL INDEX

INDEX

INDEX

Spec's deli

Katfish and grits at The Breakfast Klub

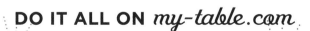

NOTES